Theorising Intellectual Property Rights from Chinese Perspectives

Handong Wu

Theorising Intellectual Property Rights from Chinese Perspectives

中国人民大学出版社
CHINA RENMIN UNIVERSITY PRESS

Springer

Handong Wu
Intellectual Property Research Center
Zhongnan University of Economics
and Law
Wuhan, Hubei, China

Translated by
Jie Zhang
School of Foreign Languages
Zhongnan University of Economics
and Law
Wuhan, Hubei, China

Ling Xue
School of Foreign Languages
Zhongnan University of Economics
and Law
Wuhan, Hubei, China

ISBN 978-981-96-5866-4 ISBN 978-981-96-5867-1 (eBook)
https://doi.org/10.1007/978-981-96-5867-1

Jointly published with China Renmin University Press Co., Ltd.
The print edition is not for sale in China (Mainland). Customers from China (Mainland) please order the print book from: China Renmin University Press Co., Ltd..

The book is supported by 2021 national B&R Book Program. The original work was first published by China Renmin University Press. It has been shortlisted in the "12th Five Year Plan" for the national key book publishing project, and won the "Book Award" in the first Chinese government awards for publishing and the second prize in the monograph category of the first Chinese Outstanding Academic Achievement Award of Law.

This Springer imprint is published by the registered company Springer Nature Singapore Pte Ltd.
The registered company address is: 152 Beach Road, #21-01/04 Gateway East, Singapore 189721, Singapore

Contents

Author and Translators

About the Author

Handong Wu is Juris Doctor, professor, doctoral supervisor, and director of the Intellectual Property Research Centre of Zhongnan University of Economics and Law—a key humanities and social sciences research base of the Ministry of Education and the national research base of intellectual property protection. He is also a member of the law department of the Social Science Committee of the Ministry of Education, honorary president of the Chinese Intellectual Property Law Research Association, a special consultant of the Supreme People's court and the Supreme People's Procuratorate, and an arbitrator of the China International Economic and Trade Arbitration Commission. He has written more than 10 books, including *On the System of Fair Use of Copyright*, *On the System of Intangible Property Rights*, *On the Basic Issues of Intellectual Property Rights*, *Multi-dimensional Interpretation of Intellectual Property Rights*, *Scientific Development and Implementation of Intellectual Property Strategy*. In addition, he has published more than 130 articles in Chinese core journals such as *Social Sciences in China*, *Chinese Journal of law*, and *Chinese Legal Science*. His monographs and papers have won the first National Excellent Doctoral Dissertation Award, the first prize of the Excellent Research Achievement Award of the Ministry of Justice, the "Book Award" in the first Chinese government award for publishing, the second prize of the Excellent Research Achievement Award of Humanities and Social Sciences of the Ministry of Education, the second prize of the national teaching materials of jurisprudence and scientific research achievement award, and the second prize in the monograph category of the first Chinese Outstanding Academic Achievement Award of Law. In May 2006, Professor Wu gave a lecture on "legal and institutional construction of intellectual property protection in China" for state leaders at the 31st collective learning session of the Political Bureau of the CPC Central Committee. In 2009 and again in 2011 he was named on the list of "the top ten most influential persons in intellectual property protection of the year", and was selected as one of "the most influential 50 people in the world's intellectual property industry" by British *Intellectual Property Management* (MIP) magazine in 2009 and 2011.

About the Translators

Jie Zhang is Professor of Applied Sociolinguistics in the School of Foreign Languages, Zhongnan University of Economics and Law (Wuhan, China), and Honorary Professor at the Department of Linguistics, Macquarie University (Sydney, Australia). She is a core member of *Collaborative Innovation Union for Language Governance Research* and *Language on the Move* (http://www.languageonthemove.com).

Ling Xue is Associate Professor in Translation Studies at Zhongnan University of Economics and Law (Wuhan, China). She completed her MA degree in Translation and Interpreting at University of Westminster in 2009, and Ph.D. in Translation Studies at Henan University in 2014. Her translation, with Professor Jie ZHANG, *Essentials of Intellectual Property Rights: China's Experience and Contributions* has been published by Springer.

List of Tables

Part I
Basic Categories of Intellectual Property Rights

Introduction for Part I

Category is a concept of logic regarding the most general and essential connections and relations that human thoughts are reflected in the real world (Pi & Ru 1961, p.1). It is the basic element of any theory within a discipline, and the rational character of a theory is based on that of its category and content. The construction of a category system is a necessary process towards the maturity of a science; hence it is of vital importance to construct a category system (W. X. Zhang 2001, p.10). In jurisprudence, the legal category system is generally composed of six parts: the ontological category (the knowledge and generalisation of the existence and essence of law), the evolutionary category (the knowledge and generalisation of the history and development of law from its inception to evolvement), the operational category (the knowledge and generalisation of the operation of law from formulation to enforcement), the category of subjectivity (the knowledge and generalisation of the subject of practice, the subject of value and their correlations in the legal domain), the category of objectivity (the knowledge and reflection of the object of legal regulation and the object of rights and obligations as well as their influence and functions), and the category of value (the knowledge, evaluation and generalisation of the legal needs of the subject, the significance of law to the subject, and the satisfaction of law with the needs of the subject). The general theory of jurisprudence is of guiding significance to all legal sciences in terms of the classification and description of categories. However, the latter cannot simply use the former as an alternative; which is to say, in the studies of the category theory in a specific branch of law, the inherent and prescriptive principles of jurisprudence need to be followed while the qualitative particularity of its own category should be taken into consideration.

Intellectual property rights (hereafter referred to as IPRs), as an emerging type of civil law rights, are incorporeal property rights distinct from tangible property rights. The basic principles and general systems stipulated in the civil law are applicable to systems of private rights, including intellectual property law (hereafter referred to as IP law). However, as a form of right to knowledge-based assets, IPRs differ significantly from the ownership of tangible movable and immovable property. Based on the static recognition of rights from the perspective of legal systems, Part I takes the concept, nature, characteristics, subjects, subject matter, utilisation, restrictions, protection and system of IPRs as the main components of basic categories with *rights* at its core. In doing so, this part attempts to discuss the constituent elements and essential attributes, legal relations and operating mode, protection scope and system framework of IPRs.

Chapter 1
Concept of IPRs

Conceptualisation is the logical starting point of studies on jurisprudence. The concepts of IPRs, together with their characteristics, subjects, subject matters, uses, restrictions and protection, constitute the basic categories of IPRs.

In the system of civil law rights, the term "intellectual property rights (IPRs)" is used to create a distinction from conventional property ownership. *Intellectual property rights* in English, *Droits de propriété intellectuelle* in French, and *Rechte an geistigem Eigentum* in German, all refer to ownership of property of knowledge or intellect. The practice of classifying all rights relating to intellectual activities as IPRs was first seen in the works of German scholar Benedikt Carpzov in the middle of the seventeenth century. This concept was later developed by Edmond Picard, a renowned Belgian jurist. Picard believed that IPRs are a special category of rights, one that is fundamentally different from the ownership of tangible things. He (quoted in E. A. Bogart 1980) held that ownership, in principle, is eternal, emerging and terminating with the production and destruction of tangible things, but there are time constraints with regard to IPRs. The property right in a certain object can only belong to one person (or a certain range of people in the case of shared property) in each instant, while there is no restriction on the number of users of a particular intellectual product, as it can be regenerated infinitely. Since then, the theory of IPRs has been disseminated widely around the world. Following the signing of the *Convention Establishing the World Intellectual Property Organization* (*WIPO Convention*) in 1967, the concept of IPRs was recognised by most countries and international organizations. The Chinese jurisprudential community[1] used to refer to "intellectual property rights" as "智力成果权 (*zhìlì chéngguǒ quán*)" (the right to intellectual achievements). In 1986, the *General Principles of Civil Law of the People's Republic of China* was promulgated, after which the term "知识产权 (*zhī shí chǎn quán*)" was officially adopted as the translation of "intellectual property

[1] One of the representative works is the *Principles of Civil Law* edited by Tong Rou, a famous late jurist and professor of China Renmin University. The book was published by Law Publishing House in 1983 as a national textbook.

H. Wu, *Theorising Intellectual Property Rights from Chinese Perspectives*,
https://doi.org/10.1007/978-981-96-5367-1_1

rights" in mainland China. In contrast, the term is translated as "智慧财产权 (*zhì huì cái chǎn quán*)"[2] in China's Taiwan Province.

1.1 Defining IPRs

In the study of jurisprudential category and even in legal debates, different perspectives often lead to discrepancy in the definitions of the same concept. Many disputes and even conflicts of views are often caused by the ambiguity of concepts and categories (W. X. Zhang 2001, p. 10). Therefore, defining of concepts is the first step of IP research. Meanwhile, it also forms an important foundation for exploring the nature and characteristics of IPRs and serves as an essential prerequisite for theoretical research (Wu 2018, p. 44).

Two approaches, namely enumerationism and generalisationism, are generally employed to define IPRs. The former method defines the concept by systematically listing the rights under legal protection, which thereby delineates the scope of the right system; while the latter method defines the concept through describing the subject matter under legal protection in a general and abstract way, i.e. briefly explain the "p*er genus et differentiam*" of this specific kind of rights. Generally speaking, foreign studies mostly adopt the method of enumeration to define IPRs, while Chinese scholars tend to use the method of generalisation.

1.1.1 Enumerative Approach

The method of enumeration can be widely seen in international conventions on IPRs. According to Article 2 (viii) of the WIPO *Convention*, IPRs includes copyright and related rights, patent rights and rights to inventions, rights to discoveries, rights to industrial designs, rights to trademarks and to other business identifiers, rights to protection against unfair competition, and all other rights resulting from intellectual activities. Article 1 of Part I of the *Agreement on Trade-Related Aspects of Intellectual Property Rights* (hereinafter referred to as the *TRIPS Agreement*) stipulates that:

> for the purposes of this Agreement, the term "intellectual property" refers to all categories of intellectual property that are the subject of Sections 1 through 7 of Part II, including copyright and related rights, rights to trademark, rights to geographical indications, rights to industrial designs, patent rights, rights to layout-designs of integrated circuits, and rights to protection of trade secrets.

[2] Translators' note: Although the term "知识产权" is widely used in mainland China, the accuracy of this translation has always been controversial. Wang Chenyan (2005) argues that the Chinese translation "知识产权" does not conform to the original meaning of "intellectual property." The main controversy is that "intellectual property" is not always directly related to "知识 (knowledge)." For example, trademarks, geographical markers, domain names, packaging decoration and other symbolic rights have little to do with "knowledge."

According to Cai (2001) the scope of protection of IPRs prescribed in the *TRIPS Agreement* is comparatively in line with the needs brought about by emerging types of intellectual property, such as the protection of layout-designs of integrated circuits and the protection of undisclosed information (including trade secrets). However, in terms of the specific types delimited, given its nature as an international convention, the *TRIPS Agreement* places emphasis on the types of IPRs generally accepted by the international community. As a result, no conclusion can be drawn that the agreement has enumerated all types of IPRs. Furthermore, the *TRIPS Agreement* does not include the right to protection against unfair competition, as provided in Article 2 (viii) of the WIPO *Convention*; instead, the *TRIPS Agreement* merely regards it as one of the relief measures to protect IPRs. Meanwhile, based on its framing of "trade-related intellectual property rights", the agreement does not cover all types of intellectual property. Therefore, subject matter given protection under the label of intellectual property cannot be entirely listed in the *TRIPS Agreement*.

In addition to international conventions, many Western scholars also adopted the enumeration method to define IPRs. In the UK, the birthplace of the IPRs regime, professor W. R. Cornish (1999), of Cambridge University, defined IPRs in his textbook by enumerating the protection scope of IPRs, which includes "protecting patent rights of technological invention and design", "protecting copyrights of literary and artistic creation" and "protecting rights to trademarks" (p. 3). In the book *Intellectual Property: Patents, Trademarks and Copyrights*, American scholars Miller and Davis (1997) listed three legal fields based on the concept of abstract property, namely, "patent rights, rights to trademarks, and copyrights" (p. 4).

The enumeration method is apt by being intuitively clear in terms of expression and description, yet there are also shortcomings. First, explaining a concept through enumeration might have the shortcomings of variable scope and trivial content. With social and economic development, the content or scope of IPRs has been constantly expanding, which inevitably leads to the variability of the concept, thus undermining the scientificity of the definition. For example, whether conventional knowledge, business models, and experimental data can be subject matter under the protection of IPRs remains controversial in academic circles, and explicit provisions in that regard have not been made by international IPR conventions. Secondly, as IPRs is a dynamic and open legal system, enumeration unavoidably leads to omissions. In addition, enumeration can hardly reveal the essential attributes of things or distinguish one from others. For instance, it cannot give answers to questions such as why different kinds of rights can be collectively referred to as IPRs, and what are the internal common features among different rights (Q. Zhang, 2012, pp. 3–4).

1.1.2 Generalising Approach

The Chinese jurisprudential community mainly adopts the method of generalisation to explain the concept of IPRs. Chinese scholars have long defined IPRs as the exclusive right that people enjoy to their creative intellectual achievements based on the abstract understanding that subject matter under intellectual property protection are intellectual creations (Wu and Min 1987; Zheng 1993; Huang 1995). Similar expressions have been made by Western scholars. Michael Blakeney (1996) defines IPRs as "a kind of creation in the legal concept, which is related to the legal monopoly right authorised by the state to a certain individual during a specific period of time in case of any unauthorised use by others" (p. 10). In addition, the *WIPO Intellectual Property Handbook* (quoted in Guo 2002) also defines intellectual property through generalisation: "intellectual property, very broadly, means the legal rights which result from intellectual activity in the industrial, scientific, literary and artistic fields" (p. 5). However, since the 1990s many scholars have challenged this definition. They have argued that not every right within the domain of intellectual property results from intellectual creation. For example, in the Tokyo World Congress of the International Association for the Protection of Intellectual Property (AIPPI) held in 1992, AIPPI divided IPRs into "rights to creative achievements" and "rights to identification marks." It can be seen that IPRs are not merely about the rights to "intellectual creation." In view of this, scholars have made new generalisation of the defined subject matter, among which three viewpoints stand out: (1) IPRs is a general term for the rights generated from creative intellectual achievements and business marks under the law (Liu 2002, p. 3); (2) IPRs refers to the rights enjoyed by people under the law to the achievements of their own intellectual activities and to the marks and reputation resulting from their operation and management activities (Wu 2000, p. 1); (3) IPRs refers to the rights enjoyed by the parties to legal civil relations to dominate the information related to their intellectual activities, to enjoy the interests, and to exclude the interference of others in accordance with the law (Y. M. Zhang 2001, p. 1).

The method of generalisation features high abstractness and conciseness. The key problem lies in whether the definition given through generalisation is accurate, appropriate and inclusive to the maximum extent. At present, there are many definitions of IP and IPRs through generalisation, but no consensus has been reached. According to W. R. Cornish (quoted in Jin 2004, p. 8), no single term can satisfactorily cover all subject matter within the scope of intellectual property, as the term "industrial property" excludes copyright in most cases, while the term "intellectual property" seldom includes trademarks or business marks.

1.1.3 Alternative Approaches

Other definitions of IPRs can be made from different perspectives and emphases. Some scholars (e.g. He 1997; Su 2005) generalise and abstract the regulating object of IPRs. From the perspective of the object of spiritual wealth, they define IPRs as the exclusive rights enjoyed by natural or legal persons to their spiritual wealth created within the fields of science, technology, literature and art in accordance with the law. Other scholars (e.g. He 1997; Jin 2004) define IPRs as the legal rights of dominion and reputation enjoyed by civil subjects to specific useful information from the perspective of information subject matter.

Different research methodologies inevitably lead to distinct conclusions from different perspectives. Graham P. Cornish explains (quoted in Jin 2004):

> ...in the tangible world that people focus on, intellectual property is often a very tricky concept to grasp. Historically, the use of creations and inventions or ideological achievements was quite crucial. Since IP does not belong to tangible subject matter, it was often missed, ignored or even rejected in the discussions of academics. In its essence, intellectual property is a concept developed to protect the idea and creation of mankind, and it is classified into a series of different types in most countries, namely patents, trade and service marks, design rights and copyright. (p. 8)

1.1.4 Normative Approach

Theoretically, it is very difficult, if not impossible, to reach a consensus on the definition of IPRs, whether it is through "enumerationism", "generalisationism" or other conventional methodologies. That is because a comprehensive definition should contain the commonalities of the subordinate items and the superordinate concept of the object to be defined (Su 2005). As far as IPRs are concerned, one of the biggest commonalities of its subordinate items, i.e. the works, inventions, trademarks, layout-designs of integrated circuits and other intellectual products, is *intangibility*, which makes them distinct from copyrighted books, patented products, trademarks, integrated circuit boards and other physical subject matter. The concept of intellectual property involves copyright, patent, trademark and other subject matter. It is believed that their common feature is *intangibility* and they are all derived from the abstract concept of *property* (quoted in Miller and Davis 1997, p. 4). On the issue of defining the superordinate concept of intellectual property, Nobuhiro Nakayama (quoted in Nobuhiro 1997, p. 7) holds that so-called 'intellectual property' refers to the protection of particular information from improper imitation. Specifically, it is the generic term for the creations of intellectual and spiritual creative achievements (such as inventions and works) and marks with business reputation (such as trademarks and trade names). It is a relatively unique approach to examine intellectual property from an information perspective. However, further studies are needed to determine whether it is feasible to equate IPRs that are commonly used in international legislation with information and information property rights that are used in multi-disciplinary contexts.

The term IPRs needs to be appropriately defined by scientific methodologies on the basis of its very essence. First, IPRs are private property rights. For example, copyrights, patent rights, and trademark rights are all private rights to intellectual properties, that is, the absolute and exclusive property rights enjoyed by specific subjects. They are not the same as rights to invention and discoveries listed in the incentive system of scientific and technological advances, which are characterised by public ownership. Second, IPRs are not equivalent to the rights with respect to intellectual achievements. That is because IPRs do not necessarily originate from the knowledge domain, nor are they all based on intellectual achievements. In terms of their sources, IPRs are mainly derived from intellectual creations and industrial and commercial activities. Their subject matters are composed of creative achievements, business marks, reputation and other kinds of knowledge and information. Third, IPRs are legal rights, which will generally be recognised by law. Yet not all intellectual products can be subject matter under the protection of IPRs. The scope of IPRs differs from country to country and period to period, as affected by economic, technological and cultural factors. In other words, not all creative achievements and industrial and commercial marks can become the subject matter under the regulation of IPRs. In practice, law makers only choose to make adjustments on certain relations that have considerable influence on their economic counterparts.

1.1.5 *IPRs Definition in China's* General Provisions of the Civil Law

Article 123 of the *General Provisions of the Civil Law of the People's Republic of China* (hereinafter referred to as the *General Provisions*), issued in March 2017, stipulates: the parties to civil legal relations enjoy IPRs in accordance with the law. IPRs are the proprietary rights enjoyed by right holders in accordance with the law in respect of the following subject matter: (1) works; (2) inventions, utility models, and designs; (3) trademarks; (4) geographic indications; (5) trade secrets; (6) layout-designs of integrated circuits; (7) new varieties of plants; (8) other subject matter specified by laws. This article is known to scholars as "the intellectual property clause."

Article 123 is the general and declaratory clause of the *General Provisions* on IPRs, which manifests the system's construction of civil rights and the regression of IPRs to private law. This article defines IPRs from the perspective of subject matter through both "enumerationism" and "generalisationism." In the *General Provisions*, many articles governing property rights have relevant definitions. For instance, Article 114 stipulates that the parties to civil legal relations enjoy real rights in accordance with the law. A real right is the right holder's exclusive right over a specific object in accordance with the law, including ownership, usufructuary right, and security interest. Article 118 provides that the parties to civil legal relations enjoy the creditor's rights in accordance with the law. A creditor's right is the right holder's right to request that a specific obligor perform or not perform certain conduct, arising from contracts, torts, management of the business of another under no obligation, unjust enrichment, and other provisions of laws. The above clauses satisfy the general requirements of the definition of property rights (Wu 2011): (1) the parties to civil legal relations are the subjects of rights, which indicates that property rights are rights enjoyed by private individuals; (2) the subject matter of rights are classified based on whether they fall into the category of tangible things or behaviour, which indicates that they are different types of rights of private interests;

(3) the attribute of rights distinguishes the right of dominion from the right of claim, which indicates that although they belong to different types, they are rights to which private individuals are entitled. Article 123 solves the problem of defining IPRs from the legislative level by taking expressions such like "the parties to civil legal rights", "subject matter" and "exclusive rights" as the semantic components.

There are many merits in the definition of IPRs given in Article 123. Firstly, it stipulates that the parties to civil legal relations enjoy IPRs in accordance with law, emphasizing that copyright owners and patent holders, as subjects, are private parties. Meanwhile, it removes the restrictions imposed on the qualification of the subjects for trademark registration, which was prescribed in the *General Principles of the Civil Law of the People's Republic of China* issued in 1986. Secondly, it stipulates IPRs by enumerating the subject matter, and includes miscellaneous provisions, which leaves institutional flexibility for the future development of the scope of IPRs protection. Thirdly, it defines IPRs as "exclusive rights" to indicate the inherent character of intangible property rights, which distinguishes IPRs from the real rights featuring the right of dominance, and the creditor's rights featuring right of claims. However, there are some defects of Article 123 itself and its legislative definition of IPRs. As Li (2017) points out, the subject matter under protection provided by this article is more in line with those stipulated in TRIPS, yet have referred less to the relevant provisions of other international agreements, such as the rights to trade names and business marks and the right to protection against unfair competition which are included in the *Paris Convention for the Protection of Industrial Property* and the WIPO *Convention.* This also constitutes an inherent limitation of the enumerative approach in legislative definition.

Definitions that are not empirically grounded are mere exercises of imagination in theory, and are not conducive to theoretical research and institutional practice. The study of IPRs including its semantic category will not be suspended. Flexibility and openness in the development of IPRs are the cornerstone fuelling the progress of relevant disciplines and institutional construction. Scholars must pay close attention to this field.

1.2 IPRs and Intangible Property Rights

Within the scope of civil law rights in the non-material realm, intellectual property is known as intangible property. In some western countries, intangible property was once used to refer to the exclusive rights to intellectual creative achievements in the relevant legislation and theories. Within the conventional framework of civil rights of the continental law system, civil law serves to regulate the property relationship and personal relationship between civil parties to civil legal relations, while property law mainly focuses on tangible subject matter. However, when studying theories of civil law, scholars often employ the concept of "*incorporales*" of the Roman law as an ideological device to interpret the new subject matter such as institutional products and spiritual outcomes. In 1875, Kohlers, a German scholar, first put forward the concept of "*Immaterial Güterrecht*", namely immaterial property rights, arguing it was mistaken that previous theories refer to the right as a kind of ownership of property. He then named it as "*Immaterial Güterrecht*", an alternative kind of right different from the ownership of tangible property, to refer to copyrights, patent rights, rights to trademarks, and so forth (Yoshifuji 1990, p. 405). The concept of intangible property rights was later adopted in some countries' national legislative documents and academic studies. Since 1967, when the WIPO *Convention* was signed, the concept of IPRs has been widely used around the world, whereas some western scholars continue to use the concept of intangible property rights. Etymologically speaking, the terms "intellectual property" and "intellectual property rights" respectively refer to "the property of the human intellect" and "the rights given to persons over their intellectual creations." The reading materials compiled by WIPO (1992, p. 4) also associate "intellectual property" with IPRs. According to Shoen Ono (1992), a Japanese scholar, the term "intangible property rights" (i.e. "*Immaterial Güterrecht*") is in use in German laws, which focuses on the legal character of property, while "intellectual property rights" refer to those related to spiritual products, i.e. the rights to "intellectual property." Thus, "intangible property rights" can be considered as an alternative term to "intellectual property rights" (Ono 1992, p. 5).

1.2.1 IPRs as Intangible Property Rights Beyond the Scope of "Knowledge"

The creation of the concept of IPRs, as a profound institutional innovation and reform in the field of private rights since Roman law, is regarded as the "revolution of non-materialisation" of property brought about by the propertisation of intellectual products and the legalisation of intellectual property. Intellectual property is a new category of property, contrasting with previous ones that entailed the enjoyment of absolute dominance over the things owned. Instead, it is "intangible and limited" (Vandevelde 1980). The "non-materialisation" of properties has significantly broadened the scope of application of property laws, and the subject matter of right include all the material and non-material things that can be regarded as property. In the contemporary era where science, technology and the modern commodity economy continue to develop, the "revolution of non-materialisation" of properties has not yet to come to an end. Moreover, with the structure of social wealth undergoing ever more profound changes, more and more types of property have become intangible and immaterial (Yin 1998, p. 19), hence we have every reason to pay more attention to and offer protection to the rights that are not conventionally regarded as property or property rights (Boston 1994). With the development of modern society and economy comes greater significance for intangible property. Although some items of intangible property are non-material, they are not necessarily related to knowledge and intellectual creations. In other words, the system of intellectual property cannot cover many new types of intangible property. Such expansion of the concept of non-material property brought about by the development of the modern commodity economy and the transformation of social wealth has led to the reality that the term "intellectual property" is not universally applicable to all types of intangible properties. It can be seen that there is indeed a collection of property rights that are non-material and still cannot be classified into the category of IPRs. With the development of social activities, other new forms of intangible property may also emerge, which requires systematic integration of these new forms of property for institutional innovation. Based on the classification of "intangible assets" made in economic circles at home and abroad (Cai 1996), intangible property rights in the sense of legal system can be divided into the following three categories: (1) rights to creative achievements, including copyrights, patent rights, rights to trade secrets, rights to layout-designs of integrated circuits, new plant variety rights, and such like; (2) rights to commercial marks, including rights to trademarks, rights to trade names, rights to geographical indications, and other rights to distinctive signs that are related to the counteraction of unfair competition; (3) operational credit rights, including credit rights, goodwill rights, commercialisation rights, image rights, and so forth.

In previous studies, the scope of intangible property rights was not exactly the same as that of IPRs. In the book *Intangible Property Rights*, the Japanese scholar Yonhe Kojima (1998, p. 47) places items such as "the forms of commodities" and "business credit" in the category of intangible property rights, and he believes that their scope should be wider than those involved in the traditional IPRs. In the book *The Property Law of France*, Yin Tian (1998, pp. 59–65), a Chinese scholar of civil law, divides intangible property rights into business monopoly rights (including the rights related to intellectual achievements and distinctive signs) and rights enjoyed by customers or rights to business assets (those rights derived from the influence of commercial reputation to attract customers). Zheng Chengsi (1996, pp. 44–45) believes that there are peripheral areas between general rights of personality and copyrights, as well as between rights to signs, goodwill rights and copyrights. Therefore, it is inappropriate for these rights to fall into any of the original categories, and it is necessary to put them under a new type of right. All the above discussions involve intangible property rights which are beyond the concept of "知识 (knowledge)."

In a nutshell, not all rights within the scope of IPRs belong to the field of knowledge. Meanwhile, there are still many new forms of rights that are irrelevant to "知识 (knowledge)" in the field of intangible property. Hence, the concept of intangible property rights, which is a superordinate to IPRs, is introduced to integrate those rights, so as to meet the demand of theoretical and institutional innovation.

1.2.2 IPRs as "Exclusive" Intangible Property Rights

Both intangible property rights and IPRs are exclusive civil rights. Compared with creditor's rights, they feature the characteristics of exclusiveness and absoluteness just as ownership does. Firstly, the intangible property and its interests are directly dominated and enjoyed without the assistance of others by the obligee; secondly, the intangible property is absolutely owned or monopolised by the obligee without the interference of others. Based on the two fundamental attributes, intangible property rights, including IPRs, have the same legal effects as the ownership of the tangible property does, namely the right in one's own property which allows the obligee to independently dominate the property; the right in the property of another which shares the interests with others; and the right of claim which helps to secure relief.

Since the 1990s, the author (Wu 1997, 2001, 2003) has been advocating the establishment of a system of intangible property rights by broadening the current scope of IPRs, so as to cover all rights derived from intangible forms. The author holds that the goodwill rights, credit rights, and image rights are all immaterial property rights, but cannot be classified into the category of IPRs. With the development of social activities, other new forms of intangible property may also emerge. Therefore, it merits consideration that two types of property rights should be generalised, namely tangible property rights and intangible property rights. The classification shall be based on the materiality and immateriality of the subject matter.

In this regard, it is necessary to discuss the "immateriality" of property rights, i.e. whether it refers to the right ("incorporales") that is regarded as an object, or the spiritual product that is regarded as an object. Yuan Xiuting (2002, 2003) reviewed the theories of intangible property rights proposed by the author. Many of his opinions are quite insightful, but he expanded the scope of intangible property rights, adding creditor's rights and rights on negotiable instruments to it, which the author cannot agree with. The reasons are as follows. Firstly, the division between tangible property rights and intangible ones is under the frame of dominant and absolute property rights. According to Karl Larenz (citation needed), a German civil jurist, the subject matter of this category of rights are placed in the first line, including tangible things and intangible spiritual products; whereas the creditor's rights and rights on negotiable instruments (i.e. a special type of creditor's right) are rights of claim and are of relativity. Another German scholar Dieter Medicus (2000) held that there is no substantial difference between creditor's rights and rights of claim, and their subject matter are different from that of dominant and absolute property rights. Therefore, while some Chinese scholars regard creditor's rights as intangible property rights, they actually confuse dominant rights with rights of claim. Secondly, when creditor's rights and rights on negotiable instruments themselves are the subject matter of rights, they can be viewed as *incorporales.* The tangible and intangible things are the sub-types of subject matter stipulated in Roman law and French law. The intangible property rights refer to the rights except for the ownership. In contrast, the subject matter stipulated in German law include all tangible ones. Despite the fact that German scholars sometimes refer to the spiritual products as incorporales, they stress that such subject matter should be regulated by IP law, rather than property law (Sun 1997, p. 3).

Therefore, in Roman law and French law, creditor's rights can be regarded as incorporales, and thus are the object of alternative rights (such as rights of inheritance and stock rights), but such intangible things (i.e. subject matter of rights) are not directly related to intangible property rights (i.e. the noumenon of rights). In German law, creditor's rights cannot be regarded as incorporales, because incorporales refer specifically to intangible spiritual products. In summary, it is indispensable to distinguish IPRs from intangible property rights, and to define their respective attributes of subject matter.

1.3 IPRs and Property Rights to Information

When it comes to the basic categories of civil rights, IPRs and informational property rights are another important topic under discussion. Humanity is experiencing the transformation of society from the industrial age to the information age. The new technological revolution pivoting on the computer, Internet and communication revolutions has promoted human society to a brand-new era of information. As a result, the scope of IPRs is apt to be expanded to include informational property rights. In the 1980s, Alvin Toffler, an American sociologist, elaborated the relationship between information and changes in society in his signature work. He (quoted in Ma et al. 1997, p. 221) believed that in the third wave of technological revolution, human beings still need tangible properties such as land and machines, but these properties have become informatised and intangible, which is a revolutionary advance. There is no doubt that during the transformation of society, the production and dissemination of information will continuously exert significant and profound impacts on aspects such as socioeconomic development, politics, and culture, which will certainly transform the traditional legal system. In the process of informatization, information, like material and energy, has become an essential resource to facilitate economic, technological and social development. Moreover, both interests of information personality and interests of informational property have been stipulated as civil legal subject matter. Meanwhile, informational property rights and IPRs have been adopted as distinctively new types of property rights. In the following part, this section discusses three basic categories of the conceptual system of information from the perspective of intellectual property theories.

1.3.1 Information as Social Resource

Information, material and energy are the three major resources for the development of human society. In informatics, information can be divided into various sub-types. Buckland (quoted in Zhou and Zhang 2003, pp. 2–3) distinguishes three types of information, namely "information as process", "information as knowledge" and "information as entity." Wang Dingding (2005, pp. 178–179) also believes that knowledge is the information that has been understood. If knowledge-based information cannot be understood, then it remains information, not knowledge. Epistemologically speaking, information refers to the subject's understanding of the state of motion and its way of change and the articulation of such understanding (Zhong 2002, p. 47). The above statements demonstrate that information, being a piece of knowledge or a creative product, may be related to the subject matter of IPRs or informational property rights. However, the information, as a natural being or a thing, may be related to the interests of other civil rights. Regardless, it will not be the object receiving the protection of IPRs or informational property rights.

In legislative cases, there are provisions on the definition of information in the respective information law of many countries. Article 2 of *Russia's Federal Law on Information, Information Technologies, and Information Protection* stipulates that "information means data (messages, data) irrespective of the form of their presentation." Section 102 of the *Uniform Computer Information Transactions Act* of the United States stipulates that "Information means data, text, images, sounds, mask works, or computer programs, including collections and compilations of them." This section defines knowledge as the substantive understanding of facts. It is evident that, in the legal context, information has knowledge connotation, which is irrespective of their representation or carrier (Qi 2012, p. 19). It is also a manifestation of people's understanding of value or interests.

1.3.2 Information Interests as Civil Law Objects

In the field of private law, information refers to those with valuable information interests, or interests of information personality, or interests of informational property. In the information society, information, rather than matter and energy, has become the most important social resource. Not only can it provide the basis for government decision-making, but also generate profits for enterprises. What is more, from the perspective of private law, it is also the legitimate rights and interests enjoyed by civil subjects.

The *General Provisions* specify information interests that shall be protected by law from three aspects: personal information, private information and knowledge information. Firstly, personal information is also known as personal data. In Article 76 (5) of the *Cybersecurity Law of the People's Republic of China*, personal information refers to all kinds of information recorded in electronic or other forms, which can be used, independently or in combination with other information, to identify a natural person's personal identity, including but not limited to the natural person's name, date of birth, identity certificate number, biology-identified personal information, address and telephone number. Personal information, including basic information on personal identity, location, and behaviour, is one of the exclusive personal interests enjoyed by the natural person as a civil subject. It is of great value for maintaining human dignity and freedom of the subject. According to Article 111 of the *General Provisions*, the personal information of a natural person shall be protected by law. Any organization or individual must legally obtain and ensure the security of the personal information of other persons, and shall not illegally collect, use, process, or transmit the personal information of other persons, nor illegally buy, sell, provide, or publish the personal information of other persons. Secondly, the privacy specified in the civil law includes the secrets and the tranquillity of private life (X. B. Zhang 2017, p. 219). The privacy of private life fits into the category of privacy information that is protected by law. The contents of personal information and privacy information overlap with each other. That is, the important or sensitive parts in one's personal information also belong to the private information of one's personal life, namely privacy. Legally speaking, privacy is the personal information that the parties concerned do not want others to know or the personal information unsuitable for others to know. The privacy is the object of the protection of privacy right that protects the privacy from being illegally infringed, known, collected, used and published by others. Its rights and interests belong to the category of right of personality. Article 110 of the *General Provisions* explicitly establishes the right of privacy and other personal rights enjoyed by natural persons. Thirdly, knowledge information, i.e. creative information, or legal information on knowledge is a kind of intellectual property or informational property different from movable property and real property. It can be the object of intellectual property or informational property. As mentioned above, in the theories about IPRs, the above subject matters are abstracted and summarised as "intellectual achievements", "intellectual products" and "information related to intellectual activities." The subject matter of IPRs can be regarded as knowledge information in a non-material form. The so-called "new technical solution" protected by the *Patent Law of the People's Republic of China* means it presents certain information of the latest development of technology in a particular field. As for the "distinctive signs" protected by the *Trademark Law of the People's Republic of China*, they belong per se to the information that distinguishes different goods or services. The "original expressions" protected by the *Copyright Law of the People's Republic of China* have become the most important and extensive information source for people through newspapers, books, radio, television, computer networks and other media. In this sense, IP law can also be called information protection law (e.g. Nobuhiro 1997; Feng 2001). Through enumerating the subject matter of IPRs, Article 123 of the *General Provisions* stipulates that IPRs are intangible property rights that are distinct from rights in rem. Generally speaking, information interests can also be divided into interests of informational property and interests of information personality, which are oriented towards different subject matter of civil rights.

1.3.3 Property Rights to Information as Civil Rights

Property rights to information are an emerging form of property rights in the information society. They are intangible property rights, distinct from traditional ownership. Although they are exclusive, and are dominated by the right holder, their object is immaterial informational property. At the same time, the term "informational property rights" is also the overarching concept of IPRs. Zheng and Zhu (2006) believe that compared with IPRs, the former is more objective, advanced and inclusive.

In terms of legislation, there are two main paradigms to provide legal protection for informational property rights. One is the "mode of ownership of information resources." Russia's *Federal Law on Information, Information Technologies, and Information Protection* explicitly stipulates that information resources are the component of property and the object of ownership. The law emphasizes that the right of ownership in relation to information resources shall be regulated by the Russian civil code. The other paradigm is the "transaction mode of IPRs." According to the *Uniform Computer Information Transactions Act* of the United States, the end-users enjoy informational rights over the purchased computer information, including not only the relevant IPRs, but also the rights to dominate and control the licensed computer information. The above two paradigms employ respectively the conventional method of ownership protection and the classic method of protecting IPRs. However, Qi (2012) argues against them, advocating a new and independent system of informational property rights.

The author believes that IPRs and informational property rights are a pair of related but distinct legal concepts. In terms of informational property, there are three types of information related to it: the first is the knowledge information with creative value protected by copyright, patent and trademark rights; the second is the commercial information whose property value is presented by confidentiality without public disclosure; the third is valuable information in a non-exclusive field. It should be noted that although the latter two are now regarded as informational property, they were not subject matter under the protection of IPRs until 1994, when TRIPS first included "undisclosed information (including trade secrets)" in the IPRs protection system. In 1996, *EU Data Protection Directive* proposed that databases composed of data or information materials should be granted special protection as copyright is. It is certain that the subjects of right of such databases should be the organizers of informational materials i.e. the makers of databases, not the owners and providers of informational materials. In any event, informational property and intellectual property are so inextricably intertwined that Zheng (2005) equates IPRs to informational property rights. However, as the subject matter of IPRs protection, intellectual property belongs to intangible property, different from movable property and real property. Moreover, it is informational property on knowledge that meets legal requirements for protection. Therefore, intellectual property is neither exactly the same as ownership, nor as informational property. The informational property that cannot be classified as subject matter of IPRs includes: (1) immaterial information products generated by the enforcement of IPRs, such as electronic information products and transaction of big data; (2) information products that do not meet the requirements for IPRs protection, such as public technical information, and expression of ideas beyond the time of legal protection; (3) information products irrelevant to creative intellectual information, such as transactional information, financial information, and virtual property of online games, etc. In summary, although some attributes of IPRs overlap with those of informational property rights, they are not identical. The international community adopts the "mode of ownership of information resources" and the "transaction mode of IPRs" to regulate informational property, demonstrating that the existing laws are adequate to protect informational property. In other words, the idea of an independent category of informational property rights is not yet mature at the current stage.

The above is just a description of the changes in the category of rights of immaterial property. The paper is not intended to judge the terms "intellectual property rights", "intangible property rights", and "informational property rights." In view of the relevant international conventions, domestic provisions, and the conventions of China's legal community, the author believes that the concept of IPRs can continue to be used, but such use shall not be confined to the narrow understanding of the traditional system of rights. Through the analysis of the connotation of the concept of IPRs, it is found that IPRs and the traditional ownership are different terms to distinguish intangible property rights from tangible property rights. Meanwhile, IPRs and informational property rights are both immaterial property rights. They are interrelated but not exactly the same. When defining the denotation of the concept of IPRs, it may be difficult to cover its entire scope through enumeration. Therefore, it is appropriate to adopt the method of generalisation to provide a concise and inclusive description.

References

Blakeney, M. 1996. *Trade Related Aspects of Intellectual Property Rights: A Concise Guide to the TRIPS Agreement*. London: Sweet & Maxwell

Bogart, E. A. 1980. Patent laws in capitalist and developing countries. In China Institute of Science and Technology Information (Eds.). *Introduction to Foreign Patent Laws* (Vol. 1). Beijing: Knowledge Publishing House

Boston, R. 1994. The current development trend of property law of the US. Trans. Lihong Zhang. *Translation and Review of Foreign Laws* 3

Cai, Jixiang. 1996. *Intangible Property*. Shenzhen: Haitian Press

Cai, Mingcheng. 2001. Problems and prospects of intellectual property rights on the Internet - taking Taiwan's respective law as an example. *Taiwan University Law Journal* 30(5)

Cornish, G. P. 2005. Electronic information management and intellectual property Rights. *Information Service and Use* 25(1)

Cornish, W. R. 1996. *Intellectual Property: Patents, Copyright, Trade Marks and Allied Rights* (3rd ed.). London: Sweet & Maxwell

Cornish, W. R. 1999. *Intellectual Property: Patents, Copyright, Trade Marks and Allied Rights* (4th ed.). London: Sweet & Maxwell

Feng, Xiaoqing. 2001. Research on some basic theories of intellectual property law. *Xiangjiang Law Review*. Xiangtan: Xiangtan University Press

Guo, Shoukang (Ed.). 2002. *Intellectual Property Law*. Beijing: Central Party School Press

He, Shanlin. 1997. A comparative study on the origin of world intellectual property and copyright. *Exploration* 4

Huang, Qinnan. 1995. *Textbook of Intellectual Property Law (New Edition)*. Beijing: China University of Political Science and Law Press

Jin, Haijun. 2004. *On the Private Rights of Intellectual Property*. Beijing: China Renmin University Press

Kojima, Yonhe. 1998. *Intangible Property Rights*. Japan: Sōzō Publishing House

Li, Mingde. 2017. Commentary on the provisions of intellectual property in the general provisions of the civil law. *China Intellectual Property* 4

Liu, Chuntian (Ed.). 2002. *Intellectual Property Law*. Beijing: Higher Education Press
Ma, Haiqun, Ge, Xiaochun and Li, Songmei. 1997. *Intellectual Property and Information Management*. Harbin: Heilongjiang People's Publishing House
Medicus, Dieter. 2000. *General Theories of German Civil Law*. Trans. Jiandong Shao. Beijing: Law Press
Miller, A. R. and Davis, M. H. 1997. *Intellectual Property*. Trans. Lin Zhou. Beijing: China Social Sciences Press (Original work published 1983)
Nobuhiro, Nakayama. 1997. *Multimedia and Copyright*. Trans. Yurui Zhang. Beijing: Patent Literature Press
Ono, Masanobu. 1992. *100 Tips on Intellectual Property Rights*. Trans. Keliang Li and Qingtian Ma. Beijing: Patent Literature Press
Pi, Zhi and Ru, Xin. 1961. *Criticism on Hegel's Theory of Category*. Shanghai: Shanghai People's Publishing House
Qi, Aimin. 2012. *Information from the Perspective of Private Law*. Chongqing: Chongqing University Press
Su, Yuan. 2005. Discussion on the nature of intellectual property and its system. *Intellectual Property* 1
Sun, Xianzhong. 1997. *Contemporary Property Law of Germany*. Beijing: Law Press
The World Intellectual Property Organisation (Ed.). 1992. *An Overview of Intellectual Property*. Beijing: World Intellectual Press
Tong, Rou. 1983. *Principles of Civil Law*. Beijing: Law Press China
Vandevelde, K. J. 1995. The new property of the nineteenth century: the development of the modern concept of property. Trans. Zhanqiang Wang. *Comparative Study of Social and Economic Systems* 1 (Original work published 1980)
Wang, Chenyan. 2005. Question and reflection on the concept of intellectual property rights. *Fujian Forum (Humanities and social sciences edition)* 9
Wang, Dingding. 2005. *Lecture Notes on the Basis of Institutional Analysis II*. Shanghai: Shanghai People's Publishing House
Wu, Handong (Ed.). 2000. *Intellectual Property Law*. Beijing: Peking University Press
Wu, Handong (Ed.). 2018. *Research on the Theoretical System of China's Intellectual Property Rights*. Beijing: Commercial Press
Wu, Handong and Min, Feng (Eds.). 1987. *Introduction to Intellectual Property Law*. Beijing: China University of Political Science and Law Press
Wu, Handong. 1997. Some theoretical issues of intangible property rights. *Law Research* 4
Wu, Handong. 2001. *Research on Intangible Property Rights System*. Beijing: Law Press
Wu, Handong. 2003. Intangible revolution of property and intangible property law of revolution. *Social Science of China 4*
Wu, Handong. 2011. Multiple attributes of intellectual property rights and the research paradigm. *China Social Sciences* 5
Yin, Tian. 1998. *The Property Law of France*. Beijing: Law Press
Yoshifuji, Kosaku. 1990. *Introduction to Patent Law*. Trans. Yonglin Song and Qixue Wei. Beijing: Patent Literature Press
Yuan, Xiuting. 2002. A Review of the "Basic Theory Series" of the Research on Intangible Property Rights, *Private Law*. Beijing: Peking University Press
Yuan, Xiuting. 2003. The positioning of intellectual property rights in the property right system. *Journal of Huazhong University of Science and Technology (Social Science Edition)* 2
Zhang, Qin. 2012. *Basic Principles of Intellectual Property Rights*. Beijing: Intellectual Property Press
Zhang, Wenxian. 2001. *Research on the Categories of Philosophy and Law (Revised Edition)*. Beijing: China University of Political Science and Law Press
Zhang, Xinbao. 2017. *Interpretation of the General Provisions of the Civil Law of the People's Republic of China*. Beijing: Renmin University of China Press

Zhang, Yumin (Ed.). 2001. *Textbook of Intellectual Property Law*. Chongqing: Southwest University of Political Science and Law Press
Zheng, Chengsi. 1993. *Textbook of Intellectual Property Law*. Beijing: Law Press
Zheng, Chengsi. 1996. *World Trade Organisation and Trade Related Intellectual Property Rights*. Beijing: China Renmin University Press
Zheng, Chengsi. 2005. *Intellectual Property Rights (3rd Edition)*. Beijing: Law Press
Zheng, Chengsi and Zhu, Xiequn. 2006. Information and intellectual property. *Journal of Southwest University of science and Technology 1*
Zhong, Yixin. 2002. *Principles of Information Science*. Beijing: Beijing University of Posts and Telecommunications Press
Zhou, Qingshan and Zhang, Shouwen. 2003. *Information Law*. Beijing: China Renmin University Press

Chapter 2
Nature of IPRs

For a long time, the basic attributes of IPRs have not received sufficient academic attention in China. Textbooks and scholarly works of the 1980s defined IPR as 'one right with two attributes,' asserting that it has the dual attributes of property rights and personal rights. By the 1990s, IPRs have been differentiated in theory and practice from right of ownership over tangible property, and qualitative analysis of intangible property rights have been made from the perspective of civil law rights. It can be observed that an evolving understanding of the nature of IPRs has been achieved in China over the past decades. Nevertheless, there is still room for further research on the nature of IPRs. In light of the *Trade Related Aspects of Intellectual Property Right Agreement* (the *TRIPS Agreement*) and *the Universal Declaration of Human Rights* and with reference to classic schools of thought on human rights, this chapter discusses the private-rights and human-rights attributes of IPRs.

2.1 IPRs as Private Rights

The private nature of IPRs could hardly be overlooked since the *TRIPS Agreement* states in Preamble 1 that "intellectual property rights are private rights", and thus emphasises the IPRs' private rights legal nature. The fact that IPRs are grouped into civil law rights is also an acknowledgement of its private authority. The term "private rights" is a concept corresponding to that of public rights, referring to various civil law rights enjoyed by private persons (including natural persons, legal persons and other organisations). Private rights can be understood in the following aspects: firstly, "private" as in "private rights" here means private persons, especially the subject of civil legal relations, that is, persons on equal status. And the state also forms a mutual equal relationship with other civil subjects when it appears as a civil subject in certain cases. Secondly, "private" as in "private rights" implies private ownership. "Private" here means that as a civil law right, it is enjoyed by a particular person and particular

H. Wu, *Theorising Intellectual Property Rights from Chinese Perspectives*,
https://doi.org/10.1007/978-981-96-5867-1_2

subject of the civil law. The right of ownership is the right of the owner to directly control the property, while the creditor's right is the right of the creditor to request the action or inaction of the debtor. This means that private rights are enjoyed by particular persons in a certain circumstance, rather than enjoyed by all persons as public rights. Thirdly, "private" as in "private rights" is the right to private interests, as opposed to public interests. According to the principles of private law, "individual is allowed to form economic or other relations with others at his own will" in pursuit of legitimate self-interest (Costea 1994, p. 5). IPRs are categorised into private rights as they satisfy the defining criteria of private rights: they are "rights with respect to private interests" (from the interest theory), "rights between subjects of equal footing" (from the relation theory) and "rights established in private law" (from the theory of law) (Li and Li 1988, p. 149). It can be argued that the basic principles and rules of civil law are applicable to the creation, exercise, and protection of IPRs. Detached from civil law rights, IPRs would be deprived of their legitimacy.

The division between public and private rights can be traced back to Roman law. In ancient Rome, every citizen was entitled to *jus civitatis*, an exclusive right including both public and private rights. The term "public right" means voting right (i.e., the right to set laws and to elect officials in legislative councils) and the right to be elected (i.e., the right to be elected as officials or members of legislative councils) under the civil law, while the term "private rights" includes rights of marriage, property rights, testamentary capacity and litigation rights (Zhou 1994, pp. 99–100). In the ancient Roman system of private rights, property rights are based on the "object", including both physical subject matter (corporeal things) and institutional subject matter (incorporeal things) (Chen 1936, p. 84). During the period of the Roman Republic (509–27 BC.), there were no property rights to protect intellectual products, that is, IPRs in the modern sense. Yet the private rights legislated in Roman law, especially the rights pertaining to "incorporeal things", nourished later thinking and contemplation of the legalisation of intellectual property. The theory of "incorporeal things" is intended to "objectify" right of ownership in subjective creations, by expanding the perception of "object" to things without physical existence. The acknowledgement of intellectual property marks a shift in modern legislation. The scope of property was no longer limited to physical subject matter, but expanded to include a full range of property which does not have external physical shape. Abandoning physical existence as the defining attribute of property and acknowledging a full range of non-physical property initiated the abstraction and de-physicalisation revolution of how property was perceived. "In the case of intellectual property law, the subject matter in question are abstract object. As it happens, abstract object does not exist, or so we claim. Abstract object in intellectual property law takes the form of legal fiction. The law assumes that there are rights in certain abstractions. An algorithm and the formulae for penicillin and its derivatives are examples of abstract object. Many people need, use and depend on such subject matter" (Drahos 1996). According to Peter Drahos, an Australian scholar, therefore, a new form of property rights is emerging that is distinct from traditional rights and is based on abstract object: these are IPRs.

Defining IPRs as private rights came as the result of the legal revolution and institutional innovation of modern society. The formation of the intellectual property system occurred over a historical process in which the feudal franchising system evolved into capitalist property rights. In medieval Europe, franchising took the form of a monarchic decree or government writ, granting printers an exclusive license to publish and empowering groups and individuals to manufacture and sell licensed products. The protection of franchising offered was supported by "imperially authorised" administrative power rather than statutory rights. Later, owing to the waning of the feudalism and the evolution of private rights in Europe, the newly emerged Burgher class, who called for a new type of ownership, i.e. "moral rights", a prototype of "moral rights" in the modern sense, to be created for printed works and franchised goods to replace the administrative privilege of franchising. For example, in seventeenth century England, publishers used natural law to justify the exclusive publishing rights, which should not be subject to the king's privilege but instead obtained based on the transfer of the author's "moral rights", which holds that the author and the publisher enjoy ownership of both a work and the books materialising such work (Abe 1992; Patterson and Lindberg 1991). In France, the concept of ownership has grown in significance since its recognition during the French Revolution (1789). This was first represented in the field of IPRs, which had to adapt to changes ranging from the expansion of subject matters of IPRs, its newly established legal relationship, to the emerging heterogeneous kinds of rights. Here, the moral rights, though not an equivalence of their modern counterparts, are exclusive, inviolable rights of ownership (Yin 1998, p. 122). The expansion of right of ownership resulted from the establishment of "moral rights", is not an institutional innovation as applied in constructing the private rights system but rather a simple stretch of the existing ownership structure. This approach has distinct defects: First, applying the concept of ownership orientating to tangible assets to intangible assets is problematic for it may overload the term "ownership" in connotation and denotation that the range and scope of it are hard to pinpoint at the technical level (Morangel 1983, p. 231). Despite the fact that the ownership of intellectual works and of other tangible properties share some characteristics, the legal provisions addressing intangible property rights should be different from the legal system of ownership. Second, intellectual property ownership differs from ownership of the traditional kind, as it is not over subject matter, but over creative intellectual products which are of another kind, and non-material subject matter. Therefore, it is necessary for us to "liberate ourselves from the imprisoning concept of property as the simple ownership of a thing by an individual person" and "design forms that create claims remote from tangible subject matter" (Grey 1994). This form of right is the intellectual property right. The establishment of the IPRs regime completed the change of the non-physical, non-material or intangible property right from privileges granted by imperial power to an ownership right upheld and protected by code of laws. As a result, IPRs are transmuted into a new private property right.

The fact that IPRs are private rights provides a new way for individuals to acquire property at the institutional level. Intellectual products are distinct subject matter independent of tangible things in the traditional sense, and the intellectual property law, by establishing intellectual products as subject matter of protection, is a new property legal system which is distinct from the property ownership of corporeal things, marking an innovation in the property legal system. In describing the relationship between economy and law, Marx said, "Whenever the development of industry and commerce creates new forms of interaction…the law has to recognise them as new ways of acquiring property" (Marx and Engels 1960, p. 72). Indeed, it was precisely the development of the commodity economy and of science and technology that gave impetus to the emergence of the new types of property that are different from tangible property. The rise of the Second Industrial Revolution in the 1860s saw a surge of new technology and inventions that led to dramatic changes in the commodity economy. Intangible property, as by-products of the technological revolution, was acknowledged first by Western capitalist countries and now has been widely accepted in the legal system.

As stated, IPRs are private rights, and such rights are in fact intangible property rights. Understanding IPRs as intangible property rights is essential to our understanding of the scope of the IPRs system, which mainly involves the attribution of rights of discoveries and inventions. Some scholars within and beyond China proposed that the rights arising from all intellectual creative activities, including rights of discovery and invention, should be incorporated into IPRs, on the grounds that this is provided for in the *Convention Establishing the World Intellectual Property Organisation*, and *the General Principles of the Civil Law of the People's Republic of China* clearly stipulates that IPRs, along with rights of discoveries and inventions, are under protection (Liu 1997, p. 2). Some even stated that IPRs should not be simply defined as intangible property rights but should also include moral rights, and the rights of discovery and invention belong to the latter (Guo 2002). Yet other scholars hold opposite opinions. Some have argued that to define scientific discoveries as the object of IPRs protection is not appropriate, and that the laws and international conventions of most countries in the world do not grant private property rights to scientific discoveries (Liu 1995, p. 3). Some further argued that rights of discovery, invention and other scientific and technological achievements are not exclusive rights to the use of these intellectual achievements but only rights to obtain honours and awards, which make them fall under the jurisdiction of science and technology related laws, such as the *Law of People's Republic of China on Scientific and Technological Progress* (Wu 2000, p. 2; Zhang 2001, p. 14).

In my view, private rights guarantee the legal protection of private property, and IPRs, the literal meaning and intent of IPRs is to secure the private rights over such intellectual property. Here, "intellectual products" is the general term for products of human intellect in the fields of science, technology, culture and so on, which do not indiscriminately grant creators private property rights. In the case of scientific and technological achievements and some technical achievements (namely, discoveries and inventions), these rights are property rights subject to non-market-based mechanisms. Both rights of discovery and rights of invention intend to reward creators with certificates of honour, medals and prizes according to their social, economic and scientific contributions. In this way, the rights of the right holders have been conferred to the state, allowing free and open access for the public. That is, rewards are given to creators in a non-market mechanism in exchange for making their scientific achievements public property. If the rights of discoveries and inventions as public property were incorporated into the IPRs regime, the defining characteristics of IPRs, primarily as exclusive private rights over intangible property would no longer exist, resulting in the collapse of the institutional and theoretical framework of IPRs.

Regarding the basic attributes of IPRs, the theoretical community in China has been deepening their understanding of them. However, these various understandings of IPRs, either as one right with two attributes, or as intangible property rights or as ordinary human rights, all uphold IPRs' primary attribute of private rights. In recent years, while maintaining IPRs' position as private rights, some scholars have come up with the proposition that IPRs also feature the attribute of public rights in respect to the development and reform of the modern IPR infrastructure in China. IPRs have been identified as private rights with public-rights attributes or, expressed differently, with both private-rights and public-rights attributes. The recognition of IPRs' dual attributes witnesses the evolution of modern private law in which the standard concepts of "right" and "private" in traditional private law have been challenged. Private law with public law attributes derives from the state's intervention in the economy, which is manifest in two ways. First, new legal divisions and legal regimes have been established successively in China. For instance, the state's intervention in the relationship between employers and the employees has led to the enactment of *Labour Law* (1995); the state's support for and regulating of business activities have led to that of *Anti-Monopoly Law* (2008) and *Anti-Unfair Competition Law*(2022); the state's intervention in the relationship between business operators and consumers has led to that of *Product Liability Law* (2018) and *Law on the Protection of Consumer Rights and Interests* (1994); and the state's coordination of business and natural environment has produced *Law on Energy Conservation* (2008)and *Environmental Protection Law* (2015). Second, restrictions have been placed on the principle of autonomy in private law, the original meaning of which was that a private individual shall enjoy rights and obligations and perform all civil acts in accordance with his own will without intervention by the state or others. From the perspective of modern framework of civil law, the principle of the autonomy of private individuals infuses each system within the civil law and is embodied in property autonomy (right of ownerships system), freedom of contract (contract system), freedom of marriage (marriage system), freedom of inheritance (inheritance system), freedom of establishment of groups (legal person system) and so on. Having private law with public law attributes restricts the autonomy in private law, but it does not undermine the essence of civil law as private law. For the same reason, the state's intervention in the IPRs regime manifests in certain limitations on the scope of the right and effect of IPRs. The IPRs regime has involved the adjustment of protection of related rights and limitations of related laws from its beginning, including the state's restrictions on monopoly rights and efforts to establish a balanced mechanism between the individual interest of creators and the interest of the public. However, these do not amount to a fundamental transformation of IPRs from private rights to a combination of private and public rights.

Finally, the *TRIPS Agreement* stipulates IPRs are private rights, which strengthens developed countries' claims of protecting intellectual property as private assets. However, TRIPS also takes into account the appeal of developing countries by highlighting the public policy objectives of IPRs. In most Western countries, the inviolability of private rights is axiomatic and a fundamental principle of law. Acknowledging IPRs as private rights ensures, conceptually and institutionally, equal protection over tangible and intangible property (Kong 2002, p. 72). Raising the standard and level of IPRs protection is necessary and inevitable for promoting technological and cultural innovation in a knowledge-based economy. However, the expansion domestically and also internationally of intellectual property as private rights, a view led by developed countries, may also bring about unpredictable consequences. Domestically, the ever-expanding range of intellectual property as private rights in domestic law will inevitably erode the public knowledge assets base available to the public. Production skills, technology, market know-how and skills, which were previously accessible to the public, will be incorporated into the private domain, leading to the shrinking of public domain of intellectual assets and conflicts between the personal interests of intellectual creators and the public interests of intellectual product users (Yuan 1997). Internationally, the increasing privatisation of intellectual property will force developing countries, whose economic, technological and cultural development is currently in a vulnerable and disadvantageous position, to accept the expanded scope of the IPRs protection as well as higher standards of private-rights protection, further widening the gap between developed and developing countries. Therefore, the *TRIPS Agreement*, while emphasising IPRs as private rights, also acknowledges the public policy objectives of IPRs protection systems, including their development and technology objectives. TRIPS is also aware that the least developed countries in particular need the most flexibility in implementing and administering the Agreement in their countries so as to be able to create a favourable environment to achieve their development and technology goals (Introduction to TRIPS).[1] Nonetheless, limited attention has been paid by TRIPS to IPRs' public policy objectives, particularly as balanced against the high-level private-rights protection it grants intellectual property. It is a consensus among international human rights organisations that because of the conflict between fulfilling the *TRIPS Agreement* and realising economic, social and cultural development, governments of various countries should bear in mind the social function of IPRs in conformity with international human rights obligations when introducing relevant legislations.

[1] See the preamble to *The WTO agreement on trade-related aspects of intellectual property rights (TRIPS)*.

2.2 IPRs as Human Rights

The Universal Declaration of Human Rights, as well as other key international human-rights conventions have all acknowledged that IPRs and related rights have significant human-rights implications (Chapman 2001). It consists of two IPRs-related human rights, of which one is the right enjoyed by the creator to his/her intellectual creation achievements and the other is the right of the public to share the benefits brought by intellectual creations. These two rights are closely linked and are acknowledged as basic human rights by the international community.

Enlightenment philosophers of seventeenth and eighteenth centuries Europe shed new light on the relationship between property rights and human rights, providing the philosophical source of the human-rights implication of IPRs. From John Locke to Jean-Jacques Rousseau, philosophers of the Enlightenment in general associated property rights with natural human rights, and by so doing endowered property rights with an independent and central position. Their propositions highlighted the following three aspects of human rights: to begin with, human rights are embedded in human nature and embody the essence of humanity; thus, human rights are considered universal, transcending time and society, and are of eternal and inalienable significance. Secondly, by emphasising the rights of individuals, men are set against society and the state, with statements such as "human rights are the rights of the individual against the state' and 'innate rights of man counterweight the power of the state" (Locke 1964). Thirdly, they regarded property rights as the core to the innate rights of man and the individual interests were to be safeguarded, stating, "Only the egoistic individuals are genuine man with 'feelings, personalities and direct existence'" (Marx and Engels 1956). In summary, the innate rights of man are the rights of self-interest, namely, the sacred and inviolable rights of private property.[2]

Legacies of Enlightenment thinkers concerning man's innate rights inspired the exploration and interpretation of the basic attributes of IPRs in the later generations. First, as human rights, IPRs are "innate", that is, "inherent" rather than privilege granted by the state power. Second, as human rights, IPRs are "universal", that is, a "universal claim" rather than a provision of partial, administrative protection. It is capitalist property rights rather than a franchising system in feudal medieval Europe. However, interpreting IPRs in light of innate human rights has its flaws. IPRs as human rights imply not only indiscriminate protection of the private rights of intellectual property but also adequate sharing of intellectual property interests. When attaching great importance to the IPRs protection, we cannot afford to overlook the fact that intellectual products came into being through the creative work of intellectual labourers supported by the knowledge base accumulated over generations as the "productive resources." Thus, labourers' possession of public knowledge and their own creative thinking are integrated,[3] resulting in intellectual products being not only personal property of creators but also part of the collective wealth available to the public, in other words, the property of the whole society. Therefore, IPRs

---

[2] For a description of the theory of the innate rights of man, see Zheng (1994).

[3] For information on the social attributes of intellectual products, see Zhang (1992).

over intellectual creations are only exclusive rights enjoyed by private individuals under certain conditions and within certain scope. They are limited and are subject to limitations of laws.

Legal documents of various historical periods bring more clarity to the human-rights implications of IPRs with different legislative orientations. In Western countries, the basic rights and freedoms of citizens stipulated in the Constitution and constitutional laws are the reflection of natural rights in the name of positive law (Hu and Han 1993, pp. 1–2). As a result, IPRs are associated with human rights. For example, the *French Declaration of the Rights of the Man and of the Citizen* (The French Declaration of Rights) of 1789 states that 'The free communication of ideas and opinions is one of the most precious of the rights of man. Every citizen may, accordingly, speak, write, and print with freedom, but shall be responsible for such abuses of this freedom as shall be defined by law' (Ramond, 2011). This statement sends out clear a message that authorship, as a sort of IPRs, is as sacred and inviolable as human rights. Across the Atlantic in the US, framers of the Constitution established three overriding purposes of intellectual property policies, namely "the promotion of learning, the preservation of the public domain, and the protection of the author" (Patterson and Lindberg 1991).[4] In the *Amendments to the United States Constitution*, the freedoms of speech and publication is fully respected as the basic human rights, 'Congress shall make no law respecting an establishment of religion, or prohibiting the free exercise thereof; or abridging the freedom of speech, or of the press' (Congress of the United States, 1789); while on the other hand, the *Amendment* guarantees laws to be made determining the term of protection of IPRs. By stating that 'The Parliament of Canada, affirming that the Canadian Nation is founded upon principles that acknowledge the supremacy of God, the dignity and worth of the human person and the position of the family in a society of free men and free institutions' and that 'Affirming also that men and institutions remain free only when freedom is founded upon respect for moral and spiritual values and the rule of law,' the *Canadian Bill of Rights* (1960)[5] ensures that everyone has the right "freely to participate in the cultural life of the community; to enjoy the arts and to share in scientific advancement and its benefits; the right to the protection of the intellectual and material interests resulting from any scientific, literary or artistic production of which he is the author" (Reyes 1980, p. 213). Embedded in the universal human rights, IPRs relate to human rights in the following ways: to guarantee the exclusive right of creators to their intellectual products, and to ensure the public fair use of intellectual products, namely the access right of the public (*Constitution of the United States*) and 'the right of free participation' in sharing intellectual assets of the whole society (*Canadian Charter of Rights and Freedoms*).

[4] Some American scholars contend that the right of access is implied in the above three policies, namely, the general members of society have the right to use copyright works under certain conditions.

[5] Canadian Bill of Rights S.C. 1960, c. 44 Assented to 1960-08-10 An Act for the Recognition and Protection of Human Rights and Fundamental Freedoms Preamble.

Before the twentieth century, human rights were determined by declarations and constitutions of each nation. The protection of IPRs and sharing of intellectual interests tend to be regulated by national constitutional documents, adapting to the specific political, economic and cultural contexts. The turn of the twentieth century witnessed a successive formulation of international and regional human rights charters, starting with the *Charter of the United Nations* in 1945, which established international standards in protecting human rights. Domestically, intellectual property laws have followed suit, highlighting IPRs as human rights. The *Universal Declaration of Human Rights* adopted in 1948 and the *International Covenant on Economic, Social and Cultural Rights* of 1976, adhering to the human rights principles and standards established by the UN and referring to the *American Declaration of the Rights and Duties of Man*, have put forward three IPRs-related human rights: "the right to freely participate in the cultural life of the community"; "the right to benefit from scientific progress and its application"; "the right to the protection of the moral and material interests resulting from any scientific, literary or artistic production of which he is the author." Based on records, although the provisions concerning "the right to freely participate in the cultural life of the community" were widely accepted by all countries, these countries held different opinions as to whether IPRs are basic human rights. Proponents argued that the UN requires morality and authority to protect the productions of labour in various forms; and just like tangible property, intellectual property also requires protection. In contrast, opponents argued that the benefits of cultural and scientific progress enjoyed by the public were in conflict with the individual's monopoly to knowledge and they could not be lumped together which may end up restricting the public sharing and enjoyment of the benefits of intellectual achievements. IPRs-related provisions were eventually added to the *International Bill of Human Rights* mainly in consideration of their potential contributions to a cluster of human rights, namely "essential preconditions for cultural freedom and participation and access to the benefits of scientific progress" (Chapman 2001). It should be noted that the above mentioned IPRs-related provisions are closely linked. A full-fledged IPRs regime should on one hand ensure the protection of IPRs, and on the other hand promote, rather than restrict the public from participating in cultural life and accessing the benefits of scientific progress. The rights of creators and the rights of the public are therefore interdependent, not an "either/or choice", as respect for the right of creators ensures a richer knowledge base available to the public. What the *International Bill of Human Rights* provides is a declaratory statement outlining the interests of IPR holders and the public, specifying neither the scope of IPRs nor the range of interests shared by the public. However, this issue is manifest at the institutional level in relevant legislations as protection for and limitations on IPRs.

The concept and institutional function of IPRs find more comprehensive and noble explanations when viewed in the context of human rights. First, IPRs are regarded as a universal human right. This shows IPRs are no longer franchise privileges granted by a royal decree in the Middle Ages, but a universal right of any civilised society. Equality also directly reflects the human rights nature of IPRs. In the IP legislation, equality manifests as the free choice to engage in creative activities and the equal opportunity to obtain IPRs, which society has the responsibility to provide. IPRs as universal human rights require social conditions. Domestically, one can obtain IPRs by virtue of creative labour, and intellectual properties, regardless of their forms, are equally protected. In the case of IPRs involving foreigners, national treatment protection should be provided in accordance with the common international IPR conventions or with the principle of equivalent reciprocal treatment. In the international IPRs protection mechanism, intellectual achievements of all nations and all races should be given equal protection to promote scientific, technological and cultural development across countries around the world.

Secondly, intellectual creations, the subject matter of IPRs law protection, manifest human dignity and human value. In the view of human rights theories, literary, artistic, scientific and other intellectual products can become commodities, but they are not commodities in the first place. As Chapman emphasised, "... artistic and scientific works are not first and foremost economic commodities" (Chapman 2001). As the result of mental and moral production, intellectual products embody the creativity of individuals and rely on the prior collective achievements of human society. Intellectual products, represented as the systematic knowledge attained in certain domains as well as achievements of natural science and social science, in general have commercial value in a commodity economy (Zhang 1992, pp. 294–295). This shows that intellectual products only become the subject matter of IPRs under certain conditions. Limitations shall be placed on intellectual products being acknowledged as the subject matter of intellectual property laws. In other words, IP laws should restrict the scope of IPRs protection and exclude certain intellectual products from its protection. For example, intellectual products violating the public interests, public order and good customs shall not be protected by intellectual property laws. Intellectual products without the basic attributes of commodities or that are protected alternatively by non-market mechanisms shall also be excluded from the private rights-orientated IPRs regime. When the term of protection expires, intellectual products which have enjoyed exclusive rights will enter the public domain and be added to the public assets available to all members of society. Finally, the terms and standards of the IPRs protection should contribute to the realisation of human rights. As mentioned above, major human rights conventions require IPRs to be coordinated with human rights to ensure individuals have the rights "to take part in cultural life" and "to enjoy the benefits of scientific progress and its applications." This human rights factor should "go well beyond a simple economic calculus often governing intellectual property law" (Chapman 2001). From this standpoint, IPRs regimes should feature dualism in their value orientation. In the case of legislative purposes, equal emphasis should be placed on both promoting the development of science, technology and culture, and protecting the interests of intellectual property right holders. In terms of IPRs as exclusive rights, both "protection" and "limitation" need to be part of the consideration without over-emphasising one while neglecting the other. I once summarised the 'principle of balance' as the legal spirit underpinning modern intellectual property laws. This balance involves the balance between the rights and obligations of IP owners, the balance of rights between intellectual property owners, transmitters and users; and the balance between public interests and private interests (Wu 1996).

2.3 IPRs as Private Rights and Human Rights

It is meaningful to study IPRs based on the integration of private rights and human rights. To a certain extent, the humanist undertone of respecting knowledge creation and intellectual achievements is evident in the theoretical hypothesis of IPRs as human rights. In the academic community, the argument that IPRs shall not be deemed as human rights also exists. Some argue that from the new human rights perspective, human rights are fundamental, universal, moral and ultimate, while IPRs are state-granted, alienable, economic and instrumental (Song 2004). Some even hold that intellectual property creators' rights have two-fold features, namely IPRs as property rights, and IPRs as human rights of cultural rights over intellectual property (Zheng 2007). Even among scholars who argue that IPRs have human-rights implications, their arguments are not consistent. Some argue that so long as Article 17 of the *Universal Declaration of Human Rights* is in force, protection of IPRs as human rights is axiomatic. Yet, it is also worth mentioning that IPRs as human rights are primarily copyrights related to the freedom of expression, and do not include patents and trademarks which have strong economic overtone (Zhang 2004). Ideas have also been developed that IPRs are considered as human rights as they have the attributes of "right to development"—the ultimate aim of the intellectual property system shall be development—the development of people, society, the state, and all mankind (Wu 2005). In my view, the Enlightenment philosophers' exposition of the relationship between property rights and human rights has been a vital source of IPRs' human rights implications and established the legitimacy of the institutional construction of IPRs. The provisions of international human rights conventions on property rights provide the basis of international law for considering certain IPRs as human rights. As for the consideration of IPRs as the right to development and other special human rights, it also has positive theoretical significance for the establishment of an ideal intellectual property system. Therefore, we cannot simply sever IPRs from human rights, but need to seek the organic connection between the two. In short, the understanding of IPRs based on the integration of private rights and human rights is the starting point for a comprehensive examination of the values and social functions of the modern IPRs regime.

Construction of such an IPRs regime, in recognition of its private-rights nature and human-rights orientation and in alignment with an integrated legal value system not only is the preferred model in theory by scholars but, more importantly, also a necessity demanded by social development reality. The international human rights organisations have generally all noticed, "the centrality of IPRs to almost every sphere of economic life means that international treaties, national legal codes and judicial decisions about intellectual property can have significant ramifications for the protection and promotion of human rights." "This is particularly the case for the economic, social and cultural rights enumerated in the Covenant" (Chapman 2001). This impact can sometimes be negative when actual or potential conflicts arise between IPRs as human rights and social and economic rights as other human rights.

One underlying cause of such conflict is the impact of the new technological revolution on human rights. In 1968, the International Conference on Human Rights issued *The Proclamation of Tehran*, which specifically addressed the impact of modern science and technology on human rights. The *Proclamation* stated, 'While recent scientific discoveries and technological advances have opened vast prospects for economic, social and cultural progress, such developments may nevertheless endanger the rights and freedoms of individuals and will require continuing attention.' The Tehran Conference therefore urges the UN to take the initiative to research on the following issues: (1) the respect for privacy in view of sound recording technology; (2) the protection of personality and of physical and mental health in view of progress in biology, medicine and biochemistry; (3) the limitations that should be imposed on the use of certain electronic products that may affect people's rights and their use in democratic societies; and (4) more generally, the balance that should be established between the development of science and technology and the progress in human intelligence, spirit, culture and morality (Chapman 2001). The development of science and technology has a direct impact on human dignity, freedom of expression, the right to education, to life and health, to environment and so on, all of which are widely recognised by the international community as human rights. While at the same time, sound recording technology, biotechnology, electronic products and other advances in science are all under the IPRs protection. The positive and negative effects of the above-mentioned science and technology and attempt to address the conflicts between various rights, between IPRs and human rights have therefore become the issues of concern to both Human rights activists and legislators alike.

The other cause of conflict between IPRs and human rights is the impact of the new international trade system on human rights. The founding of the World Trade Organisation (WTO) in 1994 and the enforcement of the *TRIPS Agreement* in 1995 institutionalised the global protection of IPRs. Within the institutional framework of the WTO, member countries are obliged to align their national laws to the *TRIPS Agreement* standards, and by doing so, integrating the IPRs protection into the international trade system. In 2000, the United Nations Sub-Commission on the Promotion and Protection of Human Rights, the main subsidiary body of the former Commission on Human Rights, issued a resolution titled *IPRs and Human Rights*, which reviewed the impact of the *TRIPS Agreement* on international human rights and declared: Noting furthermore that actual or potential conflicts exist between the implementation of the *TRIPS Agreement* and the realisation of economic, social and cultural rights in relation to, inter alia, impediments to the transfer of technology to developing countries, the consequences for the enjoyment of the right to food of plant variety rights and the patenting of genetically modified organisms, 'bio-piracy' and the reduction of communities' (especially indigenous communities') control over their own genetic and natural resources and cultural values, and restrictions on access to patented pharmaceuticals and the implications for the enjoyment of the right to health (quoted in Weeramantry 1997, p. 2). For a human right–centred society, intellectual property creators' rights should be regarded as human rights, whether the creators be individuals, groups or associations. At the same time, protection of IPRs must be consistent with the safeguarding of human dignity and the realisation of other fundamental human rights. Human rights obligations outweigh all economic policies and trade agreements. Specifically, in the implementation of the *TRIPS Agreement*, obligations stipulated in the international human rights conventions should be taken into full consideration, and in the domestic legislation of each country to protect IPRs, its social function must be consistent with their international human rights obligations.

Within a country, the balance and coordination of IPRs-related interests of all stakeholders are realised through a system of protection and limitation of the rights conferred by IPRs. Based on a country's social reality and considering its economic, cultural, educational and science and technology policies, policymakers of a country adjust their focus on IPRs protection at certain times or on the limitations at other times. This is not difficult to achieve without violating international IPR conventions. Yet, it is worth considering whether the current international conventions on IPRs, like the *TRIPS Agreement*, adequately addresses the interests of all parties, such as the creators and the users, involved, and whether they are helpful to strike a proper balance between society and economy as well as between rights and obligations. It must be noted that in the international trading system, IPRs have provided developed countries a powerful tool to further strengthen their competitive edge to maintain their lead in technological innovation and global trade (Gao 2002). The *TRIPS Agreement*, within the WTO framework, is more favourable to the interests and requirements of developed countries, resulting in an imbalance of rights and obligations between developed and developing countries.

In recent years, in response to disputes over IPRs and public health issues, with the efforts of developing countries, the WTO Ministerial Conference in Doha passed the *Declaration on the TRIPS Agreement and Public Health*, also known as the *Doha Declaration* in November 2001. At the Doha Conference, South Africa presented an appeal on behalf of developing countries to respect people's right to life and health and to safeguard public interests, which received positive responses from developed members and these concerns in the field of IPRs were addressed. The *Doha Declaration* confirms the severity of public health crisis in many developing and least developed countries. While stressing the significance of the IPRs protection in new drug development, it also expresses concerns about the impact of such protection on drug prices. Furthermore, the *Doha Declaration* also stipulates that the *TRIPS Agreement* should not become barriers for member states to protect public health, and it permits members to exercise the right to issue compulsory license, determine and declare "state of national emergency or other extreme emergencies" and apply the doctrine of exhaustion in their IPRs regimes. *Doha Declaration* marks a major turn in international intellectual property laws with significant implications. First, it breaks new grounds in coordinating the conflicting interests between developed and developing countries to ensure that public health, a basic human right, receives appropriate attention. Besides. it takes the initiative to attach significant importance to the interests of economically and technologically disadvantaged countries in promoting the international protection of IPRs, incorporating their interests into the mainstream consciousness, and expanding rights protection to cover traditional knowledge, biodiversity, geographical markers and so on.

In conclusion, the overarching framework of unifying private rights and human rights provides new perspectives for the institutional design of IPRs, both domestically and internationally. To establish an IPRs regime that both private rights and human rights-orientated, and on tenable legal and humanitarian ground, not only safeguards the interests of intellectual property owners and encourages the growth of accumulated intellectual wealth, but also promotes public interests and the fair sharing of intellectual and technological benefits.

References

Abe, Kōji. 1992. Similarities and differences of copyright laws and their causes in different countries. Trans. Genquan Zhu. *Global Law Review*

Chapman, Audrey R. 2001. Approaching intellectual property as a human right. *Copyright Bulletin* 3

Chen, Chaobi. 1936. *Principles of Roman Law*. Beijing: The Commercial Press

Costea, Mi. 1994. The autonomy of private laws and its limits. *Jahrbuch des Deutsh-Chinesischen instituts fur wirtschaftsrecht*. Nanjing: Nanjing University Press

Drahos, Peter. 1996. *A Philosophy of Intellectual Property*. England: Dartmouth Publishing Company Limited

Editorial Board of Encyclopedia of Law of Peking University. 1999. Constitution and administrative law. In *Peking University Encyclopedia of Jurisprudence*. Beijing: Peking University Press.

Gao, Sheng. 2002. Justice – the foremost value for socialist system. *China's Foreign Trade* 4

Grey, Thomas C. 1994. The disintegration of property. *Comparative Economic & Social System 5*

Guo, Qingcun. 2002. Philosophical thinking on the attribute, scope and related issues of intellectual property rights. In *Peking University Intellectual Property Review*. Beijing: Economic Press China

Hu, Jinguang and Han, Dayuan. 1993. *Human Rights Protection System*. Beijing: China University of Political Science and Law Press

Kong, Xiangjun. 2002. *WTO Intellectual Property Agreement and Its Domestic Application*. Beijing: Law Press China

Li, Jin and Li, Fang. 1988. *The Chinese Dictionary of Practical Law*. Changchun: Jilin University Press

Liu, Chunmao. 1997. *Chinese Civil Law and Intellectual Property Rights*. Beijing: Publishing House of Chinese People's Public Security University

Liu, Chuntian. 1995. *Intellectual Property Law Coursebook*. Beijing: China Renmin University Press

Locke, John. 1964. *Treatise on Government*. Trans. Qifang Ye. Beijing: The Commercial Press

Marx, Karl and Friedrich Engels. 1956. *Marx-Engels Collected Works*. Beijing: People's Publishing House

Marx, Karl and Friedrich Engels. 1960. *Marx-Engels Collected Works*. Beijing: People's Publishing House

Morangel, Julio. 1983. French civil law coursebook. *In Selected materials of foreign civil law*. Beijing: Law Press China

Patterson, L. Ray and Stanley W. Lindberg. 1991. *The Nature of Copyright: A Law of Users' Rights*. Athens: The University of Georgia Press

Ramond, D. 2011. Liberté d'expression: De quoi parle-t-on? *Raisons Politiques 44*

Reyes, A. A. 1980. *Copyright and Fair Dealing in Canada: Fair Use and Free Inquiry*. Norwood: Ablex Publishing Co

Song, Huixian. 2004. Conflict and balance: from the perspective of human-rights implications of intellectual property. *Intellectual Property*
Weeramantry, C. G. 1997. *Human Rights and Scientific and Technological Development*. Beijing: World Affairs Press
Wu, Feng. 2005. Intellectual property· human rights· development. *Journal of university of Shanghai for science and technology* (social science)
Wu, Handong. 1996. *Research on the System of Fair Use of Copyright*. Beijing: China University of Political Science and Law Press
Wu, Handong. 2000. *Intellectual Property Law*. Beijing: Peking University Press
Yin, Tian. 1998. *French Property Law*. Beijing: Law Press China
Yuan, Yong. 1997. Intellectual property law and technological and cultural innovation. Philosophy and social sciences edition. *Journal of Peking University* 5
Zhang, Hesheng. 1992. *Intellectual Economics*. Shenyang: Liaoning People's Publishing House
Zhang, Naigen. 2004. On the relationship between intellectual property rights and human rights under the framework of TRIPS. *The Jurist* 4
Zhang, Yumin. 2001. *Intellectual Property Law Course*. Chongqing: Southwest University of Political Science and Law Press
Zheng, Hangsheng. 1994. *The History of Human Rights*. Beijing: Beijing Publishing House Group
Zheng, Wanqing. 2007. Distinguishing and analysing the intersection between intellectual property right and human rights: on questioning the idea of 'intellectual property rights belonging to basic human rights. *The Jurist* 5
Zhou, Liang. 1994. *Original Theory of Roman Law*. Beijing: The Commercial Press

Chapter 3
Characteristics of IPRs

The description of the characteristics of IPRs goes towards explaining their inherent legal properties, thereby distinguishing them from traditional property ownership. The basic characteristics of IPRs have been extensively discussed in academia, while the generalisation of which, varies slightly in various treatises, and are encapsulated as "exclusiveness", "territoriality," and "temporality." In fact, these described characteristics, relative to other property rights, and ownership rights in particular, are not unique to IPRs. The truly essential characteristic of IPRs lies in the intangibility of its subject matter.

3.1 Essential Characteristic: Intangibility

The object of IPRs, namely intellectual products (or intellectual achievements), is a kind of intangible intellectual wealth, and the essential characteristic of IPRs lies in the intangibility of the subject matter of IPRs. Zheng (1993, p. 45) believes that the distinctive characteristic that distinguishes IPRs from other property rights is their intangibility, intangibility, from which other legal characteristics derive, such as exclusiveness, temporality and territoriality. Technically speaking, the boundary and scope of conduct that a subject can perform by virtue of the law to realize a certain interest is a subjective fiction without physical form. Taking this into consideration, all, from Roman jurists to modern civil law scholars, describe rights with a certain property content (other than ownership) as incorporeal things. As such, the fundamental characteristic of IPRs different from related rights lies not in the intangibility, but in the intangibility of their subject matter, namely intellectual products. In this regard, Zeng Shixiong, a scholar in Taiwan China, shares the same view with me. The tangibility or intangibility of property right does not refer to that of the rights, but of the living resources controlled by the rights, namely, whether the subject matter have physical form. For example, in the case of housing ownership, the key to define

H. Wu, *Theorising Intellectual Property Rights from Chinese Perspectives*,
https://doi.org/10.1007/978-981-96-5867-1_3

the tangibility does not lie in the right itself, but in the fact that the house is a tangible thing. In the case of copyright, the key to define the intangibility lies in the fact that the work is an intangible intellectual object (Zeng 1983, p. 151). The intangibility of intellectual products is relative to the tangibility of chattels and real estate, intellectual products having different forms of existence, utilisation and disposal. In the first place, the possession of intellectual products does not confer tangible control. As intellectual products have no physical form and do not occupy a certain space, people's possession of them is not a kind of occupancy of real and physical subject matter, but is manifest through the acquisition of knowledge and experience. Despite their intangible characteristics, intellectual products must always be expressed in a certain objective form, and the physical carrier of this expression is the right of ownership over tangible property rather than IPRs. Secondly, the use of intellectual products does not result in tangible loss. Public access to intellectual products is a prerequisite for the creation of IPRs. As intellectual products must be openly accessible to the public, people can use the relevant knowledge once they get it, and such products can be used by several subjects at the same time and space. In addition, in contrast to the use of tangible subject matter, the above-mentioned use will not deplete such products, so the form of civil liability of restitution cannot be applied in case of the unauthorised use of the intellectual products of others. Thirdly, there is no de facto disposal eliminating intellectual products or de jure disposal of tangible delivery. Intellectual products will not be destroyed by physical consumption, but they will change from proprietary property to the public wealth upon the expiration of a certain period (namely, the legal protection period). Moreover, tangible delivery is not linked to de jure disposal. In other words, it is possible for a non-rights holder to dispose, through other means than legal ones, of intellectual products belonging to others rather than being actually possessed by him or her. Based on the above characteristics, it is necessary for the government to grant IPRs to the creators of intellectual products and to protect such rights with a legal system distinct from the traditional property right system.

3.2 Basic Characteristic I: Exclusiveness

Relative to creditor's rights, IPRs as proprietary civil law rights feature exclusiveness and absoluteness, as in the right of ownership. With regard to this attribute of IPRs, French scholars have been engaged in a purely academic and nearly pedantic discussion. Some scholars believe that intangible property right is a kind of "property right" (the right of ownership) with its own specialised name, IPR, signifying the ownership of knowledge (Yin 1998). However, many French scholars challenged the legitimacy of regarding intangible property right as right of ownership, and they generalise intangible property right as a monopolised or exclusive right based on the characteristics of the subject matter and the content thereof (ibid.). On the whole, Japanese scholars are in agreement with the above-mentioned views of French scholars. According to Yonhe Kojima (1998), intangible property right, distinct from the right of ownership, is a new and special right which can be divided into the exclusive right and the right to prohibit. The former refers to the exclusive and monopolised right to dominate its object, such as copyright, patent rights and the right to trademarks, trade name, circuit layout design, new plant variety and so on. The latter refers to the right to prohibit unfair competition involving trade secrets, images of goods, and goodwill. In fact, their proprietary nature, namely exclusivity and absoluteness, is the shared characteristic of IPRs and the right of ownership. The difference between them does not lie in the fact that the former are monopolised rights and the latter is a property right, but in the fact that the former are the ownership of intellectual property and the latter of tangible property.

The proprietary nature of IPRs is mainly manifested in two aspects, of which one is that intellectual property is exclusive to the rights holder, who monopolises this strictly protected proprietary right. The use of intellectual products of the rights holder is subject to relevant regulations or to the permission of the rights holder. The other is that the coexistence of two or more IPRs with the same attribute is not permitted for the same intellectual product. For example, in the case of two identical inventions, it is possible to grant a patent to just one of them and it is not possible for a subsequent invention unless it displays noteworthy characteristics and significant progress when compared with the existing technology. There is also a distinction between IPRs and the right of ownership in terms of the effect of their proprietary nature. Firstly, the exclusivity of the right of ownership lies in the exclusion of non-owners from unlawful appropriation, nuisance or destruction of the property of owners, while that of IPRs is the exclusion of people without proprietary rights from unlawful imitation, counterfeiting or plagiarism of intellectual products. Secondly, the absolute monopolisation of the right of ownership means that in the exercise of the owner's rights over the object interference is not allowed, nor is the active assistance of others required. In addition, there are no territorial or temporal restrictions when the object is under the control of the owner. In contrast, the monopolisation of IPRs means IPRs are additionally subject to limitations such as fair use in copyright, temporary transit uses in patent and use by the holder of prior rights in trademark; meanwhile, the exclusive right supported by IPRs is only valid within a certain space (regional restriction) and for a certain term (temporal restriction).

Their proprietary nature, a legal characteristic of IPRs, is expressed in different forms and contents for different types of IPRs. The proprietary nature of copyright is manifest as the proprietary right of the rights holder to use his or her work in various forms such as reproduction, issue, exhibition, performance, broadcasting, filming, and interpretation. The proprietary nature of copyright in the textbook prepared by UNESCO is expressed as follows: "any use of a protected work or other subject matter is lawful if proper authorisation from the copyright owner has been obtained, except in certain cases prescribed by the law. Using a work or subject matter of related rights in a way that would have required authorisation from its right owner would constitute an act of copyright (or related rights) infringement" (UNESCO 1984, p. 19). Patent rights are, in the literal sense, the monopolised rights of the rights holder to the "interests", namely, the proprietary right to the invention and creation, including the right to use, manufacture, sell, and import patented products. The proprietary nature of patent rights is described in the textbook prepared by WIPO as follows: "The right to innovative patents places the owner in the legal position where the patented invention can only be exploited with her or his permission, otherwise the exploitation is illegal. In this way, the owner of a patent can prevent others from exploiting the patented invention. The legal exploitation is subject to the permission of the patent owner, as this prevention does not require any action of him. The right of the patent owner to prevent others from exploiting the patented invention is called the 'proprietary' right' (WIPO 1992, p. 93). The trademark right, also called the proprietary right to trademark, consists in the monopolised right to use a trademark and the right to exclude others from using it. The *Model Law on Trademarks, Trade Names and Unfair Competition in Developing Countries*, drafted by the Joint International Bureau for the Protection of Intellectual Property Rights, refers to the rights related to a registered trademark as the proprietary right to trademark (Article 4). Article 18 of the law provides that the owner of a registered trademark has the following rights: First, the owner of a registered has the right to institute court proceedings against the use of a sign identical with or similar to the registered mark in relation to goods or services similar to those for which the mark has been registered, where confusion may arise in the public. Second, the owner of a registered trademark has the right to prohibit third parties from using a trademark identical with or similar to a registered one without justifiable reasons and causing damage to the interests of the owner thereof (Article 18).

3.3 Basic Characteristic II: Territoriality

IPRs, as a proprietary right, are not unlimited in their spatial effect. It is territorially limited, namely, strictly territorial in nature, and its effect is limited to the territory of the particular country. This characteristic of IPRs makes them different from the ownership of tangible property. In general, there is no territorial restriction on the protection of ownership in principle. The property transferred from one country to another, by legal persons for investment and trade, or by legal persons, still belongs to the rights holder without any prejudice to the legal effect of ownership. This is because the principle of equal foreign-related property rights is pursued internationally in the field of tangible property. This principle stipulates that the recipient country of the chattel will, based on its own possession system, presume the subject of the chattel as the legitimate owner and protect him or her, subject to his or her continuing effective possession after the chattel acquired in one country enters another country. In contrast, IPRs are recognised and protected under the laws of one country and can only have legal effects within that country. The rights holder cannot take substantial possession of intellectual products due to their immaterial nature, and thus the "presumption of right" protecting IPRs extraterritorially cannot be applied for possession, as in the case of tangible property. As such, except for international conventions or reciprocal agreements, IPRs have no extraterritorial effect, and other countries are not obligated to protect such rights. As a result, everyone can use the intellectual products freely in his country without the consent of or payment to the rights holder.

It is generally accepted that territoriality is a unique characteristic of IPRs, but in fact it has existed in many areas of civil law rights throughout history. According to research on private international law, tort litigation in the field of tort liability is mostly under the jurisdiction of the court of the locus delicti and governed by the law thereof. In the field of contract debt, the territoriality of the law previously caused rigidity in its application and difficulty in extraterritorial enforcement of judgment. The main reason behind was that such rights came at a time of few trade exchanges as most countries were in the grip of feudalism and seclusion. In this connection, occasional disputes involved in foreign affairs could be solved by domestic laws instead of resorting to extraterritorial force of rights (Liu 1998). That caused civil law rights to be unavoidably subject to territoriality.

IPRs emerged from that historical background. At the end of the feudal system in Europe, copyrights and patent rights were originally granted by the monarch as a privilege so that such rights could only be exercised in the territory under the jurisdiction of the monarch. The territoriality of the original IPRs reflects the territoriality of feudal law. Amid the development of modern bourgeois law, IPRs finally became a legal moral right instead of a feudal privilege. That said, only IPRs acquired through national laws are protected in capitalist countries under the principle of national sovereignty (Zhang 1999).[1] As such, territoriality is sustained as a characteristic of IPRs. IPRs acquired in one country have to be registered or approved in accordance with the law of other countries if they are to be legally protected there.

From the end of the nineteenth century, the international market for intellectual property transactions began to thrive amid the development of science and technology and the boom in international trade. A great contradiction came as a result between the international demand for intellectual products and the territorial limits of IPRs. In response to this contradiction, countries have signed some international conventions for the protection of IPRs, established some global or regional international organisations, and set up an international IPRs protection regime across the world. There are three critical principles for the international protection of IPRs, of which one is the principle of minimum protection. That is, substantive international standards for IPRs protection are agreed upon and then adopted by the domestic laws of each country through global or regional multilateral negotiations among governments, thus forming a relatively unified international protection regime of IPRs. Subject to the requirements of the principle of minimum protection, the protection level of IPRs by the contracting parties shall not be lower than that stipulated in the international conventions in terms of the scope of subject matter, content of rights and terms of protection. The second is the principle of independence, which means the rights of the same intellectual product acquired by the nationals of the contracting parties in several countries shall be independent of and not interfere with each other. On

[1] The territoriality of intellectual property protection lies in the territorial restrictions of both national sovereignty and the authorization of intellectual property. (For example, the authorization is subject to state examination and registration.)

the premise of meeting the minimum protection requirements under international conventions, the protection level and judicial remedies of the rights of the owner of the intellectual product shall be governed by the laws of relevant contracting countries that provide protection. In accordance with the theory of private international law, the protection of copyright is governed by the law of the place of claim, and that of industrial property by the law of the place of registration (Zheng 1992, p. 16). The principle of independence reflects the fact that relevant international conventions are still subject to the territoriality of IPRs. The third is the principle of national treatment, which means that all contracting countries shall give equal treatment to nationals of other contracting countries on the basis of the international protection of IPRs, thereby ensuring that nationals of these countries shall enjoy the equal treatment in all contracting countries. The provisions of international conventions on the principle of national treatment serve as an important supplement to and coordination of the territorial limits of IPRs. This principle makes it possible IPRs recognised or granted by one country to have extraterritorial force in other contracting countries under international conventions. That said, domestic laws of contracting countries still determine whether to grant rights and how to protect them, as the territoriality of IPRs has not yet been ruled out.

By the second half of the twentieth century, the legislation of IPRs had been increasingly modernised and integrated, as a result of the integration of regional economies and the development of modern science and technology. As such, the rigid territoriality of IPRs has been challenged. This is mainly manifest in two aspects. (1) the emergence of transnational IPRs. The integration of regional economies has united countries, making possible the free flow of goods, capital, human resources and labour force in a large unified market. That thus goes a long way towards the unification of related countries in the IPRs protection. For example, the *Uniform Benelux Law on Marks* enacted by the Union Economique Benelux in 1968 and the *Bangui Agreement* adopted by the African Intellectual Property Organisation in 1977 have made it possible for patents or trademarks applied for or registered in one country to enjoy proprietary rights in all contracting countries at the same time. That said, the most representative document is the *Maastricht Treaty* signed by the member states of the European Union (EU) in 1991. As part of its efforts to realise economic integration, the EU has established a broad European protection system in the field of industrial property and copyright, namely to work towards the 'illusion of common European IPRs' under the impetus of the integration of regional economy (Dietz 1986). In one case, the European Court of Justice stated that the territorial limits of the exhaustion of a rights regime[2] must be interpreted in the context of the common market. That means the exhaustion of rights throughout the EU is formed once the goods are first sold in a contracting country (Wu 1998, p. 20). That reflects the fact that IPRs have extended beyond the territory of the country which has granted the right

[2] The regime for exhaustion of rights means that the obligee has no right to control the reuse or resale of the original or copy of the work that enters the market with his consent. Similarly, the obligee has no right to control the reuse or resale of the patented product manufactured or licensed by him after it is sold.

in the first place, and have taken effect in multiple countries simultaneously, which has, to a certain extent, challenged the territoriality of the right. (2) The development of jurisdiction and governing laws of IPRs concerning foreign affairs or foreign nationals. For a long time, disputes over IPRs involving foreign affairs or foreign nationals were generally under the exclusive jurisdiction of the courts in the place of claim. The advancement of the technology of satellite, Internet and recording enables infringements involving modern technology to happen in several or even a dozen countries at the same time, so the number of places where IPRs are claimed will increase accordingly. Thus, it will be inconvenient if the rights holder takes legal action in these places one by one. As a result, a new jurisdictional theory has emerged that courts in one country are entitled to jurisdiction over IPRs-related disputes both within and outside the territory of their country. In connection with this, the applicable law of the place where IPRs are claimed, has changed accordingly. In the event of infringements of IPRs in several or a dozen countries at the same time, the adherence to the law of the place of claim will result in the unreasonable application of several or a dozen applicable laws to the same case (Liu 1998). Therefore, it may be the best choice to apply a new principle of governing law, the Doctrine of the Most Significant Relationship (Li 1991, p. 281).[3] The non-exclusive jurisdiction of disputes over foreign-related IPRs and the diversified application of relevant laws will greatly challenge the territoriality of IPRs. In short, the territoriality of IPRs persists today but has been greatly challenged. It requires closer observation and further study to determine whether this legal characteristic, inherent from feudal laws to modern laws, will be completely ruled out.

3.4 Basic Characteristic III: Temporality

Just as IPRs are restricted by territory, so are they by time. The temporality of IPRs indicates that such rights are protected only within the period stipulated by law. Once beyond the valid period stipulated by law, IPRs are extinguished and relevant intellectual products become the common wealth shared and utilised by all mankind.

Temporality is one of the major differences between IPRs and the right of ownership. As we all know, the right of ownership is protected by law as long as the subject matter of ownership (things) has not been lost, as it is not restricted by time. The legal consequences arising from the acquisition prescription and the negative prescription only leads to the change of the subjects of the property right but not the status of the property (corporeal things) as the object of the right. The Roman jurists generalised this characteristic of ownership as "eternity", which means the fate of ownership begins and ends with its subject matter. It is neither like the rights over

[3] AT the beginning of the twentieth century, scholars of private international law, Pillet and Niboyet, claimed that the law of the place of claim should be applied to intellectual property protection, while the creation and survival of rights be governed by the law of the original state (namely, the law of the country where the rights were originally granted).

the property of another with a fixed term such as mortgages and easements, nor like the creditor's rights destined for extinction such as contractual rights of creditors (Zhou 1994; Chen and Yang 1931). Perpetuity, absoluteness and exclusivity constitute three characteristics of the right of ownership. In fact, it is impossible to realise the perpetuity of ownership in many cases when it is based on the existence of the subject matter. In the case of any loss or damage, the original owner may be left "without ownership." In contrast, the subject matter of IPRs, namely, the intellectual product in an intangible form, is not likely to be damaged or lost. That means it is "perpetual" in the de facto sense, but the law restricts the validity to a certain period of time (Zheng 1998, p. 88).

The temporality of IPRs has a completely distinct implication from that of the rights over the property of another and the creditor's rights. The rights over the property of another are created between specific subjects, such as between easement holders and easement providers in the relationship of easements and between mortgagors and mortgagees in the relationship of mortgage. In addition, based on the premise of ownership, the creation of the rights over the property of another cannot be separated from ownership. As for the creditor's rights, they involve the interests between the creditor and the debtor. As the purpose of debt is performance and liquidation, the law does not recognise the perpetuity of the creditor's rights, which is different from the temporality of IPRs. According to Western scholars, the owner of an intellectual product makes a bargain, namely a special social deed, with society in the form of country. The author receives a limited monopoly and is obligated to allow public access to the work and to preserve the work for the public domain in return (Patent Document Library 1980).

The temporality of IPRs is a principle commonly adopted by countries around the world in order to boost scientific and cultural progress and encourage access to intellectual products. The establishment of the IPRs regime aims to adopt special legal means to regulate the social relations arising from the creation or use of intellectual products. In addition to the wide spread of scientific, technological and cultural achievements, this regime works for the protection of the legitimate interests of creators of intellectual products and the balance between the proprietary nature of IPRs and the public access to intellectual products. In consideration of the aforementioned factors, the legislative objectives of the regime can only be achieved by balancing and coordinating various factors that may be in conflict with each other in the process of achieving its multiple value objectives, such as social progress and equity, as well as the interests of the rights holder. In this sense, the principle of balance represents one of the basic spirits of the IPRs regime. Take the copyright law as an example. The early *Statute of Anne* focused on protecting the interests of other subjects and the public interest while protecting the rights of the author. The Statute established a so-called " public domain for literature", which derives from three rules: (1) the provision that the creation of new works is necessary for copyright (to protect existing works from being withdrawn by publishers); (2) the provision of the protection term of copyright (to counter the publishers' claims of perpetual copyright); and (3) the provision of the limited rights of copyright owners in printing, publishing, and selling (namely, the exhaustion of rights upon secondary use of the work) (Patterson and Lindberg 1991, pp. 49–55). After the Anna Act, dissatisfied with this limited copyright, publishers launched a 40-year "publisher movement" in an attempt to seek the "perpetual copyright" of authors based on the common law after the expiration of the statutory period of copyright After that they acquire rights again by assignment, as a way of preventing public access to the works. This long struggle ended with the revocation of the perpetual prohibition of "copyright in the common law" which was officially abolished in England in 1911 (Wu 1996, pp. 9–13). Unlike in England, time limits for IPRs are stipulated through constitutional provisions in the United States. The Constitution of the United States of America provides that "Congress shall have power to lay and collect taxes, duties, imposts and excises, to promote the progress of science and useful arts, by securing for a certain term to authors and inventors the exclusive right to their respective writings and discoveries." The above clause was generalised as three policies starting with "P", namely, the promotion of learning, the preservation of the public domain and the preservation of the author (Patterson and Lindberg 1991, pp. 49–55). In this regard, "the preservation of the public domain" means the limitations on copyright and patent rights in terms of time and scope.

The provisions of time limit on IPRs reflect social needs and public interest in establishing this emerging regime of civil law rights. Based on the nature and characteristics of various IPRs as well as national conditions, the laws of each country have provided for different protection periods for copyright, patent rights and rights over trademark. The term of protection of copyright for a particular work mainly concerns the property right of the work, namely, the copyright owner can only enjoy the proprietary right of the work and the right of receiving remuneration within a certain period of time. Historically, in Portugal and Nicaragua, there was a provision of "perpetual copyright" within an indefinite period of time. At present, except for the copyright of unpublished works, on which no time limit is set, the copyright laws of all countries stipulate a limited term of protection for published works. As a general rule, the length of time of copyright protection is calculated by adding a number of years after the author's death (the average life span of his or her children) to the length of the author's life after the date of first publication of a work. With regard to the personal rights of the author, namely, non-property rights that are exclusively owned by the author, some countries provide for the perpetuity within an indefinite period (e.g. France), while others provide for the same term of protection for personal rights as property rights (e.g. Germany). Regarding the term of protection of patent rights, the patent laws of different countries have made specific provisions of different term of length mainly based on two grounds. One is the coordination of social interest and the benefit of the rights holder and the other is the duration of the value of the invented technology (namely, the life cycle of technology). The term of patent rights is directly related to the interest of the parties and the public. A long term of protection conduces to encouraging and attracting the investment in long-term technologies and major inventions, but restricts the public from gaining timely ad open access to inventions. On the other hand, a short term of protection allows the earlier public access to inventions, but goes against encouraging inventions and attracting investments in costly and complex advanced technologies. Regarding the terms of protection of rights over trademark, different countries have also provided for different periods of validity. In countries where the "first-to-register" principle is adopted, the validity period of rights over trademark is calculated from the date of registration. In countries where the "first-to-use" principle is adopted, the proprietary rights can only arise after the trademark has been used. As such, the validity period of the latter is calculated from the date of use. In terms of the temporality of IPRs, distinct from the validity period of copyright and patent rights, that of rights over trademark can be renewed for extension upon expiration. The reason behind such provisions of the law is that literary and artistic works and inventions are of greater significance to the development of social programs on science and culture. As such, a certain term of protection is a must to enable intellectual products to be transformed from the proprietary property of individuals to the public intellectual wealth in due course.

The above-mentioned characteristics of IPRs are generalised and described in comparison with other property rights, especially the right of ownership. This does not mean that all types of IPRs enjoy all the above characteristics. In other words, each basic characteristic has a number of "exceptions." For example, the right over geographical indications does not enjoy complete proprietary nature, and the right over trade name has its own special provisions in its territoriality, while the trade-secret right is not limited by time. For instance, the use of Geographical Indication (GI) may not be exclusive; territoriality has limited application to trade names; and trade secrets are not compatible with temporality. In essence, only the immateriality of subject matter is the common legal characteristic of the rights of IPRs.

References

Chen, Yun and Ying Shi. 1931. *Roman Law*. Beijing: The Commercial Press

Dietz, Adolf. 1986. Is common copyright an illusion in Europe. *Legal translation series*

Kojima, Yonhe. 1998. *Intangible Property Rights*. Japan: Sōzō Publishing House

Li, Shuangyuan. 1991. *Private International Law in China*. Beijing: Ocean Press

Liu, Jiarui. 1998. Comments on the territorial conflict laws of intellectual property. *Journal of Central Leadership Institute of Politics and Law*

Patent Document Library. 1980. *Introduction to Foreign Patent Law*. Beijing: World Affairs Press

Patterson, L. Ray. and Stanley W. Lindberg. 1991. *The Nature of Copyright: A Law of User's Right*. Athens: The University of Georgia Press

Trademark Bureau of State Administration for Industry and Commerce. 1984. *Foreign Trademark Law*. Beijing: China Social Sciences Press

UNESCO Culture Sector. 1984. *The ABC of Copyright*. Beijing: China Translation & Publishing Corporation

World Intellectual Property Organisation. 1992. *Background Reading Material on Intellectual Property*. Beijing: World Affairs Press

Wu, Handong. 1996. *The Fair Use System of Copyright*. Beijing: China University of Political Science and Law Press

Wu, Handong. 1998. *Study on the Copyright System of Western Countries*. Beijing: China University of Political Science and Law Press

Yin, Tian. 1998. *French Property Law*. Beijing: Law Press China

Zeng, Shixiong. 1983. *The Present and Future of General Provisions of the Civil Law*. Taipei: San Min Book
Zhang, Naigen. 1999. *Intellectual Property Law of International Trade*. Shanghai: Fudan Press
Zheng, Chengsi. 1992. *Copyright Convention, Copyright Protection and Copyright-related Trade*. Beijing: Zhongguo Renmin University Press
Zheng, Chengsi. 1993. *Intellectual Property Law Course*. Beijing: Law Press China
Zheng, Chengsi. 1998. *On Intellectual Property Law*. Beijing: Law Press China
Zhou, Liang. 1994. *Original Theory of Roman Law*. Beijing: The Commercial Press

Chapter 4
Subjects of IPRs

From the perspective of rights, the subjects of IPRs are the rights holders, including copyright owners, patent owners and trademark owners. From the perspective of legal relationships, the subjects of IPRs relationships encompass both the rights holders and obligors. The term "subject of IPRs", in this book, refers to the owner of various types of IPRs. The term "person" referred to herein may be either a natural person or a legal person and, under certain circumstances, may also include unincorporated entities or even the state. Unlike general persons of the civil law, the term "person" in the IPRs regime represents a collective reference to both natural persons and legal persons. Terms such as "copyright owner", "patent applicant," and "trademark registrant" essentially refer to natural persons and legal persons entitled to such rights.

4.1 Subject Qualification

National laws have specific provisions for the qualifications the subjects of IPRs must possess and the rights they enjoy. Subject qualification, the legal personality of the persons in civil law (including the IPRs regime), serves as the legal premise of natural persons and their organisations to become civil subjects (Li 1997, p. 54). The equal legal status and the independent personality of civil subjects are the basic principle confirming the qualification of persons of the civil law. The former is the necessary precondition for the latter, while the latter is the concrete manifestation of the former.

In private law relations, the principle of equality is expressed as follows: First, all citizens are equal in their capacity for civil law rights. Second, persons of the civil law enjoy rights, bear obligations in accordance with the law, and are equally protected by law (Tong 1990, p. 16). Equality as it pertains to intellectual property laws is equivalent to that in private law, but has a broader definition. This is manifest

H. Wu, *Theorising Intellectual Property Rights from Chinese Perspectives*,
https://doi.org/10.1007/978-981-96-5867-1_4

in two aspects: First, equality in the IPRs regime entails free choice of the subject to engage in creative activities, and an equal opportunity to obtain the creator's rights. Modern civil law pursues equality in procedures, that is, equality is achieved when the society offers people equal opportunities. In other words, equality as in the IPRs regime indicates equal opportunity to obtain intellectual properties. As for how and whether one can make intellectual achievement, this is determined by talents, capacity and opportunities, which vary from individual to individual (Peng 1994, p. 34). IPRs are originally acquired from the creative actions of the subject (including creations and inventions). A creative action is not a civil juristic act in the general sense but a de facto action, thereby is civil conduct. As long as the subject can produce an intellectual product with his or her creative act, he or she will acquire rights as the creator based on the law. Second, equality in the IPRs regime refers to a coordination of the rights and obligations of the parties and a reasonable sharing of the intellectual wealth of the society. The historical development of the IPRs regime has gone through the process of expanding from a single subject of rights to multiple subjects of rights. In the field of copyright, it is the basic consideration of copyright legislation to balance public interest and private rights on the basis of protecting the rights of the author and coordinating the relationship between all parties, with the goal of promoting the dissemination of science and culture. With regard to the creation, dissemination and utilisation of the intellectual wealth of society, the copyright regime has established multiple subjects including creators, disseminators and users and provided for their sharing of rights and interests in works. As such, American scholars have described the modern copyright law as a balancing law that coordinates the rights of all subjects (Patterson and Lindberg 1991, p. 2). In the field of patent rights, systems such as proprietary use, statutory license, compulsory license and free use have led to a situation in which two or more subjects enjoy the benefits from the separate use of the same invention. The social and immaterial characteristics of intellectual products make it possible for the majority of subjects to make use of such intellectual achievements. The IPRs regime guarantees and promotes justice in social distribution and elevates this principle of distribution into legal rights and obligations, thus ensuring the authoritative and fair distribution of intellectual resources. It is for these two reasons that the subject system of IPRs is distinguished from that of general property rights.

4.2 Original Subjects

Original acquisition refers to the first creation of property right or the acquisition thereof without relying on the rights of the original owner. The original acquisition of ownership over general property, in production, benefit, occupation and other modes, does not require any specific identity of the subject or special authorisation from state authorities, except for real property and some chattels. In contrast, the original acquisition of IPRs consists of two legal facts, namely, the creative act of the creator and the authorisation of the state authorities.[1] In the production and development of intellectual products, the act of creation or invention is essentially a de facto action, from which anyone can acquire the identity of the creator of intellectual products through his or her intellectual labour. In the relations created by private law, status used to be the basis of privilege and the antithesis of equality. In ancient patriarchal society, family was the basic unit of legal regulation, as there were more ties between families than between individuals. All public and private rights enjoyed by parents, who are entitled by the Roman law to a fully independent personality, were based on a specific identity (Henry 1959). In contrast to the Roman law, the system of IPR subjects has two characteristics regarding creator identity, of which one is that the status of the creator generally belongs to the natural person engaged in creative intellectual labour, but in some cases, it may also belong to the legal person who organises and presides over the creative activities which embody his or her will or bear the corresponding responsibilities. In contrast to the status of parents in ancient society and that of consumers and employees in modern society, the status of creator is possible for both natural beings and social organisations. The other characteristic is that the identity of the creator is not related to the ties of kinship and marriage or other social relationships. On the contrary, it comes as a result of the de facto action of intellectual creation and is a prerequisite for the actor to acquire IPRs. In disputes over rights and interests of intellectual property, the confirmation of the creator's identity is of great significance in determining the source of rights and the division thereof.

In addition, in the original acquisition of IPRs, the authorisation of the state organ is a necessary procedure for the final confirmation of subject qualification. Authorisation is, by nature, an administrative legal act. Just like the creative act, it is significant for the original acquisition of rights. According to Patterson and Lindberg (1991), the fact of creation represents the source of copyright, which in origin arises from the law (the authorisation of authorities). Indeed, IPRs are secured only with the authorisation of administrative bodies under intellectual property laws since the object of the right is intangible. Unlike traditional subject matter, it is impossible to control or possess intellectual products in a tangible form, and thus they can easily escape from the creator and be used by others. In other words, as long as intellectual products are released to the public, others can easily obtain benefits from them through illegal disposal. As such, the owner of intellectual products cannot obtain, enjoy or exercise his or her rights and interests naturally, effectively and fully by the mere fact of creation, but must rely on the special protection of national laws, namely, the granting of proprietary rights to own or use after examination and approval by competent authorities.

---

[1] All kinds of intellectual property rights are subject to the recognition of national laws, and most of them are also granted by the state. That said, in the intellectual property system, such rights as copyright and trade secret right are not subject to the examination and approval of state organs.

4.3 Subjects of Derivative Acquisition

In the theory of civil law, there are two criteria that distinguish derivative acquisition from original acquisition, of which one is the element of intention. That means derivative acquisition only takes place based on the will of the original owner of an object (or intellectual works). The other is the source of rights, which means derivative acquisition can only be achieved through the transfer of the rights of the original owner. In the regime of property ownership, the principle of "one thing, one right" means that there cannot be two or more rights of ownership with identical provisions over the same object. In the case of derivative acquisition, the transfer of rights by one party means the loss of status of the subject of the rights, and the succession of rights by another means that he or she becomes the new owner of the property. In addition, based on this principle, although several real rights (such as usufruct or security rights) may exist in one object, the real rights must not contradict each other. In other words, there cannot be several independent real rights of the same nature in one object or a part of that object (Wang 1999, pp. 191–192).

In the field of IPRs, it is common to have several subjects of right on the same intellectual product that is derivatively acquired. Such situations can be roughly divided into three categories. One is that the rights obtained through derivative acquisition can only be property rights when a subject of rights enjoys both property rights and personal rights over his or her intellectual products. That means the subsequent owner cannot acquire the personal rights belonging exclusively to the creators. In this way, the personal rights and property rights on the same intellectual product will be shared by different subjects.[2] Second, when IPRs are partially transferred by the transferor to the new owner, the subsequent owner can only enjoy the benefits of the property rights agreed by both parties. As in the case of the separation of ownership from its functions, one or more subjects with partial rights are created, while the original subject remains. That means the rights and functions of property rights are shared by different subjects. Of course, this separation of rights from the functions has a completely different content and meaning in regard to IPRs and ownership. The subject matter of ownership is an independent and specific object, which can only be controlled and utilised by a specific subject under certain time-space conditions. The separation of ownership from its functions means that the possessor, namely, the non-owner, is the actual controller of the object, while the original owner can only be a "nominal rights holder" who does not directly control the object. That said, the subject matter of an IPR, as an immaterial intellectual product, may be used by multiple subjects under certain time-space conditions, including the original subject and the subjects of derivative acquisition. Third, the transfer of IPRs takes place simultaneously in different geographical areas. For example, there will be two or more independent subjects of rights in the case of the transfer of a same copyright or the sale of a same patent in different countries. Having said that, several assignees can

[2] In the intellectual property system, copyright is typically one body with two rights. In real life, there are cases where authors transfer the property rights of their works to others while retaining the personal rights thereof.

only exercise their rights in their respective territories where the rights are effective, which demonstrates the independent status of subjects whose rights do not interfere with each other. In this case, although the original owners of IPRs lose their status of subject, several new owners of identical IPRs may arise in different territories. That means several subjects of derivative acquisition enjoy rights of the same nature over the same intellectual product independently.

For IPRs, derivative acquisition is more significant than original acquisition. Amid the increasing prosperity of the commodity economy and the gradual socialisation of property rights, ownership is often exercised and realised through non-ownership means (such as the establishment of the right over the property of another and the creditor's rights). As Dong (1991) states, the property relations of social and economic life have been transformed from the centre of static ownership to that of dynamic creditor's rights, and the ownership has lost its original status due to the conversion of various rights. The value of IPRs, in particular, is not realised through the direct domination of the creator over intellectual products, but in the process of creating, disseminating and using of intellectual products. In the modern information society, it is almost impossible for a work or invention to be used in various forms by the creator himself or herself due to the specialised division of labour. As such, the owner of the intellectual product often realises his or her own interests by relying on the expression of intention and the behaviour of others, which is the social reason why derivative acquisition of IPRs is different from that of ownership.

4.4 Subject Qualification of Foreigners

Persons/subjects of the civil law can be divided into nationals and foreigners based on their nationality. In ancient times, the status of foreigners in civil affairs was not recognised by states, which means they were not entitled to the same rights as nationals. In ancient Rome, foreigners who had not been enslaved were regarded as enjoying the status of free persons, but were not entitled to the rights provided for by the *jus civile*. With the development of international trade, countries around the world have gradually adopted the principle of "mutualism", which means they recognised each other's citizens with the rights that their own citizens enjoyed in the other country based on the treaties or laws between them. The first domestic law to establish the equal status of foreigners in civil affairs was the *French Civil Code* of 1804, which provided that a foreigner shall enjoy in France the same civil law rights as are or shall be accorded to Frenchmen by the treaties of that nation to which such foreigner shall belong. Under the influence of the classical natural law school, the *Dutch Civil Code* of 1829 also shifted to egalitarianism, namely, equal treatment of foreigners as its own nationals in principle. Since then, national laws of countries around the world have gradually affirmed the principle of national treatment, but limited the rights enjoyed by foreigners. For example, if foreigners are not allowed to acquire land rights, mining rights and fishing rights, or to engage in certain occupations in which only citizens of the country can engage, that demonstrates national treatment with restrictions.

The IPRs regime has different provisions regarding the subject qualification of foreigners. The prevailing provisions of copyright law are as follows. Foreigners' creative works which are first published in the territory of a country shall enjoy the equal protection as works of nationals of that country. Those which are not first published in the territory of that country shall be protected on the basis of bilateral treaties or international conventions between relevant countries in accordance with the principle of reciprocity. The prevailing provisions of industrial property law are as follows. Foreigners who have permanent residence or a place of business in the territory of the country enjoy the equal treatment as its own nationals. Foreigners outside the country are treated on the basis of bilateral treaties or international conventions between relevant countries in accordance with the principle of reciprocity. These provisions demonstrate that the IPRs regime mainly adopts the principle of conditional national treatment, namely, foreigners can enjoy the equal rights with no restriction on the scope and content with nationals of the country if they fall in the above-mentioned circumstances.

The principle of national treatment serves as the basic principle of the international IPRs regime. This principle is reflected in two aspects, of which one is that the member states of the international convention must give the legal treatment to the nationals of other member states equal to the treatment of their own nationals regarding the protection of IPRs. The other is that the nationals of non-member states shall receive treatment equal to the nationals of the country, as long as their works are first published in the territory of the member states of the international convention (copyright law) or they have permanent residence or an actual business premise in that country to engage in industrial and commercial activities (industrial property law). The principle of national treatment breaks the restriction of the territorial effect of IPRs, protecting the rights holders of one country in other countries. The principle works to guarantee the status of foreigners in civil affairs equal to that of nationals of the country, thereby protecting their IPR-related benefits from infringement and also attracting advanced foreign technology and culture. For such reasons, this principle has been recognised by countries all over the world.

The national treatment principle confirmed by relevant international conventions means that all people are equal under international law, and thus, foreigners are protected as the equals of local citizens. This means that each qualified subject enjoys IPRs in both his or her own country and any of the member states of the Convention. The principle of national treatment has been gradually accepted by countries since the seventeenth century and has undergone many changes to date. One of the changes is the extension of the principle of national treatment. An imbalance in the enjoyment of rights comes as a result of the inconsistent rights enjoyed by nationals of a member state of the Convention. As such, international conventions require that the relevant legislation of each member state must meet the minimum standards provided for in the Convention. This is an extension of national treatment principle in the relevant international conventions. The second is the limitation of national treatment, which comes from the principle of reciprocity. The principle of national treatment is no longer applicable in some respects, due to the disparity in the protection level among member states. In addition, the scope of operation of national treatment can be limited by the "reservation" clause, which reserves a certain right or rights when member states accede to international conventions. These situations suggest that the implementation of the principle of national treatment is facing challenges (Stewart 1983; Cao 1995).

References

Cao, Xinming. 1995. On the national treatment principle in international copyright convention. *Studies in Law and Business* 1

Dong, Kaijun. 1991. Study on the transfer of ownership. *Science of Law* 1

Editorial board of Chinese Encyclopedia. 1984. *Encyclopedia of China*. Beijing: Encyclopedia of China Publishing House

Henry, Sumner Maine. 1959. *Ancient Law*. Beijing: The Commercial Press

Li, Kaiguo. 1997. *Study on the Basic Problems of Civil Law*. Beijing: Law Press China

Patterson, L. Ray. and Stanley W. Lindberg. 1991. *The Nature of Copyright: A Law of User's Right*. Athens: The University of Georgia Press

Peng, Wanlin. 1994. *Science of Civil Law*. Beijing: China University of Political Science and Law Press

Stewart, S. M. 1983. *International Copyrights and Neighboring Rights*. London: Butterworth and Co (Publishers) Ltd.

Tong, Rou. 1990. *General Provisions of the Civil Law*. Beijing: Publishing House of Chinese People's Public Security University

Wang, Liming. 1999. *Research on Civil and Commercial Law*. Beijing: Law Press China

Chapter 5
Subject Matters of IPRs

The subject matter of IPRs cannot be adequately interpreted under the traditional theory of *res corporales* dating back to Roman law. The German legal philosopher Georg Wilhelm Friedrich Hegel once observed that intangible creations such as intellectual skills, scientific knowledge, artistic works and inventions may be traded and contracted like tangible objects, yet they remain inherently intellectual in nature, thus rendering their legal nature perplexing (Hegel 1961; Lyu 1989, p. 32). Modern jurists have distinguished "knowledge" from its "medium" in the context of property. In their view, products of intellectual labour are deemed "intellectual" properties as they are related to items of information or knowledge, which can be incorporated into tangible subject matter and reproduced at the same time in multiple locations anywhere in the world. Intellectual property does not exist in those material reproductions, but in the informational content they convey (WIPO 1992, p. 4). The inquiry into the subject matter of IPRs seeks to delineate the difference between intellectual property and tangible property, thereby elucidating the fundamental basis for the essential difference between IPRs and traditional ownership rights.

5.1 Conceptualisation of the Subject Matters of IPRs

The subject matter of IPRs remains a controversial issue in academic discourse. Divergent interpretations of the conceptual understanding of the "object of right" have led to varying definitions and generalisations concerning the subject matter of IPR. One school of thought posits that the *subject matter* (客体) and the *object* (对象) of IPR belong to distinct conceptual categories. According to this view, the *subject matter* of IPR refers to the legal interests or social relations arising from the control, utilisation, and disposition of the *object* of IPR, whereas the *object* of IPR is "knowledge itself" (Liu 2000, p. 4). This theory regards the *subject matter* as an abstract and rational category, while the object as a concrete and objective one. An

H. Wu, *Theorising Intellectual Property Rights from Chinese Perspectives*,
https://doi.org/10.1007/978-981-96-5867-1_5

alternative perspective maintains that the *subject matter* and *object* of IPR fall within the same conceptual category. In most civil law treatises, the terms "subject matter" (客体), "subject" (标的), and "object" (对象) are used interchangeably (Jin 2001, p. 64). On this basis, scholars have proposed differing generalisations regarding the subject matter of IPR, with the most representative formulations including "intellectual achievements" (智力成果), "knowledge products" (知识产品), and "knowledge information" (知识信息).

Civil law theory holds that the subject matter of civil rights refers to the entity to which both civil rights and civil obligations are directed. But what precisely constitutes such an "entity"? Whie different interpretations exist, the prevailing view does not regard abstract and rational social relations as valid subject matter. For an entity to qualify as a civil law subject matter, it must satisfy the following criteria:

(1) Objectivity

The subject matter must embody either material or intangible interests. In the case of tangible property, objectivity manifests as *physical existence*—that is, an objectively perceivable material entity. For intellectual creations, objectivity is demonstrated through *cognoscibility* and *reproducibility*—meaning it must constitute an objectively verifiable body of knowledge.

(2) Relationality

The subject matter must be intrinsically linked to the rights and obligations of civil subjects—i.e., it must correlate with the substance of the civil legal relationship. In the realm of intellectual property, absent *creative achievements*, *commercial identifiers*, or *goodwill* as subject matter, no rights or obligations could arise, rendering the legal relationship meaningless.

(3) Governability

The subject matter must be capable of being controlled and utilised by the rights-holder. Whether in tangible form (material assets, whether natural or man-made) or intangible form (products of intellectual labour), it must possess both *value* and *utility value*. It is submitted that the *subject matter* and *object* of intellectual property rights may properly be understood as synonymous in conceptual terms.

At present, theoretical generalisations by foreign scholars regarding the subject matter of IPRs remain relatively scarce. Civil law scholars in the former Soviet Union sought to classify intellectual creations (*spiritual products*) as a distinct category of subject matter, separate from tangible things. In accordance with the principles of their national civil legislation, they collectively referred to the subject matters of such rights as "products of creative activity." These products of creative activity fall into two categories, of which one is scientific, literary and artistic works and the other is discoveries, inventions and rationalisation proposals, including industrial designs that achieve a technical and aesthetic unity through novel artistic treatment (грибанов 1984, pp. 177–178). However, the concept of "products of creative activity" developed by former Soviet scholars has two major flaws: First, it fails to generalise the common features of the subject matter that various IPRs protect. The classification obviously does not encapsulate the common subject matter underlying all IPRs, notably excluding industrial property rights such as patents and trademarks. The other flaw is that it emphasises the attribute of intellectual creation of the object but neglects its proprietary value. While the classification stresses the intellectual nature of the objects, it deliberately avoids acknowledging their economic worth. This is evident in its inclusion of non-proprietary rights, such as the rights to inventions and discoveries, thereby disregarding the essential characteristic of intellectual creations as *valuable assets.*

Zentaro Kitagawa, a famous Japanese jurist, is an advocate of the concept of "intellectual property right" in Japan. Traditionally, Japanese scholars have used the terms "intangible property rights" and "intangible property" to describe relevant rights and subject matter. However, Zentaro Kitagawa (1998) believes that the term "incorporeal things" is not universally accepted as compared with the "corporeal things" defined in Article 85 of the *Japanese Civil Code.* That's why he introduced the term "intellectual property" in his article on legal protection of semiconductor integrated circuits in 1988. Almost at the same time, other scholars also used the term, and the concept was thus widely spread in Japan. According to the theory of "intellectual property", the intellectual creations are called "intellectual" properties as they are related to various kinds of information. Such information is stored in physical carriers and reproduced in large quantities in different places at the same time. Intellectual property does not exist in these copies, but rather in the information reflected in them (World Intellectual Property Organisation 1992, p. 4). Another Japanese scholar, Yonhe Kojima, proposed the theory of "intangible property" based on the theory of intangible property rights. In his book *Intangible Property Rights*, he treats intellectual property and intangible property as the same concept and refers to them as the target of intellectual property law. He (1998, p. 2) believes that intangible property is a variety of new intellectual products (sic: intellectual achievements) that have emerged and developed with the progress of the times and are still emerging now. Yonhe Kojima emphasises that intangible property is the object of intangible property law, which falls into two categories: creation and mark. It has 'the characteristics of intangible property' and 'differs from the tangible property and other intangible property (such as light and electricity)' (Kojima 1998, p. 2). The Japanese civil law upholds the principle that things must have physical forms and the so-called intangible property refers to intellectual products or achievements, which exist in contrast to things (corporeal things). They are the subject matter of the right of ownership over intangible property (or IPRs) and general property respectively. Their definition of "intellectual property" or "intangible property" emphasises the immaterial and property nature of the object, and undoubtedly has some merit. That said, the term "property" has often been used in different senses, sometimes to refer to the right of ownership over property itself and sometimes to the object of ownership (namely possessions). In this case, the term "property" is used for both the noumenon and the object of the right, which is likely to cause ambiguity.

In the early 1980s, many scholars in China referred to the rights over intellectual wealth as the "rights to intellectual achievements", and accordingly generalised the object of these rights into "intellectual achievements", whose value could not be measured in money (Editorial Department of Law Textbook 1983, p. 383). This statement is obviously flawed, more due to historical limitations than theoretical defects. It is not surprising that legal doctrine favoured the intellectual attributes of such subject matter in a situation in which the commodity economy, especially the commercialisation of technology, had not yet been established or formed. In short, the conventional terminology of intellectual achievements fails both to demonstrate their original commodity attributes and property value and to reflect the essential characteristics of the object of IPRs. Thus, it should be reviewed.

The author strongly advocates the establishment of the theoretical category of "intellectual products", namely, the generalisation of the object of IPRs into "intellectual products." Other Chinese scholars (e.g. Wu and Min 1987, p. 34; Qian 1994, p. 26; Zhang 1992, p. 294) have also, from other disciplines, elaborated the concept of intellectual products. The so-called "intellectual products" are created in intellectual fields such as science, technology and culture, together with various forms such as inventions as well as literary and artistic creations. Such products represent an object category that is distinct and independent from material products (corporeal things). The above suggestions and ideas provide the theoretical foundation and legal basis for the establishment of the category of intellectual products. The *1984 Decision of the CPC Central Committee on the Reform of the Economic System* and the *1985 Decision on the Reform of the Science and Technology Management System* not only give a correct description of the current commodity economy in China, but also explicitly acknowledge for the first time that technology is playing an increasingly significant role in the value of social commodities and more and more technologies have become independent 'intellectual products'. In 1986, *General Principles of Civil Law* was enacted in China, in which the conventional term "right to intellectual achievements" was formally replaced with the concept of "intellectual property." The above ideas and regulations provide the theoretical foundation and legal basis for the establishment of the category of intellectual products. In fact, foreign scholars have already expressed similar views regarding the term "intellectual product." Picardy, a Belgian jurist who advocated the concept of "intellectual rights", has referred to it as the right to use intellectual products (Богатых 1980). In my view, the term 'intellectual products' can better demonstrate the essential characteristics of the object of IPRs than 'things' and 'intellectual achievements'. The concept of 'things' highlights material entities other than persons, including unprocessed natural things or creations through human material labour, and this clearly demonstrates the material nature of the object. In contrast, the term 'intellectual products' generalises the essential characteristics of knowledge products, stressing that such subject matter arise in the intellectual fields of science, technology and culture and are creations of human intellect, and this clearly shows the immateriality of the object. In addition, the implication of intellectual products highlights their commodity attributes and its property nature under the conditions of commodity production and reflects the content of property rights in copyright and rights over trademark and patent. In contrast, the implication of 'intellectual achievements' as the object of rights fails to reflect the original meaning of intellectual ownership in 'intellectual property' and fails to reveal immaterial wealth in the form of commodity with its value and use value. Thus, the object of IPRs shall be expressed as 'intellectual products,' rather than 'things' or 'intellectual achievements.'

Since the beginning of the 1990s, some scholars in China have proposed a new theoretical generalisation of the object of IPRs. Liu (2000, p. 5) believes that the target of IPRs is the knowledge which exists as a "form." Zhang (2001, p. 5) argues that the object of IPR and IPRs protection is the immaterial information related to intellectual activities. Jiang (2001) describes the object of IPRs protection as intellectual property and relevant intellectual rights and interests. Although consensus has not been reached concerning the above-mentioned statements, this discussion is of academic significance, and its basic implication is expressed in the following three aspects. Firstly, knowledge and information, distinct from things, fall into the category of non-material wealth. Secondly, knowledge and information, related to people's intellectual activities, emerge from the intellectual or mental field. Thirdly, as the object of civil law relations, their significance lies in the fact that knowledge and information constitute the interest protected by intellectual property law.

5.2 Classification of the Subject Matters of IPRs

In conventional textbooks, many scholars have criticised the generalisation of the subject matters of IPRs as intellectual and creative achievements. They believe that the subject matters of IPRs should fall into two categories, one of which is intellectual achievements and the other is business marks (Liu 1995, p. 1). In view of the development of intangible property in modern society, we propose to establish a new intellectual property system distinct from the conventional scope of subject matter, namely, to divide intellectual products into three categories. The first is creative achievements, including works as well as media and industrial technology. The second is business marks. The third is commercial goodwill. Of these, the first category occurs in the field of science and technology, and of culture, while the second and third categories arise in the field of industrial and commercial operation. Under the current law, the main subject matter of IPRs are creative works and business marks. The above three categories will be elaborated separately as follows.

Creative works and their media refer to the original creative works in different forms in the field of literature and art (the subject matter of copyright), as well as various products, articles or other media associated with the original works in the process of dissemination (the object of neighbouring rights). The works, as the subject matter of copyright, can be broadly classified into literary works, artistic works and scientific works. The media, as the object of neighbouring rights, mainly encompasses artistic performance, audiovisual recording and broadcasting program. The shared characteristics of this kind of intellectual products are that they are all intellectual creations in the cultural field, as they are related to the creator's activities of creation and dissemination. They are all objective manifestations of the creator's ideas, including words, symbols, graphics, images, audio-video and related technical forms.

While ‘industrial technology’ applies mainly in industrial, agricultural and commercial domains, they are creative achievements with material carriers, manifest as skills and know-hows. It is the methods and skills developed on scientific principles and practical experience in production, as well as production tools and other material facilities that are compatible with these methods and skills. Industrial technologies are different from scientific achievements, which are the philosophical observation of human experience, and theoretical conceptualisations and discoveries on nature, society and human mindset. Both science and technology, in the forms of knowledge, belong to the intellectual wealth of society. The function of science lies in the understanding of nature (society or thinking) and technological possibilities, which are more foresighted and far-reaching. In contrast, technology features practicality and applicability as it is directly linked to the production process and its function lies in the control and use of natural resources. From the perspective of law, industrial technology can manifest as various types of patented technologies that have acquired industrial property rights, as well as technical secrets that have acquired other IPRs and industrial products that are protected by new IPRs, namely industrial copyright.

Industrial marks are generally distinguishing marks that indicate the origin of products and the specific personality of manufacturers in the fields of industry, agriculture and commerce. Such marks, including trademarks, trade names, names of origin, are the most common marks seen in our daily lives. They have the general characteristics of the art of logo design:

(1) Distinctiveness

The main function of industrial marks is to distinguish a product and the manufacturer who produces it, as a way of easy identification and preventing misidentification.

(2) Publicity

Industrial marks are mainly used in industrial and commercial activities to achieve their promotional effect on specific commodities, manufacturers or places of production.

(3) Adaptability

Industrial marks can be used on various occasions, not only on commodities or related materials, but also in the production of various types of publicity (Wu 1989, p. 6).

As the object of industrial property rights and other IPRs, industrial marks are the essential intangible property of enterprises. Business credit refers to the business qualifications, advantages and reputation obtained by industrial and commercial enterprises in their business activities, including franchise qualifications, franchise qualifications, credit and goodwill. The business capability that a subject possesses is the internal constituent factor of its business credit. Business capability is a very broad concept, including economic status, production capacity, product quality and market share (Yang 1996, p. 638). It enables a specific subject to obtain extra profits, higher than that the general profit level of other enterprises in the same industry. Its external influencing factors are either the qualification granted by the competent authorities or social organisations, or society's evaluation of and trust in the subject. The qualifications, abilities or credit involved in these subject matters of rights demonstrate obvious elements of property interests, in addition to those of intellectual interests. Unlike literary and artistic works, industrial technologies and marks, the property value of business credit has not yet been fully recognised, leading to obviously insufficient legislative protection. For this reason, some scholars refer to such subject matter as intangible property in the process of development (Zeng 1993, p. 137).

5.3 Characteristics of the Subject Matters of IPRs

The subject matter of IPRs, including creative achievements, business marks, commercial goodwill, share the following fundamental characteristics:

5.3.1 Creativity

Unlike tangible goods, intellectual products must be innovative and creative instead of being mere repetitions of existing items. Creativity is a prerequisite for intellectual products to obtain legal protection, which is not required by general property law. Here, the emphasis on the creative nature of intellectual products does not mean that tangible goods are not creative. The key to the matter is that creativity is a condition for intellectual products to constitute the objects of IPRs, whereas no such requirement exists for tangible goods to constitute the objects of ownership rights in tangible property. The degree of creativity required varies significantly across different types of intellectual products. Generally speaking, a patented invention, which must be an advanced scientific and technological achievement, requires the highest level of creativity. In addition, the technical ideas and solutions embodied in it must make a qualitative technological leap in the relevant field. Copyrighted works require the second highest degree of creativity. It requires that a work must be the product of the author's creative labour, yet any work can acquire independent copyright as long as it is independently conceived and created, regardless of whether its idea or content is the same as or similar to that of another work. In comparison, the creativity required for a trademark only needs to be easily distinguishable, namely, the trademark shall possess distinctive characteristics making it easy to identify. And its words, graphics or their combination thereof shall avoid being confused with other trademarks. This mirrors the fact that the creativity required varies with protected subject matter. As articulated by Western scholars, patents require inventions to be "technologically advanced" (or "non-obviousness"), while copyrights require works to be "creative" (or "original") and trademark rights require trademarks be "identifiable" (or "easily distinguishable").

5.3.2 Non-Material Nature

Unlike tangible goods, intellectual products are products of human intellect existing in the form of knowledge, and have intrinsic value and utility but no physical form. This non-material nature is the primary characteristic that distinguishes intellectual products from the object of the right of ownership over tangible property. The term "non-material nature" denotes that an intellectual product does not possess a specific physical form (such as solid, liquid, or gas) and thus does not occupy physical space. People's "possession" of it is not a kind of real and physical control but rather manifests as cognition and utilisation of knowledge. A tangible good, under specific spatial and temporal conditions, can only be physically possessed or used by an individual or a social organisation, which enables the right holder to effectively control his or her tangible assets and prevent others from illegal encroachment. In contrast, an intellectual product can be "possessed" concurrently by multiple subjects and utilised by them jointly. Once disseminated, an intellectual product may be "possessed" by third parties through illegal means. Intellectual products, despite their non-material nature, must invariably be expressed in a certain objective form so that people other than the creators of the intellectual products can understand them, and this objective form of expression is one of the conditions for their protection under IP law. For instance, creative works are realised as written works, stage performances, paintings, sculptures, audio-visual products; inventions as written description, diagrams, shapes and structures; trademarks as patterns, colours, symbols, and characters. These tangible media embodying these objective forms are the materialisation of intellectual products. It is crucial to recognise that the tangible medium serving as the expression of an intellectual product is not the intellectual product itself. The effectiveness and value of intellectual products, as products of human intellect, cannot be fully encompassed and represented by their tangible media.

5.3.3 Public Disclosure

Unlike tangible goods, intellectual products must be publicly disclosed or accessible to the public. Public disclosure is a prerequisite for the owner of an intellectual products to acquire IPRs, while the general provisions of civil law do not obligate the owner of tangible property to publicly disclose his or her assets. The subject matter of IPRs all exhibit this characteristic of public disclosure. One purpose of an author creating a work is to disseminate it and to exercise his or her rights and obtain benefits from doing so. The technical content of a patent must be disclosed if the inventor is to define the scope of his or her rights. The Latin root "*patere*" (patent in

English) literally means "to make it public" or "to lay open", which indicates that the technical content of a patent must be publicly accessible. In order to distinguish their products from those of others, trademark owners utilise their distinctive signs. In countries where the "first-to-use" principle is applied or where the "first-to-register" principle is adopted, the acquisition of trademark rights requires either the first use of trademark or the first application for trademark registration, both of which are linked to public disclosure. It is generally accepted that a sound IPRs regime is sustainable on the grounds that the creator of an intellectual product discloses his or her works and inventions, so that the public can have open access to the specialised knowledge contained therein. In return, the public recognises that the creator has the exclusive right to use and manufacture his or her intellectual products for a defined period of time. While the intellectual product is publicly disclosed, no one else is entitled to use it without authorisation. Doing so constitutes infringement. "Knowledge is public, but rights are exclusive" aptly describes the relationship between the public nature of intellectual products and the exclusivity of IPRs. Under western jurists' interpretation, IPRs serve as a social contract between a society, in the form of the state, and the creator of intellectual achievements. The creator is obligated to allow public access to the intellectual product: the creator undertakes the obligation to disclose the intellectual product and, in return, acquires an exclusive right of use for a specified duration (Patent Document Library 1980, p. 12). It should be noted that technical secrets (trade secrets), as intellectual products, do not possess the characteristic of public disclosure. They rely on confidentiality to maintain their proprietary rights. In Western civil law theory, patented technology constitutes a statutory monopoly, effective for the duration of the whole protection period. In contrast, a technical secret constitutes a de facto monopoly, whose effectiveness is determined by the duration of the rights holder's successful efforts to maintain confidentiality. In the legal regime, technical secrets were traditionally not under the protection of classical IPRs regimes, but only regulated by contract law or tort law. That said, technical secrets, with the defining characteristics of intangible property, have now come under the protection of IP law, as demonstrated by the trend of modern legislation.

References

Editorial Department of Law Textbook. 1983. *Principles of Civil Law*. Beijing: Law Press China

Hegel, G. W. F. 1961. *Elements of the Philosophy of Right*. Trans. Yang Fan and Qitai Zhang. Beijing: The Commercial Press

Jiang, Zhipei. 2001. Concept, development and legal protection implications of intellectual property rights. *China Civil and Commercial Law*. http://old.civillaw.com.cn/article/default.asp?id=7537 Access 7 June 2001

Jin, Baolan. 2001. *Comparative Study on Civil Legal System*. Beijing: Publishing House of Chinese People's Public Security University

Kojima, Yonhe. 1998. *Intangible Property Rights*. Japan: Sōzō Publishing House

Liu, Chuntian (ed.). 1995. *Intellectual Property Law Tutorial*. Beijing: China Renmin University Press
Liu, Chuntian (ed.). 2000. *Intellectual Property Law*. Beijing: Higher Education Press
Lyu Shilun. 1989. *Study on Hegel's Philosophy of Right*. Beijing: Publishing House of Chinese People's Public Security University
Patent Document Library. 1980. *Introduction to Foreign Patent Law*. Beijing: World Affairs Press
Qian, Mingxing. 1994. *Principles of Real Right Law*. Beijing: Peking University Press
WIPO. 1992. *Background Reading Material on Intellectual Property*. Beijing: World Affairs Press
Wu, Handong. 1989. *Theory and Practice of Industrial Property Law*. Beijing: China University of Political Science and Law Press
Wu, Handong and Min Feng. 1987. *Introduction to Intellectual Property Law*. Beijing: China University of Political Science and Law Press
Yang, Lixin. 1996. *Personal Right Law*. Beijing: China Procuratorial Press
Zeng, Shixiong. 1993. *The Present and Future of General Provisions of the Civil Law*. Taipei: San Min Book
Zentaro, Kitagawa. 1998. *Technological Innovation and Intellectual Property Legislation*. Beijing: Policies and Regulations of the State Science and Systems Division
Zhang, Hesheng. 1992. *Intellectual Economics*. Shenyang: Liaoning People's Publishing House
Zhang, Yumin. 2001. *Intellectual Property Law Course*. Chongqing: Southwest University of Political Science & Law Press
Богатых, E. A. 1980. *Introduction to Foreign Patent Law*. Beijing: World Affairs Press

Chapter 6
System of IPRs

The construction of an IPRs system involves the following key issues: The first relates to its position in the civil law systems, particularly with regard to the relationship of IPRs with other traditional property rights. The second pertains to the coherence and consistency within the IPRs framework, mainly concerning the classification and foundation of modern IPRs. The third is the future trajectory of the IPRs system, with the focus on the dematerialisation of property from IPRs to intangible property rights. This chapter seeks to discuss and explore these issues.

6.1 IPRs Within the Property Rights System

Property rights are a basic category in the system of civil rights. They are rights with property as their subject matter and economic interests as their content, encompassing proprietary rights, IPRs, personal rights and inheritance rights (Jiang 1999). The classification of civil rights into property rights and personal rights is a fundamental dichotomy based on the differing interests embodied by the rights—namely economic interests versus personal interests.

The external structure of the property rights system contributes to the differences between property rights and personal rights. Grounded in the difference between proprietary and personal interests, civil rights can be broadly classified into property rights and personal rights. Employing the dichotomy of property rights versus non-property rights within the civil rights system represents a traditional classificatory approach. However, a difficulty inherent in this technical method lies in the precise execution of the "dichotomy". Worldwide, there has been no unanimous definition of property rights. French scholars describe property in the legal sense as a kind of "interest" capable of satisfying the material needs of human beings (Yin 1998), while German scholar Karl Larenz (2003) posits that only rights possessing "monetary value" qualify as property. Thus, it is evident that for most scholars, the dichotomy

H. Wu, *Theorising Intellectual Property Rights from Chinese Perspectives*,
https://doi.org/10.1007/978-981-96-5867-1_6

of civil rights uses the presence or absence of economic interest as the evaluative criterion. However, some Japanese scholars adopt an indirect classification method, defining personality right and status right first, then categorising "all other rights" as property rights (Xie 1996). In the view of the author, regardless of the method adopted, all these classifications represent scholarly subjective evaluations concerning the interests and substantive significance of civil rights. Furthermore, this classification method aids in the design and construction of the rights system and is also applicable in legal norms. In summary, while the dichotomy is not a flawless classificatory theory, it serves as the scholarly foundation upon which we construct the property rights system.

Within the internal structure of the property rights system, further specific divisions arise based on the differing interests realised or subject matters involved:

- Where the property right is directed towards a specific "thing",[1] such a right is termed *a right over a thing* (*jus in rem*), namely *a right in rem.* (Xie 1996);
- Where the property right is directed towards a specific person's "performance" (the execution of a specific act), such a right is termed *a right against a person* (*jus in personam*), namely *a personal right.*

Traditionally, property rights consist of *rights in rem* and *rights in personam.*[2] IPRs emerged later as a novel type of property rights. Given their subject matters are intangible intellectual products, they are also termed intangible property rights. There are clear boundaries among the three types of property rights mentioned above:

- Using the materiality or non-materiality of the proprietary interest as the criterion, dominant property rights can be divided into rights *in rem* over things and intellectual property rights over intellectual creations.
- Using the direct dominium versus the claim to performance as the criterion, the former gives rise to rights *in rem* and intellectual property rights possessing the attribute of dominium, while the latter gives rise to rights *in personam* possessing the characteristic of a claim.

Here, the differentiation of the object remains the basis for classifying property rights. The German scholar Larenz (2003) classified objects of rights (*Rechtsobjekte*) into two kinds:

- The object of right to dominion or use (*Herrschafts-oder Nutzungsrecht*), also termed *primary right object* (*Rechtsgegenstand erster Ordnung*);
- An object that can be disposed of by a subject through a legal transaction, also termed the *secondary right object* (*Rechtsgegenstand zweiter Ordnung*).

[1] In its broad conception, 'things' (res) encompass both corporeal property (tangible objects) and incorporeal property, the latter denoting certain rights possessing a proprietary nature. In its narrower conception, 'things' are confined to corporeal property. Roman law and French law adopt the broader conception, while German law adopts the narrower conception.

[2] Some scholars categorise as quasi-proprietary rights those entitlements pertaining to intangible entitlements—such as fishing rights and mineral rights—alongside the right of inheritance, where the subject matter constitutes an estate as an aggregation of rights.

In Larenz's view (2003), primary right objects are factual existences independent of legal stipulation, comprising corporeal things and intangible intellectual products. The former includes movable and immovable property; the latter includes works and inventions. Secondary right objects, conversely, are rights themselves treated as objects by virtue of legal stipulation, meaning an entire property right viewed as the object of disposition. Larenz's theory of object classification holds significance for the categorisation of property rights: Ownership (*dominium*) and intellectual property rights are dominant property rights. Their object, irrespective of material attributes, is invariably a thing embodying certain material or intellectual interests; corporeal things manifest objective reality, while intellectual creations manifest cognozability and reproducibility (Wu 2003).

Adopting Larenz's terminology, the object of such rights can only be a primary object, a factual existence., As for rights *in personam* (claims), inherence rights, and other limited rights *in rem*, these may be property rights characterised as claims (*Ansprüche*), expectancies (*Anwartschaftsrechte*), or rights established over property owned by others. Their object, besides the object in the general sense (the *res*), may also involve rights treated as objects by law (incorporeal things—*res incorporales*). Larenz (2003) argued that the object of a debtor's performance is something which the debtor should provide to the creditor through his act of performance, e.g., enabling the creditor to take possession of a thing, acquire ownership or other rights in a thing, or receive a sum of money, or achieve some other 'result' brought about by the debtor. Xie Huaishi (1996) posited that the object of the right to inheritance involves a collection of rights including various *rights in rem, rights in personam.* Liang Huixing (1996) and Qian Mingxing (1994) contend that the object of ownership can only be a corporal thing; however, limited rights *in rem* (*iura in re aliena*) may have certain property rights themselves as their object, such as usufructs over rights or pledges over rights. These perspectives demonstrate that, unlike ownership and IPRs, such property rights may have other property rights, namely, incorporeal things (*res incorporales*)—as their object.

Property rights, once arranged into a comprehensive legal system, should not be understood as merely the simple sum of property rights of different kinds, but rather an organic synthesis of distinct yet interconnected rights and obligations. Property rights define the theoretical and legal ownership of resources and how they can be used. It is essential to recognise that the fundamental unity inherent in property interests determines the common object of all property rights. This unity serves not only as the nexus linking different property institutions but also as the foundation for integration of property-related laws. Furthermore, as legitimate interests vary among properties of different natures, classifications of property rights can thus be made and the foundation of a property rights system can be established.

6.1.1 Foundations for the Integration of the Property Rights System

The constitution of a property rights system starts from the public perception and legal definition of property. Roman law's recognition of corporeal things (*res corporales*) as objects of property led to the long-term prevalence of a *res corporales*-based property rights system. In such a materialised system of property rights, corporeal things were movables and immovables, whilst incorporeal things (*res incorporales*) were also based on tangible objects. Thus, it may be stated that the traditional property rights system was structed upon a materialised conception of property. With the advancement of science, technology, and the development of a commodity economy, various abstract and non-material forms of property have continually emerged, leading to an evolved understanding of the concept of property.

American scholars have noted that in the nineteenth century, courts began to recognise that the values of some intangible properties were not necessarily connected to commercial premises or tangible commercial appurtenances. In most cases, the intangible property of the interested parties was more important than the tangible one. In other words, on many occasions, what should be protected was the "value" rather than the "thing" itself (Vandevelde 1980). By the early twentieth century, Francis J. Swayze enumerated "new types of property of great value," including business goodwill, trademarks, trade secrets, copyrights, enterprise value, franchises, and rights of fair access (ibid.). Here, the objects of property rights were no longer confined to corporeal things, but extended to the incorporeal. Regardless of whether they possess an external physical form, they all possess economic utility value. Property or property interests have different forms, namely, material entities, intellectual entities and other value entities (Xu 2002). The broader vision on property calls for an inclusive framework that can integrate the diversified forms and types of properties and coordinate them with related legislation. In essence, the conceptual integration of property forms the foundation for the integration of the property rights system.

Internationally, IPRs are predominantly treated as property rights. In English, the terms "intellectual property" and "intellectual property right" refer to "knowledge-based property" and "knowledge-based property right" respectively. In some countries, "intellectual property right" is synonymous to "incorporeal property rights" (*droits de propriété incorporelle*). In addition, Specialist publications by the World Intellectual Property Organisation (WIPO) (1992) likewise associate "intellectual property" with "intellectual assets". The *Agreement on Trade-Related Aspects of Intellectual Property Rights* (The *TRIPS Agreement*) acknowledges that IPRs are private rights, thereby treating IPRs and ownership as private property rights of equal standing, proceeding from the principle of protecting private property (Kong 2002, p. 72).

6.1.2 Core Institutions and Internal Structure of the Property Rights System

The division between property rights and personal rights, along with the fundamental classification of property rights, constitutes a civil law tradition inherited from Roman law. However, the focuses and institutional arrangements of property law have varied throughout different historical periods. Ancient Roman law constructed a property law centred absolutely on ownership (*dominium*). The Romans employed "things" (*res*) as the categorical object, upon which they designed a system of "rights over things" (*iura in re*) centred on the form of ownership, establishing a system of "law of things" (*ius rerum*)—the property rights system—comprising primarily the law of property (*ius in re*) and the law of obligations (*ius obligationes*). (Bonfante 1992, pp. 13–15). The Roman property rights system was constructed upon the broad conceptual category of the object "thing" (*res*), encompassing primarily objectively tangible things (*res corporales*), but also subjectively conceived things (*res incorporales*—i.e., rights). Furthermore, the entire property rights system was governed by a broadly conceived notion of ownership, whereby rights *in personam* (obligations/claims) and limited rights *in rem* (*iura in re aliena*) were classified as incorporeal things (*res incorporales*), constituting property owned by the holder of *dominium.* This represented a property system with absolute ownership at its core.

As an heir of Roman civil law, French civil law preserved the distinction between tangible things and intangible things, and maintained the classification of property rights. Therefore, ownership remained as the central institution of the French property system. Modern German civil law established a property law based on a dichotomous structure of rights *in rem* (*Sachenrecht*) and rights *in personam* (*Schuldrecht*). The German Civil Code (*Bürgerliches Gesetzbuch*—BGB) exhibits three key characteristics in its arrangement of property rights institutions: Firstly, the independence of rights in personam. German law treats rights in personam (*Forderungsrechte*) as distinct from rights in rem (*dingliche Rechte*), existing independently and regulated in a dedicated section. Secondly, the prioritisation of rights in personam. Departing from the ownership-centric legislative model, the BGB places the chapter on rights in personam before the chapter on rights in rem; rights in personam are viewed as prerequisites for the establishment of ownership, rather than merely methods for its acquisition. Thirdly, the systematisation of the dichotomous structure. German law formally established the two principal categories of rights in rem and rights in personam. According to this model, any specific property right can be subsumed within these categories. The question of what form the property rights system should take in modern civil law is a subject that legislators and jurists across the world continue to grapple with, without yet achieving consensus. The author submits that we may adhere to the civil law tradition by continuing to use the terms of "rights in rem" and "rights in personam", without necessarily adhering rigidly to the concept of absolute ownership as the sole centre, nor strictly observing the dichotomous structure. This signifies that the modern property rights system should constitute an open institutional framework and a pluralistic categorical system of rights.

Based on the foregoing analysis, the author (Wu 2005) advocates that the property rights system of China should comprise the following three components: the system of tangible property rights with ownership as the core, the system of intangible property rights with IPRs as the main part, and the system of other property rights with rights in personam and inheritance rights as the content. Tangible property rights, in addition to ownership, should also include land use rights, rural land contractual management rights, homestead use rights, easement, space use rights, rights of Dian, rights of habitation, neighbouring rights, and security rights such as mortgages, pledges, and liens. Intangible property rights encompass IPRs such as copyright, patent rights, trademark rights, trade name rights, right to geographical indications, right to new plant varieties, right to layout-designs of integrated circuits, and right to trade secrets, as well as non-material rights such as rights in reputation, rights in creditworthiness, and rights of publicity. Other property rights comprise rights in personam, inheritance rights, and certain property rights possessing independent significance, such as shareholder's rights, rights under trusts, and rights arising out of negotiable instruments. Some of these rights are claim-based property rights, while others are special property rights with the attributes of both rights in rem and rights in personam.

6.2 Statutory Frameworks for the IPRs System

Regarding its scope, the IPRs system may be understood in a broad or a narrow sense. An IPRs system, in a narrow sense, refers to traditional IP law, comprising copyright (including neighbouring rights), patent rights, and trademark rights. In this sense, IPRs can be generally divided into two categories: one is related to literary property, encompassing copyright and associated neighbouring rights; the other is related to industrial property, consisting principally of patent rights and trademark rights. "Literary property" originates from the writings (literary, artistic and scientific) of an author and gives him/her legal rights to the exclusive use of the writings, including publication and sale or license for profit to others to whom the author gives the right to publish. With the entry into force of literary property rights, original works and their media fall within the scope of protection, marking a new area of IPRs protection including not only the "content" but the "form" of literary creations. "Industrial property," on the other hand, refers to a form of intangible property rights with practical economic significance in industry, commerce, agriculture, forestry and other industries.

The term "industrial property" (*propriété industrielle*), first introduced in France, describes the exclusive right to intellectual products in the industrial field. The French *Declaration of the Rights of Man and of the Citizen* (the Declaration) of 1789 took thought as a spiritual property, noting that it is a "natural and unalienable right of man", and that "the free communication of ideas and opinions is one of the most precious rights of man." Based on the Declaration, the French National Assembly passed the first patent law in 1791. Before this, both England and France referred to patent right as "privilege" or "monopoly right." At that time, the drafter of French patent law, Stanislas de Beaufort, thought that the expressions of "privilege" or "monopoly rights" might be opposed by the bourgeois revolutionary legislature and those opposing feudal privilege, so he introduced the concept of "industrial property." "Industrial property" was fully reflected in the French patent law of 1791 and was later accepted throughout the world, and gradually became a general term for various exclusive rights such as patent rights and trademark rights.

The distinction between literary property (or copyright) and industrial property is part of the traditional classification in IPRs systems. Since the 1960s, the domains of industrial property and copyright have increasingly overlapped and intersected, giving rise to industrial copyright, a new category of IPR that protects industrial products in a similar way to copyright (Zheng 1990, p. 20). The legislative impetus for industrial copyright arose initially to address the drawbacks of overlapping protection for industrial designs under both patent law and copyright law. Subsequently, to fill gaps in protection for certain industrial products, and to remedy the limitations of a single system of copyright protection, some countries incorporated the layout design of integrated circuits within the scope of industrial copyright. It is worth mentioning that industrial copyright represents a departure from the traditional dichotomy between copyright and industrial property, incorporating elements of both to form a hybrid right exhibiting characteristics of each system. The principal features of this right are:

- The protected subject matter must possess both novelty (as required by patent law) and originality (as required by copyright law);
- Protection is granted under a registration system (characteristic of industrial property law) and entails a shorter term of protection.
- The right holder enjoys primary rights of reproduction and distribution, but does not possess the extensive bundle of rights typically accorded to a copyright holder.

The broad conception of the IPRs system encompasses various rights including copyright, neighbouring rights, trademark rights, trade name rights (rights in trade designations), rights to trade secrets (rights in undisclosed information), rights to geographical indications, patent rights, and rights to layout-designs of integrated circuits. This broad IPRs framework is recognised by two principal international IPR conventions: The *Convention establishing the World Intellectual Property Organisation* (The *WIPO Convention*) and the *Agreement on Trade-Related Aspects of Intellectual Property Rights* (The *TRIPS Agreement*).

The *WIPO Convention*, signed in 1967, defines the scope of "intellectual property" to include the following categories:

- Rights in literary, artistic and scientific works (i.e., copyright);
- Rights in respect of inventions in all fields of human endeavour (i.e., invention patents and rights akin to inventor's certificates);
- Rights in respect of scientific discoveries;
- Rights in respect of industrial designs;

- Rights in respect of trademarks, service marks, commercial names and designations (i.e., trademark rights, trade name rights);
- Rights in respect of protection against unfair competition;
- All other rights resulting from intellectual activity in the industrial, scientific, literary or artistic fields.

The *TRIPS Agreement*, s concluded by the contracting parties to the General Agreement on Tariffs and Trade (GATT) in 1994, delineates the scope of intellectual property as covering:

- Copyright and related rights (i.e., neighbouring rights);
- Trademarks;
- Geographical indications;
- Industrial designs;
- Patents;
- Layout-designs (topographies) of integrated circuits;
- Exclusive right to undisclosed information (i.e., trade secrets).

TRIPS

Regarding the scope defined by the *WIPO Convention*, two points warrant attention: First, it provides for miscellaneous provisions, providing flexibility for the inclusion of new forms of IPRs in the future, which is considered a commendable feature. Second, its inclusion of rights concerning inventions (in the non-patent sense) and discoveries remains controversial as to their place within the IPRs system proper.[3] The rights covered by the *TRIPS Agreement* are predominantly those related to international trade, and reflect the protection priorities of developed countries. Notably, it omits rights such as trade names rights, which are stipulated in traditional industrial property conventions. As a result, the IPRs system established by the *TRIPS Agreement* is also subject to certain limitations.

Enacting national legislation through separate statues is widely adopted around the world. Therefore, legislative models codifying the entire IPRs system comprehensively under the heading of "intellectual property" remain relatively uncommon. The Italian *Civil Law Code* of 1942, while retaining a separate IP law, dedicated specific chapters within the Code to copyright, patent rights, trademark rights, and trade names rights. Following the repeal of separate IP law, the *Civil Code of Vietnam* of 1995 incorporated IPRs as a distinct Book, covering copyright and industrial property rights (including patents, trademarks, geographical indications, etc.). The *General Principles of the Civil Law of the People's Republic of China* of 1986 included a dedicated section on IPRs within its chapter on "Civil Law Rights", encompassing copyright, patent rights, trademark rights, discovery rights, invention rights (non-patent), and rights in other scientific and technological achievements. While these legislative models represent efforts towards systematising intellectual property, their narrowly defined scopes struggle to accommodate the open-ended and dynamically evolving nature of modern intellectual property regimes. The *French Intellectual Property*

[3] See more information in Chapter 1, Part I.

Code (*Code de la propriété intellectuelle*) of 1992 constructed a novel intellectual property system in the form of a specialised code. It categorises intellectual property into two main parts:

- **Literary and Artistic Property**: Covering copyright, neighbouring rights, database producer rights, etc.
- **Industrial Property**: Covering rights in industrial designs, invention patents, rights in technical know-how (trade secrets), rights in layout-designs of integrated circuits, plant variety rights, trademarks, and other distinctive signs.

The *French Intellectual Property Code* represents the most comprehensive legal framework for intellectual property systematisation enacted to date. However, while it encompasses the vast majority of intellectual property rights, it does not purport to include all conceivable rights, suggesting its scope may warrant further refinement.

6.3 Theoretical Foundations of the IPRs System

IP law is an open, dynamic, and continuously innovative institutional system. In modern society, property is increasingly becoming intangible and immaterial with transformations in the forms of social wealth. It is observable that not all rights under the name of IPRs uniformly originate from the paradigmatic domain of intellectual assets and creations. In other words, the term "intellectual property rights" serves merely as a collective designation for various non-material property rights. In this sense, non-material property rights, incorporeal property rights, and IPRs bear no substantive distinction; each represents a novel category of property rights derived from non-material objects, distinct from traditional property ownership.

Various scholars have addressed the construction of IPRs systems. French scholar Mallory (quoted in Yin 1998) divided IPRs into two categories:

- Industrial Monopoly Rights: These rights pertain to intellectual creations and distinctive signs. *Intellectual creations* encompass literary and artistic property (copyright and neighbouring rights), patents, design rights, and trade secrets (protected under civil law and unfair competition law). *Distinctive signs* include trademarks, commercial advertising, trade names, and shop signs (protected under civil law and unfair competition law).
- Clientèle Rights (Droits de la clientèle): These rights concern the clientèle as a business asset. Clientèle rights essentially represent customer "loyalty" or the enterprise's power of attraction, constituting its goodwill.

While this French classification offers a valuable exploration, it presents shortcomings: Firstly, it omits certain emerging rights, such as the right to new plant varieties and the right to layout design of integrated circuits. Secondly, the classification of certain subject matters lacks precision. For example, commercial advertisements are categorised as distinctive marks while seeking copyright protection. Thirdly, the nature of clientèle rights as intellectual property remains inadequately defined. British scholars F. H. Lawson and B. Laden (1998), employing concepts from property law, integrated "industrial and intellectual property rights" with creditor's right, commercial securities, goodwill, bonds, and shares into the category of "intangible movables." "Industrial and intellectual property" includes patents, designs, trademarks, trade names and copyrights. American scholar Michael D. Bayles holds similar views. He believes that IPRs, creditor's rights, negotiable instruments, stocks, credit, and portraits all belong to "intangible movables." It should be noted that Anglo-American formulations are also problematic: treating goodwill/reputation as a distinct type of "intangible movable" is debatable, and they fail to incorporate rights related to newer technologies.

6.3.1 Categories of Non-Material Property in the IPRs System

The author maintains that IPRs, in a broad sense, encompasses the following two categories of non-material property.

Intellectual Assets

Property of this kind mainly comprises knowledge, technology, information and other assets which contain intangible property interests. It may be subdivided into two forms: creative works and business marks. Creative works include literary and artistic works, their media of dissemination, and industrial technology. Literary and artistic works and their media are creative achievements in the field of culture, arising from the creative and communicative activities of their authors. Their objective forms of expression include texts, symbols, graphics, images, audio-visual recordings and the like. Industrial technology refers to creative achievements in industrial, agricultural, and commercial, and other productive domains capable of being embodied in material carriers. It typically manifests as methods and skills of technical operation, along with the tools of production and other material facilities adapted to these methods and skills. Business marks refer to sign used in the course of trade which are capable of distinguishing the commercial origins and manufacturers of goods and services. This includes trademarks, trade names, and geographical indications, and similar identifiers. The aforementioned intellectual assets constitute the most important type of immaterial wealth in modern society.

Credit-Based Property

Credit-based property refers to propertised commercial personality interests, such as goodwill, commercial credit, and image of a corporation. In terms of commercial goodwill and image, they are internally determined by the operating capability of an enterprise, which can be evaluated by its economic status, production capacity, product quality and market share (Yang 1996, p. 638). But external factors also matter since public evaluation and trust also weigh in on the establishment of goodwill and image. Such interests contain significant proprietary elements alongside personal (reputational) aspects. Credit-based property is also an important part of non-material wealth.

6.3.2 Constituent Rights in a Comprehensive IPRs System

Based on the above analysis, a comprehensive IPRs system comprises the following rights.

Literary Property Rights

Although in a broad sense, copyright often includes neighbouring rights, in legislative documents "literary property rights" refers to copyright and neighbouring rights.[4] Regarding rights in creative works and their dissemination media, database protection merit special attention. To protect producers' investment in databases, the international community adopts copyright law and anti-unfair competition law to protect the *sui generis* database rights, creating a new approach to protection independent of and similar to copyright (Xue 2000, p. 93). Consequently, literary property rights comprise copyright, neighbouring rights, and *sui generis* database rights.

Industrial Property Rights

According to the *Paris Convention for the Protection of Industrial Property Rights* (the *Paris Convention*) and related treaties, industrial property rights primarily include patent rights (including design rights), trademark rights, trade name rights, geographical indications, and protection against unfair competition. The 1967 Stockholm Act of the *Paris Convention* lists patented technology, business marks, and anti-unfair competition as objects of industrial property rights protection. The scope of industrial property rights extends beyond mere industry and commerce. The term "industrial property rights" is arguably better termed "industrial and commercial property rights". Given its breadth, some scholars suggest it effectively denotes all intellectual property except copyright (Zhang 1990, p. 64). However, beyond copyright and industrial property rights, some intellectual assets are protected via "specific

[4] Neighbouring Rights (also known as Related Rights) is a more literal translation of the original French droits voisins.

protection statutes" or "overlapping protection regimes", creating the distinct rights discussed below.

Sui Generis Property Rights

Sui Generis property rights are independent intellectual property rights traditionally falling outside literary or industrial property, typically taking the form of exclusive rights ("*droits exclusifs*" or "*sui generis rights*"). There are mainly three kinds of IP that merit such rights: new plant varieties, layout designs of integrated circuits and trade secrets.

- **Plant variety rights**: There are three models of IPRs protection for new plant varieties: exclusive right, patent and dual protection. The German model protects new plant varieties with exclusive rights, while the Italian model provides for patent rights, and a third and hybrid model provides for both of these forms of rights. While the *International Convention for the Protection of New Varieties of Plants* (1961) and the *TRIPS Agreement* (1994) permit any of these models to protect new plant varieties, most member states favour exclusive rights.
- **Layout design rights for integrated circuits**: Since layout-designs are neither under the protection of copyright (as graphic works) nor patent rights (as designs), the international community adopted "industrial copyright" protection[5]—a hybrid *sui generis* right absorbing elements of both copyright and industrial property.
- **Trade secret rights**: Distinct from industrial property rights, trade secret rights do not confer exclusive rights in the common sense, and their protection is not limited in time or to place of issue. The effectiveness of trade secret rights depends entirely on the degree of confidentiality upheld by their owner. Therefore, it falls into the category of alternative IPRs.

The above-mentioned rights to creative achievements and business marks are generally protected by modern legislation in various countries as core IPRs.

Goodwill

"Goodwill" signifies commercial credit and reputation attached to a business, providing it with economic benefits. While Chinese legal scholarship often employs a broad, neutral conception of goodwill, or Shang Yu (reputation of a business) in Chinese,[6] economic theory views it as a valuable, positive asset. Yang Zhongxian (quoted in S. Z. Yang 1992) held that the term "goodwill" in English implies friendly

[5] The initial legislative motivation of industrial copyright was to correct the problem that industrial product designs enjoy the overlapping protections of patent law and copyright law. To address the fact that some industrial products cannot be protected and to make up for the lack of a single system of protection, some countries later created the industrial copyright system. See Zheng Chengsi (1990).

[6] For related theories, see Liang Shangshang (1993) and Zhu Shu et al. (1996).

corporate culture and positive public evaluation. Yang's view echoes that of his Western counterparts: according to *The Oxford Companion to Law,* "goodwill" is "a good quality possessed by a business or industry" (Walker 1989, p. 381), and the jurisprudence of British courts refers to it as "the benefits and advantages of a company's good reputation, credit and relationships" (quoted in Guan 1996, p. 173). That provides a solid base for the interpretation of goodwill in China. The author argues that goodwill is a kind of property independent of material entities and falls within the category of credit-based property. In the system of intangible property rights, while goodwill is protected by anti-unfair competition law, its legislative objectives have not been clarified. Therefore, it is more appropriate to regard it as an IPR, as trade secrets and anti-unfair competition have been incorporated into the IPRs system.

Credit/Trust

In the *Oxford Companion to Law* and the *Black's Law Dictionary*, "credit" or "trust" relates to transactions involving deferred payment, and it reflects a party's economic capacity (the ability to pay debts) based on social evaluation (Walker 1989, p. 381). Chinese legal scholarship often defines "credit" more broadly as general economic capacity of a subject, viewing it primarily as personal rights.[7] Legally, however, credit refers to a positive social evaluation and reliance obtained by an entity's debt-servicing capacity, which is different from goodwill. In addition, although intangible, credit manifests via instruments (e.g. letters of credit), with which benefits are obtained in credit exchange. That distinguishes credit from general personality rights. Therefore, the credit right is an intangible property right pertaining to financial standing.

Publicity Rights

"Publicity" refers to a variety of personas (images) owned by individuals or social organisations, including images of real and fictitious characters, and social images of the organisation. These images are often related to identifying aspects such as the right holders' name, likeness and persona as well as the name, character, work or activity created by the holders (Du 2000; Dong 1998), all of which are vulnerable to misappropriation and exploitation. The right holders may use their own images or virtual images or transfer the rights to others for reasons not limited to the popularity and creativity of these images. The value of publicity lies in associating these images with specific products to make a positive impression on consumers. Such an impression enhances product recognition and grants the user a competitive advantage. Therefore, publicity rights are not purely rights over the use of someone's

[7] For relevant theories, see Wang Liming (1993, p. 299), Zhang Junhao (1991, p. 158), Yang Lixin (1996, p. 638).

image but rather rights over intangible assets. While closely related to traditional IP, real personas are not protected by copyright, and fictional personas are not under the protection of patent and trademark laws. Therefore, publicity rights are also intangible property rights of an independent category.

The above are business credit rights, which are generalised IPRs or intangible property rights related to IPRs.

References

Black, Henry C. and Nolan, Joseph R. 1979. *Black's Law Dictionary* (15th edition), West Publishing Co.

Bonfante, Pietro. 1992. *Istituzioni di Diritto Romano*. Trans. Huang Feng. Beijing: China University of Political Science and Law Press

Dong, Binghe. 1998. On publicity right. *Legal Science* 4

Du, Ying. 2000. On merchandising right. In LiangHuixing (ed.) Civil and Commercial Law Series (Vol. 13), Beijing: Law Press

Guan, Linghua. 1996. *Cognizance and Compensation for Spiritual Damage*. Beijing: People's Court Press

Jiang, Ping 1999. *Science of Civil Law*. Beijing: China University of Political Science and Law Press

Kong, Xiangjun. 2002. *The TRIPS Agreement and Its Application in China*. Beijing: Law Press

Larenz, Karl. 2003. *General Theory of German Civil Law*. Trans. Xiaohua Wang. Beijing: China Law Press

Lawson, F. H. and B. Laden. 1998. *Property Law*. Trans. Tiantao Shi. Beijing: Encyclopedia of China Publishing House

Liang, Huixing. 1996. *Civil Law*. Beijing: China Law Press

Liang, Shangshang. 1993. On goodwill and the right of goodwill. *Law Research* 5

Qian, Mingxing. 1994. *Principle of Property Rights*. Beijing: Beijing University Press

Vandevelde, Kenneth J. 1980. The new property of the nineteenth century: The development of the modern concept of property. B*uffalo Law Review*

Walker, David M (ed.). 1989. *The Oxford Companion to Law*. Trans. Shuangyuan Li, et al. Beijing: Guangming Daily Publishing House,

Wang, Liming. 1993. *Civil Law: Tort Law*. Beijing: Renmin University Press

WIPO (ed.). 1992. *A Comprehensive Discussion on Intellectual Property Rights*. Beijing: World Knowledge Press

Wu, Handong. 2003. The dematerialisation revolution of property and the revolutionary immaterial property law. *Social Science in China* 4

Wu, Handong. 2005. On property right system. *China Legal Science 2*

Xie, Huaishi. 1996. On the system of civil rights. *Chinese Journal of Law* 2

Xu, Xuan. 2002. The integrated construction of intellectual property and property law. *Jinan Journal (Philosophy & Social Science Edition)* 6

Xue, Hong. 2000. *Intellectual Property Law in the Internet Age*. Beijing: Law Press

Yang, Lixin. 1996. *On the Law of Personal Rights*. Beijing: China Procuratorial Publishing House

Yang, Shizhan. 1992. *The Treasure House of Chinese Accounting Thoughts*. Beijing: China Financial and Economic Publishing House

Yin, Tian. 1998. *Property Right Law of Germany*. Beijing: China Law Press

Zhang, Junhao. 1991. *Principles of Civil Law*. Beijing: China University of Political Science and Law Press

Zhang, Naigen. 1990. *Intellectual Property Laws in International Trade*. Shanghai: Fudan University Press
Zheng, Chengsi. 1990. *Copyright Law*. Beijing: China Renmin University Press
Zhu, Shu, et al. 1996. On the legal protection of the right of goodwill. *Modern Law* 1

Part II
Basic Theories of Intellectual Property Rights

Introduction for Part II

This part provides an overview of the most abstract and generalised academic synthesis on IPRs and IPRs regimes. Within the "general theory" framework constructed by the author, the basic categories–such as the nature, subject, subject matter, use, restrictions, and protection of IPRs–form the components of its conceptual system, each corresponding to specific institutional designs in the legislative documents. The basic theories of IPRs cover the historical evolution, theoretical basis, cultural significance, value objectives, and political functions, mainly discussing the scientificity, legality and rationality of IPRs regime construction. Furthermore, research on the interplay between IP law and related legal regimes–such as unfair competition law, antitrust law, and civil law—serves to illustrate the relevance, co-ordination, and appropriateness of IP governance. These inquiries transcend specific legal provisions or institutional mechanisms, focusing instead on discerning and articulating the essential nature of IPRs regimes. Indeed, such analysis often extends beyond IP law itself, employing comparative legal methodologies to evaluate and critique the functional efficacy of IPRs regimes.

As a specialised legal system, the IPRs regime aims to confirm, protect and utilise intellectual properties. While the *TRIPS Agreement* provides common rules for IPRs protection, countries varying in development stages and socio-economic conditions will follow their own independent discourse in understanding and interpreting IPRs. It is, in a sense, a country or a nation's "power of discourse" in its IPRs policies (Wu

2011)[1]. This part tries to make some academic interpretation of the basic issues in IPRs based on international IPRs theories and local cultural resources.

[1] Wu, Handong. 2011. Common rules and independent discourse of intellectual property rights. *Social Science in China* 5.

Chapter 7
Historical Evolution of IPRs Regimes

The IPRs regime has a history of only three to four hundred years from its emergence, and through its development and transformation. In the legal system, IP law has a special connection with science, technology and economy: in the era of industrial economy, it is a product of modern scientific advancement and commodity economy development, providing a new way for asset owners to acquire property; in the era of knowledge economy, it is a driver of progress in modern science and technology and in market economy, becoming the guardian deity for knowledge capitalism to obtain intellectual wealth. In a sense, the history of the IPRs system represents a chronicle of the dynamic interplay and mutual influence between legal reform, technological innovation, and economic development.

7.1 Social Conditions for the Emergence of Modern IP Law

The IPRs regime is generated through the development of modern science and technology and the commodity economy. In modern history, it is generally recognised that some events represent the origin of the IPRs regime: England enacted the first patent law, *Statute of Monopolies* in 1623, and the first copyright law, *An Act for the Encouragement of Learning, by vesting the Copies of Printed Books in the Authors or purchasers of such Copies, during the Times therein mentioned*, namely the *Statute of Anne* in 1709; France enacted the first trademark law, *Law Concerning the Manufacture of Marks and Trademarks on the Principles of Use and Non-examination* in 1857. These were not historical accidents.

From the seventeenth and eighteenth centuries, the bourgeoisie began to utilise the achievements of science and technology in the field of production, thus triggering a legal problem of IPRs protection in the capitalist market. The bourgeoisie demanded that the right to private possession over intellectual products should be recognised by the law to make sure that such products could be exchanged freely, the same as

H. Wu, *Theorising Intellectual Property Rights from Chinese Perspectives*,
https://doi.org/10.1007/978-981-96-5867-1_7

ordinary subject matter (tangible products). They sought a new legal system different from the previous property law as a new way of acquiring property rights. In this way, some new rights were generated: patent rights emerged in the field of scientific and technological inventions directly related to commodity production, trademark rights in the category of commodity marks that played an important role in commodity exchange, and copyright in the process of bringing literary and artistic works to the market as commodities. They were eventually collated as IPRs.

From the end of the Middle Ages to the beginning of capitalism, the modern IPRs regime developed over hundreds of years. In the midst of drastic social revolutions, and changes in politics, economy, technology, ideology and culture, an integrated IPR infrastructure came slowly but surely into being.

7.1.1 Enhancement of Manufacturing Technologies

From the beginning of the fifteenth century, with the establishment of relations of capitalist production and the development of the manufacturing industry, some Western European countries were faced with an urgent market demand for updating their production tools and machinery with new technologies. It contributed to great progress in manufacture in the fields of textile, mining, metallurgy and chemistry, which were closely related to the development of the capitalist economy (Li 1990, pp. 83–86). The emergence of new technologies consolidated industrial civilisation and brought about the need for a mechanism that would respect and protect IP products.

7.1.2 A New Outlook on Culture and Values

Launched by the bourgeoisie of Western Europe and marked by a revival of classical scholarship and art between the fourteenth and the sixteenth centuries, the Renaissance was a backlash against obscurantism and religious fervour. The era inherited the scientific culture of ancient Greece and initiated a philosophy centred on humanism (Wang 1998, pp. 85–86). The revival of science and the discovery of humanity encouraged people to study nature and focus on practical knowledge to improve their lives and the world around them. The new cultural values of Renaissance provided the bourgeoisie with necessary cultural and ideological readiness for utilising science and technology as a material weapon and a private rights system as a legal weapon.

7.1.3 Emergence of New Political Philosophy

During the English Civil War (1642–1651), a number of philosophers, including Thomas Hobbes (1588–1679), John Milton (1608–1674) and John Locke (1632–1704), advocated ideas of popular sovereignty, equality and freedom, and emphasised the inviolability of private property. In particular, Locke expounded on capitalist principles on property and political power, and described the debate over these principles between British capitalists and newly emerged aristocracy of the seventeenth century (Patterson and Lindberg 1991, pp. 49–55). A new political system of philosophy supported by Locke and others and the European Enlightenment, represented by Montesquieu then began to take shape in the UK, arming the country with an ideology that allowed it to develop its own laws, including the IPRs regime.

7.1.4 Revival of Roman Law Principles

The ancient Roman law was extensively transplanted into European countries in the twelfth century. As Karl Marx (1818–1883) and Friedrich Engels (1820–1895) wrote, "As soon as industry and trade developed private property further, first in Italy and later in other countries, the highly developed Roman civil law was immediately adopted again and raised to authority" (Marx 2019 [1932]). The main manifestations of this revival included an upsurge in research on and introduction of ancient Roman law in European countries from the fifteenth century to the sixteenth century. Although there was no IPRs regime in ancient Roman law, its concept of intangible property, the theory of public domain, and the transfer and infringement of intangible property were sources of inspiration to later legal principles and rules of property attributes, public domain, property rights trade, and intangible infringement of IPRs. In a word, through its useful legal ideas, the revival of Roman private law facilitated the development of the modern IPRs regime.

7.1.5 Conditions for the Establishment of Modern IPRs Regimes

The modern IPRs regime is rooted in the economic relations of the times. From the perspective of science and technology, economy and law, intellectual products as the object of IPRs or the establishment of an IPRs regime depends on the following conditions.

Scientific and Technologised Social Production

In the pre-capitalist period, science and technology were separated and disconnected, and their application in production was accidental and undeliberate. At that time, technology was mastered by ordinary artisans, and progressed entirely through experience. Scientific knowledge was exclusive to aristocratic philosophers, whose theories were generalisations and summaries of practice, and lagged behind production (Zhao 1998, p. 3). The natural economy transformed into the commodity economy at the end of the pre-capitalist period and the beginning of capitalism. During this time the dominant physical factors in labour products gradually gave way to intellectual factors, enabling the natural sciences to directly serve the production process for the first time. The rise of the bourgeois class across Europe came with a surge in productivity. The connection between science, technology and productivity was thus forged, pegging social production to scientific discovery and technological invention. The shift was noted in the *Economics Manuscript,* "The process of production becomes the process of applying science, and science, in turn, becomes a production factor, a so-called function. Each new discovery leads to a new invention, a new improvement in production" (Marx and Engels 1995, p. 277).

Commercialised Scientific and Technological Achievements

In the pre-capitalist period, material products created using science and technology were commodities, but science and technology were not. As science and technology had been restricted in specific fields and in independent family workshops and had long progressed mainly through accumulation of experience, it was difficult for them to be transferred and adopted on a large scale and at the social level. In such a closed socio-economic situation, science and technology could not develop systematically and successively. Instead, they were decentralised, experience-based and passed down from generation to generation within families. The development of the modern commodity economy and the establishment of capitalism broke down the barriers among technological sectors and between technology and society in the natural economy. The strong demands of the commodity economy released technology into the society, enabling large scales of transfer. Capital reduced scientific and technological achievements to ordinary equivalents in exchange and assessed their value purely in terms of economic benefit, thus emancipating science and technology from the shackles of general skills and limited application. According to Karl Marx's labour value theory, intellectual labour is also "productive labour" that "confers more values that it possesses." In the information era, "production" may be understood in a broader sense referring to the production of both tangible commodities and intangible goods such as services, knowledge, information and technology (Li 1999, p. 39). That is, in social production featuring the application of science and technology, intangible goods themselves, whether technology, knowledge or information, are of the same commodity significance as the material products, the tangible goods produced through using knowledge, information and technology.

Legalised Intellectual Property

In the pre-capitalist period, the limited spread and exchange of science and technology had no protection of property law and contract law. Commodities (including intellectual products and tangible goods) must be traded based on a definite property right and a stable transaction order. In feudal period, however, the laws, characterised by their emphasis on punishment rather than people and on "gods over people", often treated the dissemination and application of scientific and technological achievements as a private matter, and rarely regulated them directly in the name of the state. Although in the late feudal period, there was an exclusive right to print or a franchise and monopoly, but it was a feudal franchise, not a capitalist property right. The beneficiaries of this feudal franchise were mainly printers, business owners, and rulers who issued licenses, rather than authors and creators who engaged in intellectual creative activities. In some cases, the feudal ruling class also restricted the dissemination of advanced ideas through the franchise system and oppressed progressive authors and inventors (Liang 1994, p. 3). Therefore, there is a fundamental difference in nature between such feudal franchises and modern IPRs. The protection of intellectual property cannot be limited to adopting the traditional property law based on ancient Roman property law. According to Hegel (1961), such things as mental skills, scientific knowledge, art, and inventions all can be the object of a contract and be treated in the same way as the things recognised in a sale. Such possessions, although able to be traded and contracted like a tangible thing, has something of the internal spirit in it. Therefore, intellectual products are a different type of object, independent of traditional "things." In other words, IPRs are a new legal system, different from ownership of tangible property. It is under the impetus of the development of the modern commodity economy and science and technology that IPRs, as a kind of private intangible property rights, have been universally recognised and strictly protected by capitalist countries, and have gradually formed an independent and strict legal system.

Systematised IPRs Regime

From ancient Roman law to the modern civil code, the property rights regime has been centred on tangible things. The Romans established their private law system with *things* as the subject of right. An institution of "real rights", with ownership as the core, was designed, and a thing-orientated legal system was also established, with real rights and creditor's rights as the gist. From the *French Civil Code* (1804) to the *German Civil Code* (1896), things without physical existence were either partially acknowledged, referring exclusively to right, as an abstract concept over property, or excluded from propriety property as being intangible. Such new rights as copyright, patent right and trademark right are excluded from the traditional civil code.[1] IPRs are a system that belongs to the scope of civil law but is also relatively independent of it. The practice of classifying all rights relating to intellectual activities as "intellectual property rights" was first seen only in some modern academic works. At that time there was no systematic integration of copyright, patent rights or trademark rights in legislative documents. Only in the second half of the twentieth century, especially after the conclusion of the *WIPO Convention*, was the doctrine of intellectual property widely disseminated around the world, and the practice of systematising the IPRs regime under the name of IPRs recognised by legislators in various countries.

The above conditions coalesced and unified, driven by objective laws of historical development and internal logical interconnections. Looking back at the history of the creation of IPRs regimes in Western developed countries, there is indeed a clear trajectory linking the integrated development of science, economy and law: scientific and technologised social production → commercialised scientific and technological achievements → legalised intellectual goods → systematised IPRs regime. From the perspective of social progress, this basic trajectory can be generalised as the historical process from scientific and technological development to economic growth to legal system advancement.

7.2 Basic Features of Modern IP Law Development

Since the beginning of the twentieth century, IP law has matured and become a common legal system in countries around the world. During this period, social life underwent profound changes: the rapid development of modern science and technology had an unprecedented impact on intellectual and cultural life; the highly developed modern commodity economy promoted the formation of a new international economic order and world market. In response to such changes, national legislators have had to "reform and revise the law" and focus on changes to their IP laws.

7.2.1 Expansion of Traditional IPRs Protections

Copyright, patent rights and trademark rights represent the three fundamental regimes of traditional IP law. But in modern times, their coverage has been greatly widened.

In the early days, copyright protection was confined to books and maps. Thus, it was in this sense that some people referred to copyright as "the child of printing and publishing" (Duan 1988, p. 28). It was only at the end of the nineteenth century

[1] That changed in the second half of the twentieth century. Some civil law countries try to integrate a unified property right system including IPRs within the framework of the civil code. Criticisms were common among scholars. See Sect. 18.3 for discussion on basic features of the *TRIPS Agreement*.

that various countries extended the meaning of "printed works" in copyright law, extending the scope to music, drama and photography. In the twentieth century, especially since the second half of the twentieth century, "electronic copyright" has replaced "printed copyright" and various "electronic works" have been included in the protection of traditional copyright.

The main manifestations are: first, "audio-visual works" including movies, television and videos are treated as general works and protected by copyright; second, "satellite broadcasting programs" are transmitted through satellites for synchronous reception and relayed by terrestrial broadcasting are regarded as general broadcasting programs and protected by neighbouring rights; third, "cable TV programs" received and transmitted through coaxial cables are protected by copyright or neighbouring rights according to the differences in the subject matter; fourth, computer software is treated as general written works and protected by copyright as a special object (Wu et al. 1998, p. 19). In addition, folklore expressions, as special subject matter of copyright, are also an important manifestation of the development of modern copyright law.

The coverage of patent rights has been expanded and gradually specified with the advance of science and technology and the demands of economic development. The early patent system, from the *Patent Law of the Republic of Venice* (1474) to the *English Statute of Monopolies* (1623), protected technical inventions. In the nineteenth century, France promulgated the world's first local special legislation for the protection of designs in 1803; the United Kingdom enacted the *Utility Design Act* in 1843 to protect utility models for the first time. *Paris Convention* in 1883 stipulated that the subject matter of industrial property are inventions, utility models and industrial designs. A survey of 149 countries and regions shows that 97 countries and regions stipulate two patent rights: inventions and industrial designs, in their laws and regulations; 14 name three patent rights: inventions, utility models and industrial designs; and 38 only regulate inventions (Liu 1997, p. 428). Up to now, the above three categories are the main subject matter protected by patent laws. In addition, some countries also provide for the protection of plant varieties, microorganisms, etc. Some inventions and creations are not protected by patent law, one kind being intellectual achievements that do not have the characteristics of technical solutions, such as natural rules, scientific principles, natural phenomena and economic methods (Zengchen 1977, p. 33). The other kind is intellectual achievements that are not protected due to the limitation of national technology and economic level. In this regard, legislation varies greatly from country to country, but the scope of such non-patent-protected subject matter has been decreasing. The protection of chemical substances and pharmaceuticals has become a trend in modern patent legislation.

Trademark law sees the least changes in its object among all IPRs. A trademark is used to identify goods for the buyer, and so legislators' first concern is the "recognisability" of the mark. In modern and contemporary law, legislative provisions on the constituent elements of trademarks vary. It is a general rule that characters, graphics, or their combinations can be treated as trademarks; other than that, there is not an international consensus on whether colours, sounds, shapes, geographic names and numbers can constitute trademarks. In terms of the subject matter of trademark rights, there are two trends worth our attention: first, in order to promote the development of tertiary industry, distinguishing marks are protected by trademark legislation. Most countries give equal protection to such service and commodity marks; second, well-known trademarks with a high reputation among the public are provided special protection in many countries, no matter whether they are registered or not.

7.2.2 Emergence of Novel Property Rights and Regimes

The traditional IPRs regime has been enriched with new rights. For example, copyright has long expanded from the "right of publication." Associated with new communication technologies, various "electronic copyrights" have arisen, such as the "right of broadcasting" with the technical content of radio and television transmission, the "right of mechanical reproduction" with the optical and electromagnetic characteristics, and the "right of production" in photography, video and projection; associated with transmission methods, more specific and concrete rights have arisen, such as the "right of serialisation" that allows publication of a book in newspapers or magazines one or more times as a right to reproduction, the "right of adaptation" that allows adaptation of a literary work into a musical or dramatic work, or a graphic work into 3D one as a deductive work, and the "rental right" that allows distribution of copies of works to the public through lending or leasing as a transmission right. In addition to the existing exclusive right to manufacture, use and sell, the patent right adds an "import right" to prohibit others from illegally introducing patented products from abroad.

At the same time, beyond the traditional IP law, some new independent exclusive rights to intellectual property have emerged, among which the most important is the right to layout design of integrated circuits and the right to new plant varieties related to bio-engineering technology. The integrated circuit is the core of microelectronics technology, and is a comprehensive technical achievement, including layout design and process technique. Layout design is constituted by components attached to the various carriers and the lines connecting them. However, as a drawing design of electronic product, layout design of an integrated circuit is excluded from the protection of patent law, for it does not belong to industrial design; as a 3D design, it cannot be classified as a graphic work or modelling work under copyright law. Therefore, most countries have adopted special legislation and give protection to layout design of integrated circuits as an independent IPR or "quasi-patent" through international conventions, such as the *Treaty on Intellectual Property Rights of Integrated Circuits* (1989). In addition, new plant varieties, as a major achievement of bio-engineering technology in the improvement of plant varieties, are emphasised in legislation around the world. At present, new plant varieties are mainly protected by special laws or patent laws. The *International Convention for the Protection of New Varieties of Plants* (UPOV) in 1961 and *TRIPS Agreement* in 1994 emphasise the protection of new plant varieties, but allow parties to freely choose between patents or independent IPRs or to choose both.

7.2.3 Recognition of Business Marks' Property Value

In the IPRs regime, the protection of business marks (commercial identifiers) appeared the earliest.[2] Although it developed slower than copyright law and patent law, it has undergone some significant changes in modern society:

First, business marks have formed a trademark-centred mark category. In addition to traditional trademarks, trade names, industry marks, geographic indications, quality marks (e.g. pure wool marks), quality recognition marks (e.g. "national" and "ministerial" award marks) have become subject matter with property significance and protected by law.

Second, the right to trade names (i.e., the right to the name of an enterprise) has brought about the separation of personal right and property right. The right to trade names is an intangible property right, a famous trade name can bring commercial benefits to commercial subjects, and other subjects are willing to pay a consideration to be assigned this right (Nie 1999).

Third, domain names for access to the Internet, are new marks that appear in the information market and websites. There is still disagreement among scholars about the attributes of domain names. Some believe that it is an independent category of mark, different from the original trade name or trademark of Internet users; others believe that it is only the digital expression of the original mark on the Internet and a new form of mark carrier. Putting aside the disagreement, it is an indisputable fact that domain names have gained attention worldwide and protection in some countries.

Fourth, business marks and goodwill constitute the intangible property of an enterprise. Business marks are generally associated with the goodwill of a particular enterprise. Goodwill is a positive social evaluation of an enterprise, which is formed from various factors, including the quality of the enterprise, the quality of its managers, and its relationship with customers. Among the various business marks, the trade name is the carrier of goodwill, while trademark and other marks contribute to the formation of goodwill.

Fifth, the protection of business marks involves multiple branches of law. Generally speaking, special laws (such as trademark law) are the mainstay, supplemented by anti-unfair competition laws and administrative laws. In the IPRs system, the rights related to marks are mainly a kind of industrial property right.

7.2.4 Integration of Trade Secrets and Anti-Unfair Competition into IPRs Regimes

The contemporary IPRs system is a large part of modern law. Traditionally, trade secrets and anti-unfair competition were exceptions or supplements to IPRs protection, but now they are new components of the IPRs system.

---

[2] The protection of trademarks is said to have existed in ancient Roman law, allowing buyers to sue sellers who falsified their marks.

Trade secrets are a kind of intangible information property. Different from patent, trade secrets do not confer exclusive rights in the common sense, and their protection is not limited in time or place of issue. The effectiveness of trade secrets depends entirely on the degree of confidentiality maintained by their owner. That explains why trade secrets are not included in the traditional IPRs system. The civil law countries had a long history of protecting trade secrets according to contract law or tort law without the recognition of its nature of property right; at the same time the common law countries generally regarded trade secrets as intangible property in special legislation. In the 1960s, the International Chamber of Commerce (ICC) took the lead in conferring IPR attributes to trade secrets, and WIPO in its founding convention also implied that trade secrets could be included in IPRs. In the 1990s, TRIPS specifically stipulated the protection of "undisclosed information" and confirmed that trade secrets are a type of IP.

Anti-unfair competition law is closely related to the IPRs, and it is generally categorised as IP law. The 1967 Stockholm revised version of *Paris Convention* put patented technology, business marks and anti-unfair competition under the protection of industrial property rights. The *Convention on the Establishment of the World Intellectual Property Organisation*, signed in the same year, also extended the scope of IPRs protection to unfair competition. TRIPS in 1994 emphasised that parties should comply with the relevant provisions of the *Paris Convention*, i.e., the provisions on the inclusion of anti-unfair competition as part of IPRs.

The reasons why anti-unfair competition is included in the modern IP law system are as follows: First, the anti-unfair competition law protects the subject matter that are adjusted by other IP laws, including the infringement of copyright, patent right and trademark right. Therefore, in some cases, there will be overlapping of laws and the issue of the prevail of which law. Second, the anti-unfair competition law protects the subject matter related to various intellectual property that are not covered by relevant laws, so as to work as a supplement to the IPRs regime. Third, the anti-unfair competition law ensures the minimum protection when neither the existing IPRs regime nor relevant legal systems is applicable. It can be said that the coverage of this law is the most extensive in the field of intellectual property. Although the scope of anti-unfair competition is becoming broader in the current legislation, even including many areas not related to IPRs, the main task of the anti-unfair competition law is still its focus on IPRs protection.

7.3 Contemporary Trends in IP Law Reform

Human society is in a new era of knowledge economy, which is an intellectual economy with science and technology as the main factor in production. It will impact the values, distribution principles, lifestyles, management mechanisms and government policies formed in the previous resource-based economy and trigger the restructuring of the "rules of the game", i.e. reconstruction of legal regulations. The contemporary IPRs regime is facing a new trend in development and change, and in innovation and breakthrough.

7.3.1 Technological Innovation and Modernisation of IPRs Regimes

IPRs are the result of innovation and changes in the system of private rights, as well as in basic legal system for the direct protection of scientific and technological innovations. The IPRs regime has a history of only three to four hundred years, but has gone through different periods from the Industrial Revolution to the information revolution. It was generated and changed through science and technological innovation, and in this way its development represents the interaction and mutual promotion between the legal system and science and technology. Since the Industrial Revolution in Britain, four technological revolutions have taken place. The fourth revolution, beginning in the 1980s and symbolised by the information revolution and represented by the computer and the Internet, and by the biological revolution brought about through the decipherment of human genome, is still in the ascendant (Huang et al. 1998). It has brought about the world-wide "information revolution" and "knowledge revolution." As a product of the revolution in information technology, the Internet forms a "cyberspace", which is a global information media without a centre. It not only changes the lifestyles of human beings, but also poses a challenge to the existing legal system.

At present, there are three main issues in the IPRs regime that deserve attention: The first is "Internet copyrights." The key issue to be resolved in the contemporary copyright system is how to make the exclusive rights effectively "cover" the dissemination of works on the Internet, specifically the protection of right to digital works, confidential technology measures and databases (Xue 2000). The second issue is "Internet marks." Digital business marks in cyberspace are related to both changes in the traditional trademark system (such as the conflict between the regional trademark rights and the international Internet, the conflict between the classified trademark protection and the exclusive online trademark rights, the changes in the form of online trademark infringement and the determination of infringement liability, etc.), and innovations in the system of domain name protection (including the registration and examination of domain names, the nature and content of domain name rights, the conflict between domain name rights and other prior rights, the protection of domain names and the handling of domain name disputes). The third is "Internet unfair competition." Many issues arising from information dissemination on the Internet and e-commerce should be addressed in contemporary competition law, such as the commercial packaging of screen display and website interface, confidentiality measures for online trade secrets, and online false advertising (Zhang 2000, pp. 149–150).

Gene technology, comparable to the Internet, is considered to be one of the most significant technologies of the twenty-first century. Human beings "may be at the beginning of an era when genes can explain and determine everything" (Gao et al. 2000). "Genetic food", "genetic drugs", "gene therapy", and other developments and utilisation of plant and animal genes, or even human genes, will lead to a series of changes in human beings and their surroundings. Despite controversies over national customs, ethics and religions, genetic technology tends to be protected in many countries under patent right and other IPRs. Two issues are involved in gene patent. One is to define the scope of gene patent protection, including gene methods, gene products, new varieties of genetically modified plants and animals, genetically modified micro-organisms and the genes "obtained from the human body by natural detachment or technical methods." The other is to clarify the excluded areas of gene patent, especially the methods of human cloning, commercial use of embryos and the simple discovery of gene sequences. In short, the new technological revolution has had a profound impact on the field of intellectual property. As a legal system with the most "scientific and technological content", IPRs must undergo constant innovation in the process of the "knowledge revolution", so as to achieve the modernisation of the legislation.

7.3.2 Convergence of International Trade Systems and IPRs Regimes

Economic globalisation is a major trend that gradually formed in the world economy in the second half of the twentieth century, and it will have a profound influence in the twenty-first century (Xu 1997, p. 11). As a post-war economic trend, economic globalisation connects national economies, resulting in an increasingly interdependent world market. It aims to eliminate tariff and non-tariff barriers that hinder the flow of goods and services between countries, regulate the market rules of international trade and promote the liberalisation of world trade.

The WTO and its predecessor, the GATT, play an important role in this process; the objective of WTO is to promote trade liberalisation by reducing or even eliminating tariffs and other trade barriers through non-discriminatory MFN treatment, to make full use of world trade resources, and to expand the production and exchange of goods and services. Unlike other international conventions and organisations, the WTO integrates IPRs protection into the international trading system. According to a document negotiated by the US, Japan and the EU in the Uruguay Round of trade negotiations, the resolution of IPR issues within the GATT framework concerns not just the harmonisation of countries' IPR laws but rather the elimination of trade distortions caused by the failure of some countries to gear their IPRs protection systems up to international standards (Li 1996). It should be noted that the IP interests enjoyed by developed and developing countries are unbalanced, and thus, their positions and stated objectives in relevant international consultations and dialogues are definitely dissimilar. The differences in positions between countries have resulted through negotiations at Uruguay in a package of agreements including *Agreement on Trade-related Aspects of Intellectual Property Rights (TRIPS)* and making protection of IPRs part of the international trade system. In other words, within the framework of the World Trade Organisation, the *TRIPS Agreement* promises the national coercive power of the parties and the international coercive power of the WTO and its parties, thus making it possible to link closely the IPRs protection committed to by the parties with the unconditional most-favoured-nation treatment. In short, the establishment of a new international trade system directly influences the integration of IPRs regimes, which marks a new stage of unified protection standard in contemporary IP law.

References

Duan, Ruilin. 1988. *Introduction to Intellectual Property Law*. Beijing: Guangming Daily Publishing House

Gao, Jianwei et al. 2000. On the patent legal protection of genes. *Political and Legal Forum* 4

Hegel, Georg Wilhelm Friedrich. 1961. *Grundlinien der Philosophie des Rechts*. Trans. Yang Fan and Qitai Zhang. Beijing: The Commercial Press

Huang, Yajun et al. 1998. *On Knowledge Economy*. Taiyuan: Shanxi Economic Publishing House

Li, Deyang. 1990. *The Evolution of Science and Technology*. Wuhan: Hubei Education Press

Li, Jingwen. 1999. *The New Era of Knowledge Economy*. Shanghai: Shanghai Far East Publishers

Li, Xiaowei. 1996. Changes in the IPRs system and their impact. *Hong Kong Economic Journal Monthly* 6

Liang, Zhiping. 1994. *Cultural Interpretation of Law*. Beijing: Joint Publishing

Liu, Chunmao. 1997. *Chinese Civil Law - Intellectual Property*. Beijing: Chinese People's Public Security University Publishing House

Marx, Karl. 1932. The German ideology. https://www.marxists.org/archive/marx/works/1845/german-ideology/ch01c.htm. Accessed 20 Nov 2019

Marx, Karl and Friedrich Engels. 1995. *Marx-Engels Collected Works*. Beijing: People's Publishing House

Nie, Weidong. 1999. The legal protection of trade name. *Legal Science* 3

Patterson, L. Ray. and Stanley W. Lindberg. 1991. The nature of copyright: A law of users' rights. *Michigan Law Review*, 90(6)

Wang, Zhe. 1998. *A History of Political and Legal Theory*. Beijing: Peking University Press

Wu, Handong et al. 1998. *A Study on Copyright Systems in Western Countries*. Beijing: China University of Political Science and Law Press

Xu, Ming (ed.). 1997. *27 Problems to be Solved in Contemporary China*. Beijing: China Today Press

Xue, Hong. 2000. *Intellectual Property Law in the Internet Age*. Beijing: China Law Press

Zengchen, Mingru. 1977. *Selected Treatises on Patent and Trademark Law*. Taipei: Sanmin Book

Zhang, Ping. 2000. *Analysis of Internet Intellectual Property Rights and Related Legal Issues*. Guangzhou: Guangzhou Publishing House

Zhao, Zhenjiang. 1998. *Theory on Science and Technology Law*. Beijing: Peking University Press

Chapter 8
Theoretical Foundations of IPRs Regimes

The transformation from intellectual wealth to IPRs is not merely a legal issue of institutional design and the application of regulations, but also a doctrinal issue with profound theoretical connotations. Modern jurists and thinkers have provided the corresponding theoretical foundations for IP law, either by studying useful ideas from ancient legal documents, or by adopting the methodologies of economic analysis and philosophical inquiry.

8.1 Roman Law Foundations of IPRs Regimes

IP law is a product of modern commodity economy and scientific and technological development, and the result of legal revolutions and institutional transformations in the field of property rights since Roman times. The Roman property law system was fundamentally constructed upon the concept of "things" (*res*). Its objects comprised primarily both tangible entities and intangible institutional products. During the Roman era, a property rights regime specifically designed to protect intellectual creations—that is, IP law in its modern sense—had not yet emerged. Nevertheless, the private law principles and rules it bequeathed, particularly the theory of "incorporeal things" (*incorporales*), furnish crucial intellectual resources for interpreting the legal recognition of intellectual assets. The Roman jurist Gaius (about 130—180) asserted that incorporeal things (*incorporales*) consist of "relations constituted in law" (*quae consistunt in jure*). These were entities lacking physical substance, existing solely as legal fictions (i.e., rights), such as easements (*servitutes*), usufructs (*ususfructus*), and similar entitlements (Chen 1936, p. 84; Zhou 1994, p. 28). The theory of "incorporeal things" developed within Roman law encompassed the following principal tenets: **First,** rights were abstract entities, essentially representing interests formulated subjectively. Consequently, they were classified as *incorporales*, distinct from corporeal things (*res corporales*). **Second,** for an entity to qualify as a legal *incorporale*,

H. Wu, *Theorising Intellectual Property Rights from Chinese Perspectives*,
https://doi.org/10.1007/978-981-96-5867-1_8

it had to be susceptible to monetary valuation. Rights lacking proprietary content, such as paternal power (*patria potestas*), marital authority (*manus*), or the status of freedom (*libertas*), were therefore excluded from this category. **Third,** although ownership (*dominium*) was itself a subjectively abstracted institutional construct, the Romans regarded this right as inseparable from the physical thing itself. It was considered the most complete real right (*ius in re*), and thus fundamentally distinct from other general patrimonial rights.

The underlying purpose of the theory of "incorporeal thing (*incorporales*)" was to conceptualise specific rights as the subject matter of rights. The broad view of property liberated the understanding of objects from a strict focus on things capable of direct physical control or possessing tangible existence. The theoretical contribution of Roman jurists lies not only in their establishment of a property right system suited to simple commodity economies, but also in the fact that this theory "supplied certain pivotal conceptual instruments" for the subsequent development of the modern IPRs regime (Drahos 1990, pp. 16–22).

8.1.1 Non-Materiality of Res Incorporales *and Nature of IP*

As the object of rights, "*res incorporales* (incorporeal things)" do not exist physically, but are subjective fictions or legally treated as subject matter. With regard to its dematerialisation nature, intellectual property (i.e., intellectual products and products of mind as subject matter) is also created by human intelligence and stipulated or recognised by law.

In the field of IP law, IP is generally regarded as "abstract objects." According to the Australian scholar Drahos (1996), such an object exists by virtue of human mental life; it is the product of human intellect superimposed upon the physical world. It lacks physical substance and exists purely in abstract form. From a metaphysical perspective, abstract objects constitute a postulated category of existence. Yet social reality necessitates the acknowledgement of their existence; when property extends to encompass abstract objects, relationships of interest between individuals arise based upon them. In the case of IP, the subject matter of property in question is an abstract object. As we understand it, the abstract object does not exist or we might say that it is not the case that it exists. The abstract object in IP takes the form of a legal fiction. Drahos (1996) contends that the law postulates the existence of rights in certain abstract objects. The molecular formula and chemical structure of penicillin are examples of abstract objects which many individuals need, use and rely upon. This gives rise to a distinct form of property right founded upon the abstract object. This is IP, which differs from traditional property ownership.

Drahos traces the notion of "abstract object" back to the Roman law concept of "*res incorporales*" (incorporeal things), meaning "intangible objects". Within classical philosophical thought, the conceptual lineage of incorporeal things can be traced to the Stoic school. While both represent conceptual constructs of the human mind,

Roman "*res incorporales*" specifically denoted proprietary rights (other than ownership) as institutional products, whereas Drahos's notion of "abstract objects" constitute the mental conceptions underpinning intellectual products—the very material mediating IP relations. Notwithstanding these distinctions, the theoretical contribution of the Roman jurists retains significant historical import. It may be said that the doctrine of "*res incorporales*" furnished a pivotal conceptual instrument for the development of the modern IPRs regime.

8.1.2 Quasi-Possession of Res Incorporales *and Control Over IP*

Possession is the actual control and management of a thing by a person. Generally, the subject matter of possession must be corporeal things. For this reason, Roman law devised the "quasi-possession" system for "incorporeal things" (*res incorporales*). In Roman law, the acquisition of quasi-possession, like possession itself,, required both the *animus* (intention) and *corpus* (physical element) conditions: the quasi-possessor must have exercised his or her right in fact to satisfy the *corpus* requirement; and must have the intention to exercise a certain real right for his or her own benefit to constitute the *animus* requirement (Zhou 1994, p. 432). In modern civil law theory, quasi-possession, also known as possession of right, takes property rights as the object. Strictly speaking, quasi-possession is not possession in the true sense, as it does not involve a specific corporeal object and lacks an externally perceptible manifestation (Jiang 2002, pp. 448–449). The significance of quasi-possession lies in the fact that control over a right treated as the object is deemed lawful possession, even in the absence of physical control.

Quasi-possession has been used and developed in subsequent civil legislations. For instance, the *French Civil Code* extended the concept of possession of rights to relational statuses, and termed the latter "possession of status" (*possessio status*). The *German Civil Code*, though it does not have a general provision on possession of right, recognises quasi-possession of easements (*servitudes*) and servitudes (*Dienstbarkeiten*). The *Japanese Civil Code* adopts a comprehensive legislative approach and treats property rights in a general sense as the subject matter of quasi-possession. This demonstrates that the possession of "incorporeal things" (possession of rights) is common in legislation.

Theoretically, the Roman law institution of quasi-possession of "incorporeal things" may be employed to explain the specific forms of control over IP. As mentioned above, compared with corporeal movables and immovables, IP has different characteristics of existence, utilisation and disposition. First, there is no physical control in IP possession. Since intellectual products are intangible and do not occupy a certain physical space, possession of them does not constitute a tangible, concrete occupation. Instead, it manifests as the apprehension and comprehension of certain knowledge or experience. Second, there is no physical loss in IP use. Intellectual products must be publicly disclosed or published. Use occurs when individuals gain access to the underlying knowledge. Furthermore, under certain spatiotemporal conditions, they may be used concurrently by multiple parties. Such use does not deplete the intellectual product as occurs with the use of corporeal things. If an unauthorised person exploits another's intellectual product, the civil remedy of restitution (*restitutio in integrum*) is inapplicable. Third, there is no de facto disposition in destroying intellectual products and no legal disposition of the physical delivery. An intellectual product cannot be extinguished through consumption of a physical embodiment. Its existence distinguishes between exclusive property and the public domain solely based on whether the statutory term of protection has expired. Concurrently, physical delivery is irrelevant to legal disposition. In other words, a non-right holder may purport to "dispose of" another's IP which they do not physically "possess" without recourse to legal channels.

8.1.3 "Thing-Likeness" of Res Incorporales *and Realisation of IPRs Values*

In Roman law, incorporeal things (*res incorporales*) were entities conceived by the human intellect. However, within a system of material property, this abstract entity was interpreted and explained as if it were a tangible entity: namely, an incorporeal thing is a proprietary right over a tangible thing; it is an abstract object related to corporeal things. Drahos (1996) terms this phenomenon "thing likeness"—denoting the similarity and connection between incorporeal things and tangible entities within the framework of materialised property.

Abstract objects, as intellectual products, maintain a close connection with tangible property. Drahos analyses this connection in two key aspects:

First, although an abstract object does not exist within the tangible world, it acquires tangibility through its expression. This constitutes a significant metaphysical characteristic of abstract objects. Drahos (1996) contends that when an individual asserts a proprietary right in IP, the object of that right must be concretely specified. This specification may be achieved through formal procedures (such as patent registration) or informally (as in the case of trade secrets). The consequence of such specification is that, through the form of its actual expression, an entity possessing external form is brought into being. That which can be expressed is the abstract object; that which is expressed is the corporeal thing.

Second, abstract objects acquire their proprietary significance through the control they exert over related tangible objects. The non-material abstract object must have an objective manifestation. This is not only a prerequisite for the object to secure legal protection but also the means by which the intellectual labourer realises the proprietary interests inherent in the abstract object. Drahos (1996) argues that artists, writers, and inventors must convert this incorporeal property into corporeal property in order to subsist. Once property rights in the incorporeal are recognised by law, the significance of regulating relations concerning materialised property within the corporeal world becomes paramount.

This significance manifests itself in the following ways: the abstract object serves as the source for acquiring an infinite variety and quantity of tangible objects, all of which may be enjoyed by the proprietor; furthermore, the abstract object provides the means for controlling the tangible objects which reproduce it – a control effected through the grant of exclusive rights.

8.1.4 *Transaction of* Res Incorporales *and Derivative Acquisition of IPRs*

Under Roman law, the conveyance of ownership (*dominium*) took several forms. Transfer under *ius civile* (civil law) occurred through *mancipatio* (formal conveyance) or *cessio in iure* (surrender before the magistrate). Transfer under *ius gentium* (law of nations) was primarily effected through *traditio* (delivery). *Traditio*, requiring the handing over of the object (*traditio rei*) and mutual consent (*consensus*), constituted the most common method for transferring private property in sales, but was limited to *res corporales* (corporeal things). Whether referring to the simple delivery of movables, or the *traditio brevi manu* (short-hand delivery), *traditio longa manu* (long-hand delivery), *traditio constitutum possessorium* (delivery by agreement), or *traditio symbolica* (symbolic delivery) of immovables, all concerned the delivery of corporeal objects.

The transfer of *res incorporales* (intangible things) could not utilise the method of delivering the subject matter. To address this, the Romans devised *cessio in iure* (surrender before the magistrate), a method of acquiring ownership by simulating a vindicatory action (*actio in rem*) to establish title. Also termed "conveyance before the court," this procedure was mainly applied to the transfer of intangible rights such as inheritance rights (*hereditas*) and servitudes (*servitutes*) (Zhou 1994). *Cessio in iure*, as a mode of acquiring ownership, was characterised by its publicity and procedural formality. By simulating litigation to confirm the transfer of title, it provided a formal, public process for the conveyance of *res incorporales*. This public nature enhanced the efficacy of the property transfer.

Within the realm of IP, the characteristics of "virtual possession" and the multiplicity of rights often give rise to situations of "multiple rights in a single thing" (*numerus clausus notwithstanding*) and "multiple owners of a single thing." The utilisation of IPRs exhibits greater diversity concerning subjects and rights compared to tangible property. Firstly, due to the non-material nature of intellectual assets, an IP owner's possession is necessarily "virtual rather than actual control." Exploitation requires mediation through material embodiments. A single intellectual asset can be embodied in multiple identical or different tangible forms, enabling multiple parties to use the same intellectual product simultaneously. Secondly, the rights comprising various IP types are inherently diverse. For instance, copyright encompasses the rights of reproduction, rental, performance, broadcasting, and adaptation; patent rights include the exclusive right to work the invention, the right to license, the right to assign, and the right to mark. Consequently, each distinct right within a bundle can be exploited by either the same or different parties.

In such circumstances, the derivative acquisition of IPRs cannot be affected through the "physical delivery" (*traditio corporalis*) of the subject matter or by simple agreement between the parties (*traditio*). Instead, it necessitates a specialised mode of transfer, namely the rules governing the delivery of *res incorporales*. The American scholar Versteeg (2000) contends that the Roman law concept underlying the transfer of *res incorporales* aligns with the principles governing the transfer of IP in modern law: namely, that the alienation of IP rights must be affected in writing and comply with other statutory formalities, and shall be subject to registration or examination by the competent authority. It is arguable that the Roman law's imposition of publicity and procedural formality as special regulations for the transfer of intangibles offers valuable insights for contemporary IP transactions.

8.1.5 Infringement of Res Incorporales *and Remedies for IPRs*

The Roman law provided for four types of *delictum privatum* (private wrongs), namely *furtum*[1] (theft), *rapina* (robbery), *damnum iniuria datum* (damage to property), and *iniuria* (injury to the person), all of which essentially constituted injuries to property and injuries to the person. Initially, injuries to property referred solely to injuries to tangible property, i.e., corporeal things. As Roman law developed, the rules concerning injury to tangible property were gradually extended to situations of intangible injury, namely injury to *res incorporales* (incorporeal things/rights). Versteeg (2000), quoted Roman law scholar J.A.C. Thomas's translation of the definition of "*furtum*" (theft) from Thomas's *The Institutes of Justinian*: "*Furtum* is fraudulent interference with a thing, whether with the thing itself or the use or possession of it." And, Versteeg (2000) pointed out that during the Roman republic, the concept of furtum expanded further to include "any conduct designed to deprive another of his property" (p. 550).

Intangible injury is characterised not by the unlawful physical possession of the subject matter, but rather by the unlawful "possession of a right" (*juris possessio*). When subjected to an intangible injury, the right-holder could seek remedies not only through possessory interdicts (primarily *prohibitory injunctions*) but could also bring actions for a penalty (*actio poenalis*), for damages (*actio damni*), or a mixed action (*actio mixta*). This characterisation of intangible injury and its associated

[1] In Roman law, furto was the fraudulent acquire of other's movables or the unlawful use or appropriation of an object by a person who possesses it with the consent of the owner. The Romans specifically classified furto as furtum rei, furtum usus, and furtum possessions. See Bonfante (1992).

remedies undoubtedly provided a beneficial doctrinal foundation for the establishment of IP remedies. Regarding civil remedies, the protection of ownership in civil law is achieved by granting the right-holder claims such as: a claim for declaration of ownership, a claim for the removal of impediments, a claim for the recovery of specific property (*rei vindicatio*), and a claim for compensation for loss. Among these claims, except for the claim for declaration of ownership which must be pursued by litigation before a court, the others may be asserted by the right-holder directly against the infringer or pursued by the property right-holder via litigation in court (Peng 1994).

For civil remedies concerning IP, the right-holder can naturally bring the aforementioned declaratory actions, proprietary actions (*actiones in rem*), and personal actions (*actiones in personam*) to protect their infringed rights. However, unlike general property ownership, the owner of IPRs cannot invoke the traditional civil remedies of restitution (*restitutio in integrum*) or recovery of specific property (*rei vindicatio*) within proprietary actions. The claim for restitution aims to protect property from unlawful damage by others; its general conditions for application are: the object of the right must be a corporeal thing; there must exist a factual situation of physical damage to, or diminution in value of, that property; and the damaged item must be capable of repair. Intellectual products, however, are intangible mental creations. Their unlawful use does not result in the "depletion" of the intellectual product itself, and once this right is infringed, it cannot be restored to its original state through tangible "repair".

The claim for recovery of specific property (*rei vindicatio*) is a method for protecting the possessory aspect of property rights. Its conditions for application are: the specific property claimed must be identifiable (*res certa*); and this specific property must be under the control of an unlawful possessor. Due to the distinct characteristics of intellectual products compared to corporeal things, an infringer need not have physical control to constitute "possession"; mere "cognition" or utilisation suffices. This "possession" of knowledge or experience cannot be reversed through "returning" the subject matter to restore the original state of the right. Consequently, the civil remedies of restitution (*restitutio in integrum*) and recovery of specific property (*rei vindicatio*) are inapplicable to IP.

It is evident, therefore, that the remedies adopted in Roman law for injury to *res incorporales*—namely possessory interdicts (i.e., injunctions), actions for a penalty (*actio poenalis*, i.e., punitive damages), and actions for damages (*actio damni*, i.e., compensatory damages)—share significant common ground with the remedies for IP in modern law.

In conclusion, the Roman law theory of *res incorporales* provided valuable intellectual material for the establishment of the modern IP system. However, it was not a ready-made theory directly applicable. Both the simplistic application of the "incorporeal thing" conclusion and the neglect of the theory's value are lacking in balance within scholarly research.

8.2 Economic Foundations of IPRs Regimes

The theory of knowledge value, established upon labour value theory, is a fundamental instrument for analysing the economic character of IPRs regimes. Like tangible products, knowledge-based products created by intellectual labour constitute commodities possessing both value and utility, which forms the economic rationale for recognising knowledge-based products as IP. Modern legal theorists have offered diverse perspectives regarding the economic foundations of IPRs regimes.

8.2.1 Locke's and Smith's "Labor Theory of Value"

John Locke (1632–1704), the founder of modern "labour value theory", on the basis of the theory of natural rights, expounded that labour is an important way to acquire private property rights and the rationality of such acquisition. In Locke's "labour-property" theory, there are two points worth noting: first, he clearly declared that labour belongs to the worker. This is the basis of Locke's theory of property and labour. "Every man has a 'property' in his own 'person,' and the 'labour' of his body and the 'work' of his hands are properly his. Then, he removes out of the state that Nature has provided and left in it, he has mixed his labour in it, and joint to it something that is his own, and thereby makes it his property" (Locke 1690). Second, he defined the property as a kind of "materialised" labour. This is the logical starting point of Locke's analysis of property. Starting from the falling fruit in primitive woods, Locke holds that "he that is nourished by the acorns he picked up under an oak, or the apples he gathered from the trees in the wood, has certainly appropriated them to himself…That labour put a distinction between them and common. That added something to them more than Nature, the common mother of all, had done, and so they became his private right" (Locke 1690). Locke's labour value theory provides a legitimacy basis for IP (labour belongs to the worker) and the basis of human right for it (the creation is an expansion of one's personality) (Yi 2000). Although Locke only dealt with property rights in a general sense in his writing, his theories have provided a useful source of ideas for future scholars on the relationship between intellectual labour and IPRs.

Adam Smith (1723–1790), as the creator of the capitalist "principle of market economy", continued Locke's labour-property theory. He believes that human abilities are useful. Such talents "make a part of his fortune", and "may be considered as a fixed capital in the same light as convenient labour and a machine or instrument of trade which facilitates and abridges the labour" (Smith 1972, p. 257). Smith's theoretical contribution lies in his definition of property as the result of labour, "the whole annual produce, if we except the spontaneous productions of the earth, being the effect of productive labour (Smith 1972, p. 305). This view is helpful in explaining the function of the IPRs regime, namely, the legislative objective of protecting the intellectual fruits (the condensation of intellectual labour) rather than intellectual labour itself. However, Smith's theory has obvious flaws. He divided labour into "productive labour" (such as the labour of workers and farmers) and "unproductive labour" (such as the labour of teachers, physicians, and men of letters). The former can "adds to the value of the subject upon which it is bestowed", while the latter cannot produce "fixed or vendible commodities" (Smith 1972, pp. 304–305). This view was later criticised by Jean-Baptiste Say. In a word, the classical labour value theory is based on the economic analysis of "things" and ownership of tangible property, but it helps us to understand the intrinsic significance of intellectual labour for IPRs.

8.2.2 Say's Theory of "Immaterial Products"

The French political economist of the nineteenth century Jean Baptiste Say (1767–1832) has explained, disseminated and criticised Adam Smith's theories. Say's theory of immaterial products is founded upon the premise that "labour creates utility" and "utility produces wealth." He (1963) asserted that "to create objects which have any kind of utility is to create wealth; for the utility of things is the ground-work of their value, and their value constitutes wealth" (p. 59). On this basis, Say (1963) criticised Smith's narrow conception of property. He contended that property created by human labour encompasses not only "those values which, after their creation, attach themselves to material objects and are preserved for a considerable time"—tangible products—but also those "values which perish almost instantly after their creation"—"immaterial products".

What Say (1963) termed "immaterial products" included the labour of domestic servants, physicians, lawyers, musicians, and actors. Such products are of the same nature as tangible products—both possess value or "utility". The error in Smith's theory lay in his definition of wealth as comprising only values which are fixed and realised in material objects, rather than extending the term to everything possessing exchangeable value. Consequently, all that is produced and immediately consumed does not, in his view, constitute wealth.

However, immaterial products are also the fruits of human labour, and they satisfy certain human needs to such an extent that society could not exist if these professions did not. Furthermore, to satisfy such needs, individuals must utilise tangible products of wealth to procure immaterial products. Producers of immaterial products may, through repeated acts of such exchange, amass considerable fortunes. The "immaterial products" identified by Say (1963) may, in the context of modern societal life, be broadly categorised into two distinct types: firstly, immaterial commercial services, and secondly, immaterial intellectual products. Though both are immaterial products, in the former instance, what is purchased is the labour itself (including intellectual labour); in the latter instance, it is the product of intellectual labour which possesses exchangeable value. Although Say's theory did not delineate the distinction between service activities and intellectual creations, both being immaterial products, and merely addressed "property of an immaterial nature" in a preliminary manner, his doctrine significantly enriched the concept of property created by labour. It revealed the inherent value residing in what was termed "unproductive labour", thereby laying the intellectual groundwork for constructing the theoretical framework of "intellectual labour"→"intellectual products"→"intellectual property".

8.2.3 Macleod's and Veblen's Theories of "Incorporeal Property"

In his book *Institutional Economics: Its Place in Political Economy*, the American economist John R. Commons evaluated the theory of "incorporeal property" of MacLeod and Veblen, two prominent early 20th-centuryscholars. H.D. Macleod distinguished between "corporeal property" and "incorporeal property" in his book *The Principles of Economics*. He posited the existence of a species of property or right entirely separate and distinct from any particular subject or tangible object possessed. Although the product itself might only come into existence at a future time, the property right in that future product exists *in praesenti* and may be bought and sold like any material property. Consequently, it constitutes property; in both Roman and English law, it is termed *res incorporales* (incorporeal property) because it is purely an abstract right, wholly detached from any physical entity (Commons 1962).

MacLeod's theory comprises two principal tenets: Firstly, there exists a connection between corporeal and incorporeal property. From the correspondences he cited, past corporeal property is manifested in future returns as various types of incorporeal property. For instance, immovables such as land and houses are corporeal property, whereas their permanent annual income yield therefrom is incorporeal property. Similarly, books and machines, as tangible embodiments of intellectual creations, are corporeal property, whereas copyright and patent rights derived from such intellectual creations are incorporeal property. Secondly, incorporeal property is essentially a kind of "ownership of debt." In his view, any ownership is a "commodity" that can be exchanged, and the ownership of physical things is corporeal property, while that of debts (institutional products) is incorporeal property. Incorporeal property is enjoyed not through physical possession, but through performance of an obligation to realise its exchange value (such as the payment of dividends, rents and copyright fees). MacLeod's framework of incorporeal property contains a wide range of subject matter, including both rights such as creditor's rights and intellectual rights, and subject matter such as bonds and shares. His economic perspectives bear substantial affinity with the concepts of "incorporeal chattels" and "chose in action" in the common law. It may be argued that Macleod's doctrine of incorporeal property provided an incisive economic analysis underpinning the Anglo-American legal system of incorporeal property.

T. Veblen was the first who built upon the modern concept of intangible property (Commons 1962, p. 310), which is different from MacLeod's "debt-based theory of incorporeal property." His principal propositions were as follows: First, incorporeal property is the capitalisation of "immaterial equipment." Corporeal property comprises "material means of production with specific uses", whereas incorporeal property consists of "immaterial wealth, immaterial facts, which are capitalised on the basis of the gain to be derived from their possession". "This immaterial equipment lies in the technological proficiency of the engineers and the workmen" (Commons 1962, pp. 324–325). Second, incorporeal property is the present value of future purchasing power. The buying and selling of this anticipated earning capacity constitutes the substance of transactions in vendible capital. The scale of transactions in incorporeal property or capital vastly exceeds that of material products and yields significantly greater profits (Commons 1962, pp. 329–330). Third, incorporeal property is a means for its owner to obtain differential benefits. For a corporation, earning capacity derives not from the cost of plant and material equipment owned, but from the goodwill of the enterprise. Goodwill in the modern sense encompasses "items of very diverse character", all being "immaterial wealth" or "incorporeal assets". These include established customary business relations, reputation for honesty, privileges, trade-marks, brands, patents, copyrights, legal or customary exclusive use of special processes guarded by law or by secrecy, exclusive control of particular sources of materials. All these give their possessor a differential advantage in the competition for business. They are wealth—differential wealth (Commons 1962, p. 329).

Veblen's theory of "incorporeal property" is unique in that he inherited the "labour theory of value" from Locke and attributes the production of immaterial wealth to "technological proficiency of engineers and workmen"—human capabilities that are "the products of, handed down by, the experience of generations" (Commons 1962, p. 320). Thus, he further demonstrated the intrinsic relationship of intellectual labour to incorporeal property and keenly observed the significance of incorporeal property in social wealth. As a source of "differential advantage" or "differential wealth", for an enterprise "the central and most substantial fact… is the concern's goodwill, not its plant" (Commons 1962, pp. 310, 324–325). However, Veblen's theory contained certain biases. He contended that goodwill, encompassing various forms of incorporeal property, constituted "assets which are serviceable to their owners, but without being of use to the community at large" (Commons 1962, p. 329). His rationale was that the value of incorporeal property lay in its "strategic position to 'hold up' the community and get something for nothing" (Commons 1962, pp. 320–329). Such analysis may perhaps be pertinent within certain contexts of a "pan-incorporeal property theory". However, with specific regard to intellectual property, its institutional functions of protecting inventors/creators and promoting social progress are manifest. On this point, the "public goods" theory of modern economics provides a more balanced and equitable explanation.

8.2.4 Cooter and Ulen's Theory of "Intellectual Products"

The conceptualisation of products in relation to non-material resources such as knowledge and information (encompassing mental creations including works, inventions, marks, etc.) derives from economists' theories concerning public goods and private goods. In their seminal work, *Law and Economics*, the American economists Robert Cooter and Thomas Ulen systematically expounded upon the public goods characteristics of knowledge:

Firstly, the individual consumption of an intellectual product does not diminish its availability to others; an unlimited number of persons may share a single disclosed information resource. Analogous to a public park, both those who contribute to its upkeep and those who do not may enjoy its use, necessitating that the provider furnish access to all. In other words, the disclosure of an intangible intellectual product in a tangible medium constitutes 'non-excludability' in the economic sense (Cooter and Ulen 1994, pp. 147, 152, 191).

Secondly, the production of intellectual products entails significant cost, yet their dissemination involves relatively minimal expense. Consequently, producers of intellectual products face considerable difficulty in recouping their costs through direct sales. Once a producer sells an intellectual product to one consumer, that consumer may become a potential competitor to the original producer, or other consumers may become 'free-riders' benefiting from the product—within the sphere of intellectual property law, this manifests as the unauthorised imitation or reproduction of another's intellectual product (Cooter and Ulen 1994, p. 152).

Thirdly, producers of intellectual products encounter substantial challenges in controlling the fruits of their intellectual innovation. If an innovator conceals their intellectual product, the innovation gains no recognition and thus loses its social utility. Conversely, if the innovator discloses the intellectual product publicly, they exert little de facto control over this intangible resource. Under these circumstances, the quantity of public goods (including intellectual products) supplied by the private market is likely to be sub-optimal, resulting in an informational 'under-provision' problem.

Fourthly, given consumers' demand for intellectual products, state intervention in the market becomes necessary. This entails adopting specific public policies to augment the production of information. Government intervention in the information market operates through two principal mechanisms: (1) the state directly providing intellectual products; or (2) the state subsidising privately produced intellectual products. A key instrument within the latter approach is the intellectual property system, which grants producers exclusive rights over their intellectual products. In this sense, copyright functions as 'a tax levied on readers for the purpose of awarding a bounty to the author' (Cooter and Ulen 1994, p. 191).

Cooter and Ulen's public goods theory elucidates, from the perspective of the interplay between public goods and private property rights, that the social function of the intellectual property system resides in resolving the 'free-rider' problem associated with public resources, thereby safeguarding producers' ability to recoup their investment in intellectual products. The economic rationale for establishing an intellectual property system lies in the principle that 'legal protection of property rights creates incentives for their efficient use' (Cooter and Ulen 1994, p. 191). Just as the farmer's ability to secure property rights in the crops provides the incentive to incur and rationally economise the costs of cultivation, so too does the creator's ability to obtain a monopoly right in intangible property furnish the incentive to invest in the production of knowledge and information.

8.2.5 Summary

The aforementioned theories constitute the main content of modern IPRs. The source, function and significance of IPRs have been discussed from different perspectives, and the concept of incorporeal property at different stages of social development have been demonstrated. These theories provide us with inspiring insights for our understanding and evaluation of the modern IPRs regime.

On the Originary Nature of IP

Locke, Smith and Marx all established their own "labour theory of value", which provide the essential theoretical basis for justifying IPRs. Bourgeois thinkers' labour theory of property rights contains two basic principles of modern civil society, namely, the principle of private property rights and the principle of liberalism. Conversely, the labour value theory of Marxist writers laid the basis for the theory of surplus value. Though with different social significance, their theories all correctly affirms the crucial significance that labour creates value and that the products of labour belong to the labourer. For a prolonged period, our understanding of the labour theory of value has been notably one-sided: "firstly, it was confined to direct productive labour, or even limited to simple labour—manual labour; secondly, it was confined to the value of tangible commodities." (Li 1999, p. 39). The modern "labour theory of value," particularly Marx's formulation, though derived from the analysis of productive labour creating tangible commodities, retains broad applicability in the knowledge economy era. It may be asserted that the "theory of knowledge value" which we advocate today constitutes a new development of the modern labour theory of value. The "theory of knowledge value" demonstrates that: social labour encompasses both manual and intellectual labour; the production of commodities includes not only tangible goods from material production but also intangible goods (such as services, knowledge, technology, value, etc.) from non-material production; living labour creates not only the value of materialised commodities but also the value of intellectual products. Based on the foregoing theories, it is readily apparent that intellectual products are the fruits of intellectual labour, and the intellectual labourer should consequently enjoy property rights over their intellectual product.

Recognising the originary nature of intellectual property from an economic perspective is of paramount importance. Within traditional intellectual property theory, the conclusion that "intellectual property rights must be granted by the state" was drawn logically from the premise that the intangible nature of intellectual products necessitates their special protection by state law. Undoubtedly, the original acquisition of intellectual property rights cannot be established or obtained solely by virtue of the legal fact of creative activity; it requires recognition or authorisation by a state authority. However, this circumstance does not negate the originary significance of intellectual labour for intellectual property. As Patterson and Lindberg (1991) have explained, intellectual creation is the "source" of rights, while law is the "origin" of their acquisition.

On the Proprietary Character of Intellectual Products

Modern economic theory defines property as the result of labour; consequently, the product of intellectual labour—the intellectual product—is inherently property. The primary economic imperatives for intellectual products attaining the status of intellectual property are twofold:

(1) **Utility of intellectual products**: Knowledge and information are among the most useful resources in society and an important part of social wealth. Intellectual products can work to meet the needs of people's spiritual lives and generate social benefits, and can also be transformed into tangible material products in the field of production to satisfy economic needs and yield economic benefits. Under the conditions of a commodity economy, intellectual products, like material products, possess both utility and value, and are the result of human exertion.

(2) **Scarcity of intellectual products**: Knowledge and information are not naturally occurring and inexhaustible resources. Their scarcity manifests firstly in the protracted, complex, and high-cost nature of intellectual production. The entire process demands substantial investment by society and individuals alike, requiring prolonged exploratory, creative, and continuous labour to achieve fruition. Secondly, it manifests in the limited number and high value of intellectual product creators. As the living carriers of knowledge, creative individuals engage in intellectual production, employing accumulated knowledge elements from predecessors as their instruments of labour and abstract intellectual products as their objects of labour. The production process of intellectual products has special requirements regarding the intelligence of producers: firstly, the producer must possess an intellect superior to the average, capable of undertaking highly demanding intellectual labour; secondly, they must possess considerable knowledge reserves, acquired through documented sources and cognitive retention, constituting the fundamental prerequisites for such high-level intellectual input. Relative to societal demand, there often exists a chronic undersupply of such individuals (Zhang, 1992).[2] Given the utility and scarcity of

[2] For more information about the knowledge value theory, see Zhang Hesheng (1992).

knowledge, technology, and information, it is incumbent upon society to establish an appropriate IPRs regime.

On the Value Objectives of IP

The core legislative principle of the IPRs regime is to protect the rights and interests of creators of intellectual products. Intellectual labourers are the very source from which intellectual products spring. Disregard for intellectual creation and failure to safeguard the legitimate rights and interests of intellectual labourers stifles their creative fervour, rendering scientific, technological, and cultural endeavours unsustainable. Concurrently, the safeguarding of the public interest constitutes a fundamental motivation for the relevant legislation. Intellectual property is intrinsically linked to the expression and dissemination of ideas, information, and knowledge. While safeguarding the rights and interests of creators, the imperative to promote the widespread dissemination of knowledge and advance societal civilisation—a public welfare objective—must also be considered. As articulated by a US copyright law expert in assessing American copyright law, copyright law encompasses social, political, economic, educational, and artistic dimensions. It cannot be solely preoccupied with protecting authors' rights but must also take into account the interests of the broader user community (Patterson and Lindberg 1991). In summary, the value objectives of the intellectual property system reside in the dichotomous legislative principles of protecting private intellectual property and promoting societal progress through knowledge.

Within the sphere of intellectual property, society delineates and allocates rights through the demarcation of "exclusive zones" and "free zones" (Ploman and Hamilton 1980). "Exclusive zones" encompass a vast portion of the resource of rights, with intellectual labourers being the "exclusive holders" within this domain. The establishment of this zone facilitates the recoupment of intellectual investment costs and sustains the creative passion of intellectual labourers, thereby being efficient. "Free zones" constitute a smaller proportion of the resource of rights; users are the "free agents" within this ambit, permitted under the law to utilise others' intellectual products without charge, freely, or under specified conditions. The construction of this zone does not cause detriment to the interests of intellectual creators but serves to reduce transaction costs, prevent price monopolies, and foster the free flow of information and cultural dissemination, thus also being efficient (Coase 1960).

8.3 Philosophical Foundations of IPRs Regimes

In the field of legal philosophy, the transition from intellectual assets to IP is a philosophical issue with profound theoretical implications. The subject matter of philosophical research on IPRs include the basis on which knowledge becomes the object of property rights, the state of possession and the form of rights of intellectual assets, and the social functions and goals of the IPRs regime—all fall squarely within the purview of theoretical research in the philosophy of IP law.. In this domain, modern thinkers have each advanced their own theories of property rights, thereby constructing corresponding philosophical foundations for the IPRs regime.

8.3.1 Rousseau's Theory of the "General Will"

Jean-Jacques Rousseau (1712–1778) was an eminent French Enlightenment thinker of the eighteenth century. *The Social Contract*, an important document in the history of global political thought, provided a theoretical framework for the French bourgeois democratic revolution in the political sphere and laid the philosophical foundation for the emerging capitalist system of property rights in the field of private law. Rousseau's conception of property is different from the traditional doctrine of "natural rights to property." The conventional theory of property rights, as espoused by Locke, can be distilled into three elements: "pre-emption, demand, and labour", that is: first, the land must not yet be inhabited; second, a man must occupy only the amount he needs for his subsistence; and in the third place, possession must be taken, not by an empty ceremony, but by labour and cultivation, the only sign of proprietorship that should be respected by others, in default of a legal title (Rousseau 1980, p. 32). Rousseau criticised Locke's theory; in his view, the three elements only indicated the fact of possession, but not the establishment of property rights. Building upon this critique, he proposed a new view of property grounded in social contract and general will. According to the principles of natural law, individuals voluntarily unite on the basis of complete equality, and through a social contract to establish a state and enact laws to safeguard their inherent rights, including liberty, life and property. Rousseau elaborated on the property rights system under the social contract:

> What man loses by the social contract is his natural liberty and an unlimited right to everything he tries to get and succeeds in getting; what he gains is civil liberty and the proprietorship of all he possesses. (Rousseau 1980, p. 30)

Here, Rousseau sharply distinguished between liberty and rights in the state of nature and that under the social contract. In his framework, the former is mere an existence of factual conditions, whereas the latter represented legally protected interests. In essence, mere de facto control or dominion over objects in the state of nature carried no notion of "right." The core of Rousseau's property theory lies in his doctrine of the "general will." He first made a distinction between the "general will" (*volonté générale*) and the "will of all" (*volonté de tous*):

> There is often a great deal of difference between the will of all and the general will; the latter considers only the common interest, while the former takes private interest into account, and is no more than a sum of particular wills; but take away from these same wills the pluses and minuses that cancel one another, and the general remains as the sum of the differences. (Rousseau 1980, p. 39)

In his view, the general will reflect the opinion of the majority, as individuals, acting in their own interest, would always have to consider the interests of the collective. Regarding the relationship between the general will and law, Rousseau posited:

> Law is enacted by the sovereign, and since sovereignty belongs to the people, law is an expression of the general will – an act of the sovereign and registers of our own wills. (Rousseau 1980, p. 51)

In short, the will of the sovereign (the people) embodied in law is the general will. Rousseau thus attributes the legitimacy of property rights to the general will:

> We must clearly distinguish between natural liberty, which is bounded only by the strength of the individual, from civil liberty, which is limited by the general will; and between possession, which is merely the effect of force or the right of the first occupier, and property, which can be founded only on lawful title. (Rousseau 1980, p. 30)

Evidently, mere de facto possession in the state of nature constituted only "enjoyment" (jouissance), justified by individual force or first occupation. It is only after the arrival of civil society that the fact of possession becomes a formal property right (ownership). This is as a result of an act of the law reflecting the general will. Thus, Rousseau had progressed from former explanations of the basis on which property rights are established.

In addition, Rousseau's theoretical contribution also lies in his conception of justice in property rights. This appears mainly in three aspects:

The Reciprocity of Property Rights and Obligations

Rousseau asserted that justice and property arose simultaneously. The unity of justice and property contributes to a norm, namely, a custom of respecting others' property rights within society. Once ownership is established, it not only secures property as a genuine right but also imposed restrictions on individuals.

> Every individual has a natural right to acquire everything he needs. Having his share, he ought to keep to it, and can have no further right against the community. In this right we are respecting not so much what belongs to another as what does not belong to ourselves. (Rousseau 1980, pp. 31–32)

In Rousseau's philosophy, a social order in which property rights are respected and protected is in line with the laws of justice, which needs to be observed by all: "Conventions and laws are therefore needed to join rights to duties and refer justice to its object" (Rousseau 1980, p. 49).

Equality of Property Rights

In Rousseau's theory of property, the term "equality" in no way means absolute parity in wealth but rather:

> Not the abolition of private property (which is impossible) but its confinement within the narrowest possible limits, subject to regulation, restraint, and subordination to the public good. (Rousseau 1980, pp. 60–70)

He further argued that the property right system, founded on the social contract, was:

> An equitable convention, because it is common to all…; the social contract sets up among the citizens an equality of such a kind, that they all bind themselves to observe the same conditions and should therefore all enjoy the same rights. Thus, from the very nature of the contract, every act of Sovereignty, i.e., every authentic act of the general will, binds or favours all the citizens equally. (Rousseau 1980, p. 44)

Here, equality in property rights pertains to equal status among proprietors and equal protection of property rights under the law.

The Purposes of the Property Right System

Rousseau emphasised the "common good" (*le bien commun*) and "public happiness" ((le bonheur public) in his theory of "general will." The legitimacy of property rights derived from the general will, which emerged not merely from voting but from "the common interest uniting them…or in this system, each necessarily submits to the conditions he imposes on others."

He concluded:

> "The general will must both come from all and apply to all; and that it loses its natural rectitude when it is directed to some particular and determinate object" (Rousseau 1980, p. 43). In fact, the first article of law generated from the social contract is the only truly fundamental one, i.e. each should base on the greatest happiness of the all in any conditions." (Rousseau 1980, pp. 42–43)

In summary, though Rousseau's exposition of property rights in The Social Contract primarily employed land as an example, his ideas extend to the IPRs regime. His social contract theory of property rights profoundly influenced modern "patent contract" theories, where Western scholars trace the quid pro quo of disclosure and exclusivity to Rousseau's framework. His view of general will elucidates the relationship between general will, law and property, offering a more coherent justification for property right systems than former views, and this helps us clarify the distinction between natural possession of knowledge and legal IPRs. Furthermore, his principles of justice in property—encompassing the balance of rights and obligations, equality, and the primacy of the public good—provide philosophical grounding for modern IP doctrines, including protection and limitations, dissemination and utilisation of knowledge, and the public interest principle underpinning IP systems.

8.3.2 Kant's Theory of "Free Will"

Immanual Kant, the renowned 18th-century German philosopher and a leading exponent of liberal legal thought, grounded his inquiry in human nature to explore the concepts of free will and innate rights. On this foundation, he expounded upon the volitional content of rights and the basis for their validity. In his work *The Metaphysics of Morals* (*Metaphysische Anfangsgründe der Rechtslehre*), Kant articulated his "free will" theory of property:

The Concept of Ownership Vis-À-Vis Factual Possession

Kant (1991) distinguished between two modes of possession: empirical possession (possession apprehended by the senses) and intelligible possession (possession apprehended by the intellect). The former may be understood as physical possession of an object; the latter signifies a purely juridical possession of the same object. In his view, mere sensory possession is insufficient to constitute something as "*mine*" in the sense of ownership. Ownership arises only when possession is not affected by physical grasp or personal power, but rather when an object is conceived in thought as "*mine*", and where the factual separation of person and object does not alter this relationship.

The Purpose of Ownership and Free Will

Kant (1991) posited that to achieve ownership, a subject must take possession of an object externally—that is, treat it as their own. This external object, chosen by the will of the owner, must, objectively speaking, be *masterless* (*res nullius*).

> By a unilateral act of my will... I declare that I possess something externally by incorporating it into my possessions... and I will that this possession of mine shall also be considered as rightful. (pp. 55–57)

Thus, for an object to become "mine" by right, the subject must subjectively will its exclusive appropriation; concurrently, for the object to be secured as "my" property against infringement by others, the subject must be its true possessor or owner.

The Content of Ownership and the Collective Will

Kant (1991) proposed the principle of "external acquisition" (acquisition of ownership):

> "Anything is 'mine' by right if I am so connected with it that any use of it by another without my consent would constitute an injury to me... This connection is one of 'physical

> possession' conjoined with the 'will' to have it as mine... based on the idea of a 'collective will' (*collectiv-allgemeiner Wille*) a priori.

Consequently, Kant (1991) concluded that ownership embodies a dual volitional content—possession by individual will and possession by collective will. When an individual can oppose another's possession or control of an object without physically holding it, this is attributable to the operation of the collective will. The true essence of ownership lies not in the owner's free disposition of the thing, but in the inviolability accompanying such disposition. The collective will represents the consensus or shared recognition among all members of society regarding the owner's possession and control. As Kant (1991) states, any acquisition is an act of the united will (*vereinigte Willen*) of all by which everyone is obliged to respect my act and to behave in conformity with my will.

The Validity of Ownership and the Universal Law Reflecting the Collective Will

Kant (1991) analysed two volitional components inherent in the owner: Firstly, the declaration through word or deed that an external thing is "mine", imposing on others the duty to refrain from using that specific object over which the owner has exercised their will. Secondly, the implicit promise not to infringe upon the external possessions rightfully belonging to others. This mutual guarantee against infringement derives from the universal law (*allgemeines Gesetz*) which embodies the collective will.

> Hence, only the collective, universal, and powerful will (*kollektiv-allgemeine und machthabende Wille*)... which provides security for all, can give this guarantee... When men live under such universal, public, and lawful conditions, backed by power, they are said to be in a *civil state* (*bürgerlicher Zustand*). (p. 68)

It is evident, therefore, that ownership is only possible within a legal order or civil society. Although Kant's "free will" theory of property primarily addressed corporeal objects (*res corporales*) and ownership (*dominium*), his doctrine concerning free will and property rights provides a robust philosophical foundation for establishing modern IP and its associated rights regime. Accordingly, we may reasonably conclude:

Firstly, given the incorporeal nature of intellectual products (*geistige Erzeugnisse*), the object of IPRs cannot be possessed empirically. This, however, does not preclude the subject's "purely juridical possession" of this object.

Secondly, an intellectual product is an "external object" chosen by the creator's will. The creator is the possessor or owner of this object, entitled to treat it as "mine" free from interference by others.

Thirdly, an intellectual product becomes IP not merely by the creator's free disposition, but by virtue of the "collective will"—the recognition and consensus of all members of society regarding this proprietary status.

Last but not least, the recognition of intellectual products as objects of property rights is a consequence of economic development and social progress. Precisely because intellectual products readily elude the creator's physical control, IPRs depend upon special protection afforded by state law.

8.3.3 Hegel's Theory of "of Property and Personality"

Friedrich Hegel, succeeding Kant, stands as another great philosopher and a representative figure of idealist jurisprudence. In his work *Elements of the Philosophy of Right*, Hegel constructed his theory of private law upon the fundamental categories of "Will-Personality-Property", presented within a highly complex philosophical language. Hegel posited that the essence of law is freedom of the will and rights, while the immediate determinate existence (Dasein) of this freedom and the immediate content of rights is property in the natural world.

According to Hegel, the will constituting law is initially merely abstract or universal will. When this will develops into a real will, "the will becomes a single will – the person". (Hegel 1961). Here, he refers to individual concrete persons. The relationship between persons is, in essence, a relationship between wills. Hegel further asserted that the essence of a person is personality (*Persönlichkeit*), and personality is the freedom of the will. He emphasised the paramount importance of this freedom, stating that "a person can forfeit his life, but not his freedom" (Hegel 1982); Simultaneously, he noted its limitations, explaining that the significance of personality lies in the fact that each individual must be subject to legal stipulations and restrictions. (Hegel 1961). Building upon this "Will-Personality" theoretical foundation, Hegel then introduced property, characterised by its instrumentalist nature, as the basic form through which free will achieves its determinate existence and abstract personality gains objectivity.

The doctrine of property constitutes the essence of Hegel's view on ownership. Concerning the concept of ownership, he (Hegel 1961) provided two key explanations: First, according to Hegel's canonical formulation, "a person's putting his will into a thing – that is just the concept of property (ownership)"". From this theory, the person is free will, and free will is infinite and absolute in relation to all things (objects). Consequently, all things can become the property of a person. Every individual has the right to transform his will into a thing, or to transform a thing into his will. Following Hegel's reasoning, we can posit that intellectual products such as skills, knowledge, art, and inventions, under the dominion of the creator's free will, can be sublated (aufgehoben) to become private property. Through the action of free will, not only tangible objects but also non-material intellectual products can be transformed into something belonging to oneself. This provides the philosophical basis for a system of "intellectual property" (literally: 'property in the spiritual'). Second, ownership is the development of a single personality. In justifying ownership, Hegel stated that the rationale of property is to be found not in the satisfaction of needs but in the supersession of the pure subjectivity of personality. It is only through ownership that a person exists as Reason. In Hegel's philosophical world, the task of the will is to attain absolute freedom. The will in its initial stage is self-consciousness as personality, seeking to place itself within the external world—meaning personality requires certain concrete forms of existence in the world. Therefore, the establishment of ownership is primarily not about satisfying individual needs and desires, but is essential to the existence and development of personality. In a certain sense, personality is the personality of property, or conversely, concrete property is abstract personality; a person's personality and rationality find embodiment only in property. Based on this theory, we can further argue that intellectual products are creations of human intellectual labour, intrinsically linked to the personality of a specific subject. "IP" allows the creator's personality to exist and develop through the realisation of the IP.

It is evident that Hegel's philosophy contains an explanation for the justification of IP. Furthermore, proceeding from his "property-personality" theory, Hegel elaborated within the framework of ownership on matters concerning the transfer and protection of IP.

Conditions for the Transfer of IP

While the person itself and a person's spirit (Geist) are inalienable, certain things closely connected to them can be alienated. Hegel set conditions for such transfer, limiting it to the partial alienation of mental faculties and their products. He (Hegel 1961) stressed that a person can alienate to another individual [*entäußern*] his particular physical and mental skills and specific capabilities of action for a restricted period of time, or he can alienate the use of them for a specific period or otherwise delimited, since the use of them is restricted in time externally. In such cases, only a delimited portion of the mental capacity is alienated, one which maintains an external relationship to the individual's totality and universality, thus not constituting an alienation of the person's substantiality—their entire personality and rationality. While Hegel's immediate intention here was to analyse the distinction between a slave and a wage labourer, his emphasis on the subject retaining independent personality (their universality) holds positive significance in the context of property embodying personality being freely alienable. By extension, this theory is also applicable to the transfer of IP. IP law permits the full transfer of rights in a specific intellectual product but generally does not advocate for the transfer of all rights to all of a creator's intellectual products (including future creations). Its legislative provisions aim not only to protect the creator's proprietary interests but also to safeguard their independent personality.

The Object of the Transfer of IP

Property, being a product of the will, can be relinquished or transferred through an act of will, but the thing must be capable of externalisation (*Veräußerungsfähigkeit*). Hegel (1961) observed that the distinctive character of spiritual production may, in accordance with its mode of expression, assume immediately the form of something external (*Äußerlichkeit*). Here, Hegel's philosophy acknowledges the fundamental characteristics of intellectual products: their non-material nature and reproducibility, touching upon the distinction between the intellectual product itself and its material embodiment (vehicle). Terms like "external determinate existence" and "externality of a thing" used by Hegel in various contexts are essentially philosophical expressions for the reproducibility of intellectual products and their material vehicles. Hegel (1961) categorised intellectual products as follows:

- **Works of Art**: Where external material is shaped into a form depicting thought. It is so thoroughly the expression of the author's own individuality that even a copy is a product of the copier's own spirit and technical skill.
- **Literary Works** (Subject of Copyright): In terms of becoming an external thing, like inventions of technical devices, they belong to a mechanical kind of thing (e.g., writing, printing, binding). Here, a series of abstract symbols (like words) are used to express thought, not a concrete configuration.
- **Inventions of Technical Devices**: Where a mechanical contrivance expresses an inventive technical idea. The method and manner of producing these mechanical things belong to ordinary craft (Handwerk).
- **Intellectual Products at Various Stages between Art and Craft**: Such as industrial designs.

Rights of the Transferee of IP

The rights enjoyed by the transferee vary depending on the nature of the specific intellectual product and, crucially, the intention of the transferor. Hegel (1961) distinguished two scenarios:

- The transferee becomes the new owner controlling the intellectual product, able to make the thoughts propagated in the book or the invention contained in the machine his own and simultaneously acquires the universal ways and means so expressed, of producing such things himself and thus of making any number of them.

The creator of the intellectual product may reserve to himself the right of producing such things in the universal mode as method, etc. In this case, the transferee is only the complete and free owner of that single, specific copy. They have the right to use the acquired item as a sample and fully exploit its value, but cannot infringe the specific rights reserved by the original owner under the law.

Protection of IP

Hegel (1961) holds that the purely negative, but primary, method of furthering learning and science is to secure their workers against theft and to provide for the protection of their property. Hegel then discussed the distinction between legitimate reproduction/reiteration and plagiarism concerning copyrighted works. He noted that intellectual products are produced for apprehension by others and appropriated by them. Typically, the dissemination of science and knowledge involves largely reiterating existing ideas. The question arises: To what extent does the form of this reiteration become a transferable commodity, i.e., the reiterator's property? Or to what extent can it be deemed plagiarism? Hegel acknowledged the difficulty of precise rules. However, he strongly criticised making merely superficial alterations or insignificant modifications to another's creation, viewing it as merely stamping more or less of one's own personality on an alien property.

8.3.4 Drahos' Theory of "Abstract Objects"

Peter Drahos' *A Philosophy of Intellectual Property* is a significant work in contemporary IP scholarship. Employing the tools of analytical philosophy and tracing the emergence, development, and associated theories of property regimes, the author focuses on the characteristics of IP as "abstract objects" and the general circumstances under which IPRs are established over such objects. Consequently, he proposes a distinctive theory of IP that diverges from traditional property perspectives, offering a new philosophical framework for understanding the principles and rules of IP law from an external disciplinary viewpoint. Drahos' theory of "abstract objects" primarily comprises the following elements:

"Abstract Objects" and the Roman Law Concept of "Res Incorporales" (Incorporeal Things)

"Abstract object" is a fundamental category frequently employed by Drahos in his philosophical inquiry into IP. It is dependent on human mental life for its existence, an object brought into being by human thought superimposed upon the physical world (Drahos 1996).

It lacks physical form and exists abstractly. From a metaphysical perspective, an abstract object is a postulated category of existence. Yet, social reality necessitates the recognition of abstract objects; when property extends to such objects, interpersonal interest relationships arise based upon them.

In the case of IP, the object under discussion is an abstract object. As we know, abstract objects do not exist, or we might declare them not to exist. Abstract objects in IP take the form of a legal fiction.

According to Drahos (1996), the distinction between corporeal and incorporeal property does not stem from the nature of the rights per se, but rather from the differing nature of the objects to which those rights attach. IP is classified as a form of incorporeal property right.

The law postulates that rights exist in certain abstract objects. The molecular formula and chemical structure of penicillin are examples of abstract objects; many people require, use, and depend upon such objects. A new form of property right thus emerges based on abstract objects. This is IP, distinct from traditional property ownership (Drahos 1996). Drahos (1996) traces the concept of abstract objects back to the Roman law notion of *res incorporales* (incorporeal things), also termed "intangible objects." Within classical philosophy, the conceptual category of incorporeal things can be traced to the Stoic school. While both are fictions of the human mind, *res incorporales* in Roman law specifically referred to property rights (other than ownership) as institutional products, whereas Drahos' abstract objects are mental conceptions constituting intellectual products—the very material mediating IP relationships.

Notwithstanding the above distinction, the theoretical contribution of Roman jurists holds historical significance; it can be said that the theory of incorporeal things provided the crucial conceptual tools for the modern IP regime.

Relations Between "Abstract Objects" and "Corporeal Things" (Tangible Property)

In the Roman law, *res incorporales* were originally subjectively conceived fictions. However, within a materialised property system, these abstract entities were also interpreted and explained as if they were real entities—that is, incorporeal things were property rights over tangible things; incorporeal things were abstract objects related to corporeal things. Drahos (1996) terms this phenomenon "thing likeness," signifying the similarity and connection between incorporeal things and physical entities within a materialised property framework. Abstract objects, as intellectual products, also bear a close relationship to tangible property. He (1996) offers two key analyses:

First, abstract objects do not exist within the tangible world, but acquire tangibility through expression. This is an important metaphysical characteristic of abstract objects. Drahos (1996) states that when a person asserts an IPR, the object of the right must be concretely specified. This specification may occur through formal procedures (e.g., patent registration) or informally (e.g., trade secrets). The result of such specification is that, through an actual form of expression, an entity with an external form is created. An object that can be expressed is an abstract object; the object of actual expression is a corporeal thing.

Second, abstract objects acquire their property significance through the control of related corporeal things. Non-material abstract objects must have an objective manifestation; this is not only a condition for the object to obtain legal protection but also the means by which the intellectual labourer realises the property interest inherent in the abstract object. Drahos (1996) contends that artists, writers, and inventors must convert this incorporeal property into corporeal property to survive. Once property rights in incorporeal objects are recognised by law, the significance of regulating relationships concerning materialised property within the world of corporeal things becomes even more important. The significance manifests thus: abstract objects are the source for acquiring an infinite variety and quantity of corporeal objects, all of which can be enjoyed by the property owner; abstract objects are the means of controlling the tangible manifestations of themselves, and the grant of exclusive rights enables this control.

Abstract Object and IPRs Regime

IPR is an exclusive form of property right generated based on abstract objects. Through an analysis of early modern English law, Drahos (1996) expounds the justificatory grounds for the existence of the IP system. He (ibid.) writes:

> Individuals must labour to survive. Inventors and authors, like others, are entitled to remuneration. But this remuneration can only be a temporary privilege; interests extending beyond this scope constitute an invasion of the labour of others and violate the fundamental law of the nation. In other words, an inventor or author can only expect a temporary advantage over others, the nature of which is a privilege. (pp. 32–33)

Drahos (1996) insists that this privilege must not be exceeded, as it may lead to the following consequences:

(1) **Endangering individual liberty**

Allowing private individuals to establish exclusive rights over abstract objects can create a "person-dependent relationship" within a society. Drahos analyses that as the exclusive power of individuals grows, it impacts the negative liberty of others—the right to be free from interference becomes imperilled. In short, when property extends to abstract objects, conflicts of interest may arise. He illustrates: a farmer requires seeds to plant rice; if those seeds embody an abstract object protected by a patent or plant variety right, the farmer must seek the consent of the owner of that abstract object before using them. This overlays a personal dependency relationship upon the material dependency. Consequently, Drahos concludes that when certain resources essential to the public are controlled by right holders as abstract objects, a formal, legal person-dependent relationship is added to the resource dependency relationship. Drahos therefore expresses concern about the legal mechanisms established between abstract objects and property rights. If civil society pursues exclusive rights without restraint, the person-dependent relationships implicit in the utilisation of abstract objects create a danger that this property rights system will restrict, rather than promote, freedom within the social community. In this sense, Drahos concludes that IP is a charter of liberty which is inimical to liberty.

(2) **Threatening distributive justice**

The exclusivity of IP not only enables owners of abstract objects to control numerous tangible reproductions of the same abstract object but also incentivises them to control more abstract objects. Both scenarios may enable a minority to utilise the property rights mechanism over abstract objects to gain control over resources upon which society is generally dependent. Drahos argues that, from the perspective of distributive justice, the scope of exclusive rights should be constrained. The disequilibrium in social distribution caused by rights expansion is an empirical conclusion Drahos draws based on a socio-economic analysis of the modern era. In his view, possessing certain abstract objects in some technological fields requires high-level scientific capabilities and large-scale capital investment. When such abstract objects constitute vital resources upon which society is generally dependent, their owners effectively wield immense "threat power." This "threat power," founded on the exclusivity of abstract objects, is a form of power backed by law. When society creates property rights over abstract objects, it potentially faces a scenario where vast amounts of "threat power" become concentrated in the hands of a few. Drahos' fundamental position is that exclusive rights over abstract objects enhance the factional tendencies and dangerous potential of individual power; therefore, there are grounds for strictly limiting the scope of such rights, or even abolishing some of them.

In summary, Drahos' philosophical theory of "abstract objects" provides novel perspectives for understanding the fundamental attributes of IP objects, analysing the relationship between incorporeal and corporeal property, and exploring the social function of the IP system. As he himself states, the book contains "no effort to provide a justification for private property"; instead, it emphasises the "threat power" IP may generate and the "danger" of creating distributive disequilibrium. These concerns, of course, do not constitute grounds for denying the existence of the IP system, and Drahos does not intend this. However, through the above analysis, it is necessary to reflect upon the current state of IPRs protection and, consequently, to affirm the balance of interests and public interest objectives inherent in IP law. This is undoubtedly the valuable insight offered by Drahos' philosophical thought.

8.3.5 Summary

Modern thinkers constructed the IPRs regime within a metaphysical philosophy framework. Metaphysics, as a tool for philosophical analysis, concerns itself with the nature and origins of things beyond experience and perception. Unlike the empirical "cost–benefit" studies of economists, philosophers employ abstract reasoning to address the general questions concerning the IP system.

The Non-Material Nature of IP

The legal recognition of IP signifies a transformation in the concept of property from the concrete to the abstract. Property is no longer confined to tangible objects but extends to numerous assets lacking physical form, representing the abstraction and dematerialisation of property. The dematerialisation of property received considerable attention as early as Locke's era. In his *Two Treatise of Government*, Locke employed the term "property" in several senses: property, in a narrow sense, denoted material possessions owned by an individual, expressed using terms like "possessions," "estates," "fortunes," and "goods"; broadly, termed "property," it encompassed not only material goods but also a person's body, mind, life, and liberty, and even included their labour and conduct. It represented the totality of an individual's possessions, comprising both physical and mental aspects, existing in corporeal and incorporeal forms (Mei 1994). For the German philosophers Kant and Hegel, property rights were linked to will and personality; the possession of things was merely the externalisation of free will. This view comes remarkably close to the understanding of IP as abstract property. Kant's brief discussions on IP primarily concerned copyright works. He emphasised that a work is an expression of the author's thought and personality; protecting IPRs thus meant protecting the author's personality rights (Qu 2002). To some extent, a work is not merely a commodity, but an extension of the person—the author; it is a reflection of personality (Liu and Liu 1987). Here, Kant distinguished intellectual achievements embodying the author's personality from traditional tangible property. Hegel noted the distinction between material carriers and intellectual products, designating the latter as "things reduced to an external form through the mediation of mind," including mental aptitudes, scientific knowledge, art, and inventions (Hegel 1961). Such mental products require an external "existence" to be recognised by others and become objects of transaction. Consequently, they are not immediately given but become immediate only when the internal is reduced to immediacy and externality through the mediation of mind. Admittedly, the contemporary scholar Drahos' theoretical formulation of "abstract objects" carries a more distinctly modern legal character. An abstract object is a postulated category of existence, or a subjectively conceived entity. This fundamental category originates from the Roman "*res incorporales*", but Drahos imbues it with a new meaning distinct from institutional products: abstract objects are intellectual products, the material mediating IP relationships. Philosophers observed the changing forms of property and extended its scope to encompass all utilisable material and immaterial objects. However, it should be noted that rendering all interests, opportunities, qualifications, etc., as property or commodities, or equating social rights and personal rights with property rights, is inapposite, as an overly broad conception of property risks undermining the scientific foundation of non-material property. In sum, IP can be understood as non-material property, but the scope of non-material property must be rigorously defined.

The Rationale for IPRs

The establishment of the IP system was, from a socio-historical impetus, the result of scientific, technological, and commodity economic development; from an institutional construction perspective, it was the product of legal revolution and innovation. Thinkers have offered diverse explanations for the justification of the IP system. Within economic discourse, figures from Locke and Smith to Marx developed their own "labour theories of value." Although their works primarily addressed material production and tangible goods, this theory possesses particular theoretical appeal when arguing for the origins and justification of IP. Within legal philosophy, the "social contract" theory and the "property-personality" theory offer alternative perspectives on the justification of IP. Rousseau traced the basis of property rights to the general will embodying the sovereign's (the people's) will. Law is the record of the social general will; justice is the law of property rights. Rousseau's "social contract" theory provides one justification for the IP system: it realises a contractual exchange between the monopoly of rights and the disclosure of knowledge. According to some Western scholars, the social conditions giving rise to the IP system are: the owners of intellectual products disclose their works and inventions, enabling the public to access the specialised knowledge within; in return, the public recognises the owners' right to enjoy that specialised knowledge for a limited period. This constitutes a special contract between society, represented by the state, and the owners of intellectual products (Bogart 1980). Only thus can everyone enjoy greater wealth and security. Philosophers term the agreements ultimately reached through such negotiations the "social contract," as it establishes the fundamental terms of social life. (Cooter and Ulen 1994, p. 132). Hegel's "property-personality" theory intriguingly complements Locke's "labour-value" theory. This is because justifications for IP, whether based on "personality" or "labour," are morally acceptable. Within fundamental philosophical categories, personality can be expressed as the "self," the "unique existence." Personality is the qualification of being human, which should be the qualification for an individual to exercise their own will (Li 2000). In the theoretical sense of legal philosophy, personality is essentially the legal status of the will; its essence lies in being the existential qualification of the will. It is precisely within this metaphysical system of will-personality ("personality is the freedom of the will") that Hegel expounded his view of property. Hegel emphasised that free will manifests itself primarily through private property ownership.

"The task of the will is to realise absolute freedom";

"This task requires several stages":

"At the primary stage, the will appears in the form of personality";

"Personality must attain a more concrete form of existence in the world";

"This concrete form comes into being through the use of things";

"The category of 'things' includes intellectual resources, learning, and artistic skill";

The above mental conceptions "once externalised, become objects capable of legal possession" (Drahos 1996, pp. 75–82).

Hegel's statements are interpreted as supporting the existence of property rights, including IP. Within this complex philosophical language, Hegel conveys a simple meaning: property rights are essential for individual existence. Furthermore, the property right distinguishing "mine" and "thine" in intellectual products is not only a distinction required for personality to exist in the world as a free-willed individual entity or characteristic, but also an institutional form necessary for the individual to survive in the world. Hegel's personality theory not only served as a doctrinal perspective corroborating the justification of intellectual ownership (*geistiges Eigentum*), but also directly influenced the ideological foundation for the establishment of modern continental European IP systems.[3]

[3] In modern times, civil law countries conducted their copyright legislation based on the "value of personality", and established a system of "authorship" that is different from the English "copyright law" system. See Abe (1992).

The Public Interest Objective of IP Law

The concept of "public interest" (*bonum publicum*) originates in Rome; as the Roman thinker Cicero stated, "the welfare of the people is the supreme law" (*Salus populi suprema lex esto*). Incorporating the public interest principle within the IP system does not negate the private right nature of IP, but rather emphasises the balance between private exclusive rights and the public interest. Philosophers have offered different interpretations of this. Rousseau embedded the idea of justice within his conception of property. In his view, the establishment of ownership aims to construct a social order where property is respected and protected, which accords with the laws of justice; the property rights system is a fair convention common to all; to maintain the natural equity of the property rights system, law should be oriented towards the common interest of all members. Hegel expounded his view of IP from the perspective of intellectual production and dissemination. He believed that mental products "peculiar to us," once externalised, may be reproduced by others—this is not a problem, but a positive development. For through the appropriation of externalised intellectual products, more new intellectual products can be generated. The purpose of producing intellectual products lies in their recognition by others and their utility as a foundation for others' learning. In the process of social transmission of knowledge, "universally recognised thoughts" are modified and imbued with new individual form. When a particular intellectual form is utilised and disseminated by individuals across different eras, it contributes to the interests of others. Regarding how an individual can assert rights over intellectual forms within the process of human intellectual development, Hegel saw no "universally determinate principle." Based on experience, he advocated delineating legal boundaries within the intellectual system, establishing a certain intellectual common (a "public domain"), arguing this would better safeguard the learning needs of others or future generations. It should be noted that while Hegel stressed that the best way to promote science and art was to protect scientists' and artists' intellectual products from misappropriation, he simultaneously advocated the importance of the intellectual commons as a collective resource. Thus, Hegel's IP perspective clearly incorporates a public interest dimension. Drahos does not explicitly discuss the public interest principle of IP law in his work, but he describes the consequences of establishing IPRs over abstract objects. He acknowledges the justification for IP's existence but worries that establishing such a system in an imperfect society may lead to adverse consequences: the growth of private exclusive rights may create person-dependent relationships alongside thing-dependent relationships; if the scope of rights is not limited, it may cause distributive inequity. Drahos' warning implicitly advocates for establishing the spirit of balance and the public interest principle within the IP system. Regarding the relationship between the public interest principle and legal systems, the contemporary American legal philosopher Edgar Bodenheimer (1987) offers a more incisive exposition. He argued that the term "common good" is an indispensable conceptual tool, denoting an external boundary beyond which the distribution and exercise of individual rights must not extend, lest the general populace suffer serious harm. He advocated creating an appropriate balance between individual rights and social welfare. While the realisation of individual rights is deeply rooted in the needs and inclinations of personality, limiting certain rights is equally necessary for the sake of the public interest. Although the above views pertain to the public interest principle and general legal justice, they offer valuable insights for understanding the value objectives and functional role of the IPRs regime.

References

Abe, Kōji. 1992. Similarities and differences of copyright laws and their causes in different countries. Trans. Genquan Zhu. *Global Law Review*

Bodenheimer, Edgar. 1987. *Jurisprudence—The Philosophy and Method of the Law.* Trans. Zhenglai Deng and Jingwu Ji. Beijing: Huaxia Publishing House

Bogart, E. A. 1980. Patent law in capitalist and developing countries. *Patent Law.* Beijing: Knowledge Press

Bonfante, Pietro. 1992. *Istituzioni di Diritto Romano.* Trans. Feng Huang. Beijing: China University of Political Science and Law Press

Chen, Chaobi. 1936. *Principles of Roman Law.* Beijing: The Commercial Press

Coase, Ronald. 1960. The problem of social cost. *Journal of Law and Economics* 10

Commons, John. 1962. *Institutional Economics: Its Place in Political Economy volume 2.* Trans. Shusheng Yu. Beijing: The Commercial Press

Cooter, R. and T. Ulen. 1994. *Law and Economics.* Trans. Jun Zhang et al. Shanghai: SDX Joint Publishing Company and Shanghai People's Publishing House

Drahos, Peter. 1990. *A Philosophy of Intellectual Property.* England: Dartmouth Publishing Company Limited

Drahos, Peter. 1996. *A Philosophy of Intellectual Property.* England: Dartmouth Publishing Company Limited

Hegel, Friedrich. 1982. *Philosophy of Fine Arts volume 1.* Trans. Guangqian Zhu. Beijing: The Commercial Press

Hegel, Friedrich. 1961. *Philosophy of Right.* Trans. Fan Yang and Qitai Zhang. Beijing: The Commercial Press

Jiang, Ping. 2002. *Civil Law.* Beijing: China University of Political Science and Law Press

Kant, Immanual. 1991. *The Metaphysical Elements of Justice: The Science of Right.* Trans. Shuping Shen and Rongyuan Lin. Beijing: The Commercial Press

Li, Jingwen. 1999. *Embracing the New Era of Intellectual Economy.* Shanghai: Shanghai Far Eastern Publishers

Li, Xihe. 2000. *On Philosophy of Civil Law.* Shanghai: Fudan University Press

Liu, Chuntian and Liu Bolin. 1987. Theoretical issues on copyright law. *FaLu XueXi Yu YanJiu* 2

Locke, John. 1964 (1690). *Two Treatises of Government (volume 2).* Trans. Qifang Ye et al. Beijing: The Commercial Press

Mei, Xueqin. 1994. On the concept of property by John Locke. *World History* 6

Patterson, L. Ray. and Stanley W. Lindberg. 1991. *The Nature of Copyright: A Law of Users' Right.* Athens: The University of Georgia Press

Peng, Wanlin. 1994. *Science of Civil Law.* Beijing: China University of Political Science and Law Press

Ploman, Edward W. and L. Clark Hamilton. 1980. *Copyright: Intellectual Property in the Information Age.* London: Routledge and Kegan Paul Ltd.

Qu, Sanqiang. 2002. Traditional property theory and views on intellectual property rights. *Studies on Intellectual Property Rights.* Xi'an: Xi'an Jiaotong University Press

Rousseau, Jean-Jacques. 1980. *The Social Contract.* Trans. Zhaowu He. Beijing: The Commercial Press.

Say, A. 1963. *Treatise on Political Economy*. Trans. Fusheng Chen et al. Beijing: The Commercial Press

Smith, Adam. 1972. *An Inquire of the Nature and Causes of Wealth of Nations*. Trans. Dali Guo. Beijing: The Commercial Press

Versteeg, Russ. 2000. The Roman law roots of copyright. *Maryland Law Review*

Yi, Jiming. 2000. Property right and its philosophical foundations. *Political and Legal Forum* 3

Zhang, Hesheng. 1992. *Knowledge Economics*. Shenyang: Liaoning People's Publishing House

Zhou, Nan. 1994a. *Principles of Roman Law*. Beijing: Commercial Press

Zhou, Nan. 1994b. *The Original Treatise on Roman Law*. Beijing: Commercial Press

Chapter 9
Cultural Dimensions of IPRs Regimes

The culture of IPRs is a form of legal culture characterised by inclusiveness, openness, and multidimensionality, as well as a private law culture rooted in individualism, the spirit of free will, and the pursuit of rationality. The term "IPRs culture" has both a narrow meaning, referring to conceptual and institutional cultures, and a broader sense, referring to cultures at the ideological level. According to Lee S. Weinberg and Judith W. Weinberg, legal culture reflects the will of the public in terms of attitudes, beliefs, evaluations, perceptions and expectations towards legal systems and legal authorities (Liu 1999, p. 36). As such, IPRs culture may be regarded as general opinions of and behavioural patterns surrounding IPRs and IPRs protection. Based on previous studies of legal culture, this chapter looks into the cultural basis of Western IPRs regimes in the hope of shedding light on the cultural requirements for establishing a sustainable IPRs regime in China, and it also attempts to visualise the transformation and reconstitution of China's IP culture for the present-day and the foreseeable future.

9.1 Western Cultural Foundations in IP Law Construction

From the privilege system towards the end of the Medieval period (900–1400) to the private property rights system established with the rise of capitalism, legislation on IPRs in the West has had a history of several hundred years. In the midst of drastic social transformation, the development and changes in politics, economy, science and technology, and ideology constitute the necessary social conditions for the survival and flourishing of this emerging legal system.

Law is interconnected with culture; thus, it may be said that the IPRs regime illustrates IP culture and that the latter serves as the ideological basis of the former. The Renaissance, launched by the bourgeoisie of the western Europe and marked by a revival of classical scholarship and art between the 14th and the sixteenth centuries in

H. Wu, *Theorising Intellectual Property Rights from Chinese Perspectives*,
https://doi.org/10.1007/978-981-96-5867-1_9

Western Europe, was a backlash against obscurantism and religious fervour. The era inherited the scientific culture of ancient Greece and initiated a philosophy centred on humanism (Wang 1998, pp. 85–86). The cultural values proposed during this period laid the cultural and ideological groundwork for the western intellectuals to use science and technology as a material weapon and the private right system as a legal weapon against the ignorance, tyranny and authoritarianism prevailing at the time, all of which led to the legislation of Western IPRs between the seventeenth and nineteenth centuries.

As concepts are the building blocks of legal doctrines, innovation in a legal system follows the advancement of legal concepts. A good example of this is the modern concept of IP formed during the Industrial Revolution (1775–1880), allowing IP creators to enjoy private rights to their intellectual achievements and to dispose of their IP at will. The IPR legislative documents of this period embodied/are permeated with the values of the Natural Law School, highlighting rights, individual freedom and human rationality. In a word, individualism, liberalism and rationalism may be viewed as the humanistic foundation and spiritual propositions of IPR laws, all of which are elaborated in the following section:

9.1.1 Individualism

The concept of individualism covers a wide variety of ideas, attitudes and doctrines whose common factor is the systematic attribution of centrality to the individual (Miller and Bogdanor 1992, pp. 353–354). As the opposite of 'collective,' the concept of the 'individual' may be expressed in many ways. Research perspectives based on various definitions of individualism may be divided into axiological and methodological approaches.[1] 'Axiological individualism' refers to claims of individual rights. It stresses an individual's freedom and rights, advocates for an individual-based ideological system and insists that in the relationship between an individual and a group or that between a subject and a society, the individual or subject has indisputable priority over the group or society, ensuring individual freedom and rights while the group or society is only a mean or tool of safeguarding individual freedom and individual rights.

The value of individualism is represented in atomism in both social and political theories. It is "a view of society as constituted by individuals for the fulfilment of ends that are primarily individual, which gives priority to the individual and his rights, seen as existing antecedently to any particular form of social life." This view is typically seen as stemming from the seventeenth century and as exemplified in the Social Contract theories of Hobbes and Locke and later in the utilitarian tradition. Thus "atomism" is seen as rooted in both philosophical traditions and economic

[1] For a classification of axiological individualism and methodological individualism, see Yi Jun (2006).

meaning. And the "possessive individualism" is based on "a concept of the individual as essentially the proprietor of his own person or capacities (Liu 1999, p. 36).

Methodological individualism, however, is a social theory emphasising research on the 'social nature of individuals and individual behaviours' (Hayek 1958, p. 14). Holding that a proper explanation of a social regularity or phenomenon is grounded in individual motivations and behaviour, methodological individualism makes the individual the basic research unit in analysing society and exploring the general principles and laws of society. In social sciences, methodological individualism is a framework to understand social phenomena through the explanation of the properties, goals, beliefs and actions of individuals (Miller and Bogdanor 1992). The individualistic methodology advocated by John Locke (1632–1704), David Hume (1711–1776), Adam Smith (1723–1790) and Friedrich A. von Hayek (1899–1992) involves many fields, including philosophy, politics, economics and law. Of these, Hayek (1958) considered individualism primarily as a social theory and "the great discovery of classical political economy which has become the basis of our understanding not only of economic life but of most truly social phenomena" (p. 8).

There are indeed conceptual and perspective differences between axiological and methodological individualism; however, their basic views and main content are similar. In the area of private law, values of modern individualism are also the values of modern civil law. In his book *Ancient Law*, Henry Sumner Maine (1901) proposed two pivotal points in the transition from ancient law to modern law: the shift from status to contract and the turn from family to individual. Modern thinkers refer to the establishment of the individual as the centre as the "the discovery of man" and "human liberation." It is worth mentioning that, as a research paradigm, the application of methodological individualism in private law, still has practical significance even today. "The emphasis laid upon the individual, individual rights, individual autonomy and self-reliance in private law is necessary to achieve methodological individualism" (Yi 2006, pp. 39–41).

The constitution of modern private law features individualism as its cultural foundation. Specifically, the basic features of individualism are present in the legal relationship between private individuals in modern society. For example, countries are composed of individuals, and legal persons are granted the collective status of individuals who are all considered independent, free, with sacred, unalienable rights. The overarching principle of modern civil law is thus the principle of the independence of personality.

This leads to the second principle of modern civil law, the principle of equal rights. No subordinate relationships are found in the domain of private law; everyone enjoys equal legal status, and no one is at the mercy of others. Equality in personal relationships is based on the disintegration of patriarchal families and relationships shaped by the exchange of commodity, both of which emerged with the decline of the natural economy (Liang 1997).

The third principle of modern civil law is that personal relationships are free from interference. In modern society, only governments and laws have the power to influence, even to dominate, personal relationships. However, modern governments in general attempt to protect personal relationships rather than interfere with them.

The third principle, known as the principle of autonomy of private law, is a product of respect and protection of relationships and falls within the category of private law.

Modern Western legal systems feature individualism and protect intellectual property on the basis of laissez-faire capitalism. Above all, IPRs are the private property rights of those who engage in creative activities as opposed to rights endowed by absolute monarchy. In the "dematerialisation of properties"[2] since Roman law, IPRs that were specific to the public law domain have been grouped into the private law domain, making IPRs legally required and transferable rather than chartered exclusive rights (Wu 2003). At the same time, IPRs are not public rights shared by all but rather private rights owned by specific civil subjects,[3] which indicates that an individual, as the basic unit of a civil society enjoys rights independently. Examples are in abundance in modern copyright legislation: The first copyright legislation, the *Statute of Anne* (1709) (long title: *An Act for the Encouragement of Learning, by Vesting the Copies of Printed Books in the Authors or Purchasers of such Copies, during the Times therein Mentioned)*, recognised that authors should be the primary beneficiaries of copyright law though it protected publishers' rights, which are not original rights, but derivative rights, within a limited duration of time (14 years). The *French Copyright Act* (2001), however, highly values the centrality of the author and imposes comprehensive regulation on the author's position as a natural person and the first copyright owner.

9.1.2 Liberalism

Liberalism is presently the most popular and influential mindset in Western countries and in other countries influenced by European culture (see the entry on 'liberalism' in Miller and Bogdanor 1992, pp. 415–418). With the pursuit of freedom as its kernel, liberalism dates back to the city-states of ancient Greece and Rome. Both Aristotle (384–322 BC) and Marcus Tullius Cicero (106–43 BC) described civil society as "a public ethical–political community of free and equal citizens under a legally defined system of rule" (Cohen and Arato 1992, p. 84, as cited in He 1994). Liberalism is an ideological prop of the city-state. The city-state is a community of freemen, wherein each occupant possessing citizen rights is his own master, not a slave to others. Laws ensure the development of the city-state, thus gaining the voluntary support of its free citizens; the mission of a city-state is to meet everyone's need of freedom to

---

[2] The "propertisation of knowledge", also known as the "dephysicalisation of property", is regarded as an institutional creation of the greatest revolutionary significance in private rights. For further discussion on "new property", see Nico Stehr (1998) and Kenneth Vandevelde (1980).

[3] In terms of a scientific research reward system, the right of invention and discovery is not a private property right but rather a reward system of a non-market mechanism in exchange for the public property right of scientific achievement. In addition to the declarative provisions of the *WIPO Convention* on the right of invention and the right of discovery, most of the national legislation and international conventions from modern to contemporary times do not regard the above rights as IPRs with the nature of private rights.

the maximum extent. It should be noted that the pursuit of freedom that emerged in ancient Greece and Rome was based on the classical models of citizenship rather than the freedom and liberation of personality in the modern sense.

The pursuit of freedom prevailed in European countries through the Middle Ages. It was firmly believed that the law was independent of and above the government, and "freedom under the law" was considered a concept of natural law. Influenced by that a liberal policy system was established in the field of economics through the efforts of Christian philosophers (Hayek 2001, pp. 56–57). During the eighteenth and nineteenth centuries, the pursuit of freedom reached its apex in Western countries, forming a comprehensive system of liberalism underpinned by ideological and theoretical resources. Reviewing the history of the West, the concept of liberalism has varied by time and region. For instance, the liberalism of the secular class differed from that of the religious world—Hobbes and Locke's classical liberalism differed from the new social liberalism proposed by Thomas Hill Green (1836–1882) or Leonard Trelawney Hobhouse (1864–1929). Further, the spirit of freedom can be found in various social science fields, in forms including freedom of thought, political liberty and economic freedom (Miller and Bogdanor 1992).

In the formation of modern private law culture, liberalism manifest in the form of "the discovery of man", i.e. propositions concerning free individuality and the development of the individual's capability and principal status. Under "liberalism" in the *Enciclopedia del Novecento*, Hayek systematically expounded on the legal concept in four aspects, as detailed below.

Liberalism and Natural Rights

Private rights are guaranteed by the liberal constitutional politics expressed by natural rights and the separation of powers. That is, liberal constitutionalism advocates that individuals enjoy rights or natural rights (such as rights to freedom, property and security) free from deprivation. Liberalism emphasises the separation of powers and opposes unlimited or sovereign power.

Liberalism and Legal Justice

The rationality of private law is based on particular views of justice. Liberalism is primarily concerned with justice in social exchange, rather than distributive justice. The former is a natural distribution justice, a natural distribution status shaped spontaneously out of .../Liberalism, with its primal concern on justice in social exchange, involves a market-centred distribution mechanism nurtured and shaped spontaneously out of commercial interests, rather than distributive justice, which provides ethical guidance for a mandatory distribution mechanism in consonance with the merits of individuals, and the best interests of society by the single order of a certain authority.

Liberalism and Equality

In the field of private law, equality is a legal requirement for subjects participating in private relationships. Liberalism traditionally opposes discriminatory treatment and instead advocates the equality of opportunity in obtaining private rights. Such equality may take the form of freedom of choice to establish private relationships or an equal opportunity to obtain private rights; however, it need not guarantee the same result from private law activities, namely substantive equality.

Freedom to Pursuit Material and Spiritual Things

Everyone has the right to freedom of thought and the pursuit of material possessions, which underpin the principle of autonomy in private law. Liberalism, in essence, encourages human communication and exchange of ideas, enabling freedom of thought, the improvement of cognitive abilities and progress of knowledge/intellectual progress. In addition, the freedom to participate in the economy, i.e. the availability of means (resources) to achieve one's behavioural purposes, is of great significance, similar to the freedom of thought (Hayek 2001, pp. 48–98).

The private legal system based on individual freedom highlights the autonomy both of private law and of the will. The principle of autonomy of private law emphasises that "the subject of right is the subject of will", meaning that all civil acts depend on the wills of the parties involved, without interference by the government or other parties. This principle runs throughout various civil rights systems and is seen in property autonomy (ownerships system), freedom of contract (contract system), freedom of marriage (marriage system), freedom of testament (inheritance system), freedom of establishment (legal person system) and so on.

Freedom of thought is at the core of liberalism and is the soul of modern IP law. As presented in *the French Declaration of the Rights of Man and of the Citizen* (1789; the Declaration), freedom of thought once was a political right in the fields of creation, academy, art, speech, publishing and so on. Article 11 of the Declaration states, "The unrestrained communication of thoughts and opinions being one of the most precious rights of man, every citizen may speak, write, and print with freedom".[4] Framers of the United States Constitution likewise included three IP policies: "the Promotion of Learning, the Preservation of Public Domain, and the Protection of Author's Rights" (Patterson and Linberg 1991, pp. 49–55).

Such provisions in constitutional documents embody the freedom of thought lacking in the franchise system of the Middle Ages. In the case of the copyright system, for example, the early feudal franchise was closely related to feudal censorship. The emergence of the printing industry in Europe not only gave birth to the chartered publishing right but brought about the government control of printed publications. Feudal states stipulated that works must be submitted for examination before

[4] *The Universal Declaration of Human Rights*, Available at ccnmtl.columbia.edu/projects/mmt/udhr/article_19.html, accessed 7 Jan. 2020.

publication, subjecting publishing privileges to government censors. The publishing privilege, being a private right established without consideration of political needs, thus became a tool for ideological examination under feudal autocracy. The *Statute of Anne* took the initiative in abandoning the system of feudal franchise and feudal censorship of books, reflecting the legal values of the free dissemination of works and the protection of freedom of thought (Wu 2005, pp. 84–86). Modern Western constitutional documents thus incorporate IPRs principles of economic significance as well as the freedom of thought, which has political significance.

9.1.3 Rationalism

Rationalism, with value rationality and instrumental rationality as its core, defines the Western philosophical tradition and forges Western legal culture. Thanks to the contribution of Max Weber, value rationality and instrumental rationality refer to mental processes through which people give coherence and meaning to fragmented, ongoing experience and instil regularities in patterns of social action. Weber's philosophical stance is inspiring for legal infrastructure since value rational action capacities are closely related to social justice, which is the primary aim of any social institutions (Shen 1993). Humans are rational by nature and bound by reason. Thus, a legal system responding to the capacity for innate action in humans, and simultaneously referring to a reasonable value system reflects the value of justice. On the other hand, instrumental rationality, which deals only with the most effective and efficient means to reach given ends, provides an important indicator in evaluating the justice within social institutions. Reason is the best test of knowledge, and with rationality human beings are capable of arriving at the ultimate "truth" and finding configurations of it with the help of language. In a similar way, through adopting instrumental rationality, a complete, coherent and reasonable legal system, is established.

The terms "rational" and "reasonable" are derived from the same Latin root, "ratio", which means reckoning, numbering and calculation. In the past, "rational" and "reasonable" were used interchangeably in theoretical social research. Rationality as an attribute in belief and action is the successful exercise of the rational faculty, or common sense. A person holds a belief rationally if he or she can justify it with facts and, more importantly, is prepared to reassess it in light of arguments against it, which is known as practical rationality (see the entry on 'rationality' in Miller and Bogdanor 1992, pp. 630–631). Reason may be identified and judged according to the value orientation of human purposes. "Non-utilitarian, pure rationality" refers to going beyond selfish desires. In the legal sense, non-utilitarian rationality is the original meaning of "reason", that is, "reasonable", "in line with truth" and "in accordance with law."

Chinese scholars generally believe that "rationality", or "reason", has a twofold meaning. One refers to inevitability and law as they pertain to human subjects. Mankind is characterised by the unity of naturality and sociality, meaning that people generally act according to their values and nature in pursuit of personal needs and purposes (principal status in society or nature, interests, values and other purposes) as well as according to the conditions necessary to attain these needs and purposes. As noted above, reason and rationality define the nature of law. Whereas the second refers to inevitability and law in society and the natural world. Rationality in society pertains to social development, while reason in nature pertains to the regularities and coordination of the relationship between humans and nature. In short, social development and a harmonious human-nature relationship are rational goals embedded in the law (Qiao and Li 1991).

Yet it is also worth mentioning that rationality does not necessarily go against the spirit of freedom as observed by some social theorists for two flaws/loopholes can be found in their arguments. The first lies in ignoring the fact that reason is a critical tool and in viewing the spirit of freedom as an absolute and complete freedom as a requirement of a laissez-faire policy. The second error is to disregard the limits of reason, viewing all human systems as products created deliberately, and considering the rational spirit as the opposite of civil liberty. According to Hayek (2001, pp. 199–222), the libertarian theory is not anti-rational; it only opposes the assertion that reason is absolute and is the sole element of importance in "designing" social development. Hayek goes on to state that, as opposed to philosophy over-emphasising reason, real rationalism (classical rationalism or modern critical rationalism) does not run counter to liberalism. In terms of system design and organisation, reason itself must be limited—that is, imposing any reasonable pattern on a society runs the risk of stifling its freedom to engage in progressive improvement.

Aristotle, Thomas Aquinas (1225–1274) and Baron de Montesquieu (1689–1755) all emphasised the role of reason in the development of civilisation. Their pursuit of rationality as a cultural legacy had an important impact on the formation and development of both Roman private law and modern civil law. In ancient Greece and Rome, philosophers and jurists strove to advocate for "natural law", a positive law that is both natural and rational. Aristotle first proposed the concept of the natural law, and the Stoics, founded by Zeno of Citium about 300 B.C furthered the concept, proposing that the natural law could reflect human reason and that the wise man should be submissive to natural law.

Guided by practical rationality, Roman jurists introduced the terms *jus gentium* (universal law) and *jus civile* (civil law). *Jus gentium* refers to the law shared by all nations, whereas *jus civile* refers to the law of one nation. In *Istituzioni di Dritto Romano*, Pietro Bonfante (1864–1932) wrote that the *jus naturale* (natural law) "is not made to embody wills of legislators", and the Julius Paulus (Second to third centuries), one of the most influential and distinguished Roman jurists said that such law "is always just and kind" (Bonfante 1992, pp. 13–15). Therefore, *jus gentium* conforms to the essence of the natural law, and its status is above that of *jus civile*.

Scholasticism, the medieval school of philosophy refused was rationalistic, and the rationalism proposed by its representative figure, Thomas Aquinas (1225–1274), served as the methodological basis for the upsurge in research and the continuation and development of Roman law in the Middle Ages. Thomas Aquinas deemed human reason to be universal; however, he conceded that both pure reason and practical reason allow for exceptions, and that freedom is influenced by reason (Yan 1999,

p. 74). The natural law is fixed in that it relies on a universal concept of reason; thus, all laws should be rational and natural. Nevertheless, the legitimacy of a new law relies upon the exceptions permitted by the natural law, i.e. a certain degree of variability.

Rationalism was fully developed between the seventeenth and nineteenth centuries. Guided by rationalism, modern thinkers such as Hugo Grotius (1583–1645), Montesquieu and Jean-Jacques Rousseau (1712–1778) put forward the theory of the natural law, introducing new ideological approaches to the study of law. The principle of this theory is that human beings originated in a state of nature governed by the natural law, representing reason and justice, and enjoyed various natural rights. To better enjoy these rights, people established governments through social contracts.

Rationalism in modern times emphasises a unified law, distilling the concept to the pursuit of justice, equality, freedom, dignity, happiness and so on (Yu 1990, pp. 110–117). It requires a law to rely on a traditional and universally applicable stability and regularity rather than to yield to human wills. The essence of a law is thus the unification of subjectivity and objectivity; that is, a law should reflect the objectives of the society pursued by human wills, prioritising these over legislators' subjective wills. Modern jurists and legal reformers have thus discovered an ideal legal system by the mere use of their rational powers. It was only natural that they should endeavour to work out in a systematic form all the various rules and principles of natural law and embody them in a code (Bodenheimer 1974). In summary, rationalism provides an essential philosophical/ideological foundation for the systematisation and codification of modern laws.

IPRs permit creators to safeguard their right of ownership of their IP while securing society's rational pursuit of knowledge dissemination. Although there are parallels between traditional right of ownership over property and intellectual property, some critical differences exist in the objectives of legal value. In the traditional theory related to private law, right of ownership is defined as the unconditional control and exclusive possession of property. Although legal limitations have been imposed on the exercise of such ownership to protect the public interest and to ensure social order, no limitations have been imposed on the elements of time, territory and legal capacity with respect to right of ownership. In traditional theory related to ownership and in modern legislation, right of ownership is entirely relegated to the domain of private rights.

IPR law, however, seeks a balance between personal interests, i.e. creators' rights, and social interests, e.g. the dissemination of knowledge. Such legislative tradition can be observed in the *Statute of Anne*, which stipulated the protection of authors' rights and meanwhile marked off "the public domain for literature" (Patterson and Linberg 1991, pp. 49–55). Thus, IPR law does not provide for absolute private ownership of creations, but rather imposes limits such as conditional exclusivity, finite exclusivity and terminable duration. It is the limits imposed on private ownership that ensure an IPRs regime always centres on fair use. And an IPRs regime as such is thus claimed to adopt "a rational principle of egalitarianism", featuring "fairness and justice" and showing "institutional flexibility" (Party 1986, p. 4). It can be concluded that modern Western lawmakers establish IPRs regimes aiming at two legislative results, namely, protecting creators' private rights and promoting knowledge dissemination. Despite variations in policies and details in legislation from time to time and from country to country, adjustments to the protections offered and the limits applied are constant topics of IP legislation.

9.2 Cultural Challenges in IP Transplantation: The Chinese Context

"Legal transplant" refers to "activities in one country or region to integrate laws of other countries or regions into its own legal system for the local implementation" (Wang 2004). As a modern approach of legislation, legal transplant takes either an active or a passive form. An active legal transplant involves direct or fundamental motivations coming from within the society, that is, countries or regions take the imitative in introducing foreign laws through their independent legislative judgement. For example, the smooth evolution of European laws in the Middle Ages benefited from the spread of ancient Roman law, which was extensively transplanted into European countries in the twelfth century. Marx and Engels (1960) observed, with the further advancement of industry and trade, private property (initially in Italy and subsequently in other countries) was revitalised; concurrently, the elaborated private law of Roman jurisprudence was promptly revived and reinstated to its former influence and authority. The main manifestations of this revival included an upsurge in research on and introduction of ancient Roman law in European countries from the fifteenth century to the sixteenth century.

Passive legal transplant, in contrast, occurs due to external pressures when countries or regions are forced to introduce foreign laws. Cases can be found among Asian countries in the second half of the nineteenth century. Western civilisation as well as Western legal rules and conventions forced their way into Asian countries, leaving them with no choice but to embrace the cultural and political colonisation by accepting these heterogeneous elements. As Xin Chunying (2007) noted, for the Western colonists, it is only natural to transplant their laws to colonies as the right thing to do, while for colonies, it is humiliating to accept such legal transplant.

The IPRs regime developed ingenuously in Western countries before it was transplanted to other regions. Following the establishment of Roman law, another milestone in legal history involved the "dematerialisation of properties", which first introduced the concept of IPRs. Deeply rooted and well nurtured in Western legal culture over 300 years, the IPRs regime was established in industrial countries as "a paragon of institutional civilisation".[5] The establishment of an IPRs regime in developing countries, however, occurred in response to external pressures. Taking China as an

[5] North and Thomas (1973) compared China in the fourteenth century with the UK in the seventeenth and eighteenth centuries, and argued that inventions and technological revolution were stimulated by the UK's establishment of the IPRs system, laying a solid foundation for the forthcoming industrial revolution, which ultimately boosted the modern economy.

example, in the late Qing Dynasty, the last of the imperial dynasties of China, IPRs were for the first time under protection, which was a product of the Qing government's New Policies[6] and the associated introduction of certain Western ideas; however, it was to a great extent a reluctant reform catering to the Western powers.

The concept of an IPRs regime has been transplanted, "chosen rationally" and localised in China over the past 100 years, ultimately facilitating the domestic development of the Chinese IPRs regime. After the establishment of the People's Republic of China in 1949, legal transplant, as a legislative tradition, has been followed, leading to a constantly updated and increasingly comprehensive IPRs regime in China for over twenty years. However, the current IPRs regime fails to fully actualise the expected policy objectives and legal benefits, with its effectiveness wanes and in question, which may be resulted from the "diminishing return of the transplanted IP laws" (Song 2006). Both legal and non-legal factors are found affecting the effectiveness of China's IPRs regime. The legal factors include whether legal ideas, legislative objectives and forms of legislation on which the IPRs regime is based are rational, scientific and up-to-date, whereas the non-legal factors occur in the implementation of IPRs, including whether the development of the economy and the technology, the public policy, the social context, and cultural conditions are consistent, coordinated and compatible. As Xin Chunying (2007)states, the ultimate goal of legal transplant is to transplant legal culture, which means the transplant of rules and regimes must take culture as its basis. Yet as a borrowed idea, IPRs have always been "exotic" for traditional Chinese culture, which exerts a far-reaching influence on the enforcement of China's IPR laws.

9.2.1 *Historical Inertia of Traditional Chinese Cultural Influences*

IPR laws come into being as the product of legal revolutions and institutional changes in modern society. As in Europe of the Middle Ages, a franchise system prevailed in imperial China; however, China's franchise system did not evolve into IP legislation, leaving China lacking historical and cultural connections with modern IPRs regimes. What kept China from catching up with its Western counterparts? Mentality and thinking patterns rooted in traditional Chinese culture may provide us with answers.

As previously discussed, individualism has been the cultural basis of private law in modern times. The culture of private law was nurtured with the development of IPRs, or more precisely, it was the "person" ("*Mensch*" in German) that was developed in private law. However, traditional Chinese culture was supported by an agrarian economy, with the patriarchal family as its basic unit and an ethical framework as its core. In traditional Chinese culture, human subjectivity was not recognised, as individuals were expected to depend on the state and the family unit; it emphasised the

[6] "New Policies" refers to a series of cultural, economic, educational, military and political reforms implemented in the last decade of the Qing dynasty to keep the dynasty in power.

value of kinship, honour given to family and the male-centred clan.[7] The individual existed essentially as part of a whole; only in the context of collectivism, no matter whether family, clan or country, did one hold significance, and only in the network of human relationships did an individual's will and emotions matter. Confucianism, the central philosophy of traditional Chinese culture, advocated not the human rights standard with citizen as its unit, but the humanist standard with the family as the basic unit (Yu 1999, p. 168). In such an environment, a person enjoyed little, if any, independent personality and therefore could not claim individual rights.

Liberalism inspires and underpins the constitution of modern private law. Freedom of thought and freedom of pursuing material life, which are expressed in the form of cultural consciousness and cultural policies are the preconditions of knowledge creation and intellectual propertisation. Freedom is a right protected by law (Montesquieu 1994, p. 154). Nevertheless, neither freemen (a social class of Western history) nor free thoughts based on the natural law existed in traditional Chinese society. One of the basic Confucian ethical concepts *li*, (ritual or the rules of propriety, is the code of conduct of Chinese people's daily life. By providing the standardised models of behaviour and ideal personalities, *Li*, to some extent, opposes the notion of individual personality, discouraging creativity, curiosity and innovation; thus, it cannot protect rights, let alone [act as] a yardstick of freedom (Liang 1999, p. 193). Furthermore, *Li* advocates for illiteracy under the notion that "people may be made to follow a path of action, but they may not be made to understand it" and under the cultural autocratic policy prohibiting unconventional behaviour. Under its influence, common people were resigned to their places in the patriarchal hierarchy and under the absolute domination of their rulers, suppressing individual freedom of thought (Song 1991, p. 233).

Besides, in traditional Chinese culture, intellectual creations are nothing but byproducts of a noble man's (*Jun zi*) self-cultivation. Accordingly, the awareness of rights regarding creations is often purposely obfuscated. For instance, Chinese intellectuals are expected and obliged to make their work available to the public for inspirational and educational purpose rather than holding them in private ownership, with traditional sayings such as "Articles are not written for profit or rewards of any kind" and "A noble man (*Jun zi)* never concerns himself with personal gain" being cases in point.

Rationalism, as the cultural pillar of private law, reflects its legislative objectives and value orientations. In fact, reason provides the most essential concept for natural law, to the point at which the two may be equated. More specifically, natural law comprises intellectual reason, valuing the pursuit of knowledge and truth based on

---

[7] In describing the distinctions of the mourning, *the Book of Rites*, one of Confucian Classics states, "[F]or the kindred who are the nearest, the honored ones to whom honour is paid, the elders who are venerated for their age, and as the different tributes to males and females; there are seen the greatest manifestations of the course which is right for men." This passage emphasises two basic principles running through the rules of propriety in ancient China, namely to maintain hierarchy and "a male-centred clan". Available at https://ctext.org/dictionary.pl?if=gb&id=10021 last accessed Apr. 22, 2022.

natural science and epistemology. The relations between natural law, reason and knowledge may be best demonstrated in the following equation:

Natural law = Reason = Knowledge (Yu 1999, p. 168)

Rationalism is not incompatible with traditional Chinese culture. Confucianism, the mainstay of China's cultural tradition for instance, embraces reason and rational thinking; however, reason in the Chinese context differs greatly from that of the West.

Confucian rationality is by nature ethical and pragmatic as human relations are attached with ontological significance. Reason, in the Confucianism context, is built from "within" since it comes from an individual's own recognition of life and the universe, and is applied only to explain and justify everyday life. Preoccupied with secular and humanist concerns, Confucian rationality makes no attempts to reveal the truth and explain the physical world, and thus easily finds itself in great need of growth potential. What's more important, the perception of such rationality relies on nothing but moral teaching. The Confucian ideal of the harmonious society, the coexistence of human beings and the universe can only be achieved by the internalisation of Confucian ethics motivated by routine moral teaching. Furthermore, Confucian rationality pursues the integration of individual, family, country and the world through cultivating individual moral character, running the family harmoniously and managing the nation for a peaceful world, rather than as a way of adjusting and judging the tensions between subject and object, between the spirit and the flesh, between humans and nature and between the individual and country through instrumental rationality. In an environment where Confucian rationality dominates, the emphasis on harmony deters people from engaging in courtroom battles to protect IPRs against infringement.

There is inertia in legal cultures, especially when they are confronted with conflicting and dominating cultural traditions. China's time-honoured traditional culture and Confucianism legacies have resulted in a cultural tenacity that challenges the development and thriving of the IPRs regime. Whereas Western IPR laws are based on individualism, liberalism and rationalism, Chinese traditional culture features standards of obligation, autocracy and human relations defined by Confucian ethical codes. These distinctive cultural foundations determine that Western laws transplanted into China have to become acclimatised to the local realities.

9.2.2 *Realistic Obstacles to Societal Acceptance of Legal Transplantation*

Past centuries have witnessed the development of IP law in the Western world, throughout the Renaissance, the Reformation, the Recovery of Roman law and the Industrial Revolution, thus laying the cultural and economic foundations for IPRs regimes. The world's first patent law, the *Statute of Monopolies*, and the first copyright law, the *Statute of Anne*, which were enacted in the UK in 1623 and 1709 respectively, and France's first trademark law, the *Manufacture and Goods Mark Act* and *Trademarks Based on the Principles of Use and Non-examination* promulgated in 1857, mark the beginning of IP legislation with a modern significance.

Legal transplant played an active role in the establishment of modern IPRs regimes in the West since most of Western countries introduced IP legislation from their Western counterparts. As a reform of the legal system and as legislation proceeding in a broad sense (Liu 2004), such transplantation had two basic characteristics. First, Western countries introduced IP laws proactively for their own development, having undergone a transformation from feudal franchise to capitalist property rights in terms of the protection of IPRs. With the establishment of the capitalist system in the West, major capitalist countries introduced IP legislation in the eighteenth and nineteenth centuries. Examples of such legislation include the *Copyright Act of 1790* in the US, the *Law of the Author's Right* (1793) in France, and the *Law for the Protection of Scientific and Artistic Works against Copy or Imitation* (1837) in Germany. Patent laws were promulgated in 1790 in the US, in 1791 in France and in 1877 in Germany, and trademark laws were introduced in 1870 in the US, in 1874 in Germany and in 1875 in the UK. All of these laws were spontaneous responses to the changes in social and legal systems in Western countries occurring at the time.

The second characteristic of the transplant of IP laws in Western countries was that it was carried out between countries with homogeneous legal and cultural traditions. The *Copyright Law* in the UK adheres to the theory of "commercial copyright" in legislation to establish laws with "property values", whereas France and Germany regard "personality values" as the ideological preconditions of a system of authors' rights (Kôji 1992). Yet despite the differences in IPR legislative strategies, these countries share the same cultural tradition honouring freedom, knowledge and individual rights.

Cultural discrepancies between the East and the West made the transplant of IP laws in China entirely different. From the fall of the Qing Dynasty in the 1840s to the rise of the Republic of China in 1912, the introduction of an IPRs regime had always been under international pressure rather than to meet its own domestic needs. The "borrowed" IPRs regime, lacking connections to the local culture, was thus hardly recognised by the public. In general, "the legal transplant between heterogeneous cultures is bound to cause collisions and frictions, and the indigenous legal culture will tenaciously resist foreign laws" (Pan 1999), resulting in a disconnect between such laws and the local society. On that, China may not be the only case in point. In the 1860s, the Meiji Restoration was enacted in Japan to meet a domestic requirement for industrialisation. Consequently, an array of social and political reforms was undertaken, including an overall legal transplant of German laws. Yet differences between the native culture and German culture resulted in ineffective implementation of the transplanted new laws and the Meiji government spared no effort in initiating a 'top-down reform' (Fu 2003) so that a favourable cultural environment might guarantee the success of its legal transplant. Such top-down reform never occurred in China. The Xinhai Revolution in 1911,[8] though it overthrew the political system of the Qing Dynasty, failed in its attempt to establish a new cultural outlook and rule-governed society based on science, democracy and law through abolishing the feudal ideological architecture. Thus, China possessed neither an institutional inheritance of an IPRs regime nor a cultural foundation to support its transplanted IPRs regime.

Noticeable changes have been experienced in modern China in adopting IPRs. Though legal transplant was still the common practice, national realities and domestic needs, both economic and political have been taken into consideration in its IP legislation. Examples can be found in China's determination to maintain minimum patent protection in order to keep pace with international economic and technological development, and in its hesitation to participating in international copyright protection due to the imbalance of power between the East and the West.

However, the conclusion of the *Uruguay Rounds Agreement* in 1993 ushered the international trade system into a new era, and the international context of IPRs protection has gone through great changes. Since its accession to the World Trade Organisation (WTO) in 2001, China has honoured its promise by updating its IP legislation so as to align with international IPR conventions. However, low public recognition of domestic IPR and international IPR conventions is still a pressing reality in China. Two factors may contribute to it. First, the country as a whole lacks a cohesive understanding of the legal transplant, as members of society differ in their perceptions and degrees of acceptance (Liu 2004). Although the protection of IPRs is a general rule in modern international trade, and thus obliging members of the WTO to protect IPRs, there is a definite imbalance of interests in the current system, which gives greater weight to the demands and experience of developed countries. Given these circumstances, opinions vary widely on legal transplant among members of Chinese society.

The second reason that China fails to identify with the legal transplant is a need for necessary resources, including time and experience, to support the transplant. In general, laws are transplanted from developed countries to less developed countries to fill a legislative gap and legal transplant is considered to be the most effective way of improving the legal architecture in developing countries. However, the gradual transition necessitated by the proposal and draft of a new law is time-consuming even developed countries. In the context of China, both the government and enterprises, with limited experience and inadequate mental preparation, have had to manage an overnight transformation. Without sufficient knowledge and capacity to make a full use of the transplanted legal system, it is thus understandable that IP law loses its vitality in China.

---

[8] The Xinhai Revolution, which overthrew China's last imperial dynasty (the Qing Dynasty), established the Republic of China. This is also known as the Chinese Revolution or the Revolution of 1911.

9.2.3 Cultural Deficiencies in Legal Localisation

The term "legal domestication" refers to the process and acceptance of transplanted laws (Xiao 2001, p. 115). The use of this term in this paper emphasises the fact that laws must be transplanted and implemented in a manner that it is likely to fit into the local cultural and ideological inheritance so as to be fully appreciated and respected.

Developing countries seeking to benefit from the global industrialisation trends, emphasise IPRs. They introduce IPRs regimes from foreign countries or from the international community. That raises issues related to the domestication of IPRs. The legal domestication often involves for the newly-introduced legal concepts not only a reflection of the form of the foreign law but also an adjustment to the local legal culture. The spirit of the law plays an important role in both the development and reform of local laws, and exerts a decisive effect on the successful domestication of transplanted laws: the spirit of the law provides an ideological yardstick, measuring and guiding the coordination and integration of the domestic laws and those transplanted (Song 2006). China's practice demonstrates that it is relatively easy to transplant IP laws, or even the "know-how" involved in IPR implementation, (the "hardware system" of the rule of law). However, to adequately adopt the system, it is necessary to fully integrate the underlying value of the IPRs regime (the "software system"), including the spirit and the concepts of IPRs that support the hardware system (Zhang 2005). China, after decades of IP legislation endeavour, has generally succeeded in introducing the "hardware system" of IPRs through legal transplants; however, in terms of "software system" that sustains its IPR infrastructure, China still has a long way to go before realising the objectives of its national IPR strategy. In China's domestication of IP laws, two main concerns merit attention: the cultivation of the spirit of the law and the promotion of consciousness of legal culture. These are detailed below.

Cultivation of the Spirit of the Law

In domesticating the transplanted IP laws, indiscriminate application of foreign rules or models may not be plausible. Rather, selections and adaptations are expected, making rules that suit a domestic IPRs regime, and incorporating the foreign laws into the constitution of existing laws (Gong 2000). The process of domestication involves the rational pursuit of legal civilisation and the reconstruction of the local legal culture. Because of the time-consuming nature of this process, although China first introduced foreign IP laws into the country a century ago, such laws have only exerted an influence on public life in China since the 1990s.

The constitution of IP laws has garnered worldwide attention and remarkable achievements have been made in this respect, as confirmed by Dr Árpád Bogsch, former Director General of WIPO. The purpose of the transplant and domestication of IP law is to advocate for a spirit of innovation and respect for IPRs. Properly domesticated IP law incorporates both advanced thought from Western culture, specifically the prioritisation of people and private rights, and a reasonable core of local tradition to achieve a balance between ideal and reality. As the cultural environment that gave birth to IP laws cannot be recreated in China, as discussed above, and the domestic legal literacy campaign has not been fully fulfilled, China has failed to achieve legal culture transformation through IPR domestication.

Promotion of Legal Culture

If regarded purely as a collection of legal norms, the value and range of an IPRs regime would to a great extent be underestimated. Besides the spirit of law, an IPRs regime should also reflect the legal consciousness of the public, including the common belief and public opinions, which should be relied on as the ideological basis of IP laws. Jean-Jacques Rousseau (1712–1778) stated that "the most important of all which is graven neither on marble nor on brass, but in the hearts of the citizens; which that creates the real constitution of the state; which every day takes on new powers; which when other laws decay or die out, restores them or takes their place, and keeps a people in the ways in which it was meant to go" (Rousseau 2003, p. 46). Such a belief in IP law may be viewed as a "live" IP law existing in the life of the society.

The transplant of modern IP laws into China is relatively recent; thus, the process of domestication has just begun. This legal transplant thrives on the public force of the government and the initiatives of elite intellectuals; however, most ordinary citizens pay little attention to the transplant beyond the extent to which it affects their own interests. It indicates that although the legal norm was established during the domestication of foreign IP laws, a strong and prevailing legal belief is still in urgent need.

9.3 Transformation of IP Legal Culture in Contemporary China

Legal culture provides a vivid representation of the internal logic and spirit of a country's legal system (Gong 1998). In contemporary China, the domestication of IP laws provides us with a glimpse into the overall modernisation of its rule of law. With the rising of a new legal system, cultural transformation and reconstruction, marked by a new orientation towards the cognition, spirit and evaluation of law, are indispensable.

The innovation of IPRs culture manifests as the recognition of the humanistic spirit of the law. The contemporary humanism developing out of the spirit of the classical natural law "refers to the supreme concept of human rights protection, and embodies the people-oriented and rights centred value" (Qu 2002). Thus, the individualism, rationalism and liberalism advocated by modern thinkers are the driving forces of private legal culture. However, these concepts call for contemporary interpretations under the present legal institution. They are explored in further details below.

9.3.1 Individualism and Legal Standards

The present-day standard outlook of private law is individualism, marking a change from previous eras. The individualist standard of modern private law is influenced by a society intent on realising individual goals. However, the new individualist standard of contemporary private law is a product of social attitudes, which emphasise that the individual, as an independent subject, is responsible to society and must therefore respect other members of society. Amid changes in the IPR legal system, the "private standard remains fixed" (Yi 2003, p. 178). However, IPR, as private rights, have changed, developing from single-subject rights to multiple-subject rights in modern laws. The private individuals entitled to IPRs (subjects of equal status) include creators, disseminators and users of intellectual achievements (Patterson and Linberg 1991, pp. 49–55). And it is the intention of IPR legislature to strike a legal balance between these stake holders.

9.3.2 Liberalism and IPRs Protection

Liberalism, or liberal thought, freedom of thought, is a doctrine of political philosophy whose fundamental aspect is the defence of individual freedom and private initiatives. Liberalism is deemed as the cornerstone of IPRs considering that it guarantees freedom of thought, which, in return, encourages intellectual creations. Therefore, freedom of thought is the premise of intellectual creation and associated rights, and IP legislation is introduced in the service of liberalism. In IP laws, liberalism is manifest in the recognition and protection of creators' and users' rights to exchange ideas and otherwise disseminate information. At the same time, autonomy of will, as a principle of private law, is the philosophical undertone of liberalism. As such, private law requires that IPRs protection guarantee freedom of thought (including freedom of creation and freedom of expression). According to American scholars, IPRs and freedom of thought are two sides of the same coin, the former addressing property ownership and the latter addressing the social nature of political rights. These two elements are bound together by their shared importance to knowledge dissemination, with one focusing on limiting unauthorised use of IP and the other defending liberalism (Patterson and Linberg 1991, pp. 49–55).

9.3.3 Rationalism and IPRs Legislative Objectives

Rationalism is an important aspect of justice in the social system. The rational pursuit of justice in IP legislation is reflected in the relationship between private rights and the public welfare. IP law serves the public interest and social justice by promoting both cultural and technological development and the dissemination of knowledge and by providing compensation for creative activities in the form of private rights, thereby addressing the social demand for intellectual achievement (Gellian 1990).

In spite of that, rationalism, which should have been instantiated in the operation of the IPRs regime has in fact not been fully appreciated. China can be taken here as an example: IPRs, taking in general the form of private property rights, have been enhanced increasingly by China's domestic legislation and international conventions, which inevitably reduce the IPRs available in the public domain and hence intensify conflicts of rights between creators and users of intellectual products. While catering to the international IPRs regime, China has no better choice but to adopt strong protection for IPRs as favoured by most industrial economies, leading to an imbalance of interests between China and its Western peers. As a result, China's current IPRs regime, beset with domestic conflicts and international pressures is in urgent need of renewal by reiterating individualism, liberalism, and rationalism as the underpinning philosophy of the IPRs regime.

Given its place in international law, the development of IPRs culture involves the interaction of pluralistic legal cultures. Recognised widely as the paragon of institutional civilisation, IP laws worldwide feature high compatibility and transplantability. Nevertheless, they reflect differing experiences of various countries in their IPRs regime construction and in the efforts made for promoting their economic and technological development. The global integration and assimilation of IPRs regimes are observed by American scholar Lawrence Friedman as "the prevailing of modern legal culture" (Friedman 1994, p. 242). The prevalence of IP culture in China depends on three preconditions, which are detailed below.

To begin with, a legal civilisation knowing no national border has to be established and accepted by all members of human communities. The protection of IPRs rightly involves a global legal infrastructure and set of norms that is approachable by every nation in the world. Legal infrastructure and norms should be a juxtaposition of valuable experience gained by every sovereign state from their trial and errors in IP legislation and enforcement. It should also respect their mutual interests despite differing legal sources that result from their various historical legacies and legal practice (Gong 2000). Therefore, the IP culture aspired to should not be Western-centred, nor should it fall prey to national chauvinism. Rather, a universal applicability of IPR principles and rules must be attained based on legal beliefs common to all countries. In the case of China, the introduction of legal values trusted by all people might be the first step ahead.

Besides this, the valuable experience of Western legal civilisations has to be drawn on heavily. The Western world is the cradle of IPRs and the major beneficiary of the international IPRs regime. Its success lies in having defined the basis of the private law system: individualism, liberalism and rationalism running throughout the IPRs regime. Among all the barricades stopping China from having a widespread IPRs culture, inadequate research into Western IPR experience is a prominent one.

Finally, the rational elements of Chinese traditional culture have to be turned to. In the history of its legal civilisation, China has achieved a full-fledged public law system while suffering from an excessively backward private law culture. Scholars attribute the contrast to China's time-honoured legal tradition valuing the group, rather than the individualist, standard and social norms rather than rules-governed political philosophy. As a result, the legal infrastructure in China has long featured "rule by law", under which the governing authorities may execute law where they find it to be convenient, rather than "rule of law", which secures a non-arbitrary form of governance. For Chinese people, in the past and present, lawsuits are in general their last resort since face-to-face confrontations clash with their collectivist beliefs (Zhang 1999). As discussed above, historical inertia in traditional Chinese culture curbs the thriving of IPRs culture.

However, values of traditional Chinese culture should never be overlooked. As a Chinese scholar aptly noted, harmonious function with human kindness, introspective nipping an evil in the bud, and the plot theory, namely, each circumstance affecting the direction of the subsequent circumstance, actually contain meanings that transcend culture and time (Ji 1999). In the re-examination of China's cultural legacies, scholars have identified certain characteristics of traditional Chinese culture that coincide with the IPRs culture of promoting knowledge innovation and sharing intellectual achievements. These include the common desire for ideal personality and aspirations to creativity and innovation (Li 2007).

Traditional culture, as an inherent mode of behaviour and ideas, has an overpowering/a pervasive influence that can hardly be ignored. However, for the survival and development of laws introduced from foreign soil, two approaches may be adopted simultaneously. The first is to analyse the traditional culture, identify positive elements in that culture that may promote the effective operation of the adopted system so as to incorporate them into the new legal culture. This may be an effective method to introduce modern systems with the power to influence the public consciousness and to promote the transformation of traditional culture through functional mechanisms. The second method involves analysing and comparing the traditional culture and the foreign culture and either imposing the recipient country's own understanding, interpretation and application of ideas on the implanted legal culture or endowing the imported ideas with entirely new meanings in theory or in practice (Huang 2001). In the present context, drawing on Western legal culture, identifying the reasonable core existing in Chinese traditional culture and integrating the common achievements of human legal civilisations are the solutions to China's IPR transformation and reconstruction.

To facilitate such reform and transformation, economic and social resources shall be made full use of (Li 2003), since the coordinated and comprehensive use of these resources, including both endogenous and exogenous variables, drives the modernisation of IPRs culture, as detailed below.

9.3.4 Knowledge Economy Market Dynamics

IP laws came into being as a result of developments in science and technology as well as in the commodity economy, which combine to form the commercialisation of sci-tech achievements. Karl Marx's labour value theory holds that the creation of a "surplus product" constitutes the material foundation for the development of a society, and the "surplus products" are created by "productive labour." From this perspective, intellectual labour is also "productive labour" that "confers more values that it possesses." In the information era, "production" may be understood in a broader sense referring to the production of both tangible commodities and intangible goods such as services, knowledge, information and technology (Li 1999, p. 39), given that tangible and intangible goods enjoy equal commercial significance. The endogenous impetus of the market economy inevitably leads to the formation of a legal culture featuring individualism, liberalism and rationalism. Therefore, "the modernisation of legal culture would be achieved in a specific country, quickly or slowly, so long as it is committed to forming a modern market economy, promoting economic modernisation, and establishing its own market economy system" (Li 2003).

Historically, modern IPRs culture is part of Western legal culture; however, from a sociological angle, such a culture may be attributed to the knowledge market in general. The commercialisation, marketisation and industrialisation of knowledge products require corresponding IPRs cultures and IPR laws. The humanist standard advocated by IPRs cultures is not unique to or solely derived from Western countries but is rather a cultural requirement of the market economy. Therefore, the transformation of China's IPRs culture is modern in quality rather than specifically Western.

The Assurance of IP Policies and Institutional Environment

IP laws serve as a social policy instrument, through which the government, in the name of the state, provides guidance and formulates rules for the creation, ownership, utilisation and management of IPR resources with institutional configuration and policy arrangement. IP policies feature a result-orientated approach, aiming at laying out feasible and agreeable guidelines towards a certain problem of public concern and bringing them into action. As American scholar Frank Fischer holds, objectives and the means to realise them are primal concerns of any public policy regardless how and where a public policy is made (Fischer 2003, p. 3). That is to say, every public policy is made and implemented for certain policy objectives.

In the ecosystem of public policies, IP policies never work alone. Other policies involving culture and education, industrial economy, science and technology, and foreign trade all serve to promote knowledge innovation and intellectual wealth. Creating such a policy and institutional environment cannot be more important for the formulation of a sound legal culture. Japan, for instance, followed German Civil

Code in the 1900s and later introduced an American Constitution in the post-World War II period, remoulding its original legal culture through political authority and the implementation of relevant policies, and thus greatly improving the compatibility of Japan's legal culture (Fu 2003). On the other hand, in China, for quite a long time, the nationwide IPR initiative, with "respecting knowledge, promoting innovation and protecting intellectual property" as its theme, has been under-performing in both social acceptance and effectiveness. With reference to Japan and China, it can be noted that only when codes of law and policies integrate with cultural renovation can the legitimate rights of IP owners be secured and non-arbitrary use of IPRs be ensured (Liu et al. 2007).

IPR Empowerment and Promotion

Legal literacy and legal empowerment pave the way for the modernisation of IP laws. Effective implementation of IP laws, as well as supporting administrative measures, are of equal significance in IPR knowledge acquisition and IPR empowerment, which cultivate public perception and awareness of IPR rules. Studies and research show that the public gains access to IPR knowledge mainly from their working experience or school education, or by self-learning, media campaign, social promotion and so on (Liu et al. 2007). From this aspect, Japan's efforts are worth learning: the Ministry of Education, Culture, Sports, Science and Technology of Japan requires universities with law schools and colleges offering IPR courses across the nation to participate in the training of IPR professionals. The Japan Patent Office also initiates a package of IPR education programs, including compiling IPR textbooks targeting senior and junior high students, adults, and people of all social strata, holding seminars, and funding research on IPR education. As for the Ministry of Economy, Trade and Industry, efforts have been made to encourage the industrial, academic and research sectors to jointly develop IPR specific courses along with corresponding coursebooks. As a result, half a million standard IPR textbooks were published in just the year 2003. Moreover, since 1974, when the first Invention Clubs for school-age children were created by the Institute of Invention and Innovation (JIII), there are now more than 159 fully functional clubs in 47 prefectures around Japan. With all its efforts, JIII reinforces its mutual understanding and cooperation with local governments, with the Ministry of Education, with schools and enterprises. In addition, activities held by JIII including IPR further education projects, invention awards, invention and innovation exhibitions, invention contests and invention clubs also contribute to the creation of a social environment that fully respects and appreciates IPRs culture (Shen 2005).

Drawing on Japan's experience, China may correspondingly start with enhancing IPR values among teenagers by integrating IPR education into the curriculum in order to foster new ideas and innovations. Besides this, for the general public, in particular entrepreneurs, extensive IPR education and empowerment should be undertaken so as to improve the market environment of IPR related products and national IPR competitiveness. Furthermore, in academic circles, studies and research on IPRs should be further enhanced to provide theoretical guidance for China's future IPR endeavour (Liu and Zhou 2006).

References

Abe, Kōji. 1992. Similarities and differences of copyright laws and their causes in different countries. Trans. Genquan Zhu. *Global Law Review*

Bodenheimer, E. 1974. *Jurisprudence, the Philosophy and Method of the Law*. Cambridge: Harvard University Press

Bonfante, Pietro. 1992. *Istituzioni di Diritto Romano*. Trans. Feng Huang. Beijing: China University of Political Science and Law Press

Cohen, Jean L. and Andrew Arato. 1992. *Civil Society and Political Theory*. Cambridge, MA: Press of MIT.

Fischer, Frank. 2003. *Evaluating Public Policy*. Beijing: China Renmin University Press

Friedman, Lawrence M. 1994. *The Legal System*. Trans. Qiongying Li et al. Beijing: China University of Political Science and Law Press

Fu, Jingkun. 2003. Legal transplant and legal culture about civil law revision. *Journal of Shen Zhen University (Humanities & Social Sciences)* 6

Gellian, Davis. 1990. Public interest in collective management of power. *Copyright Reference* 2

Gong, Pixiang. 2000. Globalisation and modernisation of China's legal system. *Chinese Journal of Law* 6

Gong, Pixiang. 1998. The conceptual framework of legal modernisation. *Science of Law* 4

Hayek, Friedrich A. 1958. *Individualism and Economic Order*. Chicago: The University of Chicago Press

Hayek, Friedrich A. 2001. *Hayek Selections*. Trans. Zhenglai Deng. Beijing: Capital University of Economics and Business Press

He, Zengke. 1994. Evolution of the Concept of the Civil Society, *Social Sciences in China* 5

Huang, Wenyi. 2001. Multiple perspectives on the interaction of multiple legal cultures. *Jilin University Journal (Social Science Edition)* 1

Ji, Weidong. 1999. Developments and inner contradictions of Chinese legal culture. In *Sociology of Law*, ed. Dun Li. Beijing: China University of Political Science and Law Press

Li, Jingwen. 1999. *The New Era of Knowledge Economy*. Shanghai: Shanghai Far East Publishers

Li, Shengwei. 2003. Motivations of the modernisation of Chinese traditional legal culture. In *Forum on Fronts of Jurisprudence*, ed. Wenxian Zhang. Beijing: Science Press

Li, Xingcheng. 2001. Traditional culture and traditional culture in the new period. In *Innovative Countries and Intellectual Property Culture*, ed. Minsheng Guo. http://www.sipo.gov.cn/dfzz/henan/tslm/xsll/200604/t20060421-36488.htm. Accessed 10 Aug 2007

Liang, Huixing. 1997. From modern civil laws to contemporary civil laws. *Peking University Law Journal* 2

Liang, Zhiping. 1999. The past, present and future of laws in China. In *Sociology of Law*, ed. Dun Li. Beijing: China University of Political Science and Law Press

Liu, Hua and Zhou Ying. 2006. The level and goal of China's IPRs construction. *Intellectual Property* 3

Liu, Hua et al. 2007. Report on Chinese people's intellectual property awareness. In *The Blue Book of IPR in China*, ed. Handong Wu. Beijing: Peking University Press

Liu, Xing. 2004. Rethinking legal transplant. *Social Sciences in China* 5

Liu, Zuoxiang. 1999. *Theories on Legal Culture*. Beijing: The Commercial Press

Maine, Henry S. 1984. *Ancient Law*. Tran. Jingyi, Shen. Beijing: The Commercial Press

Marx, Karl and Friedrich Engels. 1960. *Marx-Engels Collected Works*. Beijing: People's Publishing House

Miller, David and Bogdanor, Vernon (eds.). 1992. *The Blackwell Encyclopaedia of Political Thought.* Trans. Zhenglai Deng. Beijing: China University of Political Science and Law Press

Montesquieu, Baron. de. 1994. *The Spirit of Laws.* Trans. Yanshen Zhang. Beijing: Business Press

Pan, Dasong. 1999. An investigation on the development of legal culture in modern China. In *Sociology of Law,* ed. Dun Li. Beijing: China University of Political Science and Law Press

Party, Willam F. 1986. *Fair Use Privilege in Copyright Law.* Washington D. C.: The Bureau of National Affairs

Patterson, L. Ray. and Stanley W. Linberg. 1991. *The Nature of Copyright: A Law of Users' Right.* Athens: The University of Georgia Press

Qiao, Keyu and Li Xiaoping. 1991. *Value of the Law.* Beijing: China University of Political Science and Law Press

Qu, Maohui. 2002. The basic idea of Chinese civil code. *Seeker* 5

Rousseau, Jean-Jacques. 2003. *Du Contrat Social.* Trans, Zhaowu He. Beijing: The Commercial Press

Shen, Wenqing. 2005. Technological development and IPRs. *Bulletin of National Natural Science Foundation of China* 3

Shen, Zongling. 1993. Law, value, justice and interests. *Peking University Law Journal* 5

Song, Yuanfang. 1991. *The History of Publishing in China.* Beijing: China Books Press

Song, Zhiguo. 2006. Analysis on the decreasing effect in China's IP law transplant about its reason. *Politics and Law* 5

Stehr, Nico. 1998. *Knowledge Society.* Trans. Xiaorong Ying. Shanghai: Translation Publishing House

The Universal Declaration of Human Rights. https://ccnmtl.columbia.edu/projects/mmt/udhr/article_19.html. Accessed 7 Jan 2020

Vandevelde, Kenneth. 1980. The new property of nineteenth century: The development of modern concept of property. *Buffalo Law Review*

Wang, Lijun. 2004. The definition of legal transplant. *Legal Forum 2*

Wang, Zhe. 1998. *A History of Political and Legal Theory.* Beijing: Peking University Press

Wu, Handong. 2003. The revolution of intangible property and the revolutionary intangible property law. *China Social Science*

Wu, Handong. 2005. *Study on the Fair Use of Copyright (Revised edition).* Beijing: China University of Political Science and Law Press

Xiao, Yaohui. 2001. The correlative investigation of law transplant and domestication. In *Transplant and Domestication of Laws,* ed. Qinhua He. Beijing: Legal Press China

Xin, Chunying. 2007. Theory and practice of legal transplant. *Northern Legal Science* 3

Yan, Cunsheng. 1999. *A New History of Western Legal Thoughts.* Shannxi: People's Education Press

Yi, Jiming. 2003. *Private Law Spirit and Institutional Choice.* Beijing: China University of Political Science and Law

Yi, Jun. 2006. Methodological individualism and private laws. *Chinese Journal of Law* 1

Yu, Ronggen. 1990. Problems in natural-law doctrine. *Taiwan Studies* 1

Yu, Ronggen. 1999. Reflections on Legal Culture in Ancient China. In *Sociology of Law*, ed. Dun Li. Beijing: China University of Political Science and Law Press

Zhang, Hongfeng. 2005. Of and Above the Globalisation and Localisation of Law. *Fujian Legal Science* 1.

Zhang, Zhongqiu. 1999. *Comparative Study of Chinese and Western Legal Culture.* Nanjing: Nanjing University Press

Chapter 10
Value Dimensions of IPRs Regimes

The legal value objectives and function mechanism of IPRs not only exist in the legal documents of IPRs in the form of legislative purposes and provisions, but also should be manifested in the application of intellectual property law and legal activities in the form of operational regulations and behavioural rules. Starting from the above idea, the analysis of the legal value of IPRs is mainly concerned with the conceptual instruments of relevant legal values, their substantive objectives, and the pathways to their realisation.

10.1 Conceptual Tools for the Value of IP Law

Value is a specific relation between the needs of subjects and adaptions of subject matter and satisfaction of the needs of the subjects. Legal value refers to a specific relation of needs and satisfaction between humans and law. As Karl Marx indicates that value, a universal concept, emerges from the relation between humans and external subject matter that meet their needs (Marx and Engels 1963). As an object created by humans, that is, an institutional product, the law certainly has a value relation with humans. The more it can meet various human needs, the more valuable it will be. Otherwise, its value will be zero or negative.

The study of the value of a law features two aspects: to observe the practical performance of a law and the realisation of its values; and to prioritise values within a law so as to make law an embodiment of the value, thus legalising the values (Xie 1993). The study of the value of law stems from the contradiction between the ideal and reality – in other words, what ought to be and what is. It can be argued that values in a law are an ideal value choice in law and the philosophical concept of value is brought into the domain of law. It should be noted that values in law are historical, periodical and selective, that the value of a law does not transcend time or history; and the assessment of law may adopt different angles which very much vary

H. Wu, *Theorising Intellectual Property Rights from Chinese Perspectives*,
https://doi.org/10.1007/978-981-96-5867-1_10

by ethos of age and historical norms. Values in law in different historical periods and with different realities show different choices and tendencies. Yet a value analysis of IPRs law is necessary both for its legislation and its implementation. In a strict sense, legislation is a state act guided by certain values and doctrines of law. In order to infinitely narrow the gap between what legally ought to be, the ideals, and what is, the reality, a proper and thorough exploration of theory of values in law. Besides, the values in law are also the guiding principle in law enforcement activities and he same legal provision, enforced orienting towards different value priorities, incurs different enforcement results. Furthermore, the observance of the law is hinged on the understanding of its value since a law regime maintained purely by mandatory enforcement may not be sustainable in the long run. As the values of legal ideals are always higher than those of legal realities, values in law are also the driving force of legal evolution. At this very moment, a trend of diversity in values of law has emerged and this inevitably will give rise to conflicts of legal values. This requires us to solve, that is, coordinate, assess and choose values.

In spite of the disagreement over its definition, consensus has been reached on the fact that the value of a law is reflected and can only be properly appreciated within the social network of human beings and laws. Therefore, any value analysis of the law intrinsically involves three elements: "the relationship between the law and human beings", "the effect of law on the human beings" and" the evaluation of the law's effectiveness by human beings" (Yan 1991). Some Chinese scholars go further than the three elements and define the value of a law as values promoted by a law; values possessed by a law; and criteria to assess these values when various values are in conflict (Shen 1993).

Starting from the conceptual content of the values of a law, it is possible to have a clear understanding of the content of the basic study of values of IPR laws: Firstly, the basic source of the legal value of intellectual property. The relationship between the subject and object of legal values is established within a certain basic framework, and the formation and evaluation of legal values are inevitably influenced by social, cultural, and economic values. IP law, as an institutional norm regulating intellectual property interactions, is inevitably required to establish relevant evaluation methods, value objectives, and ways of realising them in and in accordance with a particular cultural, social, and economic environment. In the early construction of IP law, cultural and economic values have always served as the primary source of values for intellectual property, a new system of private rights. With a well-developed commodity economy and a good creative culture as the background, intellectual products with intellectual creation as the core guaranteed by IP law can be commercialised and capitalised. And also, only in an environment with a flourishing culture of private rights could, the early specially granted license for printing and franchise privilege have evolved into an institutional model with private property rights, which has in turn contributed to further improvement of the social and cultural context on which they are based. The moment for the legal value to be best expressed and realised is when the law and the environment are in harmony. The study of legal values will be vague and scattered if it is divorced from the necessary research on the underlying sources.

Secondly, the evaluation subject of the value of IP law. The subject is at the core of the evaluation: its absence deprives values of their significance, and its perspectives greatly influence the results. Therefore, the dialectic unification of subjectivity and objectivity must be respected. In other words, we need to rely on the evaluation of the subject to form relative stable value objectives and description of the subject-object relations, and at the same time we also need an absolute orientation that transcends the subject so as to form the objectivity of the value objectives. Throughout the formation, development and reform of IP laws, in fact, the evaluating subjects always adjust the relevant value objectives of relevant laws according to the relevant historical and social context. Historically, IP laws were based on rules that prioritise order and predictability in a national pursuit of market control, whereas IP laws of today's globalised world rely on justice-focused values. Furthermore, whereas developed countries have forged an international mainstream of order-first rules, developing countries tend to focus instead on reducing the injustice and unfairness of the current systems. Regardless of the perspectives of individual countries, all IP laws must be based on universal values, including the protection of private rights and the balance of conflicting interests.

Thirdly, ways to realise the value of IP law. The study on value objectives is the core of the research on legal values, and the value objectives and the corresponding value systems constitute the unity of the value of legal objectives and the value of legal means. Value objectives express abstract value relations as concrete relations of rights and obligations. In IP law, the analysis of value objectives necessarily reveals the value of IP as distinct from other systems, and the value objectives pursued by IP law are necessarily closely related to its superordinate value. For instance, the value of justice has served as a counterweight to the reality of the increasing expansion of IPRs at the level of legal theory. And a growing number of new systems and institutional studies have emphasised the reasonableness and justice of the system as the basis for value judgments, as opposed to the previous value of efficiency based on simple economic interests. The system of rights limitation and public domain, with the value of justice as its intension, has played an increasingly significant role in balancing interests and safeguarding rights at the level of IPRs regime norms. The realisation of value, which is directly tied to the value objectives, is also an essential component of the research on legal values. The realisation of value is the end of value theory and the link between value theory and institutional structure. Value realisation of IP laws is markedly different from the value realisation of other systems. In other words, values and ideas that are inconsistent with IPRs regime constantly accompany the existence of IP laws, and there are issues with the realisation of value objectives at the institutional level. For example, in certain developing countries, the mismatch between the culture of IPRs and its legal transplantation has resulted in obvious institutional exclusion and inadaptability, gravely undermining the authority and value of law. For the study on the value of IP law, the realisation of value needs to be prioritised over the conclusion.

10.2 Substantive Values of IP Law

The nature, purpose, and function of the legal system are embodied in its legal value, as can be shown from the hierarchical analysis of the concept of legal values. Each level has a unique meaning and yet they are closely related. What values a law promotes is in fact an issue concerning the nature and purpose of the law, as a law is not only a means to an end but also incorporates certain values, firstly among social values of different kinds and secondly between values of the same nature that a law promotes, there are bound to be conflicts and therefore there will be assessment, prioritisation and balance issues. Ancient and current, Western and Chinese thinkers and jurists have put forward myriad values of law, including justice, freedom, equality, security, order and efficiency. The values of IP law consist of both universal values for general laws and special values for specific area laws. It can be summarised as follows:

10.2.1 Justice

Justice is the primary value in any social institutions (Shen 1993) and its realisation is the top priority in IPRs protection. The concept of justice has accompanied the natural law theories throughout the history of Western legal thought. In a certain sense, natural law is seen as a belief in the pursuit of a just order, which has evolved into the foundation for the existence and legitimacy of rights protected by man-made laws. In modern legislation, IPRs are described as a natural right originating from intellectual activities. They derive naturally from the intellectual activities of creators and, freed from the fetter of granted feudal privileges, exist legally and are therefore in alignment with justice. Conversely, overlooking IPRs and allowing intellectual activities to go unpaid is to give rise to disorder in the field of intellectual production, leading to an unjust society.

While interpreting the value of justice, the foundation for the legitimacy of IP law is also described. Moreover, the emergence, change and development of IP law all need to be examined historically and judged in reality through the prism of justice. As far as the general legal characteristics go, IP laws contain the following justice values:

Firstly, justice in the legal personality of equal subjects. "Legal personality" refers to the subject's possession of legal rights and obligations. Equality is the presence of justice in the equal legal status of subjects. Engels once stated that "men should have equal rights in the state and in society" (Marx and Engels 1971, p. 668). He wrote that equality is a manifestation of justice and a principle in an ideal political or social system (ibid.). The spirit of equality in IP law is essentially identical to the principle of equality in private law, but also has its own value content. First, IPRs equality entails free choice in intellectual activities, and equal opportunities in acquiring a creator's rights, as any product of intellectual activities grants the creator IPRs. Second, IP law grants equal rights and obligations. This means that the subjects of interests, namely IP owners and IP users are independent, which establishes order in the structure of interests. IPRs are those of exclusive use, authorisation, statutory license and fair use. Under the principle of promoting the distribution of knowledge, IP policies and regulations grant specific legal rights and obligations to achieve fairness in the distribution of knowledge. Third, the equality of IPRs lies also in the equal protection of IPRs owned by foreigners. Copyright laws act on the principle of the "nationality of the writer" or "nationality of the works", and industrial property laws act on the principle of "residence" or "nationality." The national treatment of IP laws means that all people are equal under international law, and thus, foreigners are protected as equals.

Secondly, justice in benefit distribution. "Benefit distribution" refers to the distribution and arrangement of rights under the law. In this regard, fairness entails legal justice in sharing the benefits of intellectual wealth. It is a rather subjective criterion, as the determination of justice in terms of benefit distribution is usually based on generally accepted values, including "fairness" and "reasonableness" concerning economic interests (Zhang 1986, p. 22). In the field of traditional private law, there are classical expressions for the principle of fairness in legal language. For instance, equal treatment among subjects refers to that exchange shall be paid and mutually beneficial; reasonable consideration of economic interests means that the interests of all parties should be taken into consideration within the scope of the law; reasonable sharing of property liability means that when a person's property interest is harmed, compensation of equal value should be provided. In IPRs the principle of fairness is the manifestation of justice. It requires first of all the structure of the regime to balance and coordinate the interests of the creator, the disseminator and the user of IP. This balance and coordination are shown in the following two aspects: (1) it entails drawing a distinction between exclusive rights areas and non-exclusive rights areas. The subject matter of protection of IPRs are intellectual products, and not all intellectual products are subject matter of IPRs protection. Legislations have drawn a line between situations in which the creator enjoys the exclusive use and benefits of the property and exceptions to this rule, where IP is best left open for public use. (2) The non-exclusive areas refer to public domain of intellectual products and the excluded areas of the subject matter of IPRs, and this kind of human knowledge resources are open to use by all. Fairness is also seen in the limits imposed on exclusive rights. IPRs are exclusive and absolute rights; however, they are restricted by region, time and power. IP laws are meant to promote the distribution of IP and are thus described by American scholars as the law of balance between the creator, disseminator and user (Patterson and Lindberg 1991, p. 2).

Thirdly, justice of order in rights arrangement. To maintain order, the law must be stable, consistent and adaptable (Li 2001, p. 95). Orderliness and appropriateness are the values required by justice. Intellectual products, that is, the subject matter of IPRs, are "incorporeal" and incapable of being possessed naturally or controlled physically, and therefore need law to make institutional arrangement as "pure legal possession" in the case of intellectual property, giving special protection of the intellectual properties controlled by their creators. This is the legal order of the creation, dissemination and use of intellectual products established by intellectual property laws. Legal arrangement regarding its "rightful possession" or "possession noumenon", as Kant put it (Kant 1991, p. 58), are thus necessary to provide differentiated protection for property that is inherently out of reach of the creator's strict control. Legal order in the creation, dissemination and use of IP is thus established through IP law. The just order that IP laws impose contains the following: first of all, the order of defining rights, which means clear boundaries are defined over the intangible intellectual resources to reflect the state's unified rules to maintain the stability of intellectual property; Second, the order of transactions of rights, which means through the intellectual products use system regulating the intellectual properties transaction activities and promoting the dissemination and utilisation of intellectual knowledge and technology; Third, the order of rights protection which means through supervision over obligation fulfilment and accountability for violations provides order in protection. Protection of IPRs is the most important content of the order of justice.

10.2.2 Efficiency

Economic analysis of law provides us with a new aspect in our understanding and evaluating the institutional function of IP laws. The core idea of legal economics is efficiency According to the economic analysis of the law, the rules created by the law have implicit costs for different kinds of behaviour, so the consequences of these rules can be analysed as a response to these implicit costs (Cooter and Ulen 1994, p. 166). It is not difficult for us to conclude from the history of the evolution of the legal system that justice has always been the fundamental value objective of law, and justice is the primary value of the legal system just as truth is to the intellectual system (Qiao and Li 1991, p. 160). However, the law's justice value does not completely cover the efficiency value provided by the law, and the ultimate attainment of justice does not equate to the realisation of maximum efficiency. Studies of law and economics show that law which is deeply rooted in economic life should not only function to maintain social justice but also undertake the mission to ensure the effective distribution of rights and growth of social wealth. Therefore, justice and efficiency have become the dual value objectives of modern law. In a sense, all legal issues are essentially manifestations and requirements of economic relations, and the law itself reflects the fundamental rules and principles of economics. For example, from the aspect of legislative requirement, only what is in accordance with objectivity is right and, the top priority of the legislation that is oriented to a market economy is to respect its objective law through laws and regulations (Jiang 1995). Still, whether a legal system is accurately reflecting the conditions of economic life of society and whether it is capable of promoting social and economic development is dependent on an assessment of its efficiency, that is, the economic analysis of the law. That is to say, the fundamental spirit of the legal system should be discussed from an economic perspective and the reform of the legal system should be promoted with the goal of maximising efficiency.

Efficiency is both the ideological foundation and the value objective of IP law. The establishment and implementation of a great number of IP laws all can find their explanation under the principle of efficiency. Patent law's efficiency basis is like that of the dynamic theory of property rights and suggests that protection of property rights has the economic function of inducing efficient use of resources (Posner 1987, p. 22). Patent rights spur intellectual activity and production. However, too low standard for patents would invite "garbage" patents which generate no benefits. Granting patents to technological achievements and setting necessary threshold standards will be helpful to encourage technological innovation and raising the use value of patents and thereby maintaining the efficiency of the patent system; In copyright law, efficiency is demonstrated in the chain of creation, dissemination and use. Aiming to protect private rights and advance knowledge dissemination, legislators, through the protection, use and limitation of copyright to achieve optimal distribution of information resources. The main benefit of trademarks is a "reduced search cost for consumers by guarantee of standardised quality" (Cheng 2001, pp. 33–37). Search cost is a type of transaction cost generated by conducting research on product quality prior to purchase. Trademarks aid in reducing this cost by functioning as signs indicating the origins and reputation of the products. Proper distribution of trademark rights entails a weighing of costs and benefits. Whereas a "first use" approach, particularly one that prioritises "the actual use of designation as mark" over "a symbolic one" (Li 2003, p. 288), is more in the spirit of efficiency, a "first to file" approach focuses on the registration of trademarks. A protected yet unused trademark generates no profit; however, it also generates lower inspection and administrative costs in a "first to file" system than in a "first to use" system, rendering a "first to file" system more efficient under such circumstances.

The pursuit for efficiency in IP laws is manifest in their reasonable and effective distribution of rights in the design.in other words, achieving an equilibrium among the subjects in the rights system. In microeconomics, equilibrium is a form of interaction wherein each party achieves its maximum benefit; if achieved, such equilibrium tends to endure (Cooter and Ulen 1994, p. 22). Equilibrium is a common social phenomenon. Everyone seeks a combination of products in economic activities that can satisfy the greatest demand through the exchange; They set a price that restrains each other in order to satisfy their demands, eventually leading to a situation where supply and demand are equal. Last but not least, the price is unchanged, which is a state of continuous and efficient increase in social wealth. Equilibrium is the basic requirement of efficiency in a system design. In an IPRs regime, it is a balance between the protections and limitations of IPRs and is meant to eliminate conflicts in the creator's, disseminator's, and user's interests. In a balanced distribution system, the creator holds the primary rights. The law grants the creator private property rights, which are the most economical, effective and enduring incentive for innovation. The disseminator holds secondary rights in the intermediate between the creator and the user, and the disseminator's intellectual or material input is necessary to the efficiency of knowledge distribution. The user's rights are also important. As users are both consumers of existing products and potential creators of future products, granting them free access to IP within limits motivates their own intellectual activities. In summary, legislators seek to ensure the rights of the creator, disseminator and user, to maximise the interests of all of the parties and to strike the proper balance in the distribution of resources.

10.2.3 Innovation

IP Law arises from the combined factors of science and technology, economy and law and it solves the issue of where knowledge as a resource belongs and it is a mechanism of encouraging and regulating interests. With the legislation of IPRs, the right of ownership over knowledge is defined as a resource, which requires a mechanism of incentives and interest coordination for its full function. In this regard, the era of knowledge-based economy also means an era of intellectual property. Knowledge-based economy is an intellectual economy with science and technology as the most important factor of production. The driving force of the development of knowledge-based economy lies in scientific and technological innovation, which is inseparable from the innovation of property rights system (Wu 2001). It can be considered that IP law itself is the product of institutional innovation in the field of private law; at the same time, the value objective of IP law should be innovation-oriented.

Firstly, a fully functioning IPRs regime highlights innovation-orientated values, which finds theoretical explanation in economic theory. Joseph Schumpeter (1883–1950), an Austrian economist, reviewed innovation with economic perspective. In his work *The Theory of Economic Development* at the beginning of the twentieth century, he defined innovation as the novel combination of production factors and conditions. Since the 1950s, his theory has been developed by others to cover both technological innovation and institutional innovation. "Technological innovation" values the promotion of economic development by science and technology, whereas "institutional innovation" refers to the interplay of technology and social institution in economic development. Institutional innovation is a key factor in stimulating technological innovation and advancing the economy (Ling 2001 pp. 17–21). "Institutional innovation" generally refers to the evolution of new institutions in the pursuit of increased opportunities for profits. It includes the innovation of rules and regulations in industrial systems, property rights, enterprises, economic management and market operation system. Institutional innovation, once being sustained and accumulated, is the basis for and guarantee of a comprehensive innovation system. In the new institutional economics theory, institutional change is understood to be the process of replacing one system with a more efficient one. It includes two types: one is "induced institutional change", that is, the change or substitution of institutional construction, or the creation of new institutions, which are spontaneously initiated, organised or implemented by individuals or groups. The second is "mandatory institutional change,' which is realised by the introduction of government orders, laws and policies (Coase 1994). In the innovation system, institutional innovation is the foundation and guarantee. Intellectual innovation, including scientific and technological innovations and cultural innovations, promotes economic advancement through the integration of science and technology, culture and economy. It involves the use and commercialisation of new technologies and requires protection, regulation and limitations through relevant institutions. Thus, intellectual property laws are, in part, a response to innovation and changes in private law. They form a legal institution to protect intellectual innovative activities.

Secondly, the value of innovation is the soul value of IP law. Values of law vary with legal systems and their different development phases. In a specific era, a particular legal system will contain a number of different values, and their respective focuses will be different. For example, criminal legislation manifests order and justice, civil law directly stipulates equality and honesty; economic law focuses on efficiency and in the era of acknowledge economy, the intellectual property law system reflects is independent dominant value, that is, innovation value (Chen and Wang 2004). As the modern economy relies heavily on the production, distribution and use of knowledge and information, innovation has become a major characteristic of the knowledge economy and has attained unprecedented importance and development. Any party seeking an advantage in high-tech competition must master innovation, which has become a standard of modern human activity. Innovation is present not only in human–nature interactions but also in human–human and human–society interactions. Indeed, innovation has become a major category of relations in general. And "innovation" as a concept in the "historical view" is a result of the pursuit of human aspirations. The historical view needs to respond to and resolve the basic issues of driving force, mechanism, and laws in the process of historical development, while innovation continues to evolve in the long process of historical movements and broad social practices. In a word, the concept of "innovation" is a comprehensive and insightful explanation of the knowledge-based economy, so it can be regarded as the basic value category of IP law.

Thirdly, the value of innovation is demonstrated in both IPR policymaking and legislation. China has elevated innovation to the strategic level, overarching the setting of its blueprint, and guiding the making of national policies including that of IP. Innovation-prompted social relations aim to respect innovation while protecting private rights. It should be noted that the IPR laws mainly regulate the social relations arising from innovation, showing respect for innovation, and protection of private rights as their purposes. For example, in patent law, this means protecting the first commercial use and profits of a novel technological invention, which are the fruits of "technology commercialisation." In copyright law, the first publication and profits of creative works, the outcomes of "works commercialisation", are protected. Likewise, trademarks protect interests such as product reputation. Trademarks in themselves may not represent innovation; however, they protect the first commercial use and profits along with the consumer's interests in first recognition. IP laws establish IPRs as private property rights and provide prior right protection, which protect individual innovation and promote the sustainable development of social innovation. Meanwhile the cost of innovation can remain at a rational level. These laws also set boundaries on private property rights, such as by defining a limited duration of patents and the exhaustion of rights, thereby bringing IP into the public domain, where it may encourage further creative activities.

In conclusion, innovation is the cause of and the ideal pursued by the establishment of IP law. In the process of realising this value, institutional innovation and reforms are also accomplished in IP law. As a result, in the age of the knowledge-based economy, the value of innovation is the dominating value expressed and promoted by IP law.

10.3 Core Values of Modern IP Law

It has taken nearly four hundred years for IP law to mature from its inception to become a universal legal system in the world. Throughout this time, human social life has undergone profound changes: the rapid development of modern science and technology has had an unparalleled influence on people's knowledge and culture; the highly developed modern commodity economy promotes the formation of a new international economic order and the world market. As a result of the development of this situation, legislators from different countries have to concentrate on reforming their IP laws. At the same time, the values of IP law have also undergone significant changes throughout time, from the early ethics of distribution to the later ethics of creation to the modern ethics of development. As the contemporary IP law adopts the property order and justice in distribution as its values, then the modern IP law, due to legal globalisation and economic integration, has turned to justice in creation and the development order as the core values.

10.3.1 Benchmark of Legal Values

Modern IP law establishes a criterion for evaluating legal values with the sanctity of private law and the balance of interests as the core. The dual value objectives of protecting the legitimate rights of creators and promoting the widespread use of intellectual products are represented in the legislative purpose of IPRs. It resolves the conflict between the exercise of the exclusive rights of creators and the promotion of the full use of intellectual resources in terms of the fundamental institutional functions and balances the interests of creators, disseminators, and users. Based on these value objectives, modern IP law should create the following fundamental principles to evaluate legal values:

The first principle is the inviolability of private rights. Private rights, as corresponding to public rights, or state power, involves various civil law rights enjoyed by private individuals (including both natural and legal persons). The inviolability of private rights espouses that various private rights, including IPRs, are respected and fully protected by national laws. Such principle reflects in every aspect the achievement of 'human rightism,' which, as the humanism of the twenty-first century, safeguards human rights, embodies the values of people-oriented and rights-based, and regards private rights as the basic right of human rights (Qu 2002, p. 5). In practice, the establishment of an IPRs regime is guided by the following principles. First, an IPRs regime is private rights orientated. IPRs are rights of intellectual intangible property with basic attributes which are the same as that of property ownership, both of which should be classified as civil law rights. The primary objectives of human rights are to safeguard and realise private rights, as they are the foundation of political rights, social rights and other fundamental human rights. Second, an IPRs regime is based on institutionalised private rights. Although it establishes a series of procedural and public laws, it remains a private rights-orientated and substantive law-based system. Procedures of rights acquisition, alteration, management, remedy and so on. are all centred on the IP holders' rights, establishing a distinctive institutional and normative framework consistent with private rights. Third, an IPRs regime establishes its standard as rights centred. This legal standard refers to the relationship between rights and obligations. In an IPRs regime, rights determine obligations but not vice versa. To summarise, an IPRs regime is rights-centred, enabling legislation, with the protection of the IP owners' rights as its legislative priorities.

The other principle is the balance of interests between parties involved, rights and obligations, individuals and society. The balance of interests is the requirement of a civil and moral code, and reflects the guiding values of human rights and the public interests (Chapman 2001). Interests are the fundamental elements of rights. They are the precondition and the contents of rights, defining the orientation of rights and reflecting the legislative objectives. IP laws aim to strike a balance between interests of stakeholders by imposing limits on IPRs and regulating the use of IPRs. From the perspective of human rightism, the balance of interests pursued by an IPRs regime involves the following aspects. First, the rights over one's own IP should be balanced with the rights over others' IP. The rights over one's own IP are the IPRs of creators or inventors, that is, their exclusive rights over the use of their IP under the law. The rights of others' IP are disseminators' and users' rights to exercise limited control over others' IP according to legal provisions or under the authorisation of the rights owner. For balancing interests, the rights over one's own IP should coordinate with the rights over others' IP. To achieve that, equality and mutual respect should be adopted to ensure a mutually beneficial position for the exchange between IPRs holders and users, with the only exception of fair use. The reasonable sharing of IPRs interests should take into account the interests of all involved parties within the legal framework, which coordinate the rights of the creator, the disseminator and the user. Also, private interests are to be balanced with public interests. It is necessary to limit the exclusive rights of creators to ensure the fair use of intellectual products by the public. The use of others' intellectual products, be it for the freedom and dignity of humankind, for public education or for public health is legitimate and justifiable, in line with the major human rights conventions. Jillian Davis quotes a senior official of the World Intellectual Property Organisation (WIPO), saying that 'public interests, as good intentions, imply that the interests of the majority outweigh those of the individual, and individuals should give up personal gains for the common interests of society' (Davis 1990, p. 2).

10.3.2 Selection of Legal Values

In designing and implementing its intellectual law objectives and values, each country has gradually moved from universal values to particular values. Legislators as subjects of value also apply these values when they select and evaluate the established IPR values according to the unique social contexts and stages of development stages of their respective countries. The value of modern IP law has changed from the value of Western culture to the value of world civilisation and the Western model of the traditional IPRs regime is experiencing many revisions and adjustments due to value transplantation and value realisation. For instance, issues like the IPRs protection of traditional knowledge, the right to life and health, and the patent protection of pharmaceuticals all reflect important shifts in the value of modern IP law at the institutional level. As opposed to what the extreme radicals who are opposed to IPRs advocate, these changes, are not intended to subvert the existing and important legal systems, but hope to reexamine the fundamental value of IP law, its value objectives, and the correct ways of transplanting and realising the value of IPRs, in order to transform and change the value system of traditional IP law to meet the requirements of the current social, economic, and cultural environment, and to ensure the existence and value of IPRs.

The differences between the values of relatively disadvantaged countries and those of their more privileged counterparts escalate conflicts in modern IP law. Particularly with respect to legal claims related to the ethics of development and ethics of distribution: developing countries aspire to be incorporated into the international economic and legal order through IPR laws and to fully enjoy the benefits brought about by a global civilisation and advancements in science and technology. They believe that IPR laws should not set up new technological barriers and rights gaps through the means of private rights or monopoly (Zhang 2010, p. 82).[1] These countries propose that the law should instead focus on human rights protection, promoting the scientific and technological, cultural and economic development of the whole of human society and more reasonable distribution of intellectual resources. On the other hand, developed countries, based on their interest of maintaining their current advantages, tend to utilise the current IPR rule systems to restrict and exclude the attempt of redistribution of intellectual property sources. They therefore out of consideration of

[1] There exist great differences in the applications of digital technologies around the globe. The imbalance in Internet development is called the 'digital gap'. Digital industries such as film, television, music, radio, games, animation and publishing dominate the copyright industry. A great number of technological standards are controlled by developed countries or by their transnational enterprises. Zhang Xinhong finds that the overall digital gap index between China and the EU was 0.69 in 2007, indicating that China's overall development and application of information was 69% lower than that in the EU. See Zhang Xinhong (2010).

their countries' interests, emphasise the justice and priority of IPRs creation theories and property theories on the basis of the inviolability of private rights. There is a clear line between the value orientations of developing countries and those of developed countries, with the former emphasising the human rights elements of IPRs and the latter favouring its private rights attributes.

10.4 Pathways for Realising the Values of IP Law

In general, realising the underlying values of IP law requires the coordination of various social conditions, including politics, the economy, culture, education and the legal institution itself, comprising internal driving force and external variables such as the development of a knowledge economy market, the birth of a policy and system environment and the nurturing of a legal cultural environment, all of which are important conditions for the compliance and enforcement of IP laws. Here, the main focus is on the functional mechanism of IP laws, i.e., the relationship between the institutional functions and the value objectives of IP.

The basic systems of IP laws, centring on the objective of legal value, play the social function of protecting rights, balancing interests, and promoting scientific and technological progress and economic growth. The mechanisms of IP law encompass the following:

10.4.1 Rights Identification and Innovation Incentives

IP law is an effective institutional arrangement for property rights over intellectual products. Intellectual products are the general term for creative intellectual achievements in spiritual fields such as science, technology, and culture. They cannot adopt a single type of property rights due to the variety of their categories. Among intellectual products, scientific and some technological advancements take the form of non-market mechanisms of property rights, and the government frequently develops specific legal instruments to promote and stimulate the intellectual activities of creators. It has been chosen to establish what economists refer to as a priority reward system, which is a system of various forms of awards related to priority (Yuan 1999, pp. 72–74), for the aforementioned scientific and technological achievements. This system consists of two parts: first, the right to name scientific discoveries and technical inventions; and second, the right to receive prizes for discoveries and inventions. In essence, this system grants the discoverer or creator the right to get the "name" and the prize money, and in exchange for this benefit, society receives public property rights over scientific and technological achievements. This is the system of the right to discover or invent. In a broad sense, IPRs include the right to discover or invent. As was already mentioned, the rights listed above are a scientific and technological reward system, rather than private property rights. As far as major intellectual products are concerned, their rights are all in the form of private property rights. The condition of consideration for private property rights is that inventors publish their intellectual achievements so that the public can see and understand their unique knowledge and only then can society recognise that they have the exclusive right to use their intellectual products for a certain time (Bulgartehe 1980, pp. 10–14). While intellectual products are open to the public (the attribute of public products), IPRs are monopolistic (the attribute of private property rights). IP law gives inventors and creators benefits by granting them private property rights. It unquestionably also gives inventors the most economic, effective, and long-lasting incentive to innovate, ensuring that scientific and technological innovation activities continue to develop at a new level and thus fostering the rapid growth of advanced productivity entailed the innovative achievements.

10.4.2 Rights Transfer and Resource Allocation

The primary legislative purpose of IP laws is to define relevant property rights and protect the legitimate rights and interests of inventors and creators, while at the same time, regulate the transactions of property rights and promote the wide dissemination and utilisation of knowledge and technology. According to the theory of supply and demand in economics, intellectual creation is also a production activity. The purpose of mental production is also exchange and only through the exchange can individuals obtain the best combination of all kinds of goods and achieve the maximisation of efficiency or benefits. In terms of scientific and technological innovation activities, the commercialisation and marketisation of new technologies is a key part and its fundamental purpose. An invention may be supplanted by a newer technology and lose its economic value if it is not put into practice as soon as possible. The transaction of property rights in the relevant laws is expressed in the use of IPRs with three systems use being authorised use, statutory use, and fair use. Authorised use, often known as licensed use, means that the owner of IPRs grants permission for another party to use their intellectual products in a particular way. Internationally, this transaction is called licensing. The economic function of the authorised use contract is it summarise people's transaction habits, provides uniform trading norms and terms, and prevents the parties from the need to make complex contract terms, so as to reduce the transaction costs and help parties to reach an agreement. Both statutory use and compulsory use are a form of involuntary authorised use. The former refers to the compensated use of publicly available intellectual products in the way directly stipulated by the law, which is internationally known as "legal license"; the latter refers to the compensated use of publicly available intellectual products in the way that has been specifically approved by competent authorities of the state, which is internationally known as "compulsory license'. The two types of transactions mentioned above are actually "cooperative games" set up by the government. The goal is to significantly increase the chance of a successful transaction between the parties by lowering the information cost of the transaction such as cost involved in finding out who trades, what is traded and how to trade and the negotiation cost such as cost involved in the negotiation to secure authorisation (Cooter and Ulen 1994, p. 27). Fair use is a special case in the utilisation of intellectual property. It is a system of using others' intellectual products for legitimate purposes without the owner's or the creator's consent and without paying compensation to the owner or the creator in accordance with the law. Only a limited percentage of information resources are available for free and without charge, and they are all essential for the use and dissemination of knowledge. Different from the above-mentioned uses, the transaction of rights between users and creators in fair use is not a "one-to-one" transaction, but an exchange of information resources between specific creators and unspecified users under the social system of distribution arrangement. In a word, the transaction systems of IPRs aim to coordinate the rights allocation relations among information creators, disseminators, and users, so as to achieve the optimal benefits of scientific and technological progress and economic growth.

10.4.3 Rights Limitation and Interest Balancing

The limits of IPRs mean limitations on the exercise of proprietary rights, which functions to balance the interests between rights holders and the public to ensure the public access to intellectual products. The property rights system of the modern days should not only focus on its initial objectives of protecting the rights of IP holders, but also, while acknowledging the creators' right to own and control their intellectual products, promote the dynamic use of the intellectual wealth of the society. In economics, the paradox of information property rights has been raised: due to the monopoly of information property rights, on the one hand, it will encourage information producers to create new information, but on the other hand, the producers of monopoly information will demand high prices, preventing the information from being fully utilised. The dilemma has been summarised as follows: "Without legal monopoly not enough information will be produced, but with the legal monopoly too little of the information will be used" (Cooter and Ulen 1994, p. 185). The legal solution to this dilemma is to impose necessary limitations on the monopoly right while protecting IPRs. The protection and limitation of property rights involves the interests of different parties. So, the system design should accurately identify the primary and secondary status of interests in addition to its attention to the overall objective of social development. At present, there are two factors worth considering: First, the national conditions of different countries need to be taken into consideration. Generally speaking, developing countries and developed countries have different positions on the level of protection and product utilisation. Developing countries should consider their own economic, scientific, and technical development as well as the minimum protection criteria stipulated in international conventions when determining what limits on IPRs should be imposed and to what extent. It is inappropriate to merely copy the existing regulations of developed countries. Second, adaptation to the requirements of new technology development is needed Due to the emergence of new technologies, the way in which knowledge products are utilised has changed greatly, and the law must readjust the division of social interests and focus on the protection of the interests of creators. This is a restriction of the limitation on IPRs.

10.4.4 Rights Enforcement and Market Regulation

What IP law protects is the creative intellectual achievements with property rights. The ownership of a technology and brand by the producers and operators is only a kind of natural or factual possession, which only indicates that they have obtained certain technological and operational advantages. Technology and brands cannot be legally protected and cannot be considered to be in the exclusive "possession" of their producers and operators unless they gain IPRs, such as patents and registered trademarks. Only in this way can producers and operators transform such technological and business advantages into market competition advantages, so as to resist all counterfeiting, imitation and plagiarism. Cracking down on infringement is not only to protect the interests of property owners but also to regulate and control the market competition order. Infringement of IPRs occurs directly in the process of the production, dissemination and consumption of mental products. An IPRs regime with ineffective implementation and enforcement would fail to curb the occurrence and spread of IPRs infringements, dampen creators' enthusiasm for producing and developing intellectual products, and eventually lead to a reduction of social benefits accessible to the public. As such, a solution from an economics perspective is to regulate the cost and benefit relationship of IPRs transaction and protection so as to deter the rational economic person from engaging in IPRs abuse and other illegal conducts (Lyu 1998). In the field of IPRs at this stage, the legal system directly determines and specifies the statutory cost of infringement, because it designs and regulates the sanctions and punishment schemes, measures and methods for infringement. If the punishment stipulated in the relevant system for a certain infringement is too light, the statutory cost of the act of infringement will naturally be low, which will weaken the punitive function of the infringement, and the infringement of IPRs will continue despite repeated prohibitions. From the perspective of modern IP legislation in various countries, it is a common practice to increase the penalties for infringement, such as increasing the criminal sanction provisions to severely punish infringement, specifying the amount of statutory compensation for infringement, and improving administrative measures. This legislative trend is essentially the legislator's adjustment of the ratio of costs and benefits of infringement, which aims to with institutional arrangements control the market for property rights transactions, maintain the order of competition, and restrict the spread of infringement.

10.4.5 Rights Administration and Governmental Guidance

IP management is the general term for the state organs' examination, supervision, coordination, services and other activities in the acquisition and utilisation of IPRs in accordance with the law. Property rights management is one of the marks that distinguish the IPRs regime from other property rights systems. The existence of such management activities is not only due to the influence of the traditional operation mechanism but also reflects the characteristics of intellectual property itself and the appropriate intervention of the state in the field of civil activities. Various management activities related to IPRs reflect the purposes of relevant national legislation and form a guiding mechanism for the government to promote scientific and technological progress and economic growth in the field of private rights. Specifically, it is mainly manifested in the following aspects. First, the mechanism of policy objectives. The government first of all acts as a policy maker in the process of protecting and managing knowledge-based property rights (Chen 2000). The IPRs regime itself is part of the national economic, scientific and cultural policy. Naturally, the overall policy objectives of the state determine the type of IPRs protection that should be offered and the degree of protection that should be given to intellectual products. Additionally, issues related to IPRs will be present to various degrees in the states development plans and specific policies, such as plans for the development of science and technology, cultural policies, industrial policies, investment policies, and foreign investment policies. Therefore, the government's policy guidance is conducive to achieving the objectives of promoting social development and IP legislation. Second, the mechanism of scientific review. A specific examination and review by national authorities is required for the majority of intellectual products, apart from copyright, which is automatically obtained as of the date the work is completed. Implementing the examination review system can exclude the public domain technologies and those that violate public order and good customs from the scope of exclusive rights protection, thus improving the quality of granting IPRs; In addition, it can also define the boundary of intangible intellectual property, specify the scope and category of the IPRs, so as to grant IPRs to intellectual achievements. Third, the mechanism of information release. Under the premise of protecting property rights, creators or inventors are required to disclose the content of their inventions. This is the patent documentation system. In fact, the allocation of technologically innovative resources takes place through information disclosure. Utilising information resources of IPRs can prevent repeated investment, save research funds, elevate the starting point of technological innovation, and realise a leapfrog in the development of technology. Fourth, the mechanism of behaviours supervision. IP use generally includes the rightsholder's own use, authorised or licensed use and transferred right of use to others and so on. The management activities of national authorities are intended to regulate the transaction of property rights, maintain the market order and protect the legitimate rights and interests of the parties. Fifth, the mechanism of administrative remedies. In the field of intellectual property, the state administrative department has the right to take administrative remedies for illegal acts or impose administrative penalties on the persons subject to administrative measures or order the infringer to compensate the aggrieved party for the loss of interests.

References

Bulgartehe, E. A. 1980. *Patent Law in Capitalist Countries and Developing Countries: Introduction to Foreign Patent Laws*. Beijing: Intellectual Property Publishing House

Chapman, Audrey R. 2001. Treating intellectual property rights as human rights: Obligations relating to article 15, paragraph 1, item 3. *Copyright Bulletin* 3

Chen, Chuanfu. 2000. On the government strategy of intellectual property system. *Journal of Law and Technology* 1

Chen, Yi and Wang, Tianliang. 2004. On the value of intellectual property laws. *Innovation, Administration and Law* 9

Cheng, Xiao. 2001. Reflections on basic problems of intellectual property law. *Journal of Renmin University of China* 1

Coase, R. H. 1994. *Property Rights and Institutional Change*. Trans. Shouying Liu. Shanghai: Shanghai SDX Publishing Company

Cooter, Robert and Thomas Ulen. 1994. *Law and Economics*. Trans. Jun Zhang et al., Shanghai: Shanghai SDX Publishing Company

Davis, Jillian. 1990. *Public Interests in Collective Management of Rights*. Copyright Reference Materials

Jiang, Ping. 1995. Roman law and modern Chinese legislation. *China Legal Science* 1

Kant, Immanuel. 1991. *The Metaphysical Elements of Justice—The Science of Right*. Beijing: The Commercial Press

Li, Long. 2001. *Good Law*. Wuhan: Wuhan University Press

Li, Mingde. 2003. *US Intellectual Property Law*. Beijing: Law Press

Ling, Binghui. 2001. Intellectual property system in national innovation. *Intellectual Property* 3

Lyu, Meizhong. 1998. *The Legal and Economic Analysis of Economic Law*. Beijing: China Procuratorial Press

Marx, Karl and Friedrich Engels. 1963. *Marx-Engels Collected Works*. Beijing: People's Publishing House

Marx, Karl and Frederick Engels. 1971. *Marx-Engels Collected Works*. Beijing: People's Publishing House

Patterson, L. Ray and Stanley W. Lindberg. 1991. *The Nature of Copyright: A Law of Users' Right*. Georgia: The University of Georgia Press

Posner, Richard A. 1987. *Economic Analysis of Law*. Kentucky: Little Brown Company

Qiao, Keyu and Li, Xiaoping. 1991. *Value of the Law*. Beijing: China University of Political Science and Law Press

Qu, Maohui. 2002. Basic concepts of Chinese civil code. *Seeker* 4

Shen, Zongling. 1993. Law, value, justice and interests. *Law Journal* 5

Wu, Handong. 2001. IP law in the coordination mechanism of science, technology, economy and law. *Chinese Journal of Law* 6

Xie, Hui. 1993. Legalisation of value and value of law. *Science of Law* 4

Yan, Cunsheng. 1991. *The Value of Law*. Shanxi: Shanxi People's publishing House

Yuan, Zhigang. 1999. On the production and consumption of knowledge. *Economic Research* 6

Zhang, Xinbao. 1986. *Basic Principles of Civil Activities*. Beijing: Law Press

Zhang, Xinhong. 2010. *Spotlight on the Fourth Difference: A Comparative Study of the Digital Gap between China and Europe*. Beijing: Commercial Press

Chapter 11
Risks Dimensions of IPRs Regimes

In the context of risk discourse, an IPRs regime represents both a "paragon of institutional civilisation" and potential institutional risks—primarily "endogenous" risks inherent in the IPRs regime, such as cultural risks, ecological risks, genetic technology risks, and cyber risks. It has therefore become a shared mission of the international IP community to address the congenial deficiencies and laten crises within the current legal framework and IP order by enhancing risk awareness, strengthening the capacity to identify risks, and building risk-management mechanisms. More specifically, countries, both developed and developing, should initiate a reform of their current IPRs regimes based on the unity of value rationality and instrumental rationality, the unity of rights and obligations, and the unity of legal control and technical regulation.[1] In addition, IPRs regimes should be further enhanced with policies to protect traditional knowledge, preserve public domain, creative commons licences, and reward innovators. These measures point to a way out of risk society and to a legal pathway for realising the value objectives of the IPRs regime.

11.1 Risk Society Theory and IP Research

The theory of risk society, a worthy contribution to contemporary philosophy and social science, was first developed by the German scholar Ulrich Beck (1944–) in his 1986 book *Risk Society: Towards a New Modernity*. According to Beck, after the first stage of "simple" modernisation, which transformed an agricultural society into an industrial society, human beings entered a second stage of "reflexive" modernisation, which has transformed an industrial society into a risk-ridden one. In a risk society, people are exposed to dangers and insecurities that are brought by society itself. Furthermore, the economic, legal and social settings in the society get involved not

[1] Detailed discussion on IPRs' value rationality and instrumental rationality see Chapter 10: Value Analysis of IPRs Regimes.

H. Wu, *Theorising Intellectual Property Rights from Chinese Perspectives*,
https://doi.org/10.1007/978-981-96-5867-1_11

only in generating, but also concealing risks. Hence, "modernisation is becoming reflexive; it is becoming its own theme" (Beck 1992, p. 19). After Beck, the theory was further developed by British scholars, including Anthony Giddens (1938–) and Scott Lash (1965–),[2] and evolved into a classical theory in social science on the cusp of the twenty-first century. Risk society has since become the focus of many international and interdisciplinary studies of twentieth- and twenty-first- century modernity.

"Risk" is the basic category in the risk society theory and the foundation in the construction of this theoretical system. In fact, risks and mankind coexist, but the connotation and structure of risks in the modern sense are fundamentally different from those in the past: one difference is the humanisation of risks. With the increasing frequency and expanding scope of human activities, the impact of their decisions and actions on nature and human society is greatly increased, thus in terms of the structure of risks, the uncertain man-made risks have superseded the natural risks and played a dominant role. Essentially, mankind has become the main producer of risks, in other words, the humanisation of risks. The other difference is the institutionalisation of risks. Mankind has the natural inclination for adventure and also the instinct of seeking safety. Many systems related to market provide incentives for risk-taking behaviours, while various systems established in modern countries provide protection for human safety. Both risk-oriented and safety-oriented systems bring about the risks of malfunction, namely, the institutionalisation of risks. In the field of risk society theory, there exists the opposition between objectivism and subjectivism among theorists. The former holds that risk is an indisputable objective fact in the era of globalisation, which demonstrates that human society is in the transformation from a classical industrial society to a risk society; while the latter believes risk society can be regarded as the result of people's subjective awareness because people's awareness of the increasing risks leads to the emergence of risk society. No matter what kind of opinion they hold, all theorists in the field of risk society try to show that in the era of globalisation, paying attention to and dealing with risks has become an unavoidable reality with the development of society.

The characteristics of the risk society are an important part of risk society theory. The term "risk society" is not restricted in its application to a specific time scale or geographical location; instead, it paints a whole picture of the risks faced by all of mankind today. Specifically, these risks have the following three features. (1) *They are inherent in society*. In risk society, the nature of risk has undergone tremendous changes: whereas the significant risks in the first stage of modernisation are produced by non-human forces, those in the second stage are created by human activities, such as through the establishment of industrial and legal systems and the application of science and technology. These are called "institutional" and "technological" risks, respectively (Yang 2005, pp. 77–82). (2) *They have global consequences*. Risk society is a worldwide society, as globalisation sends risks across borders and spreads their

[2] The representative work of Anthony Giddens is *Runaway World: How Globalization Is Reshaping Our Lives* (Giddens 2003); the representative work of Scott Lash is *Risk Culture, The Risk Society and Beyond: Critical Issues for Social Theory* (Lash 2000).

influence to every culture. According to Giddens, risks are globalised in the age of globalisation (Giddens and Pierson 1998). Beck reminds us that this globalisation of risks is to be ascribed to human decisions (Beck 2004, pp. 40–47). (3) *They vary greatly.* As its risks are man-made, the seeds and occurrence are influenced by a wide range factors like cultural, social, economic and political factors (Zhang 2010). It can be said that the risks are various and diverse. Beck believes that the knowledge gaps and fissures between social and scientific rationality lead to many negative elements of modernity. From this perspective, the "knowledge economy" is actually a "risk economy" and the "knowledge society" is actually a "risk society." He divides the risks into economic risks, political risks and cultural risks, and "trust issues" as well (Xue and Liu 2005, pp. 25–37).

Avoiding and dealing with all kinds of globalised risks is the main task in the study of risk society theory. In terms of coping strategy, Beck and Giddens show the tendency of institutionalism, that is highlighting institutional and normative measures in the risk society theory. And their ideal approach is to establish a set of orderly rules in the faulty risk society to perform the function of early warnings and controls. Mary Douglas, on the other hand, based on a subjective view, believes that the key is who perceives and increases risk awareness rather than the real risks themselves. In terms of risk response, she advocates preventing and resolving risks through sub-political movements including environmental movements and green movements. It should be noted here that risk society theorists do not see risk in an entirely negative light but emphasise that risk has a dual nature: it represents uncertainty and danger while also serving as a source of motivation for societal advancement and innovation (Giddens 2002, p. 139).

In sociology, the risk society theory emerged from the theoretical background of reflecting upon and criticising modernity, and its theoretical motivation was to examine and reflect on the crisis and subsequent problems brought about by industrial modernisation, and then construct new theories of social modernisation. This theory offers us a fresh vision through which we may examine and comprehend the development of modern society, which is a new way of thinking for human beings to reflect on themselves. Several issues, including how to understand the impact of intangible risks (or institutional risks) on the survival and development of human society, and how to grasp the moral, cultural and legal issues arising from the globalised risks, are new fields for the development of the risk society theory, and also provide new analytical tools for the study of legal systems, including IPRs.

The study of risk society from a jurisprudential perspective focuses on legal institutions and legal order. This is because society should be governed primarily by law, and the reason why modern society must be governed by law is because legal norms in comparison with other social norms have advantages necessary for social stability and progress (Zhang 2003, pp. 341–342). Beck observes that the significance and value of legal institutions are that they aim to manage and pursue every detail of technically manageable risks even if they have a small chance to happen or have limited impact (Beck 2003, pp. 31–35). The legal order is the result of the implementation of legal institutions that regulate every aspect of life in a society. According to T. M. Шамба (1987), the legal order is about the practice of law, that is, the implementation and realisation of law in social relations. In modern societies under the rule of law, studies of risk society from a jurisprudential perspective pinpoint the legal capacities of controlling institutional risks.

The IPRs regime is both a "paragon of institutional civilisation" with over three hundred years of history and an institutional risk with man-made uncertainties. Created in the process of modernisation, it poses threats to human beings (Beck 1999). On the one hand, the IPRs regime was created by humans to encourage and protect knowledge-based innovations; on the other hand, the rise of these knowledge-based innovations, accompanied by related technological, economic and legal decisions, creates risks that are beyond human control (Cheng 2007). In this sense, knowledge is the root cause of modern risks, and the choice of institutions is in fact a risk-based decision. In light of Beck's view that "risks are primarily risks in knowledge" (Beck 1992, p. 55), it can be assumed that IPRs present and even increase risks in a risk society. Studies of IPRs against the background of risk society mainly examine the following three risks.

11.1.1 Institutional Risks in IP Policymaking

In the theory of risk society, it is believed that civilising decisions made by humans trigger an array of problems and dangers (Beck 2004, pp. 25–37). More straightforwardly, risks arise from human decisions (Beck 1999). In terms of choosing IPRs regimes, developed countries and developing countries have different historical backgrounds. For developing countries, risks arise from the institutionalisation of IPRs because of their decision to introduce an IPRs regime from developed countries that have different histories and backgrounds. Although the borrowing also occurs by developed countries, such cases are merely "another form of domestic legislation or law reform" (X. Liu 2004, pp. 10–13) as a response to the need to promote their own development. The enabling cultural environment in these countries also paves the way for the successful and effective implementation of the regime. However, for developing countries with neither a precedent nor a favourable cultural environment for IP legislation, there is a risk of ineffective implementation of an IPRs regime introduced under external pressure. Additionally, radical changes in the international environment make it impossible for developing countries to follow developed countries in making a gradual transition from weak to strong IPRs protection. As a result, governments in developing countries are ill-equipped to fully appreciate and effectively implement an IPRs regime, and the public lacks the awareness to obey IPRs protection rules, leading to the "institutionalisation of IPRs violation" (Merton 2011, p. 86). Put in another way, the "rules fail" and the IPRs regime becomes counterproductive to IPRs protection (Yang 2005, p. 86).

11.1.2 Technological Risks of IP Objects

Risk society is both shaped and characterised by the rapid development of science and technology. Risk society thus consists of "man-made risks" that are "created by the very impact of our developing knowledge upon the world" (Giddens 2003, p. 44). Max Weber (1864–1920) described modernity as an "iron cage" that traps individuals in systems based on technological knowledge (Beck et al 1994, p. 107). In light of the decisive role of science and technology in modernisation, lawmakers are making relentless attempts to improve the IPRs regime to protect and encourage scientific and technological innovation. It is highly necessary to pay due respect to digital copyright and gene-related patents and provide legal protection for representative technologies of the knowledge revolution, such as information and genetic technology, laurelled as "technology of this era", for technologies as such create the sense of trust in the risk society, and it is the sense of trust that shields the public from uncertainty and insecurity (Xu 2005, pp. 26–28). However, trust and risk are intertwined in the era of reflexive modernisation, as Beck points out. Although trust in technology can build up public confidence in dealing with risks, it can also engender risks because of the drawbacks of technologies. One such drawback is conflicts between different rights. For example, as cyber-technology develops, conflicts occur between exclusive rights and the public domain, between the right to create digital content and the right to develop communications technology, and between intellectual property and traditional knowledge. Moreover, the exclusive use of technology will lead to undesirable consequences. The application of genetic technology to food, medicine, plants, animals and even directly to humans may impact a human body and a living environment positively but can also have underlying adverse effects.

11.1.3 Global Risks in IP Operations

The globalisation of the economy, technology, information and governance mechanisms brings with it the globalisation of risk. Anti-globalists criticise globalisation as representing a new imperialism that is no longer characterised by territorial expansion but by market expansion. Based on this idea, they see the Internet as "informational imperialism", the World Trade Organisation as "market imperialism", the International Monetary Fund as "financial imperialism" and the United Nations as "political and diplomatic imperialism" (Xue and Liu 2005). Unlike anti-globalists, (who judge globalisation by its concept), Beck (Ibid) judges globalisation by its results and consequences. Some of these results are beneficial but others are harmful and are even threats to the very existence of human beings, such as the decline of social identity, conflicts of values and interests, antagonism between major organisations, conflicts of national interests and the destruction of the natural environment. The globalisation of IPRs also has pros and cons: on the one hand, it universalises the rules for IPRs protection; on the other hand, it changes the IPRs regime into a global institutional risk featuring two aspects. First, the international IPRs regime clearly favours developed countries, causing an imbalance in the interests of developing countries and developed countries. While the creative works of developing countries are put in the public domain, those of the developed world are held tightly in the hands of their private companies (Chander and Sunder 2004, pp. 81–89). Second, IPRs are in conflict with international human rights. As the United Nations Sub-Commission on the *Promotion and Protection of Human Rights* declared, "since the implementation of the *TRIPS Agreement* does not adequately reflect the fundamental nature and indivisibility of all human rights", "there are apparent conflicts between the IPRs regime embodied in the *TRIPS Agreement*, on the one hand, and international human rights law, on the other" (United Nations 2000). Given the various flaws revealed in the process of formulation and implementation of the *TRIPS Agreement*, it is not surprising that the international community questions its reasonableness and appropriateness. It is true that the current international IPRs protection regime has a positive impact, however, it also has a real and potential negative impact. In a word, in a global risk society, civil decisions made by humans, one of which is instituting an IPRs regime, have global consequences (Beck 2004, pp. 19–22).

11.2 Institutional and Technological Risks of IP

The worldwide expansion of the knowledge economy and the application of cyber-network and genetic technology have fundamentally changed the environment of the existence of IPRs. This view is based on two facts: First, the side effects of technology are a factor of uncertainty. The latest technologies protected by IPRs may have substantial benefits for humans but may also inflict harm, such that "The gain in power from techno-economic 'progress' is being increasingly overshadowed by the production of risks" (Beck 1992, p. 13). This is the connection between the negative effect of technology and the uncertainty of risks. Second, the certainty of law collides with the uncertainty of risk. The traditional systems of social governance including the IPRs regime cannot address the problems brought by overdevelopment in the industrial society. As Giddens points out, "The impotence we experience is not a sign of individual failure but rather a reflection of the impotence of our systems. We need to reconstruct those systems we had or create new ones" (Giddens 2003, p. 37). It is safe to say that the current IPRs regime has inherent defects and potential risks.

11.2.1 Cultural Homogenisation and Cultural Erosion

With economic globalisation also comes cultural globalisation, whose arrival not only accelerates cultural integration but also provokes cultural conflicts (Xiao 2011, pp. 25–37), "not only between the west and the east, and also between the ethnic culture and the dominant culture within the Western society" (Xue 2004, p. 9). The issue of the safety of national cultures and the diversity of world culture is a manifestation of the social risks in the cultural fields. As a result, countries are forced to face up to a decline in their cultural security and the world experiences a decrease in cultural diversity. We are now in an "era of risk culture", of which Scott Lash warns that "risk sub-politics will be dealing with a whole new set of unintended consequences, no longer from material goods producing industry but from the information sectors, from bio-technology, from the communications and software sectors" (Lash 2000, p. 61). Today's "cultural risks" are the weakening of national cultural sovereignty and the marginalisation of traditional culture. Throughout the world, there has been a certain tension between the traditional cultures of many nations and tribes and the so-called mainstream and powerful cultures, which is seen not just between the developing and developed countries but also within European and American cultures.

Cultural globalisation should not erase the ethnic and national specificity of cultures nor their diversity, as there are more than ten thousand cultural groups living in about two hundred countries. At the domestic level, many countries have diverse ethnic and cultural groups, and their focus is mainly on maintaining their diverse cultures and on respect for the rights of the minority groups. Meanwhile, at the international level, cultural diversity means different languages, religious beliefs, and ways of life. Acknowledging this cultural diversity means acknowledging the independence and autonomy of the cultural sovereignty of different countries. "Respect … for cultures – for their equal dignity, for their diversity, for their variegated vigour and for different paths of development" (UNESCO 1995) is not only adherence to the ethical principle of pluralism[3] but also a legal requirement for safeguarding cultural sovereignty.

The deficiency in the international IPRs protection system, with the *TRIPS Agreement* at its core, is that it prioritises novelty and originality but ignores the diversity of innovations. There is no better evidence of this shortfall than the global dominance of Western culture, which, characterised by modernity and novelty, is eroding indigenous cultures and traditions and thus placing global cultural diversity in real danger. Accentuating this is that activities in the international community at large are governed by the Western spirit of law and Western norms (Yan 2006). Dominated by Western countries, the international IPRs protection system offers comprehensive protection for their modern innovations while leaving the traditional innovations of other cultures unprotected. Therefore, "while the system provides protections for intellectual properties against economic hazards, it does not protect them against cultural harm" (Tsosie 2002, pp. 91–97).[4]

---

[3] The World Commission on Culture and Development (1995) states that "pluralism is a basic principle of global ethics. And cultural pluralism is an all-pervasive, enduring characteristic of societies, and that ethnic identification is a normal and healthy response to the pressures of globalization."

[4] It is argued that IP laws cannot provide adequate protection for cultural diversity because in a case where the appropriation of culture causes a cultural harm rather than a commercial harm, the law does not have a category to redress the harm. See Rebecca A. Tsosie (2002).

Under the current international IPRs regime, the cultural risk that threatens the cultural diversity is mainly manifest in two ways: One is that a small number of countries, drawing heavily on advanced technologies and vast amounts of capital, with their advantageous culture, tend to produce and distribute cultural products that are appropriated from other less advantageous cultures, with the long list ranging from intellectual property, distinctive cultural expressions to knowledge and cultural products of other perceivable forms. Apart from cultural appropriation, cultural monopoly, which results from the expansion of the cultural influence of Western countries by continuously enlarging the magnitude of their export of cultural products, is also jeopardising indigenous cultures. Thus, on balance, the globalisation of culture, which is supported by IPRs, has surfaced as a menace to the world cultural diversity and therefore constitutes cultural risks in the global risk society.

11.2.2 Ecological Impacts and Biodiversity Threats

The conservation of biodiversity, which has ecological, genetic, social, economic and cultural values, is a common concern of humankind, and the root of the biodiversity crisis, or rather the depletion of biological resources, is not natural disasters but man-made uncertainties, or rather, "institutionalised risks."

In the current IPRs system, the patentability requirements are that the invention itself must be non-obvious, novel and useful with little, if any, regard to the source of the resources that gives rise to the invention. On this basis, biotechnology can be patented without consideration of the source of the genetic resources employed. However, one of the characteristics of biotechnological creation is its reliance on the resources and the information of the resources. Just as some scholars point out, those who have access to exhaustible genetic resources will be in an advantageous position to build up an enormous fortune in the era of biotechnology (Zhu and Yang 2003, pp. 53–56).

The reality, however, is that developing countries have 80 percent of the world's biological resources, and developed countries own and control 95 percent of biotechnology patents (Feng 2012). With the loss of "national sovereignty" of biotechnological resources, under the current IPRs regime, there is a serious imbalance in the biological interests: developing countries' biological resources advantage cannot be shown in the patent applications and nor can they obtain the advantages of using patents. Furthermore, the international regime turns a deaf ear to developing countries' calls for sharing the benefits that developed countries have received from biotechnology. Meanwhile, the high standards of IPRs protection set by the international regime push up the costs that developing countries bear for importing biotechnology from developed countries (Sun 2007, pp. 19–24).

In 1992, the United Nations adopted *the Convention on Biological Diversity* (CBD), which covers all aspects of biological diversity: "the conservation of biological diversity, the sustainable use of its components and the fair and equitable sharing of benefits arising from the use of genetic resources".[5] However, the WTO's *TRIPS Agreement* does not share the same objectives of the Convention, and some developed countries even negotiate special "TRIPS-Plus" agreements on biotechnology with developing countries that go far beyond the obligations already imposed by TRIPS (GRAIN 2001). Given these visible loopholes in the above-mentioned systems and policies, it is only natural to worry that the world is faced with considerable ecological risks and a high degree of uncertainties (Xue and Liu 2005, pp. 120–131).

11.2.3 Genetic Technology Governance Challenges

The increasingly abundant array of science and technology leads to a risk society in which technology itself becomes an inherent risk. Technological risks arise when human beings employ technologies in a way that it deviates the development of science and technology from their natural course (Wang 2008, pp. 44–48). The reason that this can occur is that humans, bounded by their cognitive capacity, can sometimes barely discern the nature of every technology and that sometimes they deviate from the proper use of the technology out of consideration of certain interests. For example, humans may choose to use technology to satisfy political ambitions or realise economic profits, even if being fully conscious of the peril such uses may lead to. In any case, the benefit so lost is the consequence of possible social risks that technology poses.

Gene technology, when abused and perverted, runs the risk of pain, losses and sense of insecurities, damaging the environment, disturbing the social order and endangering public health. That is because, first, in the risk society, the chief threat to the environment is by no means natural disasters but rather human activities. Environmentalists argue that human beings may be driven to abuse gene technology by the handsome profits it generates and that this abuse will lead to species' extinction, genetic mutation and ecological imbalance. Second, after scientists have successfully mapped the human genome, thus unravelling the genetic code for human chromosomes, gene technology is expected to be developed further to reveal humans' genetic information and to be used in testing for health, intelligence and potential. However, the misuse of genetic information may give rise to "genetic discrimination", which in turn will lead to endangering human beings. Third, the application of transgenic technology has introduced genetically modified food into the human diet. Although there are benefits from the application of this technology—genetically modified crops, for example, are high-quality, high-yielding and disease- and pest-resistant—there is also a concern that genetically modified food may contain excess protein that cannot be absorbed by the human body and will be therefore damaging to health. This is the issue of food safety in the era of gene technology.

In a word, the IPRs regime has fully demonstrated its capacities in protecting gene technology and confidently granted patents to gene technology, yet it is helpless at the

[5] See the preamble of the United Nations Convention on Biological Diversity (1992).

entailed gene technological risks. In terms of preventing the abuse of gene technology and managing its risks, enacting relevant laws and regulations is necessary but its effect will be limited. We may need to target the inadequacies of the regime and build a comprehensive system of social governance. Only then can we hope to deal with the technology risks in the era of gene technology.

11.2.4 Cybersecurity Vulnerabilities

Information globalisation is based on the socialisation of information networks. Networks constitute the new social structures, forms and modes of our times. As Manuel Custer notes, "As a historical trend, dominant functions and processes in the Information Age are increasingly organised around networks" (Castells 2000, p. 500), as networks shape the new social morphology of our societies and underpin the globalisation of information. This new form of society, known as the 'network society',[6] is in essence a risk society, as the effects of Internet technology on society, culture, politics, economy and law are unpredictable and uncontrollable. It has thus been argued that digitalisation, a trend in the network society, will not only lead to an industrial revolution but also a social revolution (2008, pp. 31–34).

Network security risks come from "inherent" risks of network technologies and the impact it exerts on copyright. Three major network security risks can be observed in modern society. First, there is a risk of distrust in formal institutions, as risk society "is not only a factual concept but also a cultural concept" (Xue and Liu 2005). To maintain order in cyberspace, both formal and informal institutions have roles to play. Formal institutions are the laws and regulations enacted and enforced by official authorities; informal institutions are social norms such as customs, practices, morals and ethics. In relation to copyright, however, formal institutions are largely powerless, as the network is inundated with copyright infringements. It is difficult to impose any penalty on copyright infringers when any click could constitute an infringement and the infringer could be any network user. Copyright infringement becomes a common practice (an "informal institution" or unspoken rule) that not only contradicts but also overrides the law (the "formal institution") which only exists in name (Wang 2005, pp. 50–54). From a legal perspective, indifference to copyright is a reflection of a lack of faith in the rule of law, and according to the theory of risk society it is a crisis of confidence in formal institutions. Second, there are the risks of technology protection measures. Digital technology facilitates the rapid and wide spread of information on the Internet. From this follows a waning of the control that copyright holders have over their digital works, which are illegally disseminated as a result. Technology protection measures are thus adopted as a part of the copyright system to curb the illegal dissemination of content. However, some scholars

---

[6] Translators' note: Network society is an expression coined by Jan van Dijk in 1991 related to the social, political, economic and cultural changes caused by the spread of networked, digital information and communications technologies.

argue that the widespread implementation of these measures may not only fail to curb the spread of digital information but also lead to an imbalance between public and private interests. Furthermore, replacing digital copyright licensing with digital rights management or other technology protection measures will restrict people's access to information (Gao 2011, pp. 67–72). Third, there is the risk of the "digital divide": the uneven development of the Internet arising from unequal access to digital technology around the world. A widening of the digital divide generates risks on all fronts. In the copyright industry, which is now primarily dealing with digital content, such as movies and television, music, broadcasts, games, animation and publication, developing countries are overshadowed by developed countries, with the latter owning most of the core technologies to produce digital products and even defining the production standards. According to the *Comparative Study on the Digital Divide between China and Europe*, the general index of the digital divide between China and Europe was 0.69 in 2007, showing that the European Union performed 69% better than China in developing and applying information technology. In a word, the digital divide in the information age reinforces inequalities (Zhuang 2004, pp. 103–117), embodied in the imbalance of copyrights interests and in the disparity in information access between the West and the East.

11.3 Risk Consciousness in the Construction of IPRs Regimes

The study of the risks of IPRs regimes, from identifying and evaluating through to managing risk, involves a synthesis of objective analysis and subjective judgement. As building an IPRs regime is a risk-based choice of policies, it is important to raise risk awareness and improve the ability to identify risks when developing the regime and establishing the order.

The development of the IPRs regime in China has moved from being forced by external powers to introduce the IPRs regime to choosing to introduce the IPRs regime on its own initiative for the purpose of building China into an innovation-driven country. Transplanting foreign or international legal systems is not just about making a rational choice, it is also a process of further localising the system, helping it to fully take root (Zhang 2005, pp. 57–62), However, when an IPRs regime is transplanted into developing countries from developed countries, it usually fails to deliver completely desirable outcomes. There are two factors that influence the effectiveness of a system in a country: legal factors, such as whether the ideas, content and forms of law that pertain to the system are sound and reasonable, and non-legal factors, such as whether the country's economic and technological development, public policy system, and social and cultural surroundings are in tune with the system. The uncertainty surrounding these factors are the risks that a country faces when it establishes an IPRs regime. It is necessary to reform and improve the IPRs regime based on the ideas of "controlling and defusing risks with law" and "dealing with risk society in the context of rule of law" (Yang 2011, pp. 30–36). Accordingly, while accepting the IPRs regime, China must address the institutional risks IPRs regime brings, emphasises local situations and adopt reforms that better suit its domestic realities in the trend of IPRs' internationalisation so as to foster the slow, phased but sure modernisation of its IPRs regime. These reforms should adhere to the following three principles.

11.3.1 Integration of Value Rationality and Instrumental Rationality

The contrast between value rationality and instrumental rationality has developed from Max Weber's conceptualisation of 'rationality'. According to Weber, value rationality is when "one has the self-conscious conviction that an action has an absolute or intrinsic value so it must be taken regardless of the conditions and outcomes" (Chen 2001, pp. 40–46), whereas instrumental rationality is when "one takes actions based on his anticipated ability to achieve some considered end" (Ibid.). Value rationality is thus concerned with the value of the action itself and instrumental rationality with the efficiency of an action to achieve its ends. Weber believed that instrumental rationality emerged from the intellectual evolution of the Enlightenment, with the flourishing of science and technology and the growth of rationality itself. However, as instrumental rationality increases dramatically, efficiency becomes the focal point of society and technology is thus widely applied. Rationality then changes from a tool for emancipating to a tool for dominating man and nature, causing a rift between technological rationality and value rationality (Weber 1958). In a capitalist society, technological rationality soars, as demonstrated in the impressive progress in technology, but with the alienation of man, the people-centred value rationality falls. Similar ideas can be found in risk society theory. According to Beck, "scientific rationality" is an important principle of modernity. Although it is outwardly infallible, scientific rationality is in essence a kind of "partial and monopolistic" instrumental rationality that causes a range of problems. Guided by this scientific rationality, society becomes economic society and nations become technological nations. With the rise of industrial rationality and the application of technology, the nature of modernisation completely changes, as human relations are dominated by instrumental rationality (Beck 1999). In a word, scientific rationality, which is believed to be value-neutral, collides with social rationality, which embodies social value in a broader context (Xu and Mao 2007).

Philosophically speaking, value rationality manifests as substantive justice and legal ends and instrumental rationality as formal justice and legal means. However, some legal systems are designed in a way that is contrary to this rule, as they take value rationality as the means and instrumental rationality as the ends, which results in social problems. For that, the modern IPRs regime contributes a vivid example: to a certain extent it is designed with instrumental rationality displacing value rationality as its end, the regime gives rise to several risks (Gao 2006, pp. 8–13). The international IPRs protection system mainly accommodates the interests of developed countries in the West, which demand high-level IPRs protection standards. As little attention is paid to the interests of developing countries in the East, the system causes an imbalance of interests, as substantial injustice is covered up by formal justice. The UK's Commission on Intellectual Property Rights provides a good explanation of the relationship between the two natures of IPRs, namely as private property rights and public policy: "Regardless of the term used for them, we prefer to regard IPRs as instruments of public policy which confer economic privileges on individuals or institutions solely for the purposes of contributing to the greater public good. The privilege is therefore a means to an end, not an end in itself" (Commission on Intellectual Property Rights, 2002). From this explanation, it is safe to say that pursuing the unity of instrumental rationality and value rationality should be the guiding principle of building a global risk governance mechanism for the IPRs regime and for reforming the current IPRs regime. Value rationality in this context means not only balancing the interests between parties in IP creation and utilisation and between the West and East in knowledge sharing, but also safeguarding the public interests in knowledge dissemination.

11.3.2 Balancing Rights Consciousness with Responsibility Consciousness

The concepts of right and obligation are the core of modern law and underpin the establishment and implementation of the IPRs regime. There are two major concepts governing the use of law to deal with the risk society: the "certainty of law" and the "uncertainty of risk." In a risk society, the rights (powers) granted by law should be used to pursue certainty by offsetting the shock and harm brought by risks (Yang 2011, pp. 27–29). The original purpose of legislating protection for IPRs is to clarify the scope of IPRs and obligations and determine the elements of ownership or possession so that the interests of IPR holders can be guaranteed. However, with the application of modern technologies, the scope of rights under the traditional legal system becomes blurry, creating a number of risks. As a result, doubts over the justice and the scope of IPRs become a major problem confronting the IPRs regime (Xiong 2010, pp. 27–29). The scope of rights in this context involves the distinction between the "exclusive domain" and "public domain" for intellectual works, between creators and disseminators and between creators and disseminators and users. The risks arise from the expansion or abuse of IPRs or from the infringement or conflicts of IPRs. According to the theory of risk society, IPRs should be conceived in such a way that the scope of rights is clear, rights are respected and protected, and, just as importantly, rights are exercised in a prudent and proper way.

Any IPRs-related problem, whether it be the abuse of rights or the violation of obligations, involves the attribution of liability. In the science of law, legal liability, also known as "secondary obligation" (Zhang 2004), is a direct and mandatory obligation triggered by a violation of legal right or a breach of legal obligation, determined by a specific state organ and attributed to a particular liable party. In the theory of risk society, however, there are two differences in the definition of liability. First, the theory gives a broader definition of the liable party, including creators of technological products, who are liable for the products' research and development, evaluators of technological products, who are liable for the assessment of the products' adverse effects, and policymakers, who are liable for the social risks brought by the policies related to the products. Risk society theorists believe that multiple liable parties can give rise to a situation of "organised irresponsibility" that Beck strongly criticises, which is an avoidable phenomenon in the risk society. Second, liability in the risk society theory is not restricted to legal liability. For instance, among the types of behaviour that cause social risks, such as the abuse of technology, misuse of technology and the interest-driven choices of technology, some constitute an abuse of right or a violation of obligation and thus involve legal liability but others may only involve moral liability, which will be punished not by law but by the public.

An IPRs regime in the risk society should give equal weight to rights (power) and responsibility, and the same applies to rights holders and the authorities. While enjoying their rights, rights holders should shoulder the responsibility to create, disseminate and utilise intellectual products in a right and proper way. Meanwhile, the authorities should establish a risk governance mechanism in which they not only exercise their decision-making power but also take responsibility for the risks brought by their decisions.

11.3.3 Integration of Legal Control and Technical Regulation

The prevention and control of risks in modern society call for a new set of social values and a new knowledge system. To manage the risks associated with the IPRs regime and with technology, a coordinated approach should be adopted that combines IP laws and technology regulations.

Laws are a vital part of the risk governance mechanism. By establishing organised social sanctions, the law ensures, including through the possible use of coercive force, that individuals follow the basic requirements for proper behaviour (Bodenheimer 1974). By expanding and protecting private rights, IP law provides incentives for innovation. However, the theory of risk society also highlights the role of IP law in controlling risks. To be more specific, legislators need to improve the legal system, especially in the areas of exclusions from patentability, the abuse of IPRs and the limitations on the exercise of IPRs. Additionally, mechanisms for limiting, prohibiting and punishing the illegal development, use and spread of technologies should be set up to supplement the legal system.

The regulation of technology, in the form of legal norms, policies, rules and codes of ethics, also plays an indispensable role in managing risks. Regulations of technology guided by the theory of risk society have the following three features. First, the guiding principle to deal with risks is to prevent them from happening, rather than to look for remedies after risks begin to take their toll. In other words, to forestall the adverse effects, technologies should be regulated from the very beginning of their development. Second, the model for preventing risks is to build an accountability system for the development and application of technologies, including social responsibility, moral responsibility, scientific ethics and legal responsibility. Third, a risk-prevention measure is to involve the public in managing technologies, meaning that the public has access to information on technology and is allowed to participate in the decision-making process (G. Liu 2011, pp. 9–13).

In conclusion, a multi-pronged approach should be taken to prevent risks arising from the IPRs regime and from the application of technology. Apart from upgrading the traditional IPRs regime, an IPRs-oriented public policy system should be developed with risk prevention as its object. Furthermore, a code of scientific ethics that values both social and scientific rationality should be widely adopted.

11.4 Legal Responses to Institutional Risks of IP

In a risk society, as the "inherent defects" of the IPRs regime become gradually more noticeable, the regime is plunged into an unprecedented crisis and is facing unprecedented challenges. People have developed trust issues in the regime, doubting its legitimacy and rationality, and some even have adopted extreme views against it completely, such as calls for the "abolishment of the patent system" and the "abrogation of copyright" (Wang 2011, pp. 21–29). That being said, the author maintains that the IPRs regime will not wither away, provided that it is reformed and relevant institutions are built to support it.

The IPRs regime should respond to the knowledge revolution, focusing on solving the problems brought about by cyber network technology and gene technology so as to prevent uncertainties due to a gap in the regulation. Four major considerations to guide such reform are as follows. First, and above all, the subject matter of IPRs protection have changed with the evolution of intellectual products. For instance, the primary subject matter of copyright protection has changed from traditional printed works to electronic works and now to digital works, and the primary subject matter of patent protection have changed from microorganisms to animal and plant species and now to genetic technology. Meanwhile, the domain name, as the symbol of digital business, has become the new focus of trademark protection. Second, the scope of IPRs has broadened with the emergence of new types of intellectual property. Not only has the range of conventional IPRs been extended, but there are also new types of IPRs. For example, copyright now covers the right of communication through information networks and the rights of data producers, and new types of IPRs have been established in the right over the layout design of integrated circuits and the right to plant varieties. Third, the original rules for IPRs protection have to be updated before regulating the new ways of utilising intellectual products. For instance, facing the expansion of the Internet, traditional IPRs rules fail to determine the legitimacy of technologies and measures used to protect confidential information or define the liability of people who spread and consume digital works. Furthermore, the territoriality principle of trademark rights does not apply on the Internet, and the classified protection of trademark rights does not pertain to an exclusive trademark right across the network. Fourth, there are challenges to conventional ideas about IPRs. When biotechnology blurred the distinction between discovery and invention, the conventional thinking that patents can only be granted to inventions but not discoveries was brought into question (Reisman 1995, pp. 101–106). Meanwhile, the concept of a right to traditional resources has drawn peoples' attention to the protection of traditional knowledge. In short, although the four problems mentioned above form only a part of what needs to be dealt with in IPRs reforms, they should be taken as focal points for such reforms.

The priority in reforming the IPRs regime is to remedy its defects by adding supplementary systems and improving existing ones. In this way, a comprehensive mechanism will be built to address IPRs in the risk society. The major supplementary systems to be established are as follows.

11.4.1 Traditional Knowledge Protection Systems

The World Intellectual Property Organisation uses the term "traditional knowledge" to refer to "tradition-based literary, artistic or scientific works; performances; inventions; scientific discoveries; designs; marks, names and symbols; undisclosed information; and all other tradition-based innovations and creations resulting from intellectual activity in the industrial, scientific, literary or artistic fields" (WIPO report 2001, p. 15). Traditional knowledge is a relative concept defined in the context of modern society as a contrast to modern knowledge: Modern knowledge is a body of universal knowledge developed from the Western scientific, philosophical and socio-economic system, possessing a dominant position in the world. In comparison, traditional knowledge is developed by people through generations within a specific social and ecological environment, demonstrating a high level of diversity (Li 2008). The preservation and development of traditional knowledge holds the key to the conservation of biodiversity and cultural diversity and is the mainstay of the sustainable development of human society. Nevertheless, the current IPRs regime places emphasis only on the protection of modern knowledge (innovation) and fails to protect traditional knowledge (the source of innovation). The regime's neglect of the importance of protecting cultural diversity and knowledge diversity has meant that some countries, nationalities and races are deprived of rights to which they are due. In recent years, the international community has begun to attach great importance to the protection of traditional knowledge and has conducted valuable discussions in this respect. There are two approaches of the institutionalisation of traditional knowledge protection. One is that the current IPRs regime should be upgraded to cover traditional knowledge protection, meaning that the scope of copyright and neighbouring rights protection would be extended to cover folk art and literature, the scope of patent protection to cover products and methods related to the use and development of genetic resources, the scope of plant variety right protection to cover new plant varieties developed from Protophyta, the scope of design right protection to cover traditional handicrafts, the scope of trademark protection to cover individual and collective marks used for products and services with traditional elements, the scope of geographical indication protection to cover community marks used for natural and traditional products and handiworks, and the scope of protection against unfair competition to cover undisclosed traditional knowledge (Correa 2001). The other view, held by some scholars and non-government organisations, is that a specialised regime is needed for traditional knowledge protection to cover its nature and characteristics. There is, however, disagreement over whether such a specialised regime should be subject to the IPRs regime. Some argue that despite the specialised regime differing greatly from the conventional IPRs regime in terms of its theoretical basis and social norms, it should be regarded as a special IPRs regime; others hold that the specialised regime should be subject to a broader system of rights, thus constituting a traditional resources rights regime, on which there are heated discussions among the international community. The IPRs regime and the traditional resources right regime would have different roles, as the former provides an incentive for innovation and the latter provides protection for the source of innovation (Long 2004). The protection of traditional knowledge requires international coordination, but it remains a divisive issue and is thus an uncertainty factor in the risk society. The outcome of the debate over traditional knowledge protection will not only set a new pattern of interest but also orient the future development of the international IPRs regime.

11.4.2 Public Domain Preservation Systems

Creations in the public domain are those to which no exclusive IPRs apply. The public domain system can be traced back to the UK's *Statute of Monopolies (1623)* and *Statute of Anne (1709)*. According to these statutes, as soon as the protection of patents and copyrights expires, the intellectual products are placed in the public domain. After the UK, the US also adopted the public domain system to restrict the term and scope of IPRs protection. The constitutional grant of power to US Congress manifests three policies for copyright, one of which is "the preservation of the public domain" (Patterson and Lindberg 1991, pp. 49–55). Whereas IPRs represent private interests, the public domain represents public interests. Given that the purpose of the IPRs regime is to protect both private and public interests, it must not only guarantee IPRs but also preserve the public domain. It can be said that the dualistic purposes of IP legislation constitute the practical foundation of the preservation of the public domain. In China's legal infrastructure, most scholars conclude that the public domain consists of three types of intellectual resources: first, it contains intellectual products for which the protection term has expired; second, it contains intellectual products that fail to meet the substantial requirements for granting IPR; and third, it contains the knowledge shared by all humans, including unprotected “ideas”, scientific theories, mathematical theories and so on. Within the international conventions, the public domain mainly consists of freely reproducible forms of expression, freely applicable technologies, signs and symbols freely used to denote or connote in the marketplace, functional and aesthetic designs free to apply to products; ideas and ephemeral news and accessible knowledge (Zhang 2011). It must be noted, however, that as the IPRs regime develops, IPRs expand and the public domain contracts, provoking a conflict between private interests and public interests. And IPRs “have become a means of recycling public information into private monopolies” (Drahos and Braithwaite 2002, p. 165). This risk of the IPRs regime is primarily realised by legislators and governments giving priority to copyright protection and thus leaving the public domain unattended (Feng 2006, pp. 30–34). To address this risk, the public domain system must be rebuilt to balance the interests of stakeholders and to identify and control the expansion of exclusive rights.

11.4.3 Open Access Movement and Creative Commons Licensing

As mentioned above, the expansion of IPRs and the imbalance between private and public interests plague the reform of the IPRs regime. US scholar Henry C. Mitchell argues in his work *The Intellectual Commons* that the harm done by the overexpansion of IPRs to the ecosystem is as great as that done by the overexploitation of natural resources. Therefore, for the sustainability of ecosystems, there is a need to communalise intellectual resources and halt the trend of privatisation (Mitchell 2005, pp. 67–173). To ensure the availability of intellectual resources, some organisations and individuals have launched “sub-politics” movements (Beck 1999),[7] of which the most representative are the Open Access movement and the Access to Knowledge movement. The Open Access movement, supported by people in academic circles, the publishing sector and library and information industry around the globe, aims to use the Internet to facilitate the spread of scientific and technological achievements. According to the Budapest Open Access Initiative in 2001, “by ‘open access’ to literature, we mean its free availability on the public internet, permitting any users to read, download, copy, distribute, print, search, or link to the full texts of these articles, crawl them for indexing, pass them as data to software, or use them for any other lawful purpose” (H. X. Liu 2006, pp. 55–56). However, it is worth mentioning that in the Open Access movement, the freely available literature mainly refers to academic literature that will be used for teaching, research and study. Thanks to the Open Access movement, a platform for “intellectual commons” has been built on the Internet. As an improvement to the traditional copyright system, it has directly

[7] In risk society theory, global ‘sub-politics’ refers to forms of politics outside and beyond the representative institutions of the political system of nation-states. It is a means for dealing with the risk society. See Ulrich Beck (1999).

promoted the exchange and spread of academic literature. The Creative Commons licence is another improvement to the traditional copyright system. Based on the idea of an "anti-patent", the license is an extension of the open-source license from the software industry into other cultural industries. Since the licence was produced by Creative Commons in 2001 as a public copyright licence, it has been applied to all work falling under copyright. Copyright owners can confer rights to use a work they have created through different types of Creative Commons licences. In short, the Open Access movement and Creative Commons licence are improvements to the traditional copyright license and have opened up a new approach to the free and widespread and the recreation of intellectual works (Yang 2007).

11.4.4 Knowledge Innovation Incentive Systems

The problems caused by the drawbacks of the patent system are a representative "institutionalised risk" in the risk society. To overcome these problems, especially the decline in the quality of patents, the explosive rise in patent litigations, patent thickets and patent races, work on building a risk management mechanism with supplementary institutions is underway. Although the patent system plays a major role in encouraging and protecting intellectual innovation, it needs to be supplemented by a reward system, of which there are two types. One type is a "patent reward system" connected to the patent system. Under such system, patented inventions become state-owned and are placed in the public domain when the government pays the patent holder monetary compensation equivalent to the social value of the invention (Y. H. Liu 2011, pp. 33–36). This system is mainly applied to technology industries in which the protection of exclusive rights will produce strong adverse effects in society. For example, the pharmaceutical industry for inventions concerned with public health and some other industries in which the large scale and high density of inventions patents have exerted a negative influence on technological innovation. The other type is an "invention reward system" running in parallel to the patent system. Under this system, the government gives inventors tangible or intangible rewards for their inventions based on their social or economic value. The inventions then become state-owned but freely available to everyone. As a non-market mechanism, this reward system is a supplement to the patent system.

The value of an IPRs regime lies in the protection it provides to private intellectual property and in its contribution to the progress of society and knowledge. Reform and improvement of the IPRs regime has now become a major concern for the international intellectual property community, not only as a measure to control the risks of the IPRs regime but also to open a legal pathway to fully achieve its value objectives.

References

Anupam, Chander and Sunder, Madhavi. 2004. The romance of the public domain. *California Law Review* 9

Beck, Ulrich, Anthony Giddens, and Scott Lash. 1994. *Reflexive Modernization: Politics, Tradition and Aesthetics in the Modern Social Order*. California: Stanford University Press

Beck, Ulrich. 1992. *Risk Society: Towards A New Modernity*. London: Sage

Beck, Ulrich. 1999. *World Risk Society*. Cambridge: Polity Press

Beck, Ulrich. 2003. From industrial society to the risk society: Questions of survival, social structure and ecological enlightenment. *Marxism & Reality* 3

Beck, Ulrich. 2004. The silence of words and political dynamics in the world risk society. *Marxism & Reality* 4

Bodenheimer, E. 1974. *Jurisprudence: The Philosophy and Method of the Law*. Cambridge: Harvard University Press

Castells, Manuel. 2000. *The Rise of the Network Society*. Oxford: Blackwell Publishers

Chen, Zhigang. 2001. Marx's criticism of instrumental rationality. *Studies in Philosophy of Science and Technology* 6

Cheng, Boqing. 2007. Social problems in risk society. *Journal of Nanjing University (Philosophy, Humanities and Social Sciences)* 2

Commission on Intellectual Property Rights. 2002. Report of the commission on intellectual property rights, integrating intellectual property rights and development policy. http://iprcommission.org/papers/pdfs/final_report/ciprfullfinal.pdf. Accessed 20 Jul 2007

Correa, Carlos M. 2001. *Traditional Knowledge and Intellectual Property: Issues and Options Surrounding the Protection of Traditional Knowledge: A Discussion Paper*. Geneva: Quaker United Nations Office

Drahos, Peter and Braithwaite, John. 2002. *Information Feudalism: Who Owns the Knowledge Economy?* London: Routledge

Feng, Fei. 2012. China is more than 15 years behind developed countries in bio-industry. http://blog.sina.com.cn/s/blog_674923790100jnzy.html. Accessed 14 Feb 2012

Feng, Xiaoqing. 2006. A theory of public domain in copyright law. *Journal of Xiangtan University (Philosophy and Social Sciences)* 1

Gao, Fuping. 2011. The development of copyright law in the digital age. *Intellectual Property* 2

Gao, Mingliang. 2006. Value rationality in comparative law. *Journal of Comparative Law* 5

Giddens, Anthony and Pierson, Christopher. 1998. *Conversations with Anthony Giddens: Making Sense of Modernity*. California: Stanford University Press

Giddens, Anthony. 2002. *The Third Way and Its Critics*. Beijing: Central Party School Press of the Communist Party of China

Giddens, Anthony. 2003. *Runaway World: How Globalization Is Reshaping Our Lives*. New York: Routledge

GRAIN. 2001. *TRIPS-Plus Through the Back Door: How Bilateral Treaties Impose Much Stronger Rules for IPRS on Life Than the WTO*. Saskatchewan: Grain Publications

Lash, Scott. 2000. Risk culture. In *The Risk Society and Beyond: Critical Issues for Social Theory*, eds. Barbara Adam, Ulrich Beck and Joost van Loon. Thousand Oaks, Calif.: SAGE.

Li, Fayao. 2008. *An Empirical Study on the Protection Mechanism of Traditional Knowledge from Multiple Perspectives*. Beijing: Intellectual Property Publishing

Liu, Haixia. 2006. A review on the research of open access. *Library and Information* 1

Liu, Tieguang. 2011. Shift of the fundamental paradigm of technology regulation in risk society. *Modern Law Science* 4

Liu, Ting. 2008. Risk control in the network society. *Journal of Ningxia University (Social Science Edition)* 5

Liu, Xing. 2004. Some new insights into legal transplantation: From "history" to "present". *Social Sciences in China* 5

Liu, Youhua. 2011. The future pattern of the patent system: Being replaced, reformed or globalised. *Journal of South China Normal University (Social Science Edition)* 4

Long, Wen. 2004. *The Way of Protecting Traditional Knowledge as Intellectual Property, Research on Patent Law, edited by the Department of Law and Treaty of China National Intellectual Property Administration.* Beijing: Intellectual Property Publishing

Merton, Robert K. 2011. *Social Research and Social Policy.* Trans. Mengren Li. Shanghai: SDX Joint Publishing

Mitchell, Henry C. 2005. T*he Intellectual Commons: Toward an Ecology of Intellectual Property.* Maryland: Lexington Books

Patterson, L. Ray and Stanley W. Lindberg 1991. *The Nature of Copyright: A Law of Users' Right.* Georgia: University of Georgia Press

Reisman, Joseph M. 1995. Physicians and surgeons as inventors: Reconciling medical process patent and medical ethics. *High Technology Law Journal* 10

Sun, Fabo. 2007. International intellectual property protection for biotechnology. *Journal of Political Science and Law* 6

Tsosie, Rebecca A. 2002. Reclaiming native stories: An essay on cultural appropriation and cultural rights, *Arizona State Law Journal* 34

UNESCO. 1995. *Our Creative Diversity: Report of the World Commission on Culture and Development.* France: EGOPRIM.

United Nations. 2000. Sub-Commission on Human Rights resolution 2000/7

Wang, Xixin. 2005. A case study on the problems in China's administrative law enforcement. *Chinese Journal of Law* 3

Wang, Taiping. 2011. Intellectual property system in the future. *Chinese Journal of Law.* 3

Wang, Xuezhong. 2008. The control of technological and social risks with law. *Journal of Science, Technology and Law* 4

Weber, Max. 1958. *The Protestant Ethic and the Spirit of Capitalism.* New York: Scribner

WIPO. 2001. *Intellectual Property Needs and Expectations of Traditional Knowledge Holders* (WIPO Report on Fact-Finding Missions, 1998–1999)

Xiao, Qing. 2011. Issue of national cultural security from perspective of "risk society". *Studies in Culture & Art* 2

Xiong, Wencong. 2010. A study on the legitimacy and scope of copyright from the perspective of postmodernism. *Political Science and Law* 6

Xu, Doudou. 2005. Technology knowledge and risk society. *Journal of Fujian Provincial Committee Party School of CPC (Fujian Academy of Governance)* 9

Xu, Zhijin and Mao, Baoming. 2007. Scientific and technological development in the risk society. *Forum on Science and Technology in China* 2

Xue, Xiaoyuan and Liu, Guoliang. 2005. An interview with Ulrich Beck on the present and future world risk society. *Marxism & Reality* 1

Xue, Xiaoyuan. 2004. Research on globalisation and the cultural industry. In *Report on the Development of Global Cultural Industry (2003–2004)*, ed. Tuo Lin. Beijing: Social Sciences Academic Press

Yan, Yonghe. 2006. *The Protection of Traditional Knowledge as Intellectual Property.* Beijing: Law Press

Yang, Chunfu. 2011. Understand risk society from a jurisprudential perspective. *Law and Social Development* 6

Yang, Hongjun: *The System of Copyright License* (Dissertation). Wuhan: Zhongnan University of Economics and Law (2007)

Yang, Xuedong. 2005. A review on risk society theories. *Journal of Chinese Academy of Governance* 1

Zhang, Hongfeng. 2005. The globalisation and localisation of law. *Fujian Journal of Legal Science* 1

Zhang, Wenxian. 2003. *Marxist Jurisprudence-Theory, Method and Frontier.* Beijing: Higher Education Press

Zhang, Wenxian. 2004. *Jurisprudence: Marxist Theory, Methods and Points of Law*. Beijing: Higher Education Press

Zhang, Xiulan. 2010. Understand risk from the perspective of social science. In *Social Amplification of Risk*, ed. Xiulan Zhang and Peter Taylor-Goody. Beijing: China Human Resources & Social Security Publishing

Zhang, Yanmei. 2011. A study on the international public domain under the international IPRs treaty system. *Contemporary Law Review* 4

Zhu, Xuezhong and Yang, Yuanbin. 2003. Sharing mechanism of IP interests produced on the basis of hereditary resources and choice of China. *Journal of Science*, Technology and Law 3

Zhuang, Yougang. 2004. The Internet Age and risk society. *Journal of Huaiyin Teachers College (Social Sciences Edition)* 4

Шамба, T. M. 1987. Legal order and democracy. Trans. Bin Chang et al. *Legal Translation Series* 4

Chapter 12
Policy Dimensions of IPRs Regimes

An IPRs regime constitutes a vital component of a government's public policy. It protects legitimate IPRs and promotes the advancement of human knowledge. In the modern era, the UK and US governments have formulated and implemented IP policies effectively, whereas developing countries, in general, are confronted with the challenge of developing their own IPRs regimes capable of performing within the framework of the international trade system and also yielding the highest net benefits for their nations. Over the past century, IP legislation in China has undergone a transition from passive transplantation of Western experiences to indigenous innovation. Today, the national strategy of establishing China as an innovation-oriented country determines that further adjustments and improvement of China's IP policies must be accomplished.

12.1 IPRs Regime Within Public Policy Frameworks

At the state level, the IPRs regime functions as an instrument of social policies (Liu 2004, p. 46). It is shaped by the choices and decisions a government makes on public policy concerning whether to protect IPRs, and if so, the scope and level of protection, in accordance with the nation's current development circumstances and potential future development needs. Nourished and evolved in developed countries, IPRs, with a history spanning more than 300 years, are thriving in the West as an achievement of institutional civilisation. It has played a significant role in promoting economic development, scientific and technological advancement, as well as cultural and educational progress. Establishing an IPRs regime has become an inevitable policy choice for a country seeking to modernise.

"Public policy", a common term in policy science, refers to "a system of laws, regulations, rules, programmes, plans, measures, or projects made by policy-making institutions on cost-effectiveness analysis to restrain or guide private or public behaviours

H. Wu, *Theorising Intellectual Property Rights from Chinese Perspectives*,
https://doi.org/10.1007/978-981-96-5367-1_12

at a certain period" (Wu 2004, p. 4). According to this definition, the IPRs regime is also an IP policy in the public policy system.

12.1.1 Policy-Making Entities

The US scholar and President Woodrow Wilson (1856–1924) said that "public policy is made by politicians, that is, by legislators, and enforced by the executive" (Wu 1985, p. 4). In essence, intellectual property policies are formulated, implemented and promoted at the national level. In other words, the government guides and regulates the creation, ownership, utilisation and management of intellectual resources by means of institutional allocation and policy arrangements in the name of the state. Public policy actors play three main roles. First, they formulate laws and regulations to protect relevant intellectual property in the form of property rights. With regard to an IPRs regime, as an independent law, a legislator will initially take into account the local realities regarding the country's economic, scientific, cultural and educational development; however, once an international IPRs protection system has been formed, domestic laws are often affected by the trend of legal integration, so the legislator must then consider the coordination between integration and localisation in the choice and management of the system. Second, they provide preconditions and means that are essential for the implementation, and establish supporting mechanisms for judicial adjudication, administrative management, social services and so on. Although IPRs are a form of property rights of the market mechanism, they cannot exist without the regulation of the government mechanism. Because of the nonphysical existence of intellectual products, the judicial organs, administrative bodies, social service agencies and others need to intervene in the acquisition, utilisation, protection and management of IPRs to ensure the benefits of implementing the system are realised. Third, supported by the public, they serve the goal of the "general policy"[1] (Wu 2004, p. 5) with the support of other relevant public policies. In the public policy network, the goal of promoting economic growth and social improvement is undertaken not only by IP policies but also by other public policies. Some norms of IP policies are reflected in other public policies and rely on the support of other policies for their implementation. Public policies related to IPRs mainly include those in the domains of culture and education, industry and economics, science and technology, and trade. The tasks of the government, as the agent of policymaking, are to formulate, improve, unify and coordinate this range of policies.

[1] A general policy is one that holds a commanding position in the public policy system and plays a fundamental and decisive role in guiding the social operations of a country. It is a policy that affects the whole situation and runs through a specific historical period, always with strong generality and stability.

12.1.2 Regulatory Functions

According to theories of policy science, the process of implementing public policies inevitably faces the question of "who has the vested interest in the policy, and who is the loser of the policy?" Therefore, public policies must strike a balance between conflicting interests to ensure their smooth implementation and the stable development of society (Wu 2004, p. 3). IP policies are thus concerned with the allocation and adjustment of interests. It concerns the rights and obligations of creators, disseminators and users of intellectual products as "stakeholders" and the balancing of the proprietary rights of creators with the public interests. In striking this balance, policymakers must consider that intellectual property takes the legal form of private intellectual property. Therefore, in the relation of rights and obligations, right is the basis, authorisation is the main content of the method, and the protection of the creator's right is central to legislation. At the same time, however, intellectual property is a legal means to the end of sharing intellectual benefits. The interests between the subject of rights and the subject of obligations and between the individual and the society are thus adjusted by means of the limitation of rights and the design of the system for utilising rights; that is, policy is tasked "to carry out purposeful and directional regulation of various objective interest in social relations, in order to promote the formation and development of interests" (Sun 1995, pp.26–29). Based on the adjusting functions mentioned above, two basic underlying legal principles have formed around the IPRs regime: the sanctity of private rights and the balance of interests. In the intellectual property infrastructure, it is of special significance to emphasise the principle of balanced interests, which refers to the interests between the parties, between the subject of rights and the subject of obligations, and between the individual and the society, and which accords with the kernel idea of fairness. The balance of interests is not only a requirement in the spirit of civil law and social morality but also a reflection of human rights and the public interests (Chapman 2001, p. 3). The IPRs regime emphasises the balance of interests, aiming at protecting the interests of IP creators while ensuring that the reasonable use of intellectual products by the public. The definition of "fair use" may be based on freedom of expression, on the need for public education or on necessity for public health and social life. American scholars describe the modern copyright law as a "balanced law" (Patterson and Lindberg 1991, p. 2) that coordinates the interests of all parties, and this appraisal is applicable to the whole intellectual property system.

12.1.3 Policy Objectives

Franklin M. Fisher (1935–2019), professor emeritus of economics at Massachusetts Institute of Technology noted that "Whether public policy is formulated by political debate or formal voting, it involves both the goal of public policy and how to achieve the goal" (Fischer 2003, p. 3). The formulation and implementation of public policy always correlates with its goal. In general, public policy aims at promoting the stability, justice, and development of society. However, different public policies have their respective specific goals to solve specific related social problems. Taking IPR policy as an example, its aims are justice and efficiency. As "justice is the primary goal of a social system" (Shen 1993), realising justice may be a priority in the establishment of an IPRs regime, and establishing an IPRs regime satisfies the demand for justice as it formalises what is deemed in modern legislation as a right in natural law, existing naturally based on the creators' intellectual property and legally based on the aim of freedom from feudal constraints. To ignore creators' rights would deny compensation for their intellectual input and produce a state of disorder in mental production and injustice in the whole society. Therefore, an IPRs regime rooted in economics should satisfy the pursuit of justice, effective allocation of intellectual resources and promotion of nonmaterial wealth. Efficiency-oriented targets make great contributions in the field of IPR, including the dissemination of knowledge, technology and information and the achievement of a number of systems, such as exclusive use (creators' right) of intellectual property, licensed use, statutory license (disseminators' right) and fair use (users' right). Therefore, the purposes of the IPRs regime are to maintain the just order of intellectual rights and implement an efficient system of knowledge dissemination.

To measure the rationality of IP policies, economists adopt a cost–benefit analysis (CBA). For instance, the emergence and choice of any institution are the result of a comparison of its costs and benefits according to the relevant parts of the new institutional economics. In other words, the institutional arrangement of IPRs should bring a net benefit in knowledge management. CBA can also explain why an IPRs regime is required. An IPRs regime costs less than relying solely on the market to solve problems with knowledge products. According to Ronald Coase (1910–2013), public policy is an alternative when a market offers a solution that has costs that are too high (Coase 1994). The definition of property rights on knowledge products originates from their attribute of being a public good. Unlike private goods, public goods are non-rivalrous in consumption and may be used by different subjects at a certain time and place. A bus, for example, might carry both payers and non-payers, but the bus company cannot discern them and shall accommodate both. Those who do not pay for public goods are called "free riders" (Cooter and Ulen 1994, p. 147). In the field of knowledge, production is expensive, but dissemination costs relatively less. Once one consumer pays for a knowledge good, others may become free riders, which "is a phenomenon that someone duplicates others" products gratuitously" (Ibid., p. 152). In view of such a situation, it is necessary for governments to intervene in the market of knowledge goods by adopting specific public policies: one is that the government provides knowledge goods itself, and the other is that the government subsidises private persons who provide knowledge goods. A significant measure of the latter set of policies is to grant exclusive rights to creators of knowledge goods through an IPRs regime.

The above scientific analysis of IP policies is static and inward looking, and IP policies rely on two prerequisite assumptions for their justification. First, the general social conditions that IP policies depend upon must exist, namely the basic conditions that enable the production, dissemination and use of intellectual products, including adequate economic, technological, cultural and educational infrastructure and environment. Without this foundation, it would be impossible to make and enforce IP laws and its related policies, and IP policies would fail to achieve their goals and may even exert negative influences. Second, IP policies shall cater to and only concern a nation's domestic realities. That is, policymakers need only consider the country's internal circumstances when constructing the country-specific IP policies or enacting customised and tailor-made IP laws. However, since the implementation of international IPRs protection, it is difficult to isolate a nation's IP policies from international practices. It is thus more likely that a country's IP policies end up conflicting with or decoupling from their domestic circumstances and thus fail to bring their expected benefits. It must be noted that certain countries, in certain contexts, have been unable to fulfil the two conditions discussed above simultaneously. Consequently, some governments, governments of industrial countries in particular, have adopted a pragmatic attitude towards IPRs protection and constantly adjust and improve their IP policies for the benefits of their own nations.

12.2 National IP Policy Approaches of Major Countries

IP laws are a result of the constant reform and innovation of property law and property law can trace its origin back to ancient Rome. The regime of IPRs itself, after 300 years of development in industrial countries, has become "a paragon of institutional civilisation"[2] (North and Thomas 1973, pp. 114–124). More recently, it has been used by industrial countries as a policy instrument to promote economic growth, technological advancement, cultural prosperity and educational progress. It has now become a strategic policy for innovation-oriented economies to maintain their technological edge, protect trade interests and strengthen international competitiveness.

In the seventeenth and eighteenth centuries, the UK, as the birthplace of IP laws (mainly patent and copyright law) as well as the cradle of the European Industrial Revolution, had a great success in implementing IP policies. IP laws in the UK have gone through a transition from the franchise system of the Middle Ages to a capitalism-based regime of property rights. The former includes the product franchise (granted by the royal members as an industrial franchise of production and circulation) and printing franchise (an administrative privilege mainly benefiting publishers). In 1623, the UK Parliament enacted the *Statute of Monopolies*, which abolished the franchise system and introduced provisions on the creation of technologies and innovation of newly founded industries, functioning, de facto, as the patent

---

[2] North and Thomas (1973) compared China in the fourteenth century with the UK in the seventeenth and eighteenth centuries argued that the UK had by then established an IPRs system that stimulated inventions and a technological revolution, laying a solid foundation for the forthcoming industrial revolution that would ultimately introduce the modern economy.

law. *The Statute of Anne* aimed to grant the exclusive right to copy to authors and publishers so as to encourage creation, and its purpose was to protect and encourage investment in the creative writing and publishing industry. The mercantilist policies of the seventeenth and eighteenth centuries in England served as a significant ideological foundation for IP legislation. The *Statute of Monopolies* encourages the creation and application of new technologies. The purpose of patents is not to create a trade monopoly, but to achieve technological progress and industrial development through temporary "monopoly rights." The enforcement of the *Statute* signified a shift from the printing franchise to a capitalist "property right" by adhering to copyright as exclusive property and introducing provisions such as duration of copyright, effectiveness of copyright and price control, for the sake of commerce (Patterson and Lindberg 1991, pp. 49–55). Complementary to and consisting of public policies on industries, commerce science and culture, IP laws in the UK made institutional preparation for the Industrial Revolution beginning in the 1770s. As American economist and Nobel Prize laureate Douglass C. North (1920–2015) noted, the UK's phenomenal economic success during the eighteenth century was founded on an environment favouring the evolution of property rights and the right of ownership over IP, under which inheritance rights, unlimited ownership of land, free labour, private property protection and patent law as well as measures mitigating defects in IP products and market were nourished. Taking China in the fourteenth century as the reference to the UK in the seventeenth and eighteenth centuries, North pointed out that the IPRs regime in the UK pioneered the new domain of the property rights system and protected the interests of creators and innovators, encouraging them to produce multitudes of creations and technological innovations, and thus triggered the Industrial Revolution and a surge of growth unprecedented in modern economic history (North and Thomas 1973, p. 191). The success of the UK in the early modern era proves that the ideal conditions for IP legislation involve a country's self-determination of protecting IPRs at a level that fits best with its economic and social realities, rather than the need to yield to outside pressures. That explains, to a great extent, the UK's smooth and rapid transition to modern society and serves as a model for other countries to follow suit.

The modern United States of America is an effective operator of IP policies. Although founded only in the eighteenth century, the United States of America was also among the earliest countries to set up an IPRs regime. Following its independence from the UK, in 1787, USA legislators drafted a constitution to include clauses on copyrights and patent rights, stating that "the Congress shall have power to lay and collect taxes, duties, imposts and excises, to promote the progress of science and useful arts, by securing for limited times to authors and inventors the exclusive right to their respective writings and discoveries" (Article I, Section 8, Clause 1 of the Constitution of the United States). This was referred to by American scholars as the "3P" policies, that is, *promotion* of learning, *preservation* of the public domain and *protection* of the author (Patterson and Lindberg 1991, p. 55). The US Congress enacted its patent and copyright law in 1790 in accordance with the provisions of the Constitution. At that time, the USA's IP policies were pragmatism-guided and mercantilism-orientated. Domestically, it aimed to promote technological and cultural advancement by granting temperate exclusive IPRs; and when it involved foreign trade, it aimed at protecting national interests. Examples of this protectionism were manifest in practices such as leaving foreign creations unprotected and piracy of foreign works unattended, collecting high fees on foreign patent applications and delaying acceding to the Europe-initiated *Berne Convention* while supporting the American Union of Copyright. Following the First and Second World Wars, the United States of America has grown into a global power. Since then, it has succeeded in increasing its IPRs protection standards and has imposed its own standards on the world as a universal threshold. Its ambition became particularly visible in moves it has made regarding its IP policies since the 1980s. Domestically, the USA established a policy system to develop its knowledge economy and innovation in science and technology, revising its patent law to reinforce protection over technological property, enacting the *Inventors Protection Act* (1999) and the *Stevenson-Wydler Technology Innovation Act* (1980) to encourage technological innovation and developing and implementing the statutorily mandated *Technology Commercialisation Fund and Technology Transfer and Commercialisation Promotion Act*, among other legislations. These policies comprise an integral legal system covering the creation, application, and protection of IPRs. Furthermore, the USA integrated its IP policies into its industrial, technological and cultural policies to support the emerging IP-intensive industries, such as semiconductors, computers, telecommunications and pharmacology, as well as cultural industries involving software development, film-making and music-recording. Thanks to the government's successful implementation of these policies, the U.S. has built IP advantages as a patent power and a brand power, consolidating its position as the world's top economic and technological power. Abroad, the USA coupled its IPRs protection policy with the international trade regime, drawing on its massive pool of talents to create IP and earn a competitive edge in the international market. Before the *TRIPS Agreement*, mainly through Sections 301 and 337 of the U.S. Tariff Act of 1930,[3] the USA required its trade counterparts to protect USA's IPRs in exchange for most-favoured-nation (MFN) treatment, a permanent normal trade relations extending the same treatment to all. Economic and trade sanctions would be imposed on those who failed to adequately or fully protect USA's IPRs. With the adoption of TRIPS, the USA turned to its contracts with other countries and the international conventions of the WTO to enforce its IPRs abroad, linking its commitment to high-standard protection with the equal standards imposed by the MFN standards of the WTO. In this process, the USA persuaded many countries to adopt patent protection of computer software, required developing countries to start granting patents for new drugs and proposed special protection for semiconductor chips. These proposals were ultimately integrated into the rules of the international trade system. Notably, since the adoption of the *TRIPS Agreement*, the USA has conducted negotiations

[3] Sections 301 and 337 of the U.S. Tariff Act of 1930 has been a source of contention between the United States and its trading partners for the last twenty years.see 19 U.S.C. § 1337 (2001).

with the European Union, Japan, Australia and other countries to sign bilateral free trade agreements, seeking higher protection of USA's IPRs. As *Council on Competitiveness, Innovate America: Thriving in a World of Challenge and Change, National Innovation Initiative Interim Report* issued in 2006 stated, "The founding base of the United States determines that IPRs protection has been and will always be the pillar of innovation." Furthermore, it insisted that "a sound, appropriate and coercive domestic and international IPRs regime must be maintained" (Council on Competitiveness 2004, p. 7). The USA has firmly enforced its IP policies and attempted to make its domestic standard the international standard, thereby becoming a major influence in shaping the modern international IPRs regime.

Since the beginning of the twenty-first century, industrial countries have raced each other to implement IPRs strategies that both suit their own circumstances and serve their national interests. As discussed above, the USA, a forerunner of technological development, has raised its protection standards and expanded the scope of protection by constantly enhancing its IPRs regime. It has also sought to impose its own values and standards on international IPRs-related affairs. Japan released its *IPRs Strategic Outline* in 2002 and enacted the *Basic Law on Intellectual Property Rights* in the same year to "strengthen the implementation of policies on IP creation, protection and utility to make Japan a powerhouse in technology and science so as to promote its international competitiveness" (The Third Science and Technology Basic Plan of the Japanese Government (2006–2010). Across the Pacific Occean, Australia carried out its *Innovation Action Plan* under its national IPRs strategy in 2001 and undertook a new round of amendments of its IP laws in 2005 based on the *Australia-US Free Trade Agreement* (AUFTA). South Korea is among the countries that observed and followed prior practices and principles in their own IP legislation. Since setting the goal of becoming the technology research hub of Asia by 2015 and a global leader in technology development by 2025, South Korea has taken legal measures to protect its own competitive hi-tech industries. It has also paid greater attention to foreign protection of its domestic IPRs. Therefore, South Korea's legislation is close to the basic positions of the United States, Europe and Japan. These cases illustrate that the IPRs regime has become a strategic policy for developed countries to maintain technological advantages and strengthen their international competitiveness.

In contrast, developing countries have been playing a passive role in IP policy arrangement. According to studies of policy science, there are limits on all public policies, meaning that if a public policy incurs a high social cost, it will fail to meet policy goals and may even come with unintended consequences. For developing countries, to adopt a country-specific approach in terms of its IPRs regime, while bearing in mind the international legal framework is the optimal path. An economic analysis of public policy also indicates that "imposing legal protection on properties creates incentives for efficient utility of resources" (Cooter and Ulen 2011). Furthermore, appropriate protection of IPRs is conducive to knowledge augmentation. However, changes to the international context have made it impossible for developing countries to make independent choices concerning their own IP policies. The reality for developing countries is that IP legislation in countries has advanced to a new stage where standards are unified. Globalisation has ushered in an era of 'standardised' IPRs protection. Minimum standards were written into the *International Convention on Intellectual Property Protection.* It must be noted that setting minimum standards was initially intended to confirm solidarity of principles and norms in IPRs protection but not to require a 'one size for all' approach for IPRs protections. However, taking the developed countries' requirements and their practices as the reference, the "minimum standards" is now universally consistent in protection standards, including both the scope and level of protection. Consequently, developing nations are left to struggle as they make continuous effort to develop their economy, technology and society to meet the high standards. Certainly, protecting IPRs is the cornerstone of global trade and developing countries must comply. Yet, when adopting minimum standards, what developing governments should, and can do is to undertake a cost–benefit analysis to seek a lower social cost to maximise the benefit. A cost–benefit analysis of compliance with international minimum standards of protection must be conducted at two levels, horizontal and vertical. At the horizontal level, the benefits of embracing globalisation must equal or outweigh the costs of integrating into the international IPRs regime. Adopting international standards of IPRs protection raises two major concerns for developing economies. The first is that high standards impose heavy financial and administrative burdens that these countries may not be able to afford. The second is that the new international trade regime imposes more pressure on developing country policymakers than they already suffer in attempting to develop their countries. Despite these concerns, developing markets' decisions to accept the WTO standards of IPRs protection as a cost of participating in global trade is made in their own interests after careful consideration, as it ensures their undifferentiated MFN treatment and access to certain favourable policies (for instance, extension of the tariff reduction period and compulsory licensing of their IPRs) committed to by developed members during the Uruguay Round.[4] It also earns the developing nations a place in future trade talks and various forums on IPRs protection, which are among the major benefits gained by developing members in this cooperative game.

At the vertical level, the benefits in future development shall outweigh the current costs. Developing countries, particularly emerging industrial countries, are under pressure not only from the international community but also from within to strengthen their IPRs protection for economic and technological promotion. An effective IP policy aligns with other related public policies and creates the physical/material

[4] Translator'S note: The Uruguay Round (1986–1994) was the eighth round of multilateral trade negotiations (MTN) under the General Agreement on Tariffs and Trade (GATT). It established laws and concepts that applied to all aspects of global commerce, from banking to consumer goods. Tariffs, non-tariff measures, tropical products as a priority area, natural resource-based products, textiles and clothing, agriculture, review of GATT articles, safeguards, Tokyo Round agreements and arrangements, subsidies and countervailing measures, dispute settlement, trade-related aspects of intellectual property rights, trade-related investment measures, and the Functioning of the GATT System were among the topics discussed during the round, which was the largest of any GATT round (FOGS).

conditions and social environment that facilitate the creation, administration, protection and use of IPRs, ultimately promoting intellectual creation and social economic development. According to the UK Commission on Intellectual Property Rights, if other conditions concerning cultural outcomes are satisfied, stronger private rights protection stimulates local cultural business in developing countries in the long term (Commission on Intellectual Property Rights 2002, pp. 237–239). This suggests that traditional developing countries seeking new industrialisation must strengthen their IPRs regimes to sustain domestic economic and social development and to effectively participate in international competition. This approach guarantees significant future gains in exchange for necessary current costs. It is challenging for developing countries to choose an appropriate IP policy that fits the WTO framework. The 2005 UN Report states that "protecting intellectual rights is a critical aspect of technology innovation, but overly protective systems can constrain creativity" (United Nations 2013). In light of this, experts striving for United Nations Millenium Development Goals (MDGs) proposed a three-tiered regime based on differences in countries' respective levels of development, under which countries with a per-capita gross domestic product (GDP) above $5,000 USD are classified in Tier A, those with a $1,000–$5,000 USD per-capita GDP are in Tier B, and those with a per-capita GDP of less than $1,000 USD are in Tier C. Tier A countries must observe all TRIPS provisions, including the legal framework and the enforcement provision, Tier B countries must adopt the entire legal framework and may need limited coercive enforcement, and Tier C countries may establish their own legal framework but under the guidance of TRIPS (Ibid.). The experts' opinion indicates that developing countries may choose their own IPRs protection standards based on their economic and social circumstances as long as they observe the minimum standards set in the international convention on IPRs (Wu 2005).[5] The World Bank Institute report included similar advice:

It has been concluded that in most low-income countries, with a weak scientific and technological infrastructure, IPRs protection at the levels mandated by TRIPS is not a significant determinant of growth. On the contrary, rapid growth is more often associated with weaker IPRs protection. In technologically advanced developing countries, there is some evidence that IPRs protection becomes important at a certain stage of development, but that stage is not until a country is well into the category of upper middle income developing countries (World Bank Institute 2005).

The above analysis shows that high protection standards are not beneficial to less developed countries as this institutional framework makes it difficult for them to

[5] Wu (2005) noted that when formulating IPRs regimes, developing countries should—while adhering to the minimum protection standards of international conventions—integrate a stage-specific approach with a scope-specific approach. The stage-specific approach requires that the level of IPRs protection be commensurate with a country's economic and social development. Such protection must not fall below nor exceed the level warranted by the state of technology and economic conditions at a given historical stage. The scope-specific approach demands that the coverage of IPRs protection align with a country's economic and social development. The scope should be neither inappropriately narrowed nor unduly expanded.

access the science and technologies needed for development. However, for industrial developing countries, strengthening IPRs protection plays a vital role in stimulating technological innovation, promoting culture and sustainably developing the economy. In summary, IP policies are not policy instruments exclusive to developed countries' use. If developing countries want industrialisation and modernisation for their countries, they should make good use of them.

12.3 Evolution of China's IP Policy

An IPRs regime is an institutional arrangement of the commodity economy and technological development. As early as in the seventeenth and eighteenth centuries, two to three centuries earlier than China, Western industrial countries initiated IP legislation. Major developing countries such as India and Brazil also preceded China by an entire century in setting up an IPRs regime. China, as a latecomer, has, over the last century, undergone the change process from foreign IP norms initially imposed on China's legal system to actively adopted and adapted to ultimately facilitate domestic economic and social development.

This "hundred years' history" of China's IPRs evolution can be divided into four periods, as detailed in the following sections.

12.3.1 Passive Acceptance Period (1870s–1948)

It is generally agreed that China's IP legislation began in the last years of the Qing Dynasty (1870s), when the tottering regime, out of an intention/desire to learn from the West, but more under pressure from foreign imperial powers, initiated its "New Policies" reform for an institutional westernisation as the last attempt to revive its sclerotic system of rule.[6] Among 40 edicts enacted by the emperor Quangxu (1871–1908), there was the *Statute of Awarding New Technologies* (1898), the first patent law in China. However, the law, as well as many other ambitious policies were soon aborted because of the failure of the 1898 Reform Movement.[7] Later, the Qing government, with the help of Western powers, formulated pilot regulations on trademark registration (1904) and the *Copyright Law of the Qing Dynasty* (1910) based on the IPRs-related terms and clauses of the *China–UK Boat Trade Treaty* (1902)

[6] Translators' note: The New Policies (1861–1895) occurred after China's defeat in the Sino-Japanese War (1894–95) and the ensuing rush for concessions in China on the part of Western imperialist powers. More than 40 edicts were issued, which if enacted would have transformed every conceivable aspect of Chinese society.

[7] 1898 Reform Movement, or the Hundred Days of Reform, as the extension of New Policies was initiated mainly by the reform proposals of Chinese intellects with Kang Youwei (1858–1927) and Liang Qichao (1873–1929) as the leading figures. It was ended by the conservative officials who argues that they were rushed, too extensive and fundamentally dangerous.

and the *China–US Boat Trade Treaty* (1903). These laws were applied until the early Republican Period (1920s). The ensuing Beiyang Government (1912–1928) and the Republic Government (1928–1948) both westernised the national judiciary by simply copying foreign IP laws. China was not the only developing country to transplant foreign laws into its own legal system. For example, India, which was once under British rule, directly applied British patent law and later enacted *Indian Patents and Designs Act* (1911) patent law, taking UK's 1911 Patent Act as a blueprint. Developing countries, with weak material foundation and inadequate social support, tend to be influenced by external forces to a large extent in their IP legislation and implementation. Therefore, their IP laws and IPRs-related laws poorly serve their ultimate social objectives and fail to function effectively.

12.3.2 Selective Arrangement Period (1949–1980s)

Despite several administrative regulations on IPRs protection put forth by the government, IPRs infrastructure has largely been absent in the People's Republic of China over the first three decades of its founding. It was not until the reform and the opening-up policy were initiated in the late 1970s and early 1990s, respectively, that China's IP legislation was put on the national agenda. A preliminary system of IP laws took shape during this period with the enactment of *China's Trademark Law* (1982), *Patent Law* (1984) and *Copyright Law* (1990). China's IPRs legislative practice highlights selective application, under which IPRs are applied selectively both in the scope of legislation and in the standards of protection and international cooperation, basing its choices on three factors. First, the urgency of the legislation made it difficult to cover all aspects of IP laws within a short time. Second, China's economic and technological circumstances required flexible standards of IPRs protection; thus, the scope of its patent protection was limited and international protection standards on computer software were not yet applied. Third, unequal international exchanges of culture and China's underdeveloped copyright law precluded China from participating in international copyright standards. This kind of selective institutional arrangement made according to different development stages and conditions was beneficial to China, and there were precedents in the international community that could be cited. One such precedent case is the USA, which, having enacted a copyright law in 1790, refused to provide protection for foreign literary and artistic works for an extended period and isolated itself from the Berne Union for 102 years based on the consideration that its culture and education lagged behind European countries, only joining the *Berne Convention* in 1988. Japan, another example, enacted its *Patent Law* in 1885, after the Meiji Restoration in 1868, a coup d'etat ending the military government for the modernisation and Westernisation of the country. At that time, the standard of protection provided by Japan's patent policy was the lowest in the world and for over half a century, the law excluded patents for medicines and chemicals and implemented favourable policies for domestic corporations to introduce foreign technologies. These cases, extensively yet not exclusively illustrate developing countries' reasonable need for a transition period of "selective protection" and "weak protection" during their IPRs development before they exercise "full protection" and "strong protection" of IPRs. Therefore, in situations where the level of national economic and social development is not high, a transitional period of low-level IP protection is necessary.

12.3.3 Adaptive Application Period (1990s–2000)

From the early 1990s until the beginning of the twenty-first century was a critical stage for China's IPRs regime. During this period, a full revision of the *Copyright Law* (2001), *Patent Law* (1992, 2000) and *Trademark Law* (1993, 2001) was accomplished, and other IPRs-related laws were enacted, such as the *Regulation on Protection of New Varieties of Plants* (1997) and the *Regulation on Protection of Integrated Circuit Layout Design* (2001). These revisions and enactments brought China's IPRs protection standards up to the requirements of TRIPS before China's accession to the WTO. Within a few decades, China managed to adjust its legislation on IPRs from a low level of protection to a high level one and accomplished the transitional tasks from domestic standard to international standard. The rapid yet smooth transition was ensured by China's commitment and self-determination within and beyond the country. At the international level, China's commitments to the *Sino–US Memorandum of Understanding on IPRs Protection* (1992) and the *Sino–US Agreement on IPRs Protection* (1995), along with other international conventions sustain its efforts to accelerate the internationalisation of its IPRs regime. Particularly, the *TRIPS Agreement* formed in 1994 reshaped China's IP legislation. As stated above, in light of the global context of IPRs internationalisation, China was not likely to develop its economy, technology and culture with an IPRs regime that did not protect foreign IPRs rights. Furthermore, the international orientation towards trade in knowledge meant that China was unable to isolate itself from the rest of the world or to remain aloof from the international protection system of IPRs led by developed economies. Yet the transition that has taken place was not primarily driven by international pressures but by internal impetuses. At the domestic level, China as an emerging industrial country, has a strong need for economic growth and technological development through strengthening its IPRs protection. Moreover, an independent and active arrangement of institutions is essential for emerging economies such as China to facilitate their general policy objectives. During this period, Chinese lawmakers conducted several rounds of revisions of laws, laying a sound foundation for the modernisation of China's legal system. For example, the year 1992 witnessed the works of applied art and acrobatic works, for the first time, included in the scope of IP; and computer programs and the rights of rental and communication through information network started to be protected thanks to the 2001 revision of the *Copyright Law*. The revision of the *Patent Law* in 1992 and 2000 ensured that it is applicable to 200 pharmaceutical products and chemical substances. Meanwhile, the protection period for patents is extended and rights of imports and promissory sales are added and a strict restriction on compulsory licenses is imposed. The scope of trademark protection was also extended through the revision of the *Trademark Law* in 1993 and 2001, to cover not only commodity trademarks but also service trademarks. In addition, the required constituent elements for trademark registration and applicable scope of trademark holders were listed / further clarified and the protection of national well-known trademarks was strengthened in the revision. *The Regulation on Protection of New Varieties of Plants* (1997) and *Regulation on Protection of Integrated Circuit Layout Design* (2001) were also enacted. Since this time period, China's IP legislation has kept up with its technological development and has been renewed/ to facilitate the modernisation of China's science and technology.

12.3.4 Strategic Decision-Making Period (2000 to the Present)

In 2004 and 2005, the National Working Group on Protecting Intellectual Property and the Leading Group on Working out National Intellectual Property Strategy were founded to reinforce and institutionalise IPRs protection in China. China thus began to strategically enact and implement IP laws adaptable to local conditions. In January 2016, at the National Conference of Science and Technology, President Hu Jintao announced the national strategy of establishing an innovation-oriented country. It was no coincidence that only four months later, IP legislation and implementation were brought under the spotlight when President Hu reiterated their significance at a study session of the Political Bureau of the Central Committee, the national decision-making body of the Communist Party of China (CPC), stating, "To establish an innovation-oriented country valuing indigenous innovations, China has to strengthen its IPRs regime so that the creation, fair use, protection and administration of IP will be promoted." This statement sent out a clear message that Chinese policymakers reviewed the function and significance of the IPRs institution from a strategic perspective. In response to the trends of global technology and economy and drawing on the experiences of innovative countries, China planned to formulate and implement its own national IPRs strategy, empowering itself with an effective IPRs institution, in hopes of catching up with developed countries within a limited timeframe.

The policy adjustment of China's IPRs regime is based on the general objective of building an innovation-oriented country (i.e., a country that establishes technological innovation as a basic strategy and engages in competition through high-technology innovation). At present, about 20 countries are regarded as innovation-oriented, including the USA, Japan, Finland and South Korea. These countries each have a high composite innovation index, with technological contribution to the economy above 70%, R&D investment to the GDP ratio over 2% and foreign technology dependence below 30% (Qian 2006, p. 25). To join this list, China faces a choice regarding its development model. Over two decades, China participated in the international division of labour, mainly in labour-intensive industries, as a producer of low-end products. This development model played an important role in promoting China's economic growth and creating jobs. However, certain deep-rooted problems surfaced and became acute as the costs of labour and environmental resources rose. For instance, China now faces a scarcity of certain natural resources, with per-capita farmland accounting for only one third of the world average; fresh water, one quarter; oil, 17%; natural gas, 13%; and even coal – a rich resource in China – only 42% of the world per-capita average (Mei 2006, p. 126). These figures indicate that China can no longer afford a resource-intensive approach to development. Furthermore, under the current economic structure, wherein developed countries offer technologies and knowledge while developing countries provide labour and materials, developed economies are unwilling to transfer their core technologies to China, either because they wish to maintain their own technological advantages or because of ideological prejudice. The lesson China has learned is that dependence on foreign technologies constrains itself from further development. Both global trends and the realities of its internal circumstances indicate that China has to embark on indigenous technological and cultural innovation, which urgently requires legal and administrative institutions necessary to support the required technological and cultural innovation. Indeed, countries or multinational corporations (MNCs) that boast strong innovation capabilities usually own their core technologies and appreciate the significance of IPRs in promoting R&D and technological updates to increase their competitive edge. For example, thanks to its IPRs regime, the USA, a leading competitive innovator in computer technology, cyber technology and biotechnology, is witnessing the rapid rise and expansion of its sunrise industries such as electronics, software and bioengineering. Particularly innovative MNCs generally own their own patented technologies, for instance, Sony's micro-electronic technology, Phillips' optical media technology and Intel's chip manufacturing technology. China lags far behind these innovative economies in both technological and innovation capability, or, more specifically, in the number and quality of proprietary technologies. China is home to one of the world's largest populations and largest manufacturing industries, ranking first in the production of approximately 200 types of commodities/goods. However, its abundance of manpower has not yet translated into an abundance of talent, and its industrial competitiveness still manifests itself in the low cost of labour it can offer. China's bottleneck lies in its weak technological and innovative achievements, specifically its lack of core technological patents, copyrights and world-famous brands. At present, China is at a critical stage in terms of its industrial restructuring, remodelling its economic growth, updating its technology and transforming its enterprises. It is thus of great importance for China's future development that it establishes an IPRs regime as a strategic pillar of its national agenda of innovation so that it can transform from an "imitator" to a "manufacturer" and, ultimately, to a "creator."

References

Chapman, Audrey R. 2001. A human rights perspective on intellectual property: Core obligations related to ICESCR Article 15(l)(c)[R]. *Copyright Bulletin* 3.

Coase, Ronald H. 1994. *The Problem of Social Cost, in Property Rights and Institutional Changes.* Shanghai: Shanghai Joint Publishing Press

Commission on Intellectual Property Rights. 2002. Report of the commission on intellectual property rights, integrating intellectual property rights and development policy. http://iprcommission.org/papers/pdfs/final_report/ciprfullfinal.pdf. Accessed 20 Jul 2007

Cooter, Robert and Ulen, Thomas. 1994. *Law and Economics.* Shanghai: Shanghai Joint Publishing Press

Cooter, Robert and Ulen, Thomas. 2011. *Law and Economics* (6th edition). London: Pearson

Council on Competitiveness. 2004. *Innovate America: Thriving in a World of Challenge and Change, National Innovation Initiative Interim Report.*

Fischer, Frank. 2003. *Evaluating Public Policy.* Beijing: China Renmin University Press

Liu, Hua. 2004. *The Rationality and Performance Analysis of IPRs regime.* Beijing: China Social Sciences Press

Mei, Yonghong. 2006. Indigenous innovation and national interest. *The Journal of Qiushi*

North, Douglass C. and Thomas, Robert P. 1973. *The Rise of the Western World.* Cambridge: Cambridge University Press

Patterson, L. Ray and Stanley, W. Lindberg. 1991. *The Nature of Copyright: A Law of Users' Right.* Georgia: The University of Georgia Press

Qian, Junsheng. 2006. *Independent Innovation and Building an Innovative Country.* Beijing: Chinese Communist Party Publishing House

Shen, Zongling. 1993. Law value justice interest. *Peking University Law Journal* 5

Sun, Guohua et al. 1995. On the choice of interests in law. *Legal Science* 4

The Constitution of the United States, Art I.S8.C1.1 Taxing Clause. ArtI.S8.C1.1.1 Taxing Power

UNESCO. 2002. Integrating intellectual property rights and development policy: Report of the commission on intellectual property rights

United Nations. 2013. *Innovation: Applying Knowledge in Development*

World Bank Institute. 2005. *Promoting Innovation in Developing Countries: A Conceptual Framework*

Wu, Handong. 2005. Post-TRIPS IPRs regime revolution and China's solution. *Studies in Law and Business*

Wu, Ming. 2004. *Economic Analysis of Public Policy.* Hunan: Hunan People's Publishing House

Wu, Qiyuan. 1985. *Public Policy.* Taipei: Taiwan Commercial Press

Chapter 13
Development Trajectories of IPRs Regimes

Within development theory, economic growth, knowledge innovation, and the advancement of the rule of law should constitute an interdependent and mutually reinforcing co-ordination mechanism. Economic growth plays a decisive role in societal transformation, driving rapid increases in material wealth and precipitating significant shifts in societal lifestyles. Within this tripartite coordination system of knowledge innovation, economic development, and legal system construction, the economy is positioned as the central axis, around which knowledge and law oscillate in their influence. Specifically, knowledge advancement serves as the dynamic mechanism propelling economic growth, while the development of the rule of law functions as its safeguarding mechanism. IP law, as a manifestation of legal civilisation arising from the dematerialisation of property, embodies the essential nature of institutional innovation. Concurrently, IP law constitutes an incentive and regulatory mechanism for creative outputs, thereby embodying the core value objective of fostering knowledge innovation.

13.1 IPRs Regime in the Context of Innovation-Driven Development

Innovation is the key to modern economic development. According to the development theory of Joseph A. Schumpeter (1883–1950), an Austrian-American economist, innovation serves as the foundation for economic growth, making it the core of the theory of economic development (Schumpeter 1911). The commercialisation and industrialisation of intellectual products and the emergence of knowledge-based economy formed thereby catalyse the establishment and implementation of IP laws. This is because knowledge production is a market-oriented activity which involves adopting and creating new knowledge. It has a strong reliance on the integration of science, technology, culture and economy and hence cannot survive

H. Wu, *Theorising Intellectual Property Rights from Chinese Perspectives*,
https://doi.org/10.1007/978-981-96-5867-1_13

without sound protection and regulation of the corresponding scientific, technological, cultural and economic institutions. The knowledge-based economy with its endogenous capacity inevitably leads to the institutional demand for IP laws. Institutional innovation is the key for the survival and development of IP law, and intellectual innovation has also become the legislative purpose and value objective of IP law. IPRs demonstrate the essence of institutional innovation and also the mission of intellectual innovation in the innovative activities of human society.

IPRs possess the inherent characteristics of institutional innovation. IP law is the nexus of knowledge (i.e. in science, technology and culture), economy and law. The emergence, reform and development of IP law is the mutually reinforcing interaction between knowledge innovation and institutional innovation. According to neo-institutional theory, one of the main theoretical perspectives used to understand organisational behaviour as situated in cultural rules and beliefs, "technological progress and institutional evolution can [both be] regarded as a process of innovation" (Wang 1992). "Innovation", as an economic term, was first put forward in the early twentieth century by Schumpeter in his work *The Theory of Economic Development* (Schumpeter 1911). He defined "innovation" as the introduction of a new combination of factors and conditions into the production system, including new products, new technologies, new markets, the control of new sources of raw materials and new enterprise organisation (Schumpeter 1911; He and Yi 1990, p. 73). Since the 1950s, Douglass C. North (1920–2015), Ronald H. Coase (1910–2013), among other scholars, adopted Schumpeter's innovation theory in analysing the supply and demand of institutional innovation. Their collective work, as a theoretical continuum of institutional economics, clarifies the multi-faceted relationship between knowledge innovation and institutional innovation, the function of nations in institutional innovation and the role institutional innovation plays in economic development. In the context of institutional economics, "institutional innovation" generally refers to "novel, useful, and legitimate change that disrupts, to varying degree the cognitive, normative, or regulative mainstays of an organisational field" (Raffaelli and Glynn 2014). It involves innovation of rules and norms in various systems, such as industrial, property rights, enterprise, economic, management and market operation. In terms of IP law, institutional innovation indicates reforming the existing system and making new institutional room for an improved way of extracting values of intellectual products. In essence, IPRs themselves are a dematerialised revolution in the field of property rights since Roman law.

IPRs possess the basic function of intellectual innovation, being the institutional arrangement of intellectual production, intellectual innovation and the development of knowledge-based economy. When explaining the economic function of the institutions, Theodore W. Schultz (1902–1998) said that 'the rise in the economic value of human agents makes new demands on institutions [and] that some political and legal institutions are especially subject to these demands" (Schultz; Liu 1999). And IP law, in responding to the knowledge-based economy, aims at defining property rights, providing an incentive mechanism for innovation activities, allocating resources, providing a trading mechanism for creative industries, protecting the property rights of creative achievements and establishing a market-regulated mechanism. IP laws address the social relations that are derived from innovation. Respecting innovation, protecting intellectual achievements and regulating the market order of the knowledge-based economy are always the objectives of IP legislation. To realise the value of innovation, policy making and policy planning on IPRs should merit the following three aspects.

First, to protect IPRs and incentivise innovation. IP laws are an effective property right system over intellectual products. By acknowledging the right of ownership over intellectual creations, an IPRs regime provides rights holders with the most economic, effective and lasting incentives to ensure the sustained development of innovative activities and bring in a rapid growth of productivity. IP laws function as a mechanism not only of incentive but also of restraint. Regulating the behaviour of market players and cracking down on infringements not only protect the interests of property rights owners but also regulate the market behaviour. A malfunctioned IPRs regime with ineffective implementation would fail to curb the prevalence of IPRs infringements, dampen creators' enthusiasm for producing and developing intellectual products, and eventually lead to the shrinking of social wealth accessible to the public. Thus, the institutional economics view provides an economic solution which helps to adjust the cost and benefit relationship between IPRs transaction and protection and leads the rational economic man to abandon infringement and other illegal activities.[1]

Second, to impose limits on IPRs and encourage innovation-based development. The limits of IPRs involve limitations on the exercise of proprietary rights to balance the interests between the rights holder and the public to ensure equal and open public access to intellectual products. The modern property rights system has outgrown its initial objectives of protecting the rights of IP holders with new orientations of promoting intellectual wealth of human communities. Therefore, the institutional arrangement of IP laws defines private property rights while stipulating a publicly available knowledge pool, protection of prior rights and fair use. By doing so, not only does private innovation secure promotion and protection but also the public innovation and an affordable cost of innovation. It is thus no coincidence that IP laws in general require private-owned IP to enter the public domain after a reasonable time through defining the period of protection and adopting the "exhaustion doctrine" to stimulate new creations.

Third, the mechanism of utilisation of IPRs and innovation achievement transaction. The utilisation of IPRs is to link the creators of intellectual products, disseminators and users, aiming at regulating the transactions of property rights between various subjects to facilitate the dynamic utilisation of intellectual products and the increase of values through the movement. Its main systems are authorised use, statutory license and reasonable use to promote the use and trade of intellectual properties. The use of intellectual products bonds IP creators with IP disseminators and users. And regulation of the use and trade of intellectual properties, including authorised use, statutory licenses and fair use, are essential for standardising stakeholders' transactions, promoting the use of intellectual products and increasing intellectual wealth of the communities. It only takes a supply and demand analysis to see that both

[1] See (Lyu 1998) for relevant discussions on institutional economics.

intellectual production and exploitation of intellectual resources reflect demand-side requests for exchange. It is through exchange that individuals obtain the optimal combination of goods they need and that producers realise maximised utility and benefit of their products.

Innovation is the core/soul value of IP law. The essence of institutional innovation and the function of intellectual innovation are intrinsically consistent in IP law. In the institutional innovation activities of IP law, a government body, as the major provider of institutions and initiator of innovations, bears resemblance to an entrepreneur. Yet, unlike an ordinary entrepreneur, a government body responsible for managing the affairs of a state plays the role of a "political entrepreneur", taking greater account of innovation of social systems, than business innovation; of the overall growth of economy, than huge profits of certain enterprises (Huang 2004). A "political entrepreneur" is an active player of innovation in the institution-building of IPRs, shouldering the following responsibilities: formulating laws and regulations on IPRs; making effective institutional arrangements for the acquisition, application and transaction of intellectual products; establishing a conducive legal infrastructure for intellectual resources by establishing operating regimes and executive bodies that make judicial decisions and provide administrative social services; setting overall targets for economic growth and social development and reaching them by a knowledge innovation oriented policy system; and promoting the commercialisation, marketisation and industrialisation of intellectual products. Regarding the intellectual innovation functions of the IP law, the law regulates the objective of innovative development and standard path to realise the objective, so as to achieve the main purpose of protecting private rights and stimulating innovation. In patent law, this means protecting the first commercial use and profits of a novel technological invention, which are the fruits of "technology commercialisation." In copyright law, the first publication and profits of creative works, the outcomes of "works commercialisation", are protected. Likewise, trademarks protect interests such as product reputation. Trademarks in themselves may not represent innovation; however, they protect the first commercial use and profits along with the consumer's interests in first recognition (Wu 2013). Intellectual property laws establish IP publishing and prior right protection, which protect individual innovation and promote the sustainable development of social innovation. Meanwhile, the cost of innovation can be maintained at a rational rate. These laws also specify a limited duration of protection and the exhaustion of rights, and other limits to the exclusive rights of the rightsholders to bring intellectual products into the public domain so as to encourage new creative activities. In a word, the existence of IPRs is linked with intellectual innovation. IP law originates from innovation being a product of the innovation of the property law institutional innovation. It changes due to innovation and holds intellectual innovation as its value objective. It can be said that persistent institutional innovation and intellectual innovation are part of the historical process of IP law and also its future mission.

13.2 Development Modes of IPRs Regimes in Modern Countries

In development theory, IPRs are regarded as an institutional tool to promote economic development. The interpretation of their functions, however, varies in the international community: one view is that IPRs should contribute to economic development by enhancing a country's fundamental strength and raising the standard of living for its citizens (Nussbaum 1997, p. 286). The other holds that IPRs should contribute to economic development by promoting trade freedom, increasing international investment and improving invention efficiency through technology transfer (Gervais 2005, pp. 528–534). When comparing the two types of economic development, the former emphasises the all-round development of human beings, believing that economic development is one of the prerequisites needed for human development and that economic development can only play its proper role if it is compatible with other development goals. By contrast, the latter emphasises economic development in a narrow sense, that is, economic efficiency and economic benefits are regarded as the main objectives of economic development, which are unrelated to other social goals.

Although different economic development theories have different understandings of the functions of the IPRs regime, in the practice of modern countries, IPRs are without exception an institutional tool for the development of the knowledge-based economy, that is, to enhance the capacity of intellectual innovation, form core competitiveness and achieve leap-forward development of the social economy through the IPRs regime. In this regard, Kamil Idris, Director General of the World Intellectual Property Organisation believed that IP is a "power tool" for economic development (Idris, accessed 2008). In the post-TRIPS era, developed countries or innovative countries such as the United States of America, the European Union, Japan, and South Korea are competing to establish their strategic objectives of IPRs, and using the IPRs regime and relevant policies to maintain their technological advantages, trading interests and core competitiveness. This is manifest in the following three aspects: first, IPRs reflect the comprehensive national strength and the advantage of IPRs is that of the national strength. A country's comprehensive strength includes hard power such as economy, science and technology, and military power and soft power like culture, which are manifest in the quantity, scale and quality of independent IPRs at the legal level. The ownership of IPRs in a country has become an important indicator to measure its strength. Second, IPRs are the choice of development strategies: the strategy of IPRs is that of becoming a powerful country. The IPRs regime in modern society was a policy tool used by European countries and the USA to promote economic development and scientific and technological progress, and in contemporary society it is a strategy for innovative countries to maintain their technological advantages and to achieve transformational/transitional development. Promoting intellectual innovation through innovative IPRs regimes and policies and using IP strategy as a tool to build a strong and prosperous country are both typical development strategies used by developed and emerging industrial countries. Third, IPRs are the tool in international competition: the competition for IPRs is that for the future world. In international trade, IPRs have become an important tool to curb competitors. It can be seen that IPRs are a system of private property rights that protect private intellectual property, but they are also a widely accepted legal norm in the field of international trade and economy. The development history of the international IPRs regime in the past 200 years is a history of the countries that developed first using IPRs to restrict and control the countries that developed later. It can be said that IPRs protection is the focus of competition between Eastern and Western countries in the field of international economy and trade, and independent IPRs are strategic tools to maintain the core competitiveness of countries.

Against the backdrop of economic globalisation and the knowledge revolution, IP laws serve not only as legal institutions but as strategic policies. The strategic cooperation of developed countries in promoting the level of international IP legislation and enforcement, the conflicts of interests between developed countries and developing countries in IPRs protection, and the selection of IPRs regimes by developing countries to follow a path that is consistent with their own economic development have all shown the dual importance of a country's IP strategy in addressing both domestic and international issues.

Internationally, IPRs protection has become a constituent component of the basic system in the field of international trade. China's IP strategy must be put into practice in such a way that it provides policy support for reforms of the current international IPRs protection system. The emergence and development of the knowledge-based economy have changed both the distribution and the governance of society. As mentioned by the American scholar Ervin Laszlo, at the beginning of the twentieth century the rules stipulating the nature of power and wealth in the world have changed. Power no longer belongs to a particular organisation, and the meaning of wealth is shifting away from tangible goods such as gold, money and land. A foundation for invisible wealth and power that is more flexible is taking shape. This new foundation is marked by ideological, technological and communication advantages (Laszlo 1997, p. 6). IPRs are taken as the institutional foundation and policy support for the emergence and development of the knowledge-based economy, one of whose features is the importance of international trade in IPRs and the widespread/prevalence of IP infringement. From the perspective of international trade, high-tech industries and cultural industries supported by IPRs have become the economic pillars of developed countries, and protecting IPRs is to maintain the major economic interests of developed countries and their industries; from the perspective of infringement, once high-cost intellectual products enter countries with weak IPRs protection, they will be subject to low-cost piracy and imitation. This deepening conflict between high-cost production and low-cost copying has made the integration of IPRs protection a primary international issue of concern to developed countries. Therefore, IPRs protection is often a key part of the competition strategy of developed countries. Developed countries continue to improve the international IPRs protection enforcement through multilateral, bilateral and even unilateral ways, with the ultimate goal of creating a business environment for their competitive industries and gaining competitive advantages.

Domestically, IPRs protection is an important institutional support for a country's strategy of innovation. Countries design and adopt IPRs regimes in their national interests and public policy positions, a macro stance transcends concerns for private rights. The development of modern economy and society has provided sufficient evidence that intellectual progress and economic prosperity have a positive correlation with sound IPRs regimes. All the countries with intellectual progress and economic prosperity have sound and proper intellectual property systems. Ever since the 1800s, IPRs regimes have been adopted across Europe and North America as policy instruments to leverage economic growth and scientific progress. Entering the 1900s, IPRs regimes have been elevated to a strategic level for maintaining technological advantages and realising innovative development. As Kamil Idris (1954–), former director-general of WIPO, stated, "IPRs is a powerful tool for economic development" (Idris, accessed in 2008). The UK was the earliest in outlining an IPRs regime in the modern sense. It was in the UK that legislation on copyright and patent was successively adopted, and it was also in the UK that the industrial revolution started. Complementary to and consisting of public policies on industries, commerce, science and culture, IP laws in the UK laid a solid institutional foundation for the Industrial Revolution beginning in the 1770s. The USA stands out as another major beneficiary of the IPRs regime. Thanks to its relentless effort to improve and optimise its IP legislation throughout the twentieth century, the USA gained the upper hand in the world market competition, positioning it as the global leader in technological innovation and economic growth. A US government report in 2004 illustrated its consistent stand on the IPRs regime, stating that "Since the founding of our nation, the protection of IPRs has been one of the underpinnings of our society and our innovation system" (Council on Competitiveness 2004, p. 7). The Obama administration (2009–2017) issued the '*Strategy for American Innovation*' in 2009 and 2011, which clearly presented IP laws as an important leverage for promoting and protecting innovation, saying that:

> The key to our success-as it has always been-will be to compete by developing new products, by generating new industries, by maintaining our role as the world's engine of scientific discovery and technological innovation. It's absolutely essential to our future.

The *Strategy* also announced that the US Patent and Trademark Office would initiate the national project "Intellectual Property in the 21st Century", to support and underpin the *Strategy* (United States Patent and Trademark Office, United States Patent and Trademark Office 2010–2015 Strategic Plan 2010). In Asia, the Republic of Korea stands outs as a strong promoter of IPRs strategy, who spearheaded the "Southeast Asian economic miracle." It initiated the "Creative Korea" campaign in 1997 and adopted "Cultural Korea" strategy in 1998, taking IPRs as a strategic leverage to transform the nation from an industrial country into an innovative power. The above cases illustrate the institutional force of IP laws in spurring knowledge innovation and transformative development.

13.3 China's New Development Philosophy and Advancement of Its IPRs Regime

IPRs are an institutional sign of a country's modernisation. As Alison Firth explained, "Although it is not always emphasised in historical records, IP laws are contingent upon and situated in the economic and political environment" (Firth 1997, p. 3). The European and American nations were the first to promote and enjoy the benefits of the IPRs regime since its inception. The IPRs regime was originally a legal civilisation generated in the Western geographical environment. Under a Eurocentric interpretation, it is seen as a necessary factor in the process of modernisation, making it a standard for social and historical progress (Liu 2002).[2] There is no doubt that in the era of economic globalisation, the WTO has shaped the legal order of the multilateral trading system, and TRIPS has provided contracting parties with uniform rules for IPRs protection. However, countries with different levels of IPRs protection have their own ideological understandings and guidance on IP institutional arrangements. In other words, guided by the principle of complying with the minimum protection criteria of international conventions, countries can express their ideas independently in the construction of their respective IPRs regime, that is, under the trend of modernisation and internationalisation, IPRs present diverse and different development patterns. In order to achieve the strategic goal of becoming a strong IP country, China's IPRs regime must, on the one hand, overcome the historical burden of having insufficient institutional experience and a weak spirit of rule of law. On the other hand, it must build a legal system and policy system that are appropriate for local conditions on the basis of IPRs integration. China has not only introduced foreign IPRs regimes since the reform and opening up; it has also paid attention to learning and absorption, and has steadily integrated them into the domestic innovation system. IPRs have become the basic legal system for intellectual innovation activities, the development of intellectual industry and the order of the intellectual market. Theories and practice of China's IPRs construction are of significance for developing countries to build a pluralistic modernisation model in the international community.

The scientific outlook on development with Chinese characteristics in the new era provides an important ideological cornerstone and guidance for the construction of China's IPRs regime. The new development philosophy has abundant connotations such as innovative, coordinated, green, open and inclusive development, involving many aspects of social development such as economy, science and technology, culture and environment. Since the reform and opening up, it is a major breakthrough in developing China's thinking and practice as well as international advanced experience and theories. In order to solve development problems, enhance development momentum and cultivate development advantages, President Xi Jinping proposed to

[2] Liu Xing (2002) contends that some frameworks of power, under the guise of modernist conceptions, are portrayed as 'progressive' developmental objectives. This transforms them into institutionally promoted constructs driven by particular interests, consequently neglecting the rightful claims of the Other under diverse historical conditions.

adhere to the people-centred development philosophy, emphasise the implementation of innovative development philosophy, and build a modern economic system. In addition, he also said that the construction of China's IPRs regime must adhere to the core concept of new development, that is, emphasising the innovative development of humanism, the coordinated development of fairness and justice, the green development of harmony between man and nature, the open development of facing the world, and the inclusive development of balancing interests, so as to maintain the correct direction of the development of the IPRs regime.

In the traditional international mainstream ideologies, development takes economic benefits as the main objective, and IPRs are considered as institutional tools to promote economic growth. The evaluation criteria of their contribution rate are to promote trade and investment freedom and improve the efficiency of technological transfer (Gervais 2005, pp. 528–534). According to the new development philosophy, development is a process that places a high value on the economy and links several social aspects, including institutional development, social development, and economic development (Yang 2017, p. 22). Therefore, the institutional functions of IPRs should take into account human problems as well as social problems like resources and environmental issues while addressing the economic problem of increasing intellectual wealth. Starting from the new development philosophy, we should clarify the basic ideas for IPRs development: First, the idea of people-centred development. Adhering to the idea of people-centred development is to take enhancing people's welfare and promoting people's all-round development as the starting point and result of development. This political proposition is humanism in the sense of legal value. On the basis of protecting the rights of creators, the humanism of the IPRs regime aims to make it possible for the entire society to benefit from the economic and social advantages brought by IPRs. It is the development of individuals, societies and countries as well as the common development of the human society (Wu 2005). Second, innovation, coordination, harmony and openness are regarded as standards to evaluate the development, that is, the innovation in the driving force of development, the coordination in the development modes, the green standard in the development quality, and the openness in the development environment should be regarded as the standards to evaluate the development status and effectiveness of the IP industry.

Under the guidance of new development philosophy, China's IP industry has formed a complete system of knowledge and experience, including realisation paths such as the overall strategy, policies and planning, as well as benefit evaluation. In terms of methodology, the transformation from ideology to system composition is mainly manifest in the following three aspects:

First, planning the national IP strategies. IP strategy is the general policy in the public policy system, or the carrier of policy strategisation. It is the overall strategy and action adopted by the main body to seek the realisation of strategic objectives through measures such as planning, implementation and evaluation. Strategy should be the basic starting point for a country to deal with IP matters and the overall arrangement on IP issues. In the process of implementing IP laws and applying IP policies, the IP strategy is in a leading position and guided by some value concepts and functional objectives. In the system of institutional norms, the development strategy plays a fundamental and decisive guiding role in a country's social operation. In a specific historical period, it always has a strong generality and stability (Wu 2004, p. 54).

China has so far basically succeeded in achieving the objectives set forth in the *Outline of the National Intellectual Property Strategy* (2008) and has established itself as a significant IP powerhouse with international influence. China's IP industry is currently in a new historical position and is transitioning from a significant IP country to a powerful IP country. In accordance with the national three-step strategic plan, China will formulate a 15-year plan (2021–2035) on the development of IP power to strengthen the coordination between IPRs and the overall national goals. Building a strong IP country is a top-level system design and strategic deployment intended to implement the socialist outlook on rule of law and development in the new era. Additionally, it serves as a transition and goal for the country's in-depth implementation of its IP strategy. In the face of the new era, new situation and new requirements, the development direction and strategic focus of the national IP strategy will be changed and adjusted accordingly, that is, in terms of IP strength and governance ability, it will achieve the goal of building a sound system, taking a lead in creativity, developing advanced industries and managing the environment properly, so as to become a modern country under the rule of law which is innovation-oriented.

Second, formulating plans to develop and promote the IP industry annually. Formulating the "Five-Year Plan" for national economic and social development is China's practical experience and institutional advantage in achieving its objective of economic and social development through medium-term planning and policy allocation. Since the reform and opening up, the basic functions of the "Five-Year Plan" are to provide a framework for macroeconomic activities and a basis for the government to perform its public service duties. It can be said that the "Five-Year Plan" is not only the basic means of national modernisation governance, but also an important standard for evaluating the effectiveness of national governance. Since 2016, China has incorporated the IP development plan into the "Five-Year Plan", which has become a national key plan. In the future, the development plan of the IP industry should be based on the "Five-Year Plan" for national economic and social development and the 15-year plan (2021–2035) on the development of IP power, and define objectives of medium-term plannings, key tasks and main measures at different stages. The annual plan, which is a specific policy document for implementing the objectives of the Five-Year Plan as well as an action plan for adjusting and refining the recent work, is formulated based on the development situation and development needs of that year and often lists key items. China, Japan, South Korea and other countries have successful experience in formulating annual plans for promoting IPRs.

Third, improving the public policy system guided by IPRs. It is a common practice for many countries, especially developed countries, to establish a system guided by IPRs and coordinated by multiple policies to enhance their capability of independent innovation and enhance their competitive advantage. In China's context, the public policies related to IP law include industrial policies that adjust and optimise industrial structures and encourage emerging industries; regional policies that cultivate local economies with their characteristics and promote coordinated development of regional economies; cultural policies that stimulate cultural innovation and promote the prosperity of the cultural and copyright industries; science and technology policies that support indigenous innovation and strengthen IPRs-centred national competitiveness; trade policies that improve the development model of trade, trade-related IPRs management, early warning and contingency planning of IPRs infringement and overseas IPRs protection; and IPRs outreach campaign that build awareness, increase knowledge of IPRs and train IPRs professionals. In addition, IPRs-related issues are also addressed in fiscal, financial, investment, government procurement, energy and environmental protection policies, creating an intertwined institutional network. In conclusion, China should learn from innovative countries in terms of policies, give full play to its own institutional advantages and policies and provide a necessary environment for the realisation of the objectives of the IP strategy.

References

Council on Competitiveness. 2004. Innovate America. Thriving in a world of challenge and change, *National Innovation Initiative Interim Report*

Firth, Alison. 1997. *Introduction, Prehistory and Development of Intellectual Property Systems.* Hongkong: Sweet & Maxwell

Gervais, Daniel J. 2005. Intellectual property, trade & development: The state of play. *Fordham Law Review* 74

Huang, Xinhua. 2004. Economic theory of institutional innovation. *Theory Journal* 1

Idris, Kamil. 2008. Intellectual property: A power tool for economic growth. https://www.wipo.int/edocs/pubdocs/en/intproperty/888/wipo_pub_888.pdf. Accessed 14 Sept 2008

Laszlo, Ervin. 1997. *Destiny Choice: Survival Options for the 21st Century.* Trans. Yinbo Li. Hongkong: Joint Publishing

Liu, Xing. 2002. The concept of modernity and modern rule of law – A diagnostic analysis. *Law and Social Development* 3

Lyu, Zhongmei. 1998. *The Legal and Economic Analysis of Economic Law.* Beijing: China Procuratorial Press

Nussbaum, Martha C. 1997. Capabilities and human right. *Fordham Law Review* 66

Raffaelli, Ryan and Glynn, Mary Ann. 2014. Institutional Innovation: Novel, Useful, and Legitimate. In *Oxford Handbook of Creativity, Innovation and Entrepreneurship: Multilevel Linkages*, ed. Christina E. Shalley, Michael A. Hitt and Zhou Jing. Oxford: Oxford University Press

Schultz, Therodore W. 1999. *Institutions and the Rising Economic Value of Man, Property Rights and Institutional Changes.* Trans. Shouying Liu. Shanghai Joint Publishing Company.

Schumpeter, Joseph A. 1990. *The Theory of Economic Development.* Trans. Wei He and Jiaxiang Yi. Beijing: The Commercial Press

Schumpeter, Joseph A. 1911. *The Theory of Economic Development.* Cambridge: Harvard University Press

United States Patent and Trademark Office. 2010. United States patent and trademark office 2010–2015 strategic plan. *Electronics Intellectual Property* 10

Wang, Dingding. 1992. The general theory of institutional innovation. *Economic Research Journal* 5

Wu, Feng. 2005. Intellectual property human rights development. *Journal of University of Shanghai for Science and Technology (Social Science)* 3

Wu, Handong. 2013. Interpreting the value of IP law from Chinese perspective. *China Legal Science* 4
Wu, Ming. 2004. *Economic Analysis of Public Policy*. Hubei: Hubei People's Publishing House
Yang, Shengping. 2017. Five development concepts: The new outlook on development of socialism with Chinese characteristics. *Studies on Socialism with Chinese Characteristics* 2

Chapter 14
IPRs Regimes and Anti-Unfair Competition

An examination of the relationships between IP law and anti-unfair competition law in the field of private law aims to elucidate the distinctive functions of anti-unfair competition law, namely, the protection of the exercise of IPRs and the regulation of their abuse. From a formal legal perspective, IP law and anti-unfair competition law appear to be two separate and incompatible systems. The former seeks to protect the "monopoly rights" of IP owners, while the latter restricts or eliminates "monopolistic positions" of a certain kind (Tomita 2000, pp. 13, 21). In reality, the two serve the same common legislative objective, that is, to protect lawful rights and foster social progress. However, their divergence lies in the means of achieving this objective. IP law fulfils this objective by protecting the legitimate rights and interests of IP owners and encouraging intellectual innovation, whereas anti-unfair competition law does so by deterring illegal competition to maintain market order. Consequently, the relationship between IPRs (as exclusive rights) and anti-unfair competition law needs to be properly handled.

14.1 Market Competition and Competition Law

Competition is the norm in economic activities, and it is an inherent attribute of a commodity economy. It should be legitimate and regulated, and this requires equal status between competitors, as well as compliance with principles of fairness and good faith. Unfair competition violates the principle of market competition and undermines the orderliness of competition, and therefore, countries around the world attach great importance to legal regulations that combat unfair competition.

The term "unfair competition" can be understood both broadly and narrowly. In a broad sense, it includes all acts that damage competition, including monopolies, restrictive competition, and other acts that violate business ethics; and in a narrow sense, it refers to acts that damage competition for all parties other than the

H. Wu, *Theorising Intellectual Property Rights from Chinese Perspectives*,
https://doi.org/10.1007/978-981-96-5867-1_14

monopolies, and restrictive competition (Xu and Meng 2008, p. 236). Monopolies and restrictive competition inherently oppose competition by obstructing or even completely excluding or preventing other market players from competition. Abuse of market dominance and concentration of undertakings are examples of "restrictiveness" in competition, while unfair competition in the narrow sense mainly refers to engaging in economic activities without adhering to the principle of good faith. Commercial confusion, false advertising, and infringement of trade secrets exemplify "unfairness" in competition.

The definition of unfair competition varies between the relevant international conventions and national legislations. The *Paris Convention for the Protection of Industrial Property* (1883) (the *Paris Convention*) provides that any competition which violates "honest practices in industrial or commercial matters constitutes unfair competition", and the *Model Law for Developing Countries on Marks, Trade Names and Acts of Unfair Competition* (1967), drawn up by WIPO, considers that any conduct which violates honest practices in industrial or commercial matters is unfair competition. In legislative practices, some countries define unfair competition by using a "generalisation plus exemplification" method. For instance, in German law, unfair competition is described as "the behaviours resorted to in competing against others that violate decent customs"; whereas some other countries simply adopt the method of enumeration. For example, Japanese law lists six types of unfair business practices. From these legislative practices we can see that moral codes like "good faith" and "decent customs" are basic standards used to assess unfair competition. In this regard, different countries have adopted similar expressions such as "transaction habits" (e.g., Belgium and Luxembourg), "principle of good faith" (e.g., Spain and Switzerland), "professional ethics" (e.g., Italy), and "decent customs" (e.g., Germany). This shows that unfair competition in essence is an illegal behaviour which violates the competition code of equity, justice and good faith.

The *Anti-Unfair Competition Law of the People's Republic of China* was promulgated in 1993, and amended in 2017, then again in 2019. Article 2 of this law specifies the fair and unfair acts of business operators. Paragraph 1 stipulates that "business operators shall, in their production and distribution activities, adhere to the free will, equality, fairness, and good faith principles, and abide by laws and business ethics"; and Paragraph 2 stipulates that "for the purposes of this Law, act of unfair competition means that in its production or distribution activities, a business operator disrupts market competition and causes damage to the lawful rights and interests of the other business operators or consumers, in violation of this Law." The aforementioned two provisions form the legal basis for defining unfair competition, whose features can be summarised as follows.

First, subjects of unfair competition are business operators. The subject of unfair competition is the business operator of the market transactions involved. The term "business operator" refers to any natural person, legal person, or non-legal person or organisation that engages in the production or distribution of commodities or the provision of services. It includes enterprises, institutions, and social organisations that are registered in accordance with law and have legal personality, partnerships, sole proprietorships and other economic entities that are registered in accordance with law but do not have legal personality, and also individual partnerships, individual business operators, and farmers engaged in business activities.

Second, unfair competition occurs in production and operation activities. Unfair competition only occurs in production and management activities, namely, in market competition; this is the difference between unfair competition and general civil tort. For example, an infringement of the corporate reputation right should be regarded as a general infringement when there is no competition between the infringer and the victim, and only treated as unfair competition when a business operator defames their opponents or excludes them from production and operation.

Third, unfair competition violates laws and business ethics. Unfair competition violates laws when the subject of market competition perpetrates specific acts of unfair competition that are expressly prohibited by laws, such as commercial confusion, commercial discrediting, false advertising, and infringement of trade secrets. As for unfair competition violating business ethics, this refers to the fact that market competitors must not violate the principles of voluntariness, equality, fairness, and integrity. Unfair competition practices occur whenever a transaction goes against these basic principles.

Fourth, unfair competition has harmed social and economic order. Its harmful consequences are mainly disruption of market competition and damage to the legitimate rights and interests of other operators or consumers. As it is a deliberate and harmful act of exclusion, aiming at infringing the legitimate rights and interests of relevant competitors by hampering the operation mechanism of market competition and the economic order of the market, the legislative objective of anti-unfair competition law is to encourage and protect fair competition, stop unfair competition, and protect the legitimate rights and interests of operators and consumers, so as to ensure and promote the healthy development of the market economy.

Competition law is a legal system that regulates the competitive relationship between business operators and regulates competition in order to establish fair and reasonable competition order. Furthermore, it also regulates monopolies and restrictions of competition. Like unfair competition, competition law has both broad and narrow meanings: in a broad sense, it includes anti-monopoly and anti-unfair competition laws, while in a narrow sense it refers only to provisions regarding unfair competition. However, the legal names and norms of the legislation of unfair competition vary greatly among countries, due to their different political and economic conditions and legal traditions. Legislative anti-unfair competition models can be summarised as follows:

The first is the special legislative model. Civil law countries mostly adopt special legislation, that is, special anti-monopoly and anti-unfair competition laws. Countries like Germany, Japan, Switzerland, Greece, and South Korea are representatives. Taking Germany as an example, it formulated the first special anti-unfair competition law in the world in 1896, and this is regarded by scholars as a significant watershed moment in modern competition law (Wang 2009, p. 56). This law received its first major revision in 1909 and has been revised more than a dozen times since. In 1957, Germany enacted the *German Act against Restraints of Competition*, forming a legislative model in which anti-unfair competition and anti-monopoly laws are split, but jointly constitute the competition law system. This has had a significant impact on the legislation of competition law in Japan, South Korea and China (Zheng and Wan 2007). Anti-unfair competition laws are usually seen as *lex specialis* within the civil scope under the special legislative mode, and are differentiated from anti-monopoly laws, which belong to economic law.

The second is the combined legislative model. The former Soviet Union, Eastern European countries, and some other countries and regions have adopted legislative models that integrate anti-unfair competition and anti-monopoly laws, combining anti-monopoly, anti-restriction of competition, and anti-unfair competition together into one law. Its representative legislative examples include Poland's *Prohibition of Monopoly Act* (1990), Hungary's *Prohibition of Unfair Market Practices and Restriction of Competition Act* (1996), Russia's *Federal Competition Act* (2006), *Australian Trade Practices Act* (1974), *Canadian Competition Law* (1985) and Taiwan's *Fair-Trade Act* (1991). Taiwan's *Fair-Trade Act* includes "free competition law" (anti-monopoly law) and "fair competition law" (anti-unfair competition law). The legislators in those countries or regions pay attention to the commonalities between anti-monopoly law and anti-unfair competition law, and therefore have chosen to integrate the two. In jurisprudence, this competition law has the dual attributes of economic law and *lex specialis* within the civil scope.

The third is the decentralised legislative model. Some common law countries have neither a formal anti-unfair competition law nor a unified competition code, and their relevant norms are scattered in various laws. For example, early British competition law was incorporated into a large number of case laws and statute laws, including contract law, tort law, consumer protection law, and commercial labelling law. Since the second half of the twentieth century, however, the UK has begun the special legislation of competition law, and currently in operation mainly includes the *Fair-Trading Act* (1973) and *Competition Act* (1998). The US has uniquely pursued a decentralised legislative model that focuses on anti-monopoly. It passed the world's first competition law, *the Sherman Act*,[1] in 1890, marking the emergence of modern competition law (Wang 2009, p. 55). Since then, the United States has successively formulated the *Clayton Act*, the *Federal Trade Commission Act*, and the *Robinson–Patman Act*, which mainly focus on anti-monopoly but also involve anti-unfair competition practices. In addition, the *Lanham Law* (a trademark law) and the *Defend Trade Secrets Act* also regulate unfair competition.

China adopted the special legislation model, enacting its *Anti-Unfair Competition Law of the People's Republic of China* in 1993 and the *Anti-monopoly Law of the People's Republic of China* in 2007. The Anti-Unfair Competition Law of PRC was modified twice, in November 2017 and April 2019. The 2017 amendment, in particular, removed some provisions that dealt with restrictive competition and monopolies from the previous version, further confirming China's special legislative model in competition law. The separate special legislation for anti-monopoly law and anti-unfair competition law in the framework of the competition law system is

[1] The full name of this act, named after Senator John Sherman, who sponsored the law, is the *Protection of Trade and Commerce from Unlawful Restraints and Monopolies Act*.

conducive to regulating different types of illegal competition activities and to realising the different legal functions of protecting free competition and protecting fair competition. Generally speaking, administrative intervention and punishment are mostly employed to regulate monopolies, while civil remedies (supplemented by administrative sanctions when necessary) are mainly for unfair competition. This leads to two conclusions about the status of China's Anti-Unfair Competition Law: first, it falls within the scope of civil law. Chong Mingzhao (1997, p. 48) stated that "economic law is legal norms with competition law as its core"; and "competition law as an integral part of economic law" is not a "market regulation law" that is distinct from macro-regulation law (Wang 2009, p. 35). In my opinion, first, China's Anti-Unfair Competition Law cannot substitute competition law in a broad sense and so cannot be defined as an "economic constitution." The Anti-Unfair Competition Law, like IP law, is a special law with comprehensive legal regulation and various legal sanctions to protect the legitimate rights and interests of operators and consumers, and to combat unfair competition. Hence, its status as an integral part of civil law is unaffected; Second, the Anti-Unfair Competition Law is a special civil law. Unlike the legal systems of Germany and Japan, China does not simply classify its Anti-Unfair Competition Law as *lex specialis* within the civil scope and special tort liability law. This is because it not only regulates the competitive relationship between equal business operators, but also provides for the legislative objective of maintaining the economic order of the market. This reflects the state's intervention in, and regulation of, social and economic life. The basic task of China's Anti-Unfair Competition Law is to maintain a fair and standardised order in market competition. To this end, its policy objective is to protect both fair competition and the interests of consumers. Unlike traditional civil law, the Anti-Unfair Competition Law represents the trend in modern civil law of the publicisation and socialisation of private law.

14.2 Interface Between Anti-Unfair Competition Law and IP Law

One of the hot issues in Chinese legal theory research in recent years is the relationship between anti-unfair competition law and IP law relating to their status and relevance in the field of private law. Examination of both the nature of and the behaviour related to rights, that is, research based on the legal characters of IPRs and unfair competition, is necessary when analysing the general relationship between the relevant laws.

IPRs are exclusive rights to IP that are enjoyed by specific subjects. The "exclusivity" of rights is usually expressed as "exclusive" or "monopoly" in English. In Chinese books or writings on IPR, they are translated as "characteristic of exclusive possession" (*duzhanxing*) or monopolistic characteristic" (*longduanxing*). Since "exclusivity" is a synonym for "monopoly", IPRs can be technically regarded as a legitimate "monopoly right" under the law, and this legitimate monopoly is manifest in two aspects: first, IPRs are an institutional product created by the state to stimulate innovation and promote the growth of knowledge wealth, and therefore their "existence" is immune to competition law, that is, IPRs are "legitimate monopolies"; second, IPRs are private property rights based on intellectual creation. The rights owners undertake intellectual works or investments for the purpose of competition, or for the intellectual fruits produced in the process of competition, and thus the protection of IPRs is conducive to enhancing the competitiveness of the owners in the market (Wang 1996). However, the "abuse" of IPRs will be punished in accordance with the Anti-Unfair Competition Law of the PRC.

Protection against unfair competition is a right of operators to seek relief and remedies when their interests are infringed. *The Convention Establishing the World Intellectual Property Organisation* (*WIPO Convention*), signed in 1967, lists (under Article 2 "Intellectual Property") rights relating to works, inventions and marks, and all other rights resulting from intellectual activities, which include "protection against unfair competition." For a period of time, under the influence of the Convention, some Chinese scholars, including Wen Xikai (1991, pp. 30–33), adopted such expressions as the right against unfair competition or the right to prohibit unfair competition to refer to protection against unfair competition, emphasising that this protection is a component of IPRs, and is in the same group as patent rights, trademark rights, and copyright. Wei Zhi (1999) argued that the term "protection against unfair competition" misinterprets the legal nature of the right against unfair competition, and that it "has neither a specific object nor a positive right content", and therefore should not be regarded as a new right in addition to copyright, patent rights and trademark rights. I consider that the term "the right against unfair competition" is prone to semantic confusion and can only be applied in limited circumstances, because it is only a type of right to relief. It derives from the original rights (such as ownership deriving from tangible properties, IPRs from intellectual properties, and creditor's right from contracts), and aims to provide remedies for the infringement of the original rights (Wei 2000). The right against unfair competition here is, in fact, a claim or request made by a rights holder that the infringer bears civil liability of the infringement. In addition, the protection of IPRs under anti-unfair competition law is only a small portion of its legal regulation, and many unfair competition acts regulated by the law have little to do with IPRs. Therefore, the view that anti-unfair competition is a positive right and can even be categorised as an IPR itself is somewhat problematic and warrants further consideration.

Although IPRs and anti-unfair competition differ in that one is an original right and the other is a right to remedies, they possess similarities in terms of functional objectives and subject matter of protection. In academic circles, there are different perspectives on the overarching connection between the two laws.

One view is that they are independent. According to this view, even if IP law and anti-unfair competition law are closely related, they cannot be merged into a single body of legislation, because IP law cannot cover all the contents of anti-unfair competition law, and vice versa. It has been suggested that the two laws have their own characteristics in terms of value orientation, functional mechanism, legislative techniques and other aspects. Therefore, anti-unfair competition law falls under economic law, while IP law belongs to civil and commercial law. Li Shunde

(1999) classifies anti-unfair competition law as the "third industrial property law", parallel to patent law and trademark law. Zheng Youde and Wan Zhiqian (2009) believe, based on the protection of trademark rights and interests, that IP law and anti-unfair competition law are parallel and equal, and they have independent subject matter of protection, regulation methods, scope of effect, and protection focus.

Another view is that they are complementary. According to this view, IP law and anti-unfair competition law are complementary and interactive, that is, anti-unfair competition is an integral part of the IPRs regime; and likewise, IPRs are an important part of the regulation content of anti-unfair competition law. Wei Zhi (1999), Yang Ming (2003), and Jiang Hui (2007) contend that anti-unfair competition law plays the role of the cover-all clause in the protection for IPRs. Japanese scholar Shigeaki Hirota (1997) believes that anti-unfair competition law is a supplement to trademark law, as it provides protection for trademarks that are unregistered and therefore not protected by trademark law.

The author is in favour of the view that they are complementary, that is, anti-unfair competition law grants additional and supplementary protection for IPRs. In German law, this is known as "the protection of intellectual achievements in competition law." In this sense, anti-unfair competition law can be classified into the system of IP law for the following reasons. First, anti-unfair competition law protects the subject matter of IP law, that is, it provides protection against the infringement of copyright, patents and trademark rights. Therefore, there may appear situations where there is an overlap and the issue of the priority of judicial applicability in some cases. Second, anti-unfair competition law protects subject matter related to various types of IPRs that are not governed by relevant laws, so as to make up for the "gap" that results from a single legal system. Third, anti-unfair competition law gives "cover all protection" to the subject matter of various IPRs in intersection. In this context, this law is a legal institution that gives broader protection to IPRs. Current legislative practices have seen a continual expansion of the regulatory scope of anti-unfair competition law, including many new areas that have nothing to do with IPRs. However, IPRs protection is still an important task for anti-unfair competition law.

Anti-unfair competition law and IP law are not the same and cannot substitute for each other; rather, they coordinate and complement each other's legal functions. WIPO declared in 1988 that anti-unfair competition law in fact protects legitimate rights that are not protected by special laws such as patent law and trademark law (Wang 2009, p. 49). When providing protection for IPRs, anti-unfair competition law differs from the special IPR laws: while a special IP law is a "law of fundamental rights", that is, it is a regulatory system with exclusive rights as its centre, involving subjects, subject matter, content, acquisition, exercise, limitations, and remedies, anti-unfair competition law is a "regulatory law on behaviours" with a core aim of maintaining the order in market competition, and it establishes a regulatory system of "unfair competition" and "anti-unfair competition." The relationship between anti-unfair competition law and a special IP law is briefly described as follows:

14.2.1 Anti-Unfair Competition Law and Trademark Law

These two laws are the most important and closely related in the IPRs regime, indeed some scholars say that trademark law and anti-unfair competition law are parallel in the protection of trademark rights and interests. Anti-unfair competition law mainly offers anti-confusion protection for unregistered trademarks with certain influences, while trademark law focuses on anti-dilution protection of well-known trademarks (Zheng and Wan 2009). In the field of commercial marks, anti-unfair competition law regulates not only the counterfeiting of trademarks but also the unauthorised use of the distinctive names, packaging, decoration, and other identifying features of goods with certain influences. In addition, anti-unfair competition law also can be used to regulate the use of other parties' trademarks (including registered trademarks and unregistered trademarks with certain influences) on similar goods (i.e., "counterfeiting"), or the substitution of one's own trademark for other parties' trademarks on their goods in the sale of goods (i.e., "reverse counterfeiting").

14.2.2 Anti-Unfair Competition Law and Patent Law

In terms of the legal protection of technology, patent law and anti-unfair competition law serve different purposes: the former grants patents for technical accomplishments, while the latter protects trade secrets. However, there is overlap between the two laws: the anti-unfair competition law can provide "temporary protection" for a technical invention during the patent application process, and "continued protection" for a design that belongs to a product with certain influences after its patent expires. It should be noted that in cases of overlap, patent law takes precedence, and anti-unfair competition law applies only if patent law does not.

14.2.3 Anti-Unfair Competition Law and Copyright Law

Anti-unfair competition law has a weaker relationship to copyright law than to trademark law and patent law. In some countries, the supposititious use of the name or title of the works of others and the commercial exploitation of a fictitious image in the works of others can be considered as copyright-related unfair competition.

14.3 Unfair Competition Practices Related to IPRs

Unfair competition is a civil tort in terms of its legal attribute, for it infringes on the interests of both legitimate business operators and the consumers. The business operators' interests include their IPRs, commercial personality rights, and business rights. "Unfair competition sometimes infringes on the interests of specific competitors, such as commercial confusion, commercial discrediting and infringement of trade secrets; and sometimes infringes on the interests of unspecified competitors, such as commercial bribery, false advertising, and improper prize-attached sales" (Wang 2009, p. 98). On the other hand, the consumers' interests relate to their personalities, property and safety, and include the rights to know information about goods, to choose to purchase, and to fair trade. Unfair competition, commercial confusion and false advertising are factors that directly harm consumers' interests, while the infringement of trade secrets and commercial discrediting indirectly harm consumers' interests as well as damaging business operators' interests.

In terms of the consequences of the infringement acts, unfair competition also damages public interest. In addition to the private rights of operators and consumers, unfair competition directly undermines the most fundamental mechanism of a market economy, namely the competition mechanism, which represents the order of the market economy and public interests maintained by the state. Thus, administrative punishments or criminal sanctions, in addition to civil remedies, may be applied against unfair competition in the legislation of many countries. With regard to the legal liabilities for infringements, anti-unfair competition law and IP law have similar provisions.

There are detailed lists of and general descriptions for the specific types of unfair competition in relevant international conventions or documents. *The Model Law for Developing Countries on Marks, Trade Names and Acts of Unfair Competition*, drafted by WIPO, lists 12 types of unfair competition: (1) bribing competitors' customers to obtain and keep their business; (2) acquiring competitors' business secrets or trade secrets through espionage or bribing their employees; (3) using or disclosing competitors' "technical secrets" without permission; (4) luring employees of competitors in order to break their employment contracts or cause them to leave their employers; (5) threatening competitors with infringement lawsuits of patent or trademark, where such threats are fraudulent and designed to reduce competitors' trading volume and prevent competition; (6) joint trade boycotts to prevent or impede competition; (7) dumping (i.e., selling below cost with the intent or consequence of preventing or suppressing competition); (8) creating an impression to the consumer that he or she is being offered an opportunity to purchase goods on favourable terms when this is not the case; (9) imitating a competitor's goods, services, advertising, or other features of trade; (10) encouraging or taking advantage of a competitor's breach of contract; (11) conducting advertisement that compares the goods or services of a competitor; and (12) violating laws that do not directly involve competition in order to obtain improper interests over a competitor. The comprehensive document on "protection of anti-unfair competition" and the *Model Provisions on Protection Against*

Unfair Competition, drafted by WIPO in 1993 and 1996 respectively, summarise unfair competition as: (1) confusing the origin of goods or services; (2) deceiving by means like exaggeration so as to mislead people about the goods or services provided; (3) derogating competitors; (4) infringement of trade secrets; (5) unreasonable use of others' achievements which have been recognised by consumers; (6) advertising in a comparative manner; and (7) other acts like prize-attached sales. The above provisions cover various aspects of unfair competition quite comprehensively. In some countries, relevant competition law legislation usually focuses on unfair competition related to IPRs, such as counterfeiting, deceptive advertising, trade libel, infringement of trade secrets, and abuse of exclusive rights of industrial property, while bribery sales and false prize-attached sales are mostly regulated by other laws.

In China, there has been changes to the specific types of unfair competition in its legislation. The1993 *Anti-Unfair Competition Law of the PRC* lists 11 types of unfair competition, including some restrictive competition and monopolies. The Anti-Unfair Competition Law was enacted when China's market economy was still in its infancy, so at the time specific anti-monopoly legislation was not necessary. However, there were already some market monopoly behaviours that needed to be regulated, including public enterprises' exclusion of competition, administrative monopolies, and low-price dumping; therefore, the legislator considered it necessary to "temporarily" incorporate these market monopoly activities into the Anti-Unfair Competition Law, with the intention of passing a separate anti-monopoly law in the future (Wang 1998). The Anti-monopoly Law of the PRC was established in 2007, and the anti-unfair competition behaviours in the two laws overlap. Therefore, the Anti-Unfair Competition Law (Amendment 2017) removed market monopolies and added "unfair competition on the Internet" into the specific types of unfair competition, in response to the development of the Internet economy. It provides for a total of seven specific types of unfair competition, namely: commercial confusion, commercial bribery, false advertising, infringement of trade secrets, improper prize-attached sales, commercial discrediting, and malicious interference on the Internet. Among the seven types of unfair competition listed in China's current law, the following acts can be categorised as relating to IPRs:

14.3.1 Confusion Regarding Business Identifiers

The "confusion regarding business identifiers" refers to the unauthorised use of the same or similar commercial marks in market transactions, so that the goods or services produced or provided by the operator are confused with those of others; or refers to the confusion that happens when an operator expresses or implies that goods or services they produce or operate have some connection with those of others. Such unfair competition is also called "deceptive trade practices", "commodity counterfeiting", and "the unauthorised use of other people's commercial marks." The administrative enforcement authorities in China customarily refers to it as "counterfeiting behaviour", while the *Paris Convention* refers to it as "confusing behaviour"

(Shao 2004, p. 53). Article 10bis of the *Paris Convention* enumerates three types of unfair competition, the first being confusion, that is, "all acts of such nature as to create confusion by any means whatever with the establishment business premises, the goods, or the industrial or commercial activities of a competitor." The WIPO *Model Provisions on Protection Against Unfair Competition* specifies "confusion of the origin of goods or services" and lists related matters of confusion, including (1) trademarks, whether registered or not; (2) trade names; (3) commercial marks other than trademarks or trade names; (4) the appearance of products; (5) expressions of goods or services; (6) a famous person or a well-known fictitious image. It can be seen that confusion is a general term for the abovementioned confusion of goods or services and consumer misconceptions. In my opinion, the term "confusion of commercial marks" is a comparatively accurate summary of the relevant unfair competition. It emphasises the competitive relationship between the confusing party and the other operators and highlights the characteristics of the infringement through the confusion of commercial origins and commercial relations. Hence, the definition is relatively in line with the legislative intent of international conventions and China's Anti-Unfair Competition Law.

According to the 1993 Anti-Unfair Competition Law, there are two types of confusion of commercial marks, namely, the confusion of commercial operators and the false indications of goods (including services). The former, defined in items 1–3, Article 5 of the Anti-Unfair Competition Law, refers to unauthorised use of the commercial marks of others, and improper use of either the commercial reputations of others, or of the reputations of goods, so that the goods or services produced or provided by the operator are confused with those of others, resulting in their misidentification by consumers. The latter, provided for in item 4 of Article 5 in the Anti-Unfair Competition Law, refers to the act of misleading other operators or consumers by false indication of the quality, reputation, origin or source of goods and of components of goods. Since there is overlap between false indication and false advertising, the Anti-Unfair Competition Law (Amendment 2017), on the basis of further improving the prohibitions against false advertising, has removed false indication from the prohibition on confusion of commercial marks. In other words, the confusion of commercial marks only refers to the confusion of commercial operators under the current law.

The Anti-Unfair Competition Law (Amendment 2017) revised and changed the confusion of commercial marks from Article 5 of the original 1993 law to Article 6 of the current law. This Article provides that the confusion of commercial marks includes the following four situations: (1) unauthorised use of signs which are identical or similar to the trade names, packaging, decoration of others' influential goods; (2) unauthorised use of others' influential enterprise names (e.g., abbreviations, font sizes), names of social organisations (e.g., abbreviations) and names (e.g., pen names, stage names, translated names); (3) unauthorised use of others' influential domain names (main part), website names, web pages and so on; and (4) any other confusing acts which can mislead people to misidentify the business operator's goods as others' goods, or to associate their goods with those of others. Compared with the original

1993 law, the current law shows three changes regarding confusion of commercial marks. First, it enhances the harmony of this law with other legal provisions. Since the act of counterfeiting a registered trademark is specifically regulated by the Trademark Law, the current law removes "counterfeiting another person's registered trademark" from the provision of confusion of commercial marks. Second, the variety of protected commercial marks has increased. Based on the experience of past legal practices and current trends in economic development, the current law makes an exemplary enumeration of enterprise names, adds names of social organisations, and adds special provisions for domain names, website names, web pages and so on. Third, the legal provisions are more flexible. Of the four types of confusion of commercial marks, the first three are given exemplary enumeration that ends with "so on", while the last one is a special cover all provision, which is a feature of a typical open legislative model.

14.3.2 False Advertising

False advertising refers to the use of advertising or other methods by business operators to create false or misleading advertisements regarding their goods or services, that is, advertisements that do not correspond to the actual situation, with the intention of deceiving and misleading consumers. False advertising is also known as "misleading the public" in international conventions and documents. The "unfair competition" of Article 10bis of the *Paris Convention* lists three types of unfair competition. It specifies that "indications or allegations the use of which in the course of trade is liable to mislead the public as to the nature, the manufacturing process, the characteristics, the suitability for their purpose, or the quantity, of the good", and this is the legal ground of "misleading the public" in international laws. Article 4, Paragraph 1 of the Model Provisions on Protection Against Unfair Competition includes a general provision regarding "misleading the public", stating that any act or practice in industrial or commercial activities that misleads or may mislead the public about the enterprise or its activities, in particular about the products or services provided by the enterprise, shall constitute unfair competition. Article 4, Paragraph 2 specifies that misleading may arise from advertising or publicity, in particular in relation to the following matters: (1) the manufacturing process of the products; (2) the rational purposes of the products or services; (3) the quality, quantity, or other characteristics of the products or services; (4) the geographical origin of the products or services; (5) the conditions promised or offered for the products or services; (6) the price of the products or services, or the calculation of the price.

China has clear provisions on false advertising. Article 9, Paragraph 1 of the 1993 Anti-Unfair Competition Law of the PRC provides that "operators shall not use advertising or other methods to make misleading false advertising about the quality, product ingredients, performance, function, producer, expiration date, origin of its goods, and so on."; and Paragraph 2 provides that "operators of an advertisement shall not deputise, design, produce or publish false advertisements when operators of advertisements have known or ought to have known the truth." The Anti-Unfair Competition Law (Amendment 2017) changes the false advertising to Article 8 of the current law, and Paragraph 1 of this Article provides that "business operators shall not make false or misleading commercial promotion for the performance, functions, quality, sales, user evaluation, and accolades so as to defraud or mislead consumers"; and Paragraph 2 of the Article provides that "business operators shall not organise false transactions to help other business operators to carry out false or misleading commercial promotion." Legal provisions on false advertising are composed of direct false advertising (Paragraph 1) and indirect false advertising (Paragraph 2), in both the old original and the current laws. The following two points are where the current law differs most from the original: First, in terms of direct false advertising, the term "misleading false advertising" in the 1993 law has been replaced with "false or misleading commercial promotion" in the 2017 amendment. In other words, the relationship between "misleading" and "false advertising" shifted from defining to parallel and selective. Second, in terms of indirect false advertising, "organisation of false transactions" that assist false advertising is highlighted for the main purpose of regulating "click farming" in e-commerce. In terms of judicial practice, the *Interpretation of Several Issues Concerning the Application of Laws in the Trial of Civil Cases of Unfair Competition of The Supreme People's Court* (2007) indicated several special types of false advertising: first, one-sided publicity or comparison of goods; second, using scientifically inconclusive viewpoints and phenomena as conclusive evidence for the promotion of goods; third, using ambiguous language or other misleading ways for product promotion. In my view, China's legislative provisions and judicial interpretation of "false advertising" and "misleading the public" are consistent with those of international laws.

We can further analyse the concept of false advertising according to the above provisions. First, the means of false advertising include advertising and other methods. False advertising usually takes advantage of advertising, using means such as newspapers, magazines, radio, television, billboards, bulletin boards, and other advertising media. Shao Jiandong (2004) names such unfair competition as "false advertising" since the aforementioned advertising media, especially the mass media, are the main carriers of commercial promotion, so false advertising is the main means of false advertising. Second, there are two sorts of false advertising, both of which contain important information about the products or services. One type is false advertising where the information contained does not match the actual situation. For example, ordinary products are exaggerated as brand products, domestic goods are advertised as imported goods, and synthetic materials are passed off as natural materials. The other type is false advertising where the information contained is misleading, such as sensational advertising that causes users and consumers to have a false understanding of the real condition of the goods and can therefore affect their choice of goods. False advertising once again misleads consumers and triggers deceptive transactions, and this is also illegal advertising, as it relies on false advertising to gain a competitive advantage while infringing on the interests of other operators.

There has been no discussion in China's academic circles the reasons why false advertising is classified as IPR related unfair competition. In my opinion, the operator influences consumers' purchasing choices by spreading untrue information to obtain competitive advantages and economic benefits in the market. This is detrimental to the interests of other operators in the same industry, and thus constitutes unfair competition. Furthermore, such behaviour damages the rights of competitors in the same industry to customers, and it is therefore regarded as IPR related unfair competition. In French civil law theory, there are two general types of intangible property rights: one is traditional IPRs, with intellectual achievements and business marks as its subject matter, and the other is "right to consumers", with customers as its subject matter. The term "right to customers" refers to a form of "business asset" (*fond de commerce*) that consists of both tangible and intangible components. Tangible components include the use of products, tools, and other tangible properties to attract consumers, while intangible components include the use of trade names, trademarks, patents, and other intangible properties to do so. The value of the *fond de commerce* depends on its attractiveness to customers, and *fond de commerce* will disappear when customers are "taken away" by others. Taking customers as its *fond de commerce*, the key to "right to customers" is the customer's "loyalty" to the enterprise, that is, the attractiveness of the enterprise to customers. Additionally, "right to customers" falls under the "business credit right." The current system of property rights includes several non-material property rights that are connected to but distinct from IPRs. Therefore, IPRs should be viewed from an inclusive perspective and treated as a dynamic, changing and developing institutional system. In this regard, jurisprudentially speaking, false advertising can be regarded as unfair competition involving IPRs.

14.3.3 Infringement of Trade Secrets

Infringement of trade secrets refers to theft, inducement, coercion, or other improper acts carried out to obtain the trade secrets of others. Trade secrets are an intangible information property. The definition of trade secrets is outlined in Article 10 of the Anti-Unfair Competition Law of the PRC as "any technical information or business operation information which is unknown to the public, can bring economic benefits to the obligee, has practical utility, and for which the obligee has taken secret-keeping measures to keep it confidential." *The Prohibition of Infringement of Commercial Secrets*, issued by the State Administration for Industry and Commerce in 1995, further interpreted commercial secrets as technical and business information, including designs, procedures, product formulas, craftsmanship, production methods, management knowhow, customer lists, resource information, production and marketing strategies, the subject matter and the content of the tender in bidding, and other information. However, this list fails to accurately and comprehensively cover the scope of trade secrets. With the development of market economy and the Internet industry, the identity of shareholders, equity ratio, user data and so on can also be counted as secret information and of commercial value. Therefore, the detailed listing of items related to technical information and business information can no longer accurately cover the scope of protection of trade secrets, for it lacks the necessary flexibility in application. In light of this, the relatively new Anti-Unfair Competition Law (Amendment 2019) adopts the defining approach of enumeration plus summary by adding the expression of "and other commercial information" to "technical information" and "business information." According to the relevant provisions of the *TRIPS Agreement* (1995), the information protected as trade secrets must fulfil the following conditions: it (1) is secret in the sense that it is not, as a body or in the precise configuration and assembly of its components, generally known among or readily accessible to persons within the circles that normally deal with the kind of information in question; (2) has commercial value because it is secret; and (3) has been subject to reasonable steps under the circumstances, by the person lawfully in control of the information, to keep it secret.

Different countries and regions have adopted different legislative models of trade secret protection, using specific trade secret laws or general tort liability laws, or anti-unfair competition laws. For a long time, civil law countries mainly invoked contract law or tort liability law to protect trade secrets, without recognising trade secrets as property rights. The US and the UK protect trade secrets through special legislation in their legal traditions in statutes: the *Uniform Trade Secrets Act* (1978) of the US and the *Trade Secrets (Enforcement, etc.) Regulations* (2018) of the UK define trade secrets as property rights. In the 1960s, the International Chamber of Commerce (ICC) was the first body to define trade secrets as IPRs. The 1967 *WIPO Convention* lists various types of IPRs, and its cover all provisions, that is, "all other rights deriving from intellectual activity in the industrial, scientific, literary or artistic fields", implicitly recognise the right to trade secrets. By the 1970s, a variety of model provisions on IPRs drafted by WIPO had established a legal regime of trade secrets; and by the 1990s, the WTO's *TRIPS Agreement* regarded trade secrets as "undisclosed information" and formally incorporated it into the IPRs system.

It is generally believed that the trade secrets regime originated in the judicial practices of the UK and the US and was later adopted by the civil law countries. As the trade secrets regime evolved, the legal framework underlying it shifted from a focus on contract theory and tort theory to a theory of anti-unfair competition, and finally to a theory of property rights.

"Contract theory" was the basis for the early protection of trade secrets in both civil law and common law systems. Although theoretical, judicial and legal circles acknowledged trade secrets as properties at the time, trade secrets were not classified as absolute rights and dominant rights (e.g., ownership), but *jus in personam* (right of legal action against or to enforce a legal duty of a particular person or group of persons) and relative rights (e.g., the creditor's right). The civil law countries, taking contract theory as the philosophical basis for the construction of trade secrets protection, attach great importance to the function of express contract in judicial practice, because the presence and content of a written contract often determine the judgement in a typical trade secrets litigation. In addition to express contracts, the United States also evolved de facto implied contracts through its judicial practice of common law; in other words, it infers that a contract limiting the use of trade secrets exists between the parties by proving the fact implicitly agreed by the parties. The US then created the concept of "quasi-contract" (the contract implied in law) in its common law. And unlike de facto implied contract, quasi-contract does not require the inference of the existence of a contractual connection by proving the facts of implied agreement. Instead, it is a specific contractual relationship imposed by law for the need to protect trade secrets. The protection of trade secrets has binding force between the rights holder and the counterparty, whether through express contract, de facto implied contract, or implied contract in law. In this regard, the *Model Provisions on the Protection of Unfair Competition Law (Articles and Notes)* (1996) issued by WIPO has provided a clear interpretation of contract theory, "Contractual obligations in connection with secret information may either be specified in oral or written contract, typically between an employer and an employee, or in the absence of an express contract, may be inferred from an employment relationship." Such a relationship may also exist between business partners or between an employer and a contractor (Note 6.12). We can see from contract theory that the owner of trade secrets always claims *jus in personam*, that is, the protection of trade secrets requires the duty and loyalty of the counterparty. As Justice Vice noted in Morrison v. Moot in 1831, it is uncertain whether the plaintiff gained more than patents from the claim, but it is clear that the plaintiff received *jus in personam* rather than right *in rem* (Jager 1985).

"Tort theory" is "the breach of confidence theory of tort liability" and was once quite popular in American trade secrets law. This theory believes that destruction of a secret relationship because of the disclosure or use of trade secrets is a tort, and the tort perpetrator shall be liable. The US *Restatement of Torts* (1939) partly accepts the "tort theory of breach of confidentiality", and Section 757 of this law provides that any person who discloses or uses a trade secret disclosed to them in confidence by another person shall be liable to that person for breach of confidence. Tort theory pays less attention to the property attributes of information and the scope of protected information, focusing more on the relationship between the parties to the trade secrets. In other words, the theory does not focus on the existence of confidentiality obligations in a contract or even the existence of trade secrets, and the essence of this theory is examination of the existence of the legal responsibility to keep secret information.

Related to tort theory is the "countering unfair competition theory", a long-adopted doctrine in the field of protection of trade secrets in civil law countries. For example, in Germany, the protection of trade secrets is incorporated into the anti-unfair competition law, which aims to both prevent enterprises' unfair behaviour in competition, and also to maintain the order of competition. Japan has added the provision of trade secrets protection in its amendment to anti-unfair competition law, which aims to prevent unfair competition behaviour and maintain the order of fair competition (Xu 1993, p. 3). In terms of the doctrine of trade secrets protection, the anti-unfair competition theories of Germany and Japan have similarities with the tort theory of the United States, that is, the legal measures for trade secrets infringement rely on tort liability. The difference lies in the fact that the anti-unfair competition theories of civil law countries hold that the unauthorised public use of other people's business secrets damages the normal order of competition. Giving trade secrets protection against unfair competition focuses on the protection of not only the interests of a single competitor, but also those of the whole society. It overcomes the limitations of tort theory which relies too much on the confidentiality of a specific relationship, thus expanding the scope of regulation.

Since the 1950s, the theory of "the property" has been gaining popularity and has gradually become the dominant doctrine in the international community in the protection of trade secrets. This theory recognises trade secrets as property rights and seeks to protect them. Nowadays, the so-called right to trade secrets is no longer a legal interest protected by contract law or tort law, but a legally recognised "intangible property" or "intellectual property." The property theory has lasted for more than a century in the judicial practice of equity law in the common law system, and its judicial precedents have incisive exposition on the property attributes of trade secrets. In the United States, the judgement of Peabody v. Norfolk (1868) declared that "whether invention or discovery of manufacturing process constitutes the object of protection of the patent rights, the holder can be confidential to this secret, and the public or people who obtain the relevant knowledge out of goodwill do not have exclusive rights, but the rights holder, after all, possesses a certain property, the court of chancery will ban the unauthorised use or disclosure to a third party by others in violation of their contractual or confidentiality obligations".[2] Since then, trade secrets have been recognised as properties in cases such as the United States v. American Bell Telephone Co. (1897), Ferroline Corp. v. DAF Corp. (1953), and Ruckelshaus v. Monsanto Company (1983). In these cases, some decisions explicitly affirm that we are dealing with an intellectual property right, in fact, a property right to the created knowledge.[3] Although the protection of trade secrets as properties has become a universal institutional design all over the world, the property theory is in conflict with the traditional theory of real rights in the civil law system. There are two specific problems with it.

The first problem is insufficient exclusivity of the right to trade secrets. The so-called property right, whether the property owned is tangible or intangible, is exclusive and follows the basic principle of "one property, one right." However, in the field of trade secrets, the same technical or business information may be enjoyed by several parties, causing the coexistence of several trade secret rights, thereby insufficient exclusivity in property rights. It must be recognised that the property theory of trade secrets protection should not be bound to the ownership of corporals. Unlike tangible properties, information property cannot be possessed absolutely and the possession can be lost quite easily. In light of this, granting legal property protection to trade secrets is an institutional arrangement in the information society, established on the principle of first possession and designed to encourage investment in and creation of new information. (Cooter and Ulen 1994, p. 185). In fact, relative exclusivity also exists in other IPR fields to various degrees. For

---

[2] See Peabody v. Norfolk 98 Mass452 (1868).

[3] See Ferroline Corp. v. DAF Corp., 207 F. 2D912 (7th cir. 1953).

example, one or more inventors can apply for patents for the same invention in different countries and obtain their respective patents, and the same trademark may be registered simultaneously by different entities on non-similar goods. It can be said that the modern system of trade secrets, even the entire IP law, is the result of theoretical and institutional innovation on the traditional system of real rights.

The other problem is the public disclosure of the right to trade secrets. It is widely known that the public must be informed of the change of real rights in order to protect the security of transactions and meet the exclusivity of real rights, and specifically speaking, the real right of corporeal movables is informed by delivery and possession, while the real right of corporeal immovables is informed by registration. Both intangible and tangible property rights are absolute rights, and any changes in them must be publicised in a certain way. Patents and trademark rights, for example, need not be subject to traditional disclosure of changes, but their transfer and licensing are subject to registration. However, the change in trade secrets requires no registration, since trade secrets are technical information that calls for confidentiality. Among intangible and intellectual properties, only technical information protected by trade secrets law has the characteristics of information property, but it is not subject to public disclosure, and the law even mandates that it be kept secret. Therefore, it is necessary to acknowledge that the disclosure rules of right changes shall be treated as an exception in the sphere of trade secrets protection, but this is not sufficient to deny that trade secrets are property rights.

14.3.4 Commercial Defamation

Commercial defamation, or commercial slander, refers to an act in which an operator uses improper means such as fabrication and dissemination of false or misleading information to damage the business and commodity reputation of a competitor in order to weaken their competitive edge. Article 14 of the original Anti-Unfair Competition Law of the PRC made clear provision regarding business defamation, saying that a business operator must not fabricate or spread false information to injure a competitor's commercial credit or the reputation of their commodities. The Anti-Unfair Competition Law (Amendment 2017) transplanted this Article into the new Article 11: "A business operator shall not fabricate or disseminate false information or misleading information to damage a competitor's commercial credit or the reputation of a competitor's commodities."

There are two forms of business defamation under the current law. One is the fabrication of false or misleading information, including both the complete fabrication of the whole false information out of thin air, and the malicious distortion and exaggeration of part of the facts or fabrication of part of the information. The other form of business defamation is the dissemination of false or misleading information, either in writing or orally, including both to specific users or operators in the same industry and to an unspecified group of people. The common methods of fabricating and disseminating false or misleading information include: publishing comparative advertisements or declarative announcements to disparage the reputation of competitors; disseminating disparaging information about competitors to business customers or consumers in business transactions; soliciting or bribing certain people to complain in the name of customers or consumers in order to discredit competitors; and holding business meetings or releasing business information to discredit the quality of a competitor's products. It is worth mentioning that the content of the fabrication and dissemination should be false or misleading information; otherwise, it does not constitute business defamation, even if it affects the reputation and credit of others.

Under Article 10bis, (3)(2) of the *Paris Convention*, business defamation is limited to false allegations, while Article 5 of the *Model Provisions on Protection against Unfair Competition* interprets business defamation as "false or unjustifiable allegations." The Anti-Unfair Competition Law of the PRC adopted the term ("false allegations") in accordance with the *Paris Convention*, limiting business defamation to "fabrication or dissemination of false information." However, the Supreme People's Court expanded the interpretation of "false facts" to "other misleading information" in the *Interpretation of Several Issues Concerning the Application of Laws in the Trial of Civil Cases of Unfair Competition* (Draft for Comment). In the process of drafting the proposed amendments to the Anti-Unfair Competition Law of the PRC, the State Administration for Industry and Commerce considered revising the expression "false information" to "false or misleading information." On the basis of this proposal, the definition of business defamation was revised to "fabricating or disseminating false information or misleading information" when the Anti-Unfair Competition Law of the PRC was amended in 2017.

Business defamation damages a competitor's commercial credit and product reputation (generally referred to as "goodwill" in legal terms). "Goodwill" evolved from the traditional rights of personality and is a general term covering commercial credit and product reputation, but it is different from "reputation" and "honour" when these terms are used in the sense of personality rights. In a legal context, "goodwill" refers to the favourable assessment of a business by members of the public about its economic potential of production and business operations. Specifically speaking, economic capacity is the comprehensive ability of an enterprise in production and management activities, and goodwill contains this subjective element; positive social evaluation is the objective element of goodwill.

The legislation of goodwill varies from country to country. Common law nations have primarily relied on judicial precedents to construct their goodwill rights protection systems. For instance, British legal precedents have developed a variety of legal proceedings, such as "action for passing off", to combat the activities of passing off goods and injuring competitors' interests. Additionally, specific procedures have been established to deal with actions that defame or damage the goodwill of others. In the United States, infringement of goodwill may constitute unfair competition, and the courts protect "goodwill of a trade or business" as a kind of "property right." The same is true for probable expectancies based on goodwill (Zengchen 1997, p. 178). In civil law countries, the protection of goodwill mainly relies on tort law or anti-unfair competition law. The right to goodwill is protected by competition law in countries like Germany and Japan, and this protection has two characteristics. First, it acknowledges that goodwill comprises property interests, but does not completely accept the property theory. Japanese scholar Yonhe Kojima (1998, p. 43) emphasises that such rights are a kind of protection against unfair competition that only has the function of prohibition, thus it is different from exclusive rights such as copyright, patents and trademarks. Second, there is a competitive relationship between the infringer and the victim, as they are business operators in competitive activities. And as for production operators, no distinction is made between natural persons and legal persons.

International conventions protect the right to goodwill mainly through curbing unfair competition. For example, the 1967 Stockholm version of the *Paris Convention* lists three types of acts, including business defamation, that should be particularly prohibited; the *WIPO Convention* (1967) provides for issues regarding anti-unfair competition in IPRs, though without listing specific acts; and the *Model Law against Unfair Competition* (1993) formulated by WIPO specifies defamation of goodwill as unfair competition.

Based on the legislative spirit of international conventions, protection against unfair competition under IPR is mainly a right of prohibition and the right to goodwill, as the infringement object of unfair competition, is a civil law right with the characteristics of property right.

The right to goodwill has been recognised as a civil law right by the legal community, but there is still disagreement as to which legal branch it falls under. There are three main theories about the legal attribute of the right to goodwill: the theory of personality right, the theory of composite right, and the theory of IPRs.

The first theory classifies the right to goodwill as a personality right to distinguish it from property rights with their economic content, and there are two schools of thought among scholars who support the notion of personality right. One school of thought is the "theory of simple personality right", which holds that goodwill is part of the legal person's reputation, and the right to goodwill is an important part of the legal person's right to reputation. The only real distinction between goodwill and reputation rights is that the laws that protect each pertain to specific types of infringers and harms. "Violation of a company's reputation by the general public (i.e., non-competitors) is known as an infringement of reputation rights, while violation of that reputation by competitors, through means regulated by laws like anti-unfair competition law, is known as an infringement of the right to goodwill" (Zhang 1997, p. 35). The other school of thought is known as the "theory of special personality right", and it posits that goodwill is in fact a personality right and not a property right, although it shares some characteristics with intangible property rights. Goodwill right includes both mental and property interests, but the latter is not a straight property interest and is contained in the goodwill interests. Therefore, the right to goodwill is a special right of personality that is different from the related rights (Wang 1999).

The second theory is the "theory of composite right", that is, the right to goodwill contains both the attributes of properties (i.e., IPRs) and the attributes related to personal rights (i.e., personality right). The infringement of the right to goodwill violates not only IPRs but also personality rights, and thus such infringement is a kind of concurrence of infringements (Guan 1996, pp. 172, 177).

The third theory, the "theory of IPRs", argues that the right to goodwill should be categorised as an IPR, since it shares characteristics with patents, trademarks, and copyright, and also contains both personal and property right attributes. As goodwill is a creation of the human mind and intelligence and relates to various information that is combined with various tangible items, it satisfies the inherent characteristics of IPRs (Liang 1993).

In my view, goodwill is a special immaterial property, and therefore rights arising from it should be considered as property rights. The theoretical defect of the "theory of personality right" lies in the fact that it ignores and even denies the property nature of goodwill. The "theory of simple personality right" makes little sense because it denies the essential difference between the right to reputation and the right to goodwill of a legal person. Goodwill is a property interest with values and has been separated from the general reputation of personal interests for the sake of special legal protection. This new type of civil law right is obviously different from the right to reputation which falls under personal rights. The "theory of special personality right" classifies the right to goodwill as a personality right, which recognises but dilutes its property nature. The right to goodwill shares some characteristics with the right to personality; nevertheless, these characteristics are not central to the right. That the right to goodwill has been affirmed by relevant documents in the economic and legal fields. In the international accounting community, intangible assets contain traditional IPRs and IPR-related intangible property rights, such as franchise rights and goodwill right (Cai 1996). Goodwill is a form of asset that can be used for investment along with copyright, patents, and trademarks in international agreements of multilateral investments (Zheng 2000, pp. 27–29). The "theory of composite right" has some merits, since it acknowledges that the right to goodwill comprises the characteristics of both property rights and personality rights. However, as the "theory of composite rights" and the "theory of IPRs" both classify rights to goodwill as IPRs, this lacks legal references and jurisprudential basis. In commercial jurisprudence, the right to goodwill is called a commercial personality right and contains the content of property interests and also moral interests. It is a kind of property right to credit, and compared with copyright, patents and trademark, does not have the basic characteristics of traditional IPRs such as determined territoriality, statutory time and constant exclusivity (Wu 2001, pp. 91–98). In relevant international conventions and legislative practices from various countries, the right to goodwill is not an IPR, but rather a protecting target under anti-unfair competition law. Therefore, the author contends that the right to goodwill, together with the right to credit and the right to image, are immaterial property rights that cannot be classified as IPRs; they are intangible property rights that are different from all ownerships but related to IPRs.

14.4 IP Considerations in China's Anti-Unfair Competition Legislation

Since its implementation in 1993, the *Anti-Unfair Competition Law of the PRC* has undoubtedly helped to promote and protect fair competition, stop and prevent unfair competition (including unfair competition related to IPRs), protect the legitimate rights and interests of operators and consumers, and ensure the continued and sustainable growth of the market economy. The *Anti-Unfair Competition Law* has been amended twice, in 2017 and 2019, and this has solved some problems that originally existed in the legal texts. However, the current Anti-Unfair Competition Law still has many shortcomings, and the following is a brief analysis of the issues of IPRs in the legislation of anti-unfair competition.

14.4.1 Separate Legislative Models for Competition Law and Prohibition of IP Abuse

China's Anti-Unfair Competition Law was first enacted on the theoretical basis of "comprehensive regulation model" in 1993. According to this legislative model, the Anti-Unfair Competition Law is not a single special law to regulate unfair competition, but a comprehensive law covering anti-unfair competition, anti-restriction of competition and certain acts of anti-monopoly. Among the eleven types of unfair competition listed in the law, restriction of competition by public enterprises, administrative restriction of competition, low-price dumping, tying and collusive bidding are usually considered to fall under anti-restrictive competition and anti-monopoly behaviour. As the Anti-monopoly Law of the PRC was introduced in 2007 specifically to regulate restrictive competition and monopolies, the legislative model of competition law in China has entered a path of separate legislation. The Anti-Unfair Competition Law (Amendment 2017) removes the restriction of competition and market monopoly from the original law, further establishing and optimising the separate legislative model of competition law in China. In view of this, IPR abuse should be regulated by the anti-monopoly (public) law, rather than the Anti-Unfair Competition Law. The legal regulation of IPRs includes regulation by private law and by public law: under private law, it is first of all the restriction of the exercise of IPRs by IP law itself (including territorial restriction, time restriction and power restriction) and then the restriction of the abuse of IPRs through the basic principles of civil law (such as the principle of good faith, the principle of prohibition of abuse of rights, and the principle of public and moral order); under public law, on the other hand, it is to solve the problem of IPR abuse within the framework of anti-monopoly law. Although IPRs are regarded as "legitimate monopoly rights", they cannot be assumed to have "market dominance" as referred to in anti-monopoly law. However, like other property rights, IPRs are not specially exempted from the application of anti-monopoly law. In other words, they do not constitute "areas of exceptions" in anti-monopoly law. In short, given the legislative model of China's competition law, IPR abuse should be regulated by the anti-monopoly law.

14.4.2 Qualification of Business Operators and Scope of Subjects Covered by Competition Law

The current *Anti-Unfair Competition Law of the PRC* provides that the subjects of unfair competition are "business operators", namely, natural persons, legal persons and unincorporated organisations engaged in the production and operation of goods or the provision of services. Critics in the academic community have pointed out the flaws in focusing solely on the operators as the main subjects of the violation. In this regard, Wang Xianlin (2009) believes that operators can be defined from two different perspectives: subject qualification and subject behaviours. The former emphasises the legal qualifications of business activities; and based on this view, employees of enterprises who infringe on commercial secrets, legal representatives of or persons handling commercial bribery, and unlicensed business operators will not be included as operators; the latter, on the other hand, emphasises the acts of business activities, and people who conduct such acts are "business operators." The latter perspective is more reasonable and feasible, because this interpretation with expanded scope is conducive to the application of the current law. However, in the future amendment to the Anti-Unfair Competition Law the scope of the subjects of regulation should be comprehensively revised. The subject of tort liability, that is, that of unfair competition, needs to be expanded from "business operators" to all subjects engaged in market economic activities. In other words, those engaged in market transactions are regulation targets of the Anti-Unfair Competition Law. Moreover, the qualification of a "business operator" is not important in the recognition of a rights holder (a victim of unfair competition); however, the term rights holder should refer to all people who have IPRs (including the creator of work names or titles, the inventor of non-proprietary technical achievements, the owner of unregistered trademarks and so on). Without limiting the qualification of rights holders and that of the subject of tort liability, the Anti-Unfair Competition Law can truly become "non-exhaustive" and play its cover-all role in the protection of IPRs (Zheng 2003, pp. 262–267). It is worth noting that *the Anti-Unfair Competition Law* (Amendment 2019) made major changes to the scope of subjects of infringement of trade secrets, specifying that "apart from business operators, natural persons, legal persons and non-legal persons committing any of the illegal acts stipulated in the preceding paragraph shall be deemed to have infringed upon commercial secrets." This newly added clause includes non-operators as the subjects of infringement of trade secrets, which expands the scope of subjects of unfair competition.

14.4.3 Enumerative Provisions on Infringement and Addition of General Clauses

The current *Anti-Unfair Competition Law of the PRC* adopts an enumerative approach to defining acts of unfair competition, but lacks generally applicable provisions, or "cover-all provisions" which would have expanded the scope of application, and this is an obvious flaw of closedness. In terms of legislative techniques, the concurrent use of generalisation and enumeration represent the prevailing model in modern legislation internationally. Specifically speaking, this model entails listing specific types of infringing acts while simultaneously establishing a general clause for infringements. Such a clause authorises law enforcement agencies to identify newly emerging infringing acts in social and commercial practice that are not exhausted in the list. Some scholars contend that Article 2(2) of China's Anti-Unfair Competition Law constitutes a general clause. This provision states: For the purposes of this Law, 'unfair competition' refers to acts committed by business operators in the course of production or business operations that violate the provisions of this Law, disrupt order in market competition, and harm the lawful rights and interests of other business operators or consumers. The author contends that this aforementioned provision lacks the essential elements of a true general clause. The reason is that, according to its wording, one acts that "violate of the provisions of this law"—meaning the seven types of conduct expressly enumerated therein—qualify as unfair competition. It may therefore be concluded that this provision functions merely as a definitional norm, and is insufficient to support an extended interpretation beyond the statutory list of infringements. Consequently, the future iteration of the Unfair Competition Law should incorporate a general clause for determining acts of unfair competition, in addition to enumerating specific, recognised types of such conduct.

14.4.4 Coordination Between Anti-Unfair Competition Law and Relevant Civil Legislation

Based on the common legislative objectives of fairness and justice, IP law and anti-unfair competition law interact and coordinate in legal regulation, and the two laws complement each other in IPRs protection. According to Professor Zheng Chengsi, the relationship between a particular IP law and the Anti-Unfair Competition Law is not about how the latter law (or the substance of the latter law) replaces the former, but rather how the former law is complemented by the latter. In terms of IPRs protection, a specific IP law grants "strong protection" in force and "narrow protection" in scope, while the Anti-Unfair Competition Law provides somewhat "weak protection" in force and "extensive protection" in scope (Zheng 2003, p. 264), which shows that the two laws are complementary in legal function but independent in legal form. There are three types of IPRs protection under China's Anti-Unfair Competition Law: first, for IPRs (such as trademark rights) that are already under the protection of IP law, the Anti-Unfair Competition Law provides only supplementary protection; second, for other IPR related rights (such as rights to trade secrets, goodwill rights, and image rights) that are not protected by special laws, the Anti-Unfair Competition Law provides special protection; third, for IPR related property rights and interests (such as the name and title of a work and the name, packaging, and decoration of well-known goods) that are not provided for in the relevant special laws, the Anti-Unfair Competition Law provides cover all protection. In this context, the IPRs and related rights and interests covered by the Anti-Unfair Competition Law can be arranged as follows in civil law: some must have special laws and regulations to cover them, such as regulations for the protection of trade secrets protection; others, such as the right to goodwill, should be provided for in principle in basic civil law; and still others should be listed in the Anti-Unfair Competition Law.

14.5 Anti-Unfair Competition Related to Digital IPRs

Network technology and genetic technology are the most representative and influential new technologies in the twenty-first century. The emergence of network technology has not only fundamentally changed the ways human beings live and changed the modes of social and economic development, but also challenged the legal regimes in countries around the world. Therefore, the IPRs regime has acquired a unique technological characteristic, "IPRs on the Internet." There are several legal challenges in the field of online copyright, such as the protection of digital works, the consideration of the appropriateness and reasonableness of technological security measures, and the definition of the responsibilities of both the disseminators and the users of online works (Xue 2000); and in the field of online trademarks, the law is faced with a conflict between the territoriality of trademark rights and the international nature of the Internet, as well as the conflict between the categorised protection of trademarks and the exclusivity of online trademarks (Wu 2002); and in the field of unfair competition on the Internet, commercial activities enter into the virtual space from the real world, and this will definitely trigger relevant legal issues. In the highly technological, virtual and instantaneous Internet environment, unfair competition can occur quickly, causing widespread damage and significant consequences. In this regard, Zhang Ping (2000) pointed out many problems that need to be solved, such as the commercial packaging of screen displays and network interfaces, the confidentiality of online trade secrets, and online false advertising. These problems not only damage the legitimate interests of the relevant business operators, but also seriously undermine the economic order of the network, therefore a response is required from anti-unfair competition laws worldwide.

The *Anti-Unfair Competition Law of the PRC* was amended in both 2017 and 2019 to respond proactively to new types of unfair competition that occur on the Internet. The two amendments involve four relevant revisions of unfair competition on the Internet. First, the Amendment 2017 added a new provision of "unauthorised use of the main part of the domain names, website names, web pages, etc. of others with certain influence" into Article 6, Paragraph 1, that is, "business operators shall not commit the following acts to mislead others to misidentify their goods as others' goods or to associate their goods with others." Second, Article 8, Paragraph 2 of the Amendment 2017 states that "business operators shall not organise false transactions to help other business operators to carry out false or misleading commercial promotion." This provision highlights "organising false transactions", and mainly aims at regulating "click farming" in e-commerce.[4] Third, Article 9, Paragraph 1 states that "business operators shall not commit the following acts infringing on business secrets", and in the Amendment 2019, "hacking" as a means to obtain the commercial secrets of a rights holder was added to the list of acts. Fourth, the Amendment 2017 adds a special clause of "unfair competition on the Internet": Article 12 of the current law, known as the "benchmark clause" of the Anti-Unfair Competition Law in the Internet era (Kong 2019, p. 529), stipulates that a business operator shall not, through manipulation of user choices or any other methods, make use of technical means to commit the following acts so as to hinder and disrupt normal operation of the network products or services provided legitimately by other business operators: (1) inserting hyperlink or forcing redirects in the network products or services provided legitimately by other business operators without their consent; (2) misleading, defrauding or forcing users to amend, close or uninstall network products or services provided legitimately by other business operators; (3) maliciously causing incomparability of the network products or services provided legitimately by other business operators; or (4) committing any other acts which hinder or disrupt network products or services provided legitimately by other business operators.

The two amendments to the *Anti-Unfair Competition Law of the PRC* are useful institutional legislative responses to unfair competition on the Internet and will promote the healthy development of China's Internet economy. However, the research and analysis of related issues cannot stop there. It must be acknowledged that the current law's institutional response to unfair competition on the Internet is still limited, and in practice there are many outstanding problems that need our attention. Furthermore, the law alone is not sufficient; the application of legal norms related to unfair competition on the Internet needs theoretical support. The current research should focus on the problems faced by the Anti-Unfair Competition Law in protecting IPRs online, and it can be summarised as follows.

14.5.1 Cybersquatting and Domain Name Infringement

There are two forms of unfair competition of domain names: 'cybersquatting' and 'domain name guide failure.' Both relate to the use of domain names on the Internet

[4] See Report of the Legal Committee of the National People's Congress on the Revision of the *Anti-Unfair Competition Law of the People's Republic of China* (Draft Revision) (October 31, 2017).

to damage the rights and interests of other trademarks, trade names or goodwill, and other commercial signs.

Domain name cybersquatting is the practice of using a commercial sign that another party owns and enjoys prior, lawful rights and interest, and registering it as its own domain name. An operator's domain name is their identity code in cyberspace. In electronic commerce activities, domain names have become a resource or wealth that enterprises compete for on the Internet, because they have symbolic recognition and commercial value. Cyber squatters typically squat repeatedly on a large number of other operators' well-known trademarks, trade names or other well-known commercial marks, and sell them publicly for profit. Cybersquatting constitutes unfair competition in the Internet sector. First, cybersquatting seriously damages the normal order of competition and transaction. For the perpetrators, cybersquatting is an act of speculation: they register domain names not for actual use but to trade them, seeking economic benefit through their transfer; and for the victims, cybersquatting is an infringement, and the legitimate owners of commercial marks will become disadvantaged in business, as they are unable to extend their brand effects to cyberspace. Second, cybersquatting constitutes the dilution of well-known trademarks and other famous commercial marks. This so-called dilution of commercial marks refers to the commercial use of others' well-known trademarks and trade names, which improperly reduces or weakens the ability of the marks to indicate their related goods or services or distinguish them from other goods or services (Li 2003, p. 267). The legal measure against dilution is to extend the protection of well-known commercial marks to non-similar goods or services. And the current judicial practice already regulates cybersquatting that dilutes commercial signs as unfair competition. In general, cybersquatting is obviously illegitimate and illegal and is a type of unfair competition that damages the legitimate rights of rights holders of commercial marks and that seeks illegal commercial interests.

"Domain name guide failure" refers to the act of weakening or disrupting the capability of other people's domain names from being connected and the improper use other people's business reputations by "embedding" technical means, such as hypertext links, framing technology, and Meta tags, so as to make improper use of other people's commercial reputation. Hypertext links, framing technology, and Meta tags and other technical means are results of the development and application of network technology, In unfair competition on the Internet, the perpetrator uses the above technical means this way: embedding hyperlinks to allow users to access information on the Internet without knowing or using the domain name, weakening the guidance function of the domain name; or framing links to "pull" other people's information into their own web pages, which damages the other people's commercial interests; or unmarking settings to bury the keywords of other people's commercial marks and taking "free ride" in a user's search, which results in misleading search results. Certainly, use of the abovementioned network technologies does not necessarily constitute unfair competition. In judicial practice, recognition of unfair competition of network operators usually takes into account two factors: first, whether there is a competition relationship between the operator embedding or framing links and the operator chained and affected; and second, whether the use of network technologies causes confusion to users, that is, whether there is misunderstanding of the origin of the chained information, or misunderstanding of the connection between the link setting word and the chained words directed to.

14.5.2 Online False Advertising

Online false advertising is a special form of false advertising, and currently the main form of unfair competition occurring online. Compared with traditional false advertising, online false advertising has the following two characteristics. One is related to the subject of liability of the false advertising. Generally speaking, there are two types of actors of false advertising, namely the business operators of goods or services (operators) and the business operators of advertising business (advertisers). The "operators of advertising business" in anti-unfair competition law includes the operators of agency, design, production and publication of advertisements. In the context of the Internet, the operators of traditional advertising business, as one of the actors of false advertising, have been replaced by the providers of online services. The Internet has now become a valuable advertising platform, and providers of online services have replaced traditional media to become advertising operators. Therefore, the providers of online services are now one of the infringement subjects in online false advertising that constitutes unfair competition. The other characteristic relates to form. The forms of promotion used online are different from those used in traditional media. Traditional media, such as newspapers, magazines, radio, and television, generally present advertising content directly to consumers, while online advertising can adopt a variety of forms. With the rise of search engine technology, bidding ranking, theme promotion and other search-related advertisements have emerged, in addition to pop-up window advertisement and web advertisement. These forms of advertising are a legitimate online business service model but may also lead to unfair competition. In short, providers of search engine services should be deemed to be operators of advertising business, that is, they qualify as subjects in the acts. And search advertising is the main form of advertising promotion in the web environment. The "notification and deletion" rule can be used to determine whether or not a search engine service provider has subjective culpability and, thus, whether or not it should bear liability for unfair competition.

14.5.3 Online Commercial Defamation

In the era of network information, the Internet has become an important information platform. BBS, blogs, and microblogs are the means of dissemination of information, and at the same time, the Internet platform is also the main carrier of commercial defamation, and the information receiver often becomes the publisher of information, making it difficult to control commercial defamation on the Internet. The emergence and spread of commercial defamation in cyberspace have brought challenges to existing laws. First, commercial defamation can now involve not only operators in competitive relationships, but also Internet users and service providers who participate in some way, either actively or passively, and this increases the complexity of the legal relations of infringement. In this regard, China's Anti-Unfair Competition Law may draw on the practices of Sweden, Belgium, and other countries, including noncompetitive actors as the subject matter of legal regulation. Second, the definition of business defamation is so restrictive that many online infringements of goodwill are not covered. The *WIPO Model Provisions on Protection against Unfair Competition* considers that there are two types of commercial defamation: one is false claims, and this has been incorporated into the Anti-Unfair Competition Law. The other is improper claims, that is, unfair, inaccurate and incomplete statements of objective facts,[5] for example, deliberately spreading the records of competitors' penalties on electronic bulletin boards, using derogatory words for similar products in comparative advertisements, and selectively publicising the side effects of certain products as toxic when scientific research results are inconclusive. It is necessary to expand the scope of China's Anti-Unfair Competition Law in light of the Model Provisions on Protection against Unfair Competition and the practical necessities.

14.5.4 Database Infringement

Electronic databases that are only accessible by computers and software are important carriers of information storage and utilisation in the Internet Age. A database which has a primary function of providing users with certain information is "a collection of independent works, data or other materials that are systematically or sequentially arranged and accessible by electronic means" (Dong 1999).

Protection of databases has become a focus of concern in IP law worldwide. The *Directive on Legal Protection of Databases* was formally enacted by the European Union's Council of Ministers in 1995. It provides two forms of protection for databases: copyright protection for "original" databases, and special rights protection for "non-original" databases. The latter is "copyright-like protection for specific subject matter that do not satisfy the requirement of copyright" (Lu 2011, p. 284), and is, in essence, a protection against unfair competition. Inspired by the EU, WIPO introduced the *Draft Database Convention* in 1996, adopting a model of special rights protection to cover databases and their contents, but not the computer programs used to produce, operate, or maintain a database. In the same year, in the United States also appeared database protection legislation, giving database producers the right to "extract" (transfer the contents of a database to another medium by any means) and "reuse" (make the contents of a database available to the public by distribution, rental, online transmission and so on), and providing protection to databases against unfair competition under "the misappropriation doctrine."

[5] For more information, see (Wu2001).

China's current IP law provides relatively limited protection for databases. Article 14 of the *Copyright Law of the People's Republic of China* (1990), revised in 2001, provides that a compilation of several works or parts of works, data or other materials does not constitute a work, but if the selection or arrangement of the content of a compilation reflects inventiveness, it shall be considered a "compilation work." This indicates that databases with inventiveness can be protected by copyright, while those without inventiveness are outside the scope of protection. In this regard, China's Anti-Unfair Competition Law can learn from the practice of the EU and provide special rights protection for "marginal works" such as non-original databases.

14.5.5 Unfair Competition Concerning Software

There are two main types of unfair competition related to software in the web environment: one is the improper use of information obtained through "reverse engineering", and the other is the use of software technology to interfere with and damage competitors' software of similar type. These situations fall into the "gap" covered by neither copyright law or patent law and therefore must resort to Anti-unfair competition law.

In the field of computer software, "reverse engineering" refers to the activity of learning or studying the function of a software in order to develop products compatible with it, or determine whether the original work is suitable by the owner of a software program or of its duplicate through reverse compilation to find the original source code. The legality of "reverse engineering" of software has become a hot issue in international research. In the United States, according to the provisions of Article 107 of the *Copyright Act* of 1976, the reasonable owner of the software can obtain the ideas, operating methods, and behavioural factors of the software through "reverse engineering" (disassembly, dismantling and so on). However, information thus obtained may not be used for any other purposes than the independent creation of the program or the acquisition of complementarity; for example, it may not be given to others or used to create, duplicate, and market programs that are substantially similar to the program (Chen 2000). In China, copyright law does not provide protection for the technical contents of software. If anyone makes improper use of the information obtained through "reverse engineering", it will dilute the inventiveness of the software and infringe on the interests of the rights holders. In this case, anti-unfair competition can offer protection as a remedy.

In the Internet services industry, the compatibility of general and conventional software is an inherent requirement for the development of the software industry, and a basic factor in the protection of the rights and interests of consumers. Operators should adhere to business ethics and legal rules when developing and promoting their own software. Some software developers take advantage of software services to intentionally break compatibility with other software that is similar to their own, force the uninstallation of the legal software of competitors, and interfere with, harm, prevent, and block the normal operation of other software during the transformation of software (Hou 2010, pp. 24–25), all of which constitute unfair competition caused by so-called "rogue software" and "malware." Such disputes have the following three characteristics. First, concealment of the technical means. The operator uses the excuse of normal conflicts of software to conceal their subjective malicious intention of incompatibility with competitors' software. Second, concealment of subject identity. The operator induces or even coerces a third party to carry out improper activities in order to conceal their own involvement in unfair competition. Third, concealment of intention. The operator conceals their illegal intention of undermining competitors and making profit by means of providing free software. The classical types and traditional rules of anti-unfair competition law cannot regulate the above cases, and this calls for institutional reform and innovation and also legislation revision and improvement.

The enumeration of the Anti-Unfair Competition Law related to IPRs on the Internet addresses the main problems rather than all the problems. Some Internet-related unfair competition problems are provided for by existing laws, and some are not. In any case, these should be particularly taken into consideration in China's future Anti-Unfair Competition Law amendment.

References

Cai, Jixiang. 1996. *Intangible Assets Study*. Shenzhen: Haitian Publishing House

Chen, Chuanfu. 2000. *High-Tech and Intellectual Property Law*. Wuhan: Wuhan University Press

Chong, Mingzhao. 1997. *The Competition Law*. Beijing: Law Press

Cooter, Robert and Ulen, Thomas. 1994. *Law and Economics*. Trans. Jun Zhang. Shanghai: Shanghhai People's Publishing House

Dong, Binghe. 1999. Legal protection of databases in China: A review of two cases involving databases in Chinese courts. In *Studies on Intellectual Property Rights*, ed. Chengsi Zheng. Beijing: China Fangzheng Publishing House

Guan, Linghua. 1996. *The Identification and Compensation of Moral Damage*. Beijing: People's Court Press

Hou, Xia. 2010. On the law regulation of new unfair competition behaviour in Internet environment. *Journal of Anhui University of Technology (Social Sciences)* 1

Jager, Melvin F. 1985. *Trade Secrets Law*. Wisconsin: Clark Boardman Company, Ltd.

Jiang, Hui. 2007. On the protection of intellectual property rights by competition law. *Academic Forum* 2

Kojima, Yonhe. 1998. *Intangible Property Rights*. Singapore: Sōzō Publishing House.

Kong, Xiangjun. 2019. *New Principles of Anti-Unfair Competition Law*. Beijing: Law Press

Li, Mingde. 2003. *Research on American Anti-Unfair Competition Law*. Beijing: China Fangzheng Publishing House.

Li, Shunde. 1999. *On the Object and Legal Attribute of Anti-Unfair Competition Law. Intellectual Property Research*. Beijing: China Fangzheng Publishing House

Liang, Shangshang. 1993. Goodwill and the right to goodwill. *Chinese Journal of Law* 5

Lu, Haijun. 2011. *On the Object of Copyright*. Beijing: Intellectual Property Publishing House

Shao, Jiandong. 2004. *Tutorial on Competition Law*. Beijing: Intellectual Property Publishing House

Shigeaki, Hirota. 1997. *Intellectual Property Law*. Tokyo: Seirin Shoin

Tomita, Tetsuo. 2000. *Intellectual Property in Market Competition*. Trans. Zhengheng Liao et al. Beijing: The Commercial Press

Wang, Najia. 1999. On the Infringement of Goodwill and its legal salvage. *Journal of Inner Mongolia Normal University (Philosophy and Social Science)* 3
Wang, Xianlin. 2009. *The Science of Competition Law*. Beijing: China Renmin University Press
Wang, Xuezheng. 1998. Theory and legislative experience of anti-unfair competition law in China. In *Intellectual Property System in China*, ed. Chuntian Liu. Beijing: Intellectual Property Publishing House
Wang, Yuankuo. 1996. A preliminary discussion on anti-competitive behaviors related to intellectual property and their legal control. *Tribune of Political Science and Law*, (4).
Wei, Zhenying (Ed.). 2000. *Civil Law*. Beijing: Peking University Press
Wei, Zhi. 1999. On the relation between unfair competition law and intellectual property law. *Journal of Peking University (Humanities and Social Sciences)* 6
Wen, Xikai. 1991. Right against unfair competition and industrial property right. *Intellectual Property* 3
Wu, Handong. 2001. The right to goodwill. *China Legal Science* 3
Wu, Handong. 2002. *Intellectual Property in a Knowledge-Based Economy*. Beijing: Law Press
Xu, Mengzhou and Meng, Yanbei. 2008. *Competition Law*. Beijing: China Renmin University Press
Xu, Yuling. 1993. *The Protection of Business Secret*. Taipei: San Min Book
Xue, Hong. 2000. *Intellectual Property Law in the Internet Age*. Beijing: Law Press
Yang, Ming. 2003. On the protection of intellectual property rights by unfair competition law. *Studies in Law and Business* 3
Zengchen, Mingru. 1997. *Selected Treatises on Patent and Trademark Law*. Taipei: self-published.
Zhang, Ping. 2000. *Analysis on Internet Intellectual Property Rights and Related Legal Issues*. Guangzhou: Guangzhou Publishing House
Zhang, Xinbao. 1997. *Legal Protection of the Right to Reputation*. Beijing: China University of Political Science and Law Press
Zheng, Chengsi. 2003. *On Intellectual Property*. Beijing: Law Press
Zheng, Xinjian. 2000. On the legal attribute of the right to goodwill. *Hebei Law Science* 1
Zheng, Youde and Wan, Zhiqian. 2007. The development and innovation of anti-unfair competition law in Germany. *Studies in Law and Business* 1
Zheng, Youde. and Wan, Zhiqian. 2009. On the parallel protection of trademark rights and interests between trademark law and anti-unfair competition law. *Studies in Law and Business* 6

Chapter 15
IPRs Regimes and Civil Legislation

The status of IP law refers to its position within the entire legal system, that is, whether it is an independent legal branch in itself or falls under a specific legal category. Chinese scholars have held different views on this matter.

Some scholars contend that IP law cannot be classified into a single legal branch, since it is a comprehensive legal regime with extensive connections to civil law, economic law, administrative law, and international law. In the author's view, IP law regulates the property and interpersonal relations of parties with equal status arising from the creation or use of intellectual products. Its methods of regulation and applicable principles are mainly those of civil law. Although administrative law, criminal law, and other legal norms apply to and have some influence on a small portion of IP law cases, they do not change the nature of IP law.

Apart from basic laws like the criminal code and the civil code, contemporary legislative practices indicate that specialised legal regimes generally employ multiple regulatory methods while still relying on primary approach based on their subject matter. Therefore, the argument that IP law is a merely a comprehensive legal regime without belonging to a specific legal branch is unconvincing.

Other scholars argue that IP law is an independent legal branch in itself, as various IPRs institutions have constituted a relatively complete law family, and the emergence of the French *Intellectual Property Code* (*Code de la propriété intellectuelle*) of 1992 is a sign of a future trend of separation from civil law. The author maintains that IPRs are a new and independent type of property rights separated from the ownership of tangible objects. They are the outcome of civil law's recognition and formalization of intangible properties in the form of knowledge. While the immateriality of the subject matter is an essential characteristic of IPRs, their attributes as rights in civil law or in private law are not substantially different from those of property rights or creditor's rights. It can be said that IP law lacks the prerequisites for establishing an independent legal branch because it lacks its own subject and methods of regulation.

Most scholars agree that IP law falls within the domain civil law. However, opinions diverge regarding how China's IPRs regime should interact with its Civil Code

H. Wu, *Theorising Intellectual Property Rights from Chinese Perspectives*,
https://doi.org/10.1007/978-981-96-5867-1_15

in the future. Many scholars advocate the incorporation of a system of property rights, including IPRs, into the Civil code for the following reasons: the means of protection of IPRs are basically of a civil nature, so such rights should be treated on a par with other property rights and regulated under the civil code. In addition, there have been legislative practices of incorporating IPRs into civil code internationally. Furthermore, the *General Principles of the Civil Law of the People's Republic of China* (1986) provide for various types of IPRs in a special section on "civil law rights" (Zhang 1999; Zhao et al. 2000). In light of these reasons, many scholars say, IPRs should be included in the civil code (Zhai 1999). However, the author holds a different view on this, which will be explained below.

15.1 Modern Civil Code Codification and Emergence of IPRs Regimes

After the introduction of the *Statute of Monopolies* (1623) and the *Statute of Anne* (1709) in the UK, and the *Manufacture and Goods Mark Act and Trademarks Based on the Principles of Use and Non-examination* (1857) in France, as the capitalist system developed in the West, various major capitalist countries introduced IP legislation from the late eighteenth century through the nineteenth century. Examples of such legislation include the *Copyright Act of 1790* in the US, the Law *of the Author's Right* (1793) in France, the *Law for the Protection of Scientific and Artistic Works against Copy or Imitation* (1837) in Germany, and the *Copyright Law* (1899) in Japan. Patent laws were promulgated in 1790 in the US, 1791 in France, 1877 in Germany, and 1885 in Japan, and trademark laws were introduced in 1875 in the UK, 1870 in the US, 1874 in Germany, and 1884 in Japan. None of the abovementioned IP legislation is directly related to the compilation of modern civil codes. Common law countries, with law derived from judicial decisions instead of statutes, honour their own legal sources and traditions. They do not have a body of written civil laws, in other words, no civil code. British and American scholars divide private laws into the laws of contracts, torts, property, trust, family and other laws, and the abovementioned norms exist in the form of case law or statute law. Whether in the UK or in the US, IP law has always been in the form of statute law, has always been an independent institution of property law, and has not involved the complications of the civil code. On the other hand, the civil law countries have inherited the tradition of codification from ancient Rome. The two-model modern civil codes, the French *Napoleonic Code* (*Code Napoléon*) (1804) and the German *Civil Code* (*Bürgerliches Gesetzbuch*) (1900), were completed in the early and late nineteenth century respectively, and their systems were based on the *Institutiones*or *Digesta* (530–533 AD) of Roman law. IP legislation was generally in place long before the codification of civil codes, and these new property regimes were mostly "transplanted" from the UK; therefore, IPRs regimes were not incorporated into the system of the exemplary civil codes of modern continental Europe.

15.2 Incorporation of IPRs Regimes in Modern Civil Code Structures

Since the twentieth century, new efforts have been made in some civil law countries to incorporate IP laws into their national civil codes, and these efforts culminated in the second civil code codification movement that emerged in the 1990s. The representative codes are:

15.2.1 Italian Civil Code

The Italian Civil Code occupies an important place in the history of the codification of the civil law system. The original code, in force from 1865, was mainly modelled on the French system. The current version, enacted in 1942, replaced the original code while retaining some parts of it (Schipani 1997). As a newly emerged legal issue that brought about new sets of legal relationships and called for new institutional arrangements, IPRs were innovatively addressed in the labour laws included in Book 6 of the current Italian Civil Code. However, this part actually covers a mixture of norms, including labour relations, corporations (partnerships), cooperatives, enterprises, IPRs, competition and monopolies. IPRs the Italian Civil Code covers are mainly copyright, patents, and the right to use trademarks and trade names. Among them, the trademarks and trade names rights are provided for in Chapter 8, "Enterprises", and creative rights are provided for in Chapter 9, "The Right to Intellectual Works and Industrial Inventions." There are two problems with the provisions of the Italian Civil Code concerning IPRs: Firstly, they are only in principle provisions, and the Civil Code emphasises that the acquisition, exercise and preservation of relevant rights are stipulated by special laws. In fact, various special laws on IPRs still exist in addition to the relevant provisions in the Civil Code, and as a result, these protections provided for in the Civil Code are ineffective in operation. Secondly, the provisions concerning IPRs in the Civil Code are treated in the chapter of "Enterprises" and that of "Right to Intellectual Works and Industrial Inventions," which undoubtedly prevented IPRs from forming one complete system. At the same time, modern IP law has become a system of numerous categories and rights, but the Civil Code only provides for four types of IPRs, which shows that it is not sufficiently inclusive.

15.2.2 Dutch Civil Code

The Netherlands is an outstanding representative in the second civil code codification movement. It formed a unique code structure, namely the Dutch Civil Code, based on the combination of "*Institutiones*" and "*Pandectae*" (a legislative technique derived from Roman law and used in the codification of civil codes in civil law countries such as Germany and Japan). The Dutch Civil Code is divided into 10 books. Book 9 covers "Intellectual Property." According to the legislative plan, the IPRs in Book 9 included patents, trademarks, copyright, trade names and so on. Those concerning private laws are in Book 9 while provisions of administrative, procedural and criminal nature are placed elsewhere. However, Book 9 on "Intellectual Property" was later abolished due to difficulties in legislative technique (Xu 2000, pp. 37–55). And another important reason is that, since the enactment of *Maastricht Treaty* in 1992, the EU has been working on a European Communities Act which will be applicable to all members. Starting with the Dutch Civil Code, the European Community has successively implemented uniform trademark law, patent law and other IPRs regulations to which all members must adhere, and which they cannot supplement or revise (Wu 1998, pp. 333–335). According to Dutch scholar Hartkamp (1998, pp. 60–70), in this context the incorporation of IP laws into Book 9 of the new Civil Code was inappropriate.

15.2.3 Russian Civil Code

Soviet Russian civil law had a wide impact on the former socialist countries. Soviet Russia's 1922 Civil Code in its chapters on property rights focuses on ownership, creditor rights, and inheritance and does not discuss IPRs. The 1961 legislative outline of Soviet civil law and the subsequent civil code of the Russian Federation were substantially revised, providing for copyright, the rights to discovery, and the rights to invention in Book 4, 5 and 6 respectively. But these three books were not combined into one book titled "IPRs", and they did not include industrial rights like patents and trademark rights. The outline of the Soviet civil legislation (1991) envisages seven books. There are two related to IPRs, one covering copyright and the other covering rights to creative works, and the latter includes patents, designs, trademarks, trade names, rationalisation proposals, authors rights, trade secrets, and new plant varieties (Yu 1995, p. 124). This model was only partially reflected in the *Civil Code of the Russian Federation* of 1994,[1] which included IPRs in its Book 5, named "Copyright and Invention Rights"; however, Russia had already enacted the *Patent Law* and *the Law on Commercial Signs* in the form of special laws in September 1992. This *Civil Code*, which has been referred to as the "model civil code" of the post-Soviet association known as the Commonwealth of Independent States (CIS), is yet to complete its section on IPRs. and the proposed volume only covers a fraction of the IPRs regime.

[1] The first part of the Civil Code of the Russian Federation was adopted in 1994 and entered into force in 1995; the second part was adopted in 1996 and entered into force in the same year; and the third part, which deals with IPRs, is being drafted.

15.2.4 Vietnamese Civil Code

The Civil Code of Vietnam of 1995 was born out of the civil law codification movement in post-socialist countries. Within it, IP law is systematically codified in a special book/section. When the *Civil Code* came into force in 1996 Vietnam's existing IP-related laws, including the *Industrial Property Law* (1989), *Copyright Law* (1994) and *Law on the Introduction of Foreign Technology* (1988) were abolished. Vietnam is one of the few countries in the world that did not make provisions for IPRs using a hybrid model of basic law and *lex specialis*, like Italy and Russia did. Book 6 of the Vietnam Civil Code, titled "Intellectual Property and Rights of Technology Transfer", contains three chapters: Chapter 1 "Copyright" provides for copyright and neighbouring rights; Chapter 2 "Industrial Ownership" provides for patents, trademarks and right to geographical indications; and Chapter 3 "Technology Transfer" provides for the subject matter of technology transfer, the right of technology transfer, and technology transfer contracts. The *Vietnam Civil Code* features the most comprehensive and centralised IPRs rules to date. However, its IP legislation exemplary effect is limited. The code includes only provisions for main traditional types of IPRs, leaving many emerging IPRs unprotected and vulnerable; and at the same time, it seems that the code, like other civil codes, is incapable of dealing with the relationship between substantive and procedural laws, leaving the procedural norms of IPRs and norms of administrative and criminal law to separate regulations or other legal divisions.[2]

In terms of legislative techniques, there are generally two approaches adopted by bodies drawing up civil codes. One approach is incorporation of all IPRs-related laws and regulations into the civil code, and this is undoubtedly a relocation move of legal norms. This approach is difficult to apply to industrial property rights system because it concerns many public law norms (as in the case of Vietnam law). The other approach is to set out broadly applicable rules and various regulations in an intellectual property section of the civil code, while also maintaining special IP laws. This latter approach has, to a certain extent, preserved the purity and formal aesthetics of the legislation of private rights, but its application is impractical and inconvenient (e.g., in Italian law). Generally speaking, incorporation of IPRs in modern civil codes is historically significant, yet this is not sufficient justification for blind imitation.

15.3 Contemporary IP Legislation Approaches

Special legislation is widely used in IP law around the world. Through special legislation, IP laws are enacted as an independent body of rules in the common law system, and as special laws falling into the civil law category in the civil law system.

[2] For an overview of the norms of the Vietnamese Civil Code and Vietnamese legislation, please see (Mi 1998; Xu 1997).

At the end of the twentieth century, legislators in France adopted specific legislation to combined 23 specific laws and regulations related to IPRs into a unified code, the 1992 *French Intellectual Property Code*. Some scholars hold that this was the first code of IPRs protection in the world, and it may serve as a model for the separation of IP laws and civil laws in the twenty-first century. However, while the accomplishments of the French IP law are noteworthy, IP law as *lex specialis* within the civil scope will remain unaffected, whether or not it is codified. First of all, the relationship of IP law to civil law and to commercial law is still that between a special law and a basic law. After France decided to adopt a separate legislation for IPRs, it made great efforts to deal with the relationship between the special laws for IPRs and the general laws like the civil law and commercial law, and has achieved good results. For example, as IPRs are intangible property rights, many rules relating to tangible property rights contained in the Civil Code cannot be applied directly. To protect the interests of authors, the freedom to contract is greatly restricted, and the labour contract of intellectual creation does not affect the author's enjoyment of the moral right and the right to freedom of thought. There are also special rules that are different from the general laws regarding the relationship between copyright and marriage and inheritance. Apart from the exceptions mentioned above, the general principles set by the Civil Code are still relevant to IP. This shows that the *French Intellectual Property Code* and the French Civil Code, even though they are two separate codes, are not two codes with parallel status. Their relationship is that of a general law and a special law It could be concluded that although the IP Code is named as a code, this does not change its basic status as *lex specialis* within the civil scope. Additionally, the IP Code is primarily a distinctive model for the systematisation of IP laws, that is, it is not a simple collection of miscellaneous IPRs-related normative documents, but a systematic legal document processed and organised on the basis of the original legal norms. French lawmakers have realised the need for code standardisation by consolidating and updating the country's many IP regulations. The French IP Code has two advantages in terms of legislative technique. First, it is arranged in a sound and orderly manner. For instance, IPRs are divided broadly into "Literary and Artistic Property Rights" (including copyright, neighbouring rights and database authorship) and "Industrial Property Rights" (including industrial design, invention, right to technical secrets, right to layout design of integrated circuits, new plant varieties, trademark rights and other sign rights). Second, the content is coordinated. The Code endeavours to coordinate the internal relations of the various IP laws, avoiding potential conflicts between their rules. However, it apparently omits one element of codification, namely, it lacks the principles and rules that are commonly applicable to all IPRs regimes.

The French intellectual property system in the form of a code has not gone far in terms of the relevant legislative practices, for *lex specialis* within the civil scope is still the preferred mode of IP legislation in civil law countries. The author argues that the choice of this mode is made mainly for the following reasons.

First, modern IP law is a comprehensive normative legal system. The IPRs regime, as a civil code, is fundamentally distinct from the basic civil law, in that it is a special law with extensive legal norms and varied legal penalties. The IPRs regime is a substantive law that protects the rights of creators; however, it also generally provides for the procedures of rights acquisition, alteration, management, remedy and so on, so the content of procedural law is provided for in the substantive law, and procedural law is dependent on the substantive law. In addition, although the IPRs regime was created as a private law to protect the rights of individuals over their intellectual property, it incorporates many principles of public law into its statutes, including administrative management, administrative penalties, and criminal sanctions (Liu 1997, p. 13), and thus it uses a hybrid legislative approach that combines the principles of both private and public law. It is true that the specificity of the legal norms of IPRs does not affect its nature as a part of the civil law system. However, on account of the specificity of the norms of IPRs, it is necessary to legislate separately for this comprehensive law outside the civil code.

Second, modern IP law is an open normative legal system. Compared with the copyright, patents and trademark rights covered by modern law, modern IP law is already a very large legal system, described in the provisions of the *WIPO Convention* as the sum of all the rights regimes arising from intellectual activities in the industrial, scientific, literary or artistic fields.[3] Since the emergence of the new technological revolution in the middle of the twentieth century, the knowledge economy has not only given birth to a new property concept of "knowledge = wealth", but also created a new IPRs regime, which is mainly manifested in two aspects: one is the "marginal protection law", that is, the adoption of certain rules of patents and copyright to create a new regime of exclusive rights, such as those related to the layout design of integrated circuits; and the other is the "separate protection law", that is, the establishment of "quasi-patent" for special knowledge products and protection for other similar IPRs, such as rights to new plant varieties and rights to domain names. While new IPRs regimes have emerged one after another, old ones have gradually evolved into new parts of the legal system of IPRs, the most significant of these being trade secret rights and anti-unfair competition law. This situation shows that modern IP law is in the process of continuous development and change, and it is obviously inappropriate to place such frequently changing laws in a civil code that requires relative stability.

Third, modern IP law is a system of constantly innovative legal norms. Modernisation and consistency are the two major trends of IP legislation, with the former resulting from developments in science and technology, and the latter from the formation of the new international economic order. As a result, IP law has been under frequent revision since the 1970s. Copyright laws in developed countries are amended on average once every less than 10 years according to studies (Wu 1998,

[3] The scope of IPRs is identified differently in several major international conventions. In summary, they can be divided into two categories. First, rights to creative works, including copyright, neighboring rights, database authorship, patents, designs, rights to layout design of integrated circuits, trade secret rights, and rights to new plant varieties. Second, rights to business signs, including trademark rights, trade name rights, geographical indication rights, and domain name rights. In addition, rights relating to fair competition, goodwill and commercialised images are also categorised as IPRs in a broad sense. As for whether the right of invention and the right of discovery are IPRs, there is still controversy in academic circles.

p. 27). The *French Intellectual Property Code* has been amended and supplemented 12 times in the six years since its promulgation. China's *Trademark Law* and *Patent Law* have each undergone two major revisions since their enactment, which occurred in the early 1990s and at the beginning of the new millennium respectively. It should be noted that these legal amendments were carried out in the form of special laws, and that it would not have been possible/easy to make such amendments within China's systematic and stable *Civil Code*.

15.4 China's IP Legislative Strategy

A debate has developed among Chinese scholars on whether IP laws should be integrated into the Civil Code. Scholars who oppose integration recommend that the present special IP laws be retained, whereas others suggest formulating a special IPRs code. Regardless of which model is to be used, IP law should be *lex specialis* of the Civil Code (See the above for its view). Scholars who, on the other hand, support integration of IP laws differ on how this integration should be carried out. One group advises that IP laws should be transplanted directly into the Civil Code, constituting a specific IP section, whereas another recommends that the Civil Code should provide only general rules on IPRs, with specific rules retained in the special laws. The author once opposed the integration of IPRs into the Civil Code, but has more recently proposed this second view of the integration of IPRs into the Civil Code based on the changing situation (Wu 2002, pp. 47–57).

The author changed his view primarily for the following reasons. First, IPRs are private rights, as was expressly stated in the preamble to the WTO's *TRIPS Agreement*. Although they are a form of intangible property related to knowledge, IPRs are by nature compatible with property rights of other types, and therefore should be classified as civil law rights. Placing intangible property rights in the civil code, together with tangible property rights, helps to form a complete and rich property rights system. Second, IPRs are rights protected by the civil code. Though there is some overlap with public law and procedural law, IP laws are framed by the private law system and subject to the civil scope. The civil code, as the basic civil law, has a higher rank and authority in legal classification. Therefore, the clear positioning of IPRs in the civil code could help maintain the sanctity of these rights. Third, IPRs provisions already exist in the basic civil law of China. *The General Principles of the Civil Law of the PRC* provide for special provisions on IPRs in Chapter 5, Section 3, however, with only enumeration of declarative terms on copyright, trademarks rights, patent rights and other rights of scientific and technological achievements, and without substantive provisions. In Chapter 5, "Civil Rights", a whole section is devoted to defining China's IPRs regime, combining IPRs with other property rights and personal rights in a special chapter on "civil law rights", which marks China's legislative innovation in civil law codification. Considering the inheritance of the legislative model, it is possible for China's Civil Code to make general provisions on IPRs in the future. Fourth, international organisation of

IPRs suggested this was a good idea. Authorities from WIPO at the 10th Shanghai International Intellectual Forum said: WIPO does not consider it a necessarily a great idea to specify IPRs rules in civil code, and countries that have done so, such as Italy, Russia and Vietnam, are reflecting on this issue, but setting general rules will be acceptable and is believed to deliver positive outcomes.

The Book *Intellectual Property Rights* in the Civil Code covers only general provisions, and the provisions of its relevant articles shall be in accordance with the following rules. First, the basic principles and general regimes stipulated in the Civil Code shall be applicable to all rights regimes, including the IPRs regime. Based on this general applicability, the Part on "Intellectual Property Rights" is not stipulated separately. Second, the general provisions stipulated in the Book *Intellectual Property Rights* shall be general and target all varieties of IP, and this part shall not affect the independent existence of relevant *lex specialis* within the civil scope. Finally, the Book *Intellectual Property Rights* should particularly describe the differences between such regimes and other regimes of civil law rights, that is, the general norms based on the characteristics of IPRs. Specifically, it should include the nature, scope, effect, utilisation, and protection of IPRs.[4]

References

Hartkamp, S. Arthur. 1998. Amendments to the Dutch civil code. *Global Law Review* 1

Liu, Chunmao. 1997. *Intellectual Property Law.* Beijing: China People's Public Security University Press

Mi, Liang (Trans.). 1998. *The Civil Code of Vietnam.* Kunming: Yunnan University Press

Schipani, Sandro. 1997. *Codice Civile Italiano.* Trans. Anling Fei and Mei Ding. Beijing: China University of Political Science and Law Press

Wu, Handong. 1998. *Studies on Copyright Systems in Western Countries.* Beijing: China University of Political Science and Law Press

Wu, Handong. 2002a. *Intellectual Property Law.* Beijing: China University of Political Science and Law Press

Wu, Handong. 2002b. Intellectual property rights system should not be incorporated into the civil code of China. *Legal Daily*, September 29

Wu, Handong. 2003. The legislative style of intellectual property and the compilation of the Chinese civil code. *China Legal Science* 1

Xu, Guodong. 2000. The framework of the draft of China's civil code. *Chinese Journal of Law* 1

Xu, Zhongqi (ed.). 1997. *Research on Vietnamese Law.* Kunming: Yunnan University Press.

Yu, Xiangyu. 1995. *Russian Civil and Commercial Law and Conflict of Laws.* Beijing: World Publishing Corporation

Zhai, Yunling. 1999. A summary of the 1999 annual meeting of the civil and economic law research association of China law society. *China Legal Science* 6

Zhao, Zhongfu, Xing, Haibao, and Bian, Jiangsheng. 2000. Review and prospect of the study of civil and commercial law in 1999. *The Jurist* 1

[4] The author has drafted eight articles on IPRs. For details, please refer to (Wu 2003).

Part III
International Protection of Intellectual Property Rights

Introduction for Part III

As a unique component of the theoretical study of IPRs, international protection is a distinctive domain, differing both from the description of basic categories and the analysis of fundamental theories, as well as from institutional theories that relate specifically to copyright, patent rights, and trademark rights. In this book, the author incorporates international protection into the "General Principles" framework for the following two reasons. Firstly, research on international protection examines the overarching IPRs regime through an international lens, addressing the origins, evolution, and changes in the international system of IPRs protection, while also introducing and commenting on the content and characteristics of major international IPR conventions. Therefore, such research requires a dynamic, holistic theoretical and empirical analysis. Secondly, research on international IPRs protection investigates the conflicts and integration, as well as the contention and co-operation within the international IPRs regime from a multidimensional perspective. It seeks to deconstruct and reflect upon the international IP order with the aid of theoretical disciplines including jurisprudence, the science of international relations, and policy science. This research aims to establish a critical and solution-oriented "Chinese perspective." In short, the section attempts to address pivotal issues in the internationalisation of IPRs through a global and strategic approach.

The international IPRs regime has a history of just over a century. While the *Paris Convention*, the *Berne Convention* and the *TRIPS Agreement* are the outcomes of international co-operation and negotiations, they were undoubtedly formulated under the dominance of Western countries, adhering to a Western-centric paradigm. In the post-TRIPS era, developed and developing countries have put forward new requirements, based on their respective stances, for the co-ordination and sharing of IP benefits, giving rise to divergent positions and propositions in international IP legislation. Against this backdrop of evolution and reform, it is crucial for Chinese scholars to engaged in research on international IPRs protection in order to reform the Western-centric international laws and build a more equitable and rational international IPRs regime, grounded in the value of international justice.

Chapter 16
International IPRs Protection System

The international protection of IPRs is an inherent component of the modern IPRs regime. Emerging in the 1880s, the international IPRs protection system has now evolved into a set of conventional practices in global economic, cultural, scientific, and trade relations. This system, primarily embodied in foundational international treaties such as the *Paris Convention*, the *Berne Convention* and the *TRIPS Agreement*, and co-ordinated by relevant international organisations including WIPO and WTO, integrates the IPRs regimes of various countries to form an international legal framework for IPRs protection. Under this framework, domestically developed IPRs regimes of various countries have gradually embarked on a path of integration and internationalisation.

16.1 Origins of the International IPRs Protection System

The international protection regime for IPRs, in a general sense, refers to a relatively unified international legal regime that takes multilateral international conventions as the basic form and international intergovernmental organisations as the coordinating body to integrate and standardise the domestic IP laws of various countries.

The formation of an international IPRs protection system marked a new era in IP legislation, as under the international framework for IPRs protection, national IPRs regimes, which arose independently in each country, have progressively converged towards integration and internationalisation. Historically, international IPRs protection did not arise concurrently with the establishment of domestic IPRs regimes. Rather, it is a product of evolving international economic and trade relations, as well as the evolution of the IPRs regime itself. The formation of the IPRs regime is attributable to two factors:

H. Wu, *Theorising Intellectual Property Rights from Chinese Perspectives*,
https://doi.org/10.1007/978-981-96-5867-1_16

16.1.1 Development of International Economic Trade and Transcending IP Territorial Restrictions

A fundamental characteristic of IPRs is their territoriality. This is manifested in two key aspects: Firstly, the IPRs recognised and protected under the law of one country only take effect within the territorial confines of that country. Beyond this jurisdiction, the intellectual asset protected therein reverts to the status of a resource within the public domain. Secondly, IPRs recognised and protected under the law of one country are not automatically accorded the same protections in any other country, unless they are recognised and protected through the domestic legal procedures of that country. This means that a rights holder cannot invoke domestic law to safeguard their IPRs interests in another country, and likewise that foreign country is not obliged to protect IPRs granted by another country. Prior to the advent of international IPRs treaties, securing IPRs protection in other countries presented significant difficulties. This characteristic of territoriality imbues IPRs with an inherent nature that segment the market and impede the development of international trade (Wan 2001, p. 13). With the progress of science and technology and the rapid development of industry and commerce, a global market for IPRs has begun to take shape alongside the expansion of the international economy and trade. Many intellectual products transcended national boundaries, flowing into other jurisdictions and thereby fostering scientific, technological, and cultural exchanges between countries. This dynamic engendered a profound conflict between the territorial limitations of intellectual property rights and the burgeoning international demand for intellectual products. In response, the international community sought to achieve international coordination on IPRs protection. The objective was to mitigate, as far as is possible, the territory-based obstruction of IPRs to the global economic and trade order. This has led to the formation of an international regime of IPRs protection, with multilateral international treaties as its core.

16.1.2 International Coordination of IPRs Protection and Transformation of Domestic Law

The protection of IPRs that were initially granted by domestic law remains a matter of national legislation. This is because international conventions, as a form of international IPRs protection regime, must pass through domestic legal procedures in order to take legal effect in certain countries (Zhang 1999, pp. 53–54). The international community has coordinated IPRs protection, leading to a shift from an isolated protection framework under domestic law to an integrated protection system under international law. Usually, it is believed that there are four ways in which IPRs are protected internationally: First, unilateral protection, that is, a country affords protection to foreign IPRs through its domestic legislation on a unilateral basis. Second, reciprocal protection, that is, protection is extended to foreign IPRs on the basis of the principle of reciprocity, conditional upon that foreign state providing equivalent protection for the protecting state's own IPRs. Third, protection by bilateral treaties, that is, a mutually acceptable IPR protection regime is established through bilateral negotiations between two states. Fourth, protection by multilateral treaties, that is, global or regional multilateral negotiations between state governments give rise to multilateral treaties establishing an international IPRs protection regime (including international substantive standards and procedural rules of IPRs). This international IPRs protection regime is then implemented through the domestic laws of the contracting parties (Zheng 1997, p. 118; Liu 2001, pp. 43–44).

Strictly speaking, the first two ways listed are merely protection of foreign IPRs in the general sense, and are based on domestic law. For instance, under unilateral protection, the *French Copyright Act* (1852) extended protection to all literary and artistic works irrespective of origin. Under reciprocal protection, the copyright laws of the United States, Spain, Sweden, and other nations incorporate provisions based on the principle of reciprocity. These examples pertain to systems of isolated domestic IPRs protection. It is argued that the latter two ways listed above constitute international IPRs protection in its true sense (even though all four fall under the category of special protection by domestic law). These international protection regimes generated through international coordination aim to overcome the territorial limitations of IPRs caused by the territorial limitations of national sovereignty, to establish an integrated bilateral or international protection regime. Its primary mechanism is conclusion of international agreements or treaties through bilateral or multilateral negotiations between governments, to establish relatively consistent standards and rules for IPRs protection, and to implement them through the domestic legislation of the contracting parties.

16.2 Basic Principles of the International IPRs Protection System

Each specific IPRs regulation has its roots in, and is based on, the values of the legal system as expressed by legal principles. These values and rules of IPRs are also abstracted from and generalised by these principles. On account of the universal applicability and hierarchical nature of legal principles, the principles of international IPRs protection may be categorised into two types: first, the principles that underpin the construction of the legal system and therefore have fundamental significance, and second, the principles that are inherent in the legal system and can be applied directly. For the former type of principles, some scholars have summarises these as: the principle of state sovereignty, the principle of equality and mutual benefit, the principle of common development, and the principle of international cooperation (Tang 1998, p. 42); or alternatively expressed as: the principle of state sovereignty, the principle of international coordination and cooperation, and the principle of equity and justice (Wan 2001, p. 42); For the latter type of principles, scholars frequently enumerate these as: the principle of national treatment, the principle of minimum protection standards, the principle of independence (for industrial property), the principle of separate protection (for copyright), the principle of compulsory licensing (for patent rights), the principle of priority (for industrial property) (Liu 2001, pp. 45, 48; Zhang 2001, pp. 49–51).

The author contends that the principles of the international regime of IPRs protection should be interpreted in the latter sense, and such principles should be stipulated in the international conventions that regulate protection of IPRs. These principles should be directly applicable, instead of being peculiar to any single specialised regime, they should be provided for in the international conventions and should apply universally to all international IPRs protection regimes. For the reasons set forth above, it is submitted that the basic principles of the international IPRs protection regime should encompass the principle of national treatment, the principle of minimum protection standards, and the principle of public interest.

16.2.1 Content of the Basic Principles

The basic principles of the international regime of IPRs protection comprise the principle of national treatment, the principle of minimum protection standards, and the principle of public interest.

Principle of "National Treatment"

The principle of national treatment is the primary principle recognised by many IPR conventions. It requires that each contracting party (Member) shall accord equal treatment to others, ensuring the nationals of other Members enjoy the same treatment as its own nationals. National treatment consists of two aspects: first, the treatment that each Member has granted or may grant to its own nationals under its national law; and second, the "special rights" (that is, the minimum protection standards) stipulated by the relevant treaty. International conventions have different expressions for the equal treatment of nationals of other Members with domestic nationals, including "not less favourable than", "with discrimination", or "shall not be prejudiced." In general, however, this does not necessarily mandate that nationals of other Members may only be granted treatment "identical" to that of domestic nationals. In other words, a Member may, in accordance with the actual situation of its economic development, accord nationals of other Members treatment more favourable than that granted to its own nationals. The principle of national treatment is a principle acceptable to countries with different socio-economic systems and varying levels of development. This principle requires neither the consistency of national laws of all countries (as it does not involve the level of IPRs protection) nor the application of foreign laws (as it does not involve the territorial limitation of national sovereignty). It merely that each country applies its own laws independently within its territory by affording equal protection to foreigners (that is, nationals of other Members) and its own nationals. Article 3 of the *TRIPS Agreement* stipulates that the principle of national treatment, mandating each Member accord to the nationals of other Members treatment no less favourable than it accords to its own nationals. According to the TRIPS regulations, the scope of foreign nationals (nationals of other Members) entitled to national treatment shall be determined, depending on the types of IPRs, by reference to the eligibility criteria set out in the *Paris Convention*, the *Berne Convention*, the *International Convention for the Protection of Performers, Producers of Phonograms and Broadcasting Organisations* (hereinafter referred to as the *Rome Convention*), *the Treaty on Intellectual Property in Respect of Integrated Circuits* (hereinafter referred to as the *Washington Convention*), etc.

- **Industrial property**: Articles 2 and 3 of the *Paris Convention* stipulate that nationals of any member of the Paris Union (i.e., the group of countries that signed the *Paris Convention*) shall, as regards the protection of industrial property, enjoy in all the other countries of the Union the advantages that their respective laws now grant, or may hereafter grant, to nationals. Even nationals of countries outside the Union who are domiciled or who have real and effective industrial or commercial establishments in the territory of one of the countries of the Union shall be treated in the same manner as nationals of the countries of the Union.
- **Copyright**: The *Berne Convention* applies the principle of "dual nationality treatment", that is, where the "nationality" of the work or the nationality of the author meets the requirements, it can be treated as a national of a member. Article 5 of the *Berne Convention* provides that Members shall grant copyright protection equivalent to that enjoyed by their own nationals to the works of three types of authors: nationals of other State Parties; persons who have their habitual residence in any of the Members; and persons who first published their works in any of the Members (even if they have no nationality or habitual residence in any Member).
- **Neighbouring rights**: The *Rome Convention* provides for performers, producers of phonograms and broadcasting organisations respectively. The prerequisites for a performer to receive national treatment are as follows: the performance takes place in the territory of another Member; the performance is recorded on a phonogram protected under the Convention; the performance is not fixed on a phonogram but is transmitted by a broadcast protected under the Convention. The prerequisites for producers of phonograms to receive national treatment are as follows: the producer of the phonogram is a national of another Member (national criterion); the first fixation of the sound occurs in another Member (recording criterion); and the phonogram is first published in another Member (publication criterion). The prerequisites for a broadcasting organisation to receive national treatment are: the broadcasting organisation is headquartered in another Member, and the broadcast is transmitted by a transmitter located in another Member.
- **The exclusive right to layout design of integrated circuits**: The *Washington Convention* imposes two prerequisites on the persons who can enjoy national treatment in a Member: first, nationals of any other Member or natural persons domiciled in the territory of any other Member; and second, legal or natural

persons having a real and effective entity in the territory of any other Member for the purpose of creating layout designs or producing integrated circuits.

In summary, international conventions mainly adopt the following three criteria on issues regarding the national treatment of foreigners (nationals of the other contracting countries):

Criterion of nationality: Nationals of any Member (whose nationality belongs to that Member) may enjoy national treatment in other Members in respect of one or more of the IPRs stipulated in the convention in question. The *TRIPS Agreement*, the *Paris Convention*, the *Berne Convention*, the *Rome Convention*, and the *Washington Convention* are all examples of conventions that include this criterion.

Criterion of domicile/habitual residency: The "domicile" or "habitual residence" of a national of any Member is the criterion used to confirm their eligibility for national treatment. The *Paris* and *Washington* conventions adopt the criterion of "domicile", while the *Berne Convention* adopts the criterion of "habitual residence."

Criterion of actual connection: The eligibility for national treatment is determined by a certain connection between a particular foreigner or their conduct, and a member. For example, the requirements of the *Rome Convention* on recording and releasing standards for the recognition of national treatment of producers of phonograms, and the criteria of the *Berne Convention* on the recognition of national treatment of authors of films and architectural works, all fall into this category.

Principle of Minimum Protection Standards

The principle of minimum protection standards requires that each Member shall, in accordance with its domestic laws, grant IPRs protection to the nationals of the other Members which cannot be lower than the minimum standards stipulated in the treaty. These standards include the subject matter of right protection, the ways of obtaining rights, the contents and limitations, the term of protection and so on. Articles 6 to 18 of the *Berne Convention* list the various moral and economic rights of authors, as well as the terms and methods of protection. The provisions of Articles 19 and 20 reflect the principle of minimum protection standards, that is, the national law in a Member of the Berne Union can grant greater protection than the Convention, or the Members of the Union concerned can grant authors more extensive rights than those granted in the Convention through bilateral or multilateral agreements. This means that the criteria of copyright protection set by a Member of the *Berne Convention* may go beyond, but not fall below the standards set by the Convention. Article 1 of the *TRIPS Agreement* sets out the obligations of the Members, namely that "Members shall give effect to the provisions of this Agreement", and those provisions include "standards concerning the availability, scope and use of trade-related intellectual property rights", "enforcement of IPRs", "acquisition and maintenance of IPRs and procedures between the parties concerned", "prevention and settlement of disputes" and so on. On this premise, "members may provide for protection in their domestic law that is [more] extensive than that required by this Agreement, provided that it does not break this Agreement." Members are obliged to protect IPRs in accordance with the criteria outlined in the *TRIPS Agreement*, and to implement the relevant provisions of the Agreement.

The principle of minimum protection standards is an important complement to the principle of national treatment. As the development of the economy, science and technology, and culture varies, the principle of minimum protection recognises that IPRs regimes differ from country to country, and thus ensures the pervasiveness and universality of international coordination of IPRs regimes. However, such international coordination requires not only universality but also effectiveness. It is impossible to effectively implement international treaties if the principle of national treatment is taken to its extreme, as this would result in vast differences in the level of protection of IPRs between countries (Luo and Gu 2002: 35–37). The principle of national treatment alone is therefore not sufficient in the international coordination of IPRs regimes, so the international conventions also include the principle of minimum protection standards, in order to avoid the adverse effects on international coordination caused by institutional differences. The principle of minimum protection standards and the principle of national treatment are different but unified in the international coordination system of IPRs regimes. The difference between the two principles lies in the fact that the principle of national treatment respects the legislative autonomy of Members with respect to IPRs, while the principle of minimum protection standards restricts such legislative autonomy. The two principles are unified in the fact that the acceptance of minimum standards in IPRs protection reflects the exercise of the legislative autonomy of IPRs among countries (ibid.). It is a basic obligation of the Members of international conventions on IPRs that they comply with these two principles. In other words, the principles are directly applicable to the Members of a convention, and the members cannot declare that they reserve their right not to apply these principles.

The principle of minimum protection standards aims to promote uniformity in the level of protection of IPRs in the Members. The relevant provisions of an international convention on IPRs (international law) are transformed into specific norms of the Member's IPRs regime (national law), which follows the principle of minimum protection standards. Appropriate application of this principle ensures that IPRs regimes have uniform protection requirements, and scholars refer to this as the "integration" or "internationalisation" of IP legislation. The international conventions have adopted a "may exceed shall not fall below" approach with regard to protection standards on IPRs. "Shall not fall below" refers to the requirement for each Member to adopt the "minimum protection standards", while "May exceed" means that each Member can choose whether to exceed the minimum standards or not. IPRs protection can exceed the minimum international standards via two models. First, the "unilateral protection" model, in which independent protection is provided by the domestic law of a Member. Second, the "bilateral protection treaty" model, in which two Members negotiate and agree on a protection treaty.[1] These two ways of exceeding international standards are an important supplement to the principle of minimum protection standards.

Principle of Public Interest

The principle of public interest dictates that the protection and exercise of IPRs shall not be contrary to the public interests of society. A balance should be struck between the public interest and the interests of the rights holder. The principle of public interest is not only the value objectives of a Member's IPRs regime, but also a basic principle of international IPRs protection. It encompasses two aspects: (1) The legal concept of balance of interests. Such a balance requires that the interests of the stakeholders—be the rights holders and obligations holders, or individuals and society—should be determined fairly, so as to achieve the goal of the public interest. (2) The legal system of limitation and use of rights. It is necessary to limit the exclusive rights of creators to ensure the fair use of intellectual products by the public, for the sake of public interest. Article 8 of the *TRIPS Agreement*, titled "Principles", stipulates that: (1) Members may, in formulating or amending their laws and regulations, adopt measures necessary to protect public health and nutrition, and to promote the public interest in sectors of vital importance to their socioeconomic and technological development, provided that such measures are consistent with the provisions of this Agreement; and (2) Appropriate measures, provided that they are consistent with the provisions of this Agreement, may be needed to prevent the abuse of IPRs by rights holders or the resort to practices which unreasonably restrain trade or adversely affect the international transfer of technology. The *WIPO Copyright Treaty* declares in its preamble that it recognises the need to maintain a balance between authors' rights and public interests, particularly those public interests related to education, research and access to information, as reflected in the *Berne Convention*. The *WIPO Performances and Phonograms Treaty* makes the same statement as the *Copyright Treaty* in its preamble regarding the balance of interests between performers and producers of phonograms on the one hand, and the public on the other. Unlike these two international conventions, previous international conventions on IPRs have mostly embodied the principle of public interest through relevant regimes of limitations on IPRs. For example, "compulsory licenses" are stipulated in Article 5 of the *Paris Convention*, and "certain free uses of works" are stipulated in Article 10 of the *Berne Convention*.

The realisation of the principle of public interest involves a balance between the interests of the rights holder and those of the public. In terms of institutional design, this is directly related to the protection and limitation of IPRs. In international conventions on IPRs, the purposes of public interest are public health, social development, freedom of expression, public education and so on, and these are achieved via limitations on, and reasonable utilisation of, IPRs within the international framework for

[1] For the four ways of international protection for IPRs, please see (Liu 2001).

IPRs protection. Naturally, these are necessary limitations and reasonable utilisations on the basis that the interests of the rights holder are protected. As American scholars have pointed out, the existence of IPRs should serve firstly the public interest, and secondly that of rights holders. The principle of public interest is important in international IPRs protection and is closely related to the aforementioned principles of national treatment and minimum protection standards. The principle of minimum protection standards restricts legislative autonomy by unifying the domestic legislation of the Members within the scope of a determined standard, while the principle of public interest limits the scope of the domestic legislation of the Members and creates a counter restriction to the principle of minimum protection standards by way of exceptional rules. In other words, certain exceptions to the limitation of IPRs may be provided for, in accordance with the principle of public interest stipulated in the relevant international conventions, when a Member applies the minimum protection standards in IP legislation.[2]

16.2.2 Relationship Between the Basic Principles and Related Principles

The basic principles of international IPRs protection embody the value objectives of the entire IPRs regime. As the primary foundation for the development of international IP law, the basic principles should reflect the highest standards of international law. In addition, the rules of various IPRs regimes should be abstracted in order to lay a foundation for the operation of the particular regime. The following provides further explanations.

Relationship with the Principles of International Law

The principles of international law are the basic norms, recognised by countries around the world and applied in all fields of international law, which constitute the basis of international law. In modern international law, the *Charter of the United Nations* (1945) and a series of documents adopted by the General Assembly of the UN have formed a sound system of principles, laying the legal foundation for the establishment of the modern international order of economics, culture, science and technology, and trade (Yang 1998, pp. 43–44). The international regime of IPRs protection is a relatively complete and independent international legal institution, yet it is also part of international law or international economic law. Therefore, the construction of the system cannot be carried out without regard to international law. Specifically, the following principles of international law have the most connection with the basic principles of international IP law:

[2] See the provisions of Article 8(1) of the *TRIPS Agreement*.

1. Principle of sovereignty

The principle of sovereignty, as the basis of the entire international legal system, is a traditional principle of international law based on the fundamental concept that all countries should respect each other's sovereignty, and have the right to determine their own political, social, economic and cultural systems. In the matter of international protection of IPRs, the functions and influence of the principle of sovereignty are manifest in the following two aspects. First, this principle indicates that each country has the autonomy to choose its legal IPRs regime and offer IPRs protection that best serves its economy and suits its scientific and technological situation. The application of national treatment embodies the spirit of the principle of sovereignty, as it does not involve the territorial limitation of the sovereignty of Members (i.e., it doesn't require the application of foreign laws), but only calls for each Member to independently apply its own laws within its own territory, and to provide equal protection for foreigners and nationals alike. Second, national sovereignty's self-constraint comes from the international conventions rather than from the dominance of certain nations, and this serves as the foundation for global coordination of IPRs protection. By applying the principle of minimum protection standards, the relevant provisions of international conventions (international law) have been transformed into the specific norms of the IPRs (domestic law) of the Members, reflecting the fact that states are willing to forego some measure of national sovereignty in order to advance economic interests. However, the problem is that developing countries' demand has not been fully met in the international regime of IPRs protection. In fact, "the international regime of IPRs protection is an international mechanism for the distribution of IPRs interests" (Wan 2001, p. 44). Against the background of economic globalisation, IPRs protection is the prerequisite for developing countries to engage in international trade and is more a legal instrument that developed countries use to maintain their advantages in trade. This major imbalance of interests and rights between countries is a serious threaten to the sovereignty of countries that are in a disadvantaged position. The international community should pay close attention to this issue.

2. Principle of the right to development

The principle of the right to development is a "principle of international law concerning the new international economic order" (Yang 1998, p. 65). The right to development is vital for protecting the third-generation human rights, that is, collective human rights. And it is the right of all peoples to "freely pursue their economic, social and cultural development" according to the *International Covenant on Civil and Political Rights* (United Nations 1966). It reflects the rise of nationalism in developing nations and their demand for redistribution of power, wealth, and other important resources globally (Xia 1993, p. 116). The *Charter of Economic Rights and Duties of States* of 1974 clearly defines the right to development as a general right, stating that "every State has the right to benefit from the advances and development in science and technology for the acceleration of its economic and social development." Development right is an urgent concern for developing countries.

The Charter requires that "all States should facilitate the access of developing countries to the achievements of modern science and technology [and] help to expand and transform the economies of developing countries." However, the right to development in developing countries has not been fully realised in the international protection regime. The International Conference on the *Establishment of an International Code for the Transfer of Technology*, held in Geneva in 1978, failed to reach an agreement between developed and developing countries due to the divergent interests of IPRs and other issues. However, when the *TRIPS Agreement* came into force in 1994, this achieved the strategic goal of the developed countries: to establish an IPRs regime with a higher standard and strong support, which further maintained the technological advantage of the developed countries in international trade—a technological advantage backed by IPRs. The principle of the right to development is instructive to the realisation of the public interests in the international regime of IPRs protection. It is not difficult to coordinate IPRs-related interests of all stakeholders within a country through the protection and limitation of IPRs, provided that those regimes do not violate the minimum protection standards set by international conventions. However, it is worth considering whether the international protection regime attempts to strike an appropriate balance of rights and obligations between developed and developing countries. It must be noted that in the international trading system, IPRs have provided developed countries with a competitive edge, helping them to maintain their lead in technological innovation and global trade (Yuan 1997, pp. 99–107). Hence, it is vital to underline the importance of the right to development as a guiding principle in international conventions, and to provide effective measures for the realisation of the principle of public interest under such circumstances.

Relationship with the General Principles of WTO

The principle of most-favoured-nation treatment (hereafter referred to as the principle of MFN) is the common basic principle of all GATT and WTO agreements, including the *TRIPS Agreement*, which aims to ensure fair competition in trade and thus constitutes the cornerstone of the entire international trading system (Tang 1999, p. 177; Zhang 1999, p. 115). According to *Draft Articles on Most-Favoured-Nation Clauses* drafted by the International Law Commission of the UN, the most-favoured-nation treatment refers to the principle that a Member's treatment of another Member, or of individuals or entities in a specified relationship with that Member, is no less favourable than the treatment given to a third Member or to individuals or entities in a specific relationship with that third Member. The MFN treatment in international trade is not typically covered by conventional IPR conventions. The *TRIPS Agreement* transplants this principle directly into IPRs, and this is an important change in the international regime of IPRs protection. Article 4 of the Agreement provides that: with regard to the protection of intellectual property, any advantage, favour, privilege or immunity granted by a Member to the nationals of any other Member shall be accorded immediately and unconditionally to the nationals of all other Members. In other words, it shall not discriminate against nationals of other countries while giving favour to a particular country. The *TRIPS Agreement* provides that the application of MFN treatment is immediate and unconditional, but it also provides for a series of exemptions from this obligation: (a) deriving from international agreements on judicial assistance or law enforcement of a general nature and not particularly confined to the protection of intellectual property; (b) granted in accordance with the provisions of the *Berne Convention* (1971) or the *Rome Convention* authorising that the treatment accorded be a function not of national treatment but of the treatment accorded mutually; (c) the rights of performers, producers of phonograms and broadcasting organisations not provided under TRIPS; and (d) derived from international agreements related to the protection of intellectual property which entered into force prior to the entry into force of the *TRIPS Agreement*, provided that such agreements are notified to the Council for TRIPS and they do not constitute an arbitrary or unjustifiable discrimination against nationals of other Members. In terms of the international IPRs protection, the principle of national treatment and the principle of MFN are both rules set up for the subjective qualification of foreigners, but they are also different: the former aims to give the same treatment to foreigners and their own nationals and to solve the problem of unequal "differentiated treatment between "internal and the external" parties", while the latter is to treat other foreigners the same as certain foreigners, which is to solve the problem of discriminatory treatment of "some foreigners as against other foreigners." The principle of national treatment is the primary principle in the *TRIPS Agreement*, while the principle of MFN is its complement. The significance of the latter is that it is non-discriminatory and equal treatment, so that the IPRs protection granted by one Member to the nationals of another Member will be granted to the nationals of all other Members. The use of the MFN principle can be attributed to international IPRs protection practices that took place in the second half of the twentieth century. At that time, preferences granted by one party to another were common practice in bilateral protection treaties. In a bilateral agreement between the US and South Korea in the mid-1980s, for instance, South Korea undertook to protect US patents on pharmaceutical and agrochemical products that were not otherwise protected under its domestic law. However, this commitment constitutes discrimination against the relevant patents of the EU countries. In the early 1990s, in the Sino–US Memorandum of Understanding on Intellectual Property Rights, China promised to give administrative protection to US patents on pharmaceutical and agrochemical products, which also triggered similar demands from EU countries and Japan. The stipulations of the *TRIPS Agreement* on the principle of MFN are intended to prevent such problems. It is worth noting that some developed countries have sought to use bilateral negotiations to obtain additional benefits or preferences above the level of protection stipulated in the *TRIPS Agreement*, outside the protection framework of the multilateral treaty. For example, the US has successively negotiated with the EU, Japan, Australia and other countries to achieve or potentially achieve a higher level of protection than that stipulated in the *TRIPS Agreement*. However, under the MFN principle, any benefits or preferences obtained in this way should benefit all Members. Developing countries should be cautious about such negotiations, however, as a high level of protection may not be a benefit but rather an obligation. It is inappropriate for economically and technologically developing countries to seek a level of intellectual property protection beyond the minimum standards stipulated in international conventions.

Relationship with Specific Principles of the International IPRs Protection System

In the field of international IPRs protection, the Members are required to adhere to the principles of national treatment, minimum protection standards and public interest, as well as a number of specific principles stipulated in the relevant conventions. The key principles pertaining to the protection of industrial property rights are as follows:

1. **Principle of independence**. When a citizen of a Member obtains patents or trademark rights in multiple countries (both Members and non-Members), those rights are considered separate and distinct from one another. This independence stems from the territoriality of IPRs protection. A patent or trademark registration obtained in one Member shall have no binding effect on the survival or abolition of the relevant rights in other Members. The independence principle is consistent with the spirit of the national treatment principle in that each Member is required to apply its own laws independently within its own territory, and foreigners are independent in acquiring a member's patents or trademark rights, but their interests are equal to those enjoyed by the nationals of that Member.
2. **Principle of compulsory enforcement**. This requires that a person who has obtained a patent in a contracting country must implement their invention in that country's territory within a certain period of time, otherwise the Member will take measures to compel the license or revoke the patent. This principle aims at promoting the application of patented technology and preventing illegal monopoly of patents. The principle of compulsory enforcement was first recognised by the *Paris Convention*, and the *TRIPS Agreement* made it an important measure in achieving public interest. According to the spirit of the *Doha Declaration* of the WTO (2001), the Members have the right to implement "compulsory licenses" for the sake of maintaining public health, and the right to decide the reasons for implementing "compulsory licensing." The principle of compulsory enforcement is related to the use of patented technology, and the object of its regulation has evolved from the private legal relationship between the patentee (licensor) and the patent user (licensee) to the international legal relationship between underdeveloped and developed countries. Hence, in this case, the implementation of the principle of compulsory enforcement should fully meet the legislative intent of the principle of public interest.

In addition, two key principles pertaining to copyright protection are as follows:

3. Principle of automatic protection. This means that the enjoyment and exercise of one's copyright without any formalities. In other words, works that are entitled to national treatment do not need to go through application or registration procedures such as patents and trademarks, and they are automatically protected in

all Members with the production or first publication of the works. The principle of automatic protection relates to how a copyright is acquired. It is stipulated in the *Berne Convention* and the *TRIPS Agreement* as a basic requirement of the minimum protection standards, which must be followed by all Members. It should be noted that the United States has a copyright registration regime, yet "such registration is not a prerequisite for copyright protection" but rather a "necessary prerequisite for filing a lawsuit against copyright infringement" (Zhang 1999, p. 89). Naturally, this rule is not applicable to works covered under the *Berne Convention* with a nation of origin other than the United States. It can be argued that the treatment of nationals of Members of the *Berne Convention*, is higher than that of US nationals in terms of copyright registration, due to the minimum treatment required by the minimum protection standards of international conventions.

4. **Principle of independent protection**. This principle stipulates that Members may, on the premise of complying with the minimum protection standards stipulated in the relevant conventions, determine at their discretion the subject matter, scope, duration, content and limitations, infringement and remedies of copyright protection. Like the principle of independence, this principle is consistent with the spirit of the principle of national treatment, which will not be discussed in further details here.

16.2.3 Implementation of the Basic Principles

The basic principles of the international IPRs protection system are rich in institutional content, and they guide the system's overall operation. Specifically speaking, realisation of the basic principles mirrors the process of coordinating the interests of the international community, and indicates the direction of development of, and changes in, the international IPRs regime.

Implementation of the Principle of National Treatment

This principle is the primary principle for international coordination of IPRs protection. Its function is to overcome the territorial limitation of IPRs based on the territorial limitation of national sovereignty, and to establish a bilateral or international protection regime with consistency, so as to eliminate the obstruction of territorial limitation to the international order of economy and trade. Regarding foreigners, laws of various countries generally recognise the principle of national treatment but restrict the scope of rights enjoyed by foreigners. For example, foreigners may not be allowed to acquire land rights, mining rights, fishing rights and other rights, and this is known as limited national treatment. IP law, unlike civil law, adopts the principle of conditional national treatment, and so long as foreigners meet the specified criteria of nationality, residence or actual connections, they can enjoy the same treatment as domestic nationals without having the scope and content of their rights restricted. The principle of national treatment recognised by international conventions embodies the concept that all people are equal under law. This principle assimilates foreigners to nationals, and thus, foreigners are protected as equals. In other words, each eligible subject not only enjoys IPRs in their own country, but also enjoys the corresponding rights in any Members. The principle of national treatment has been generally accepted in the legislation of various countries since the conclusion of the *Paris Convention* and the *Berne Convention* in the second half of the nineteenth century. Today, the practical operation of the principle has undergone several changes:

1. **Extension of national treatment**. The problem of imbalance in the enjoyment of rights occurs because the rights enjoyed by nationals of a member in other Members are not the same as those enjoyed in the home country. This different treatment of nationals and foreigners occurs because the relevant laws of each Member must meet the minimum protection standards required by the relevant convention, which means that special protection is afforded to foreign works in order to meet these standards. For example, before amending the Copyright Law, the Chinese Government promulgated the *Provisions on the Implementation of International Copyright Treaties*, which provides a higher level of protection for foreigners' computer software and practical art works than for Chinese nationals' works; another example is that the provisions of the US Copyright Law regarding the registration of works as a requirement for infringement lawsuits do not apply to works from another Member in the US. These are all examples of exceptions to the application of the principle of national treatment.
2. **Limitations on national treatment**. Such limitations emerge as a result of the principle of reciprocity. This is due to the fact that the principle of national treatment does not apply when there is a significant gap in the level of IPRs protection between different states, and instead the principle of "balanced reciprocity of interests" is used (Cao 1995, pp. 33–38). For example, only a few European countries, such as France, Germany and Italy, have explicit provisions on the protection of the right of resale. According to the principle of reciprocity, works from other countries do not enjoy this interest. This suggests that the IPRs protection in the claimant country may be subject to the relevant provisions of the country of right origin in some cases, thus making the principle of national treatment somewhat limited by the principle of reciprocity. Additionally, the emergence of reservation clauses affects the application of the principle of national treatment. The Members could declare reservations to one or several rights during conclusion of or accession to international conventions in the past, and such reservations were actually a kind of limitation on the principle of national treatment. The *TRIPS Agreement*, however, removed this limitation. Article 72 of the *TRIPS Agreement* stipulates that reservations shall not be entered in respect of any of the provisions of this Agreement without the consent of the other Members. This implies that a member must obtain the consent of the other Members before making a reservation to the *TRIPS Agreement* in its domestic law. The reservation clause

provided in the *TRIPS Agreement* is, to some extent, actually a clause prohibiting reservations.

3. **Conflict with national treatment**. Some Members attempt to circumvent the application of the principle of national treatment by special legislation. These provisions for exceptions are not provided by international conventions, but the creation of the domestic legislation of a member. This pragmatic approach, taken by some countries in order to circumvent their obligation as regards IPRs protection, poses certain challenges to the principle of national treatment (Stewart 1983). For instance, some Western nations have revised their copyright laws, or added new rights in addition to the existing ones, in light of the rapid development of contemporary communication technologies, with the "public lending right" and the "right to reproduction" being the most representative examples. The public lending right is not yet recognised by international conventions, so it cannot enjoy the principle of national treatment. The right to reproduction, on the other hand, is a basic right recognised by international conventions. However, some countries use public funds or taxes as a way to compensate for copying, which makes foreign works de facto ineligible for national treatment.

Implementation of the Principle of Minimum Protection Standards

The minimum protection standards provide a consistent standard of IPRs protection for Members, and this is conducive to overcoming the imbalance of rights and obligations among Members and to ensuring effective international IPRs coordination. The principle of minimum protection standards stipulated in international conventions is the basis for the internationalisation and integration of the IPRs regime. It is worth noting that the cornerstone of such integration and internationalisation is the global unification of protection standards. From the *Paris Convention* and the *Berne Convention* in the second half of the nineteenth century to the *TRIPS Agreement* and the Internet Treaties[3] at the end of the twentieth century, the international agreements all provided minimum protection standards that were generally applicable to all Members, thus leading to the integration of the IPRs regime. However, the integration of modern laws has three distinctive features.

1. Supremacy of international law. Applying minimum protection standards fundamentally requires that international law prevails over domestic law. International conventions on IPRs signed in the second half of the nineteenth century established the basic standards of IPRs protection and recognised the primacy of domestic law in IPRs protection on the basis of the principle of national treatment. The integration of laws during this period was mainly manifested by the formation of interstate laws (international law) and the interaction between international laws and domestic laws. In contemporary times, however, international

[3] *The WIPO Copyright Treaty* and *the WIPO Performances and Phonograms Treaty* are collectively referred to as the Internet Treaties by the international intellectual property community.

conventions—especially the *TRIPS Agreement*—have set new international standards for IPRs protection that will serve as overarching principles and references for its members' domestic legislation. In the integration of laws in this period, domestic law follows international law, and domestic laws are congruent with one another.

2. **Shift from substantive to procedural rules**. Contemporary minimum protection standards encompass detailed procedural rules. The *Paris Convention* and the *Berne Convention* administered by WIPO provide mainly for the substantive contents of international IPRs protection, but less for the procedural provisions of IPRs enforcement, which particularly lacks necessary enforcement measures and dispute settlement mechanisms, so that some treaties have become "soft laws" without sufficient legal binding force. In terms of IPRs enforcement, the above-mentioned conventions do not have uniform international rules to follow; rather, it is largely up to each Member to adopt different measures to sanction infringement through domestic legislation, which often results in IPRs not being fully and effectively protected, and in the degree of protection varying from country to country, that is, not a universal and consistent protection. In contrast, the WTO, as an international organisation which can be described as an "Economic United Nations", has become the new leader and maker of rules on IPRs protection, beyond the sovereign jurisdiction of legislators of Member countries. The *TRIPS Agreement*, which is overseen by the WTO, differs from international treaties that place a premium on coordination, and by doing so it has realised the consistency of IPRs protection laws on both substance and procedures. In terms of substantive norms, the *TRIPS Agreement* provides institutional standards for IPRs protection, mainly in terms of: (1) the expansion of the scope of protectable subject matter and rights; (2) the extension of terms of protection; and (3) limitations on permitted exceptions. In terms of procedural norms, the *TRIPS Agreement* strengthens the enforcement procedures and protection measures of IPRs, which mainly include: (1) judicial review regimes; (2) fair and equitable civil procedures; (3) damages; (4) provisional measures; and (5) border measures (Wu 2005, pp. 126–140). In short, the *TRIPS Agreement* has for the first time transformed the implementation procedures of IPRs protection, which were originally part of domestic legislation, into international rules stipulated in the convention, making them, together with the substantive norms, into international standards that must be strictly followed by the Members.
3. **High level of IPRs protection**. This is a defining feature of contemporary minimum protection standards. The cornerstone of minimum standards required by international conventions is the consistency of the protection standards among the Members, and these have little to do with the actual level of protection applied by individual Members. The protection level varies among international conventions with types of convention and historical backgrounds. For example, both the *Berne Convention*, advocated by European countries in 1889, and the *Universal Copyright Convention* (1952), led by the United States, provide minimum protection standards. However, the former clearly offers a better level of copyright protection than the latter. Unlike the initial stage of the international regime of

IPRs protection, the minimum standards required under the *TRIPS Agreement* are by no means low standards for developing countries. Catering mainly to the needs of developed countries, the interests of IPR holders have been further strengthened, raising even the minimum level of protection to an unprecedentedly high level which goes well beyond what developing countries can afford. From the perspective of international protection, the integration of the modern IPRs regime, that is, the institutional design of the minimum protection standards, is in fact an institutional arrangement actively led by developed countries and passively accepted by developing countries.

Implementation of the Principle of Public Interest

This principle is an indispensable principle of the international protection regime, as it embodies the highest value objectives of the IPRs regime. The realisation of this principle is also the direct motivation for the reform of the contemporary international IPRs protection regime. To serve the public interest and achieve a balance between individual rights and social interests, countries have adopted the principle of prohibition of abuse of rights in private law. In line with the spirit of this principle, the IPRs regime has also established its own objectives of public interest. In the Constitution of the United States, there are three policy-based provisions for the protection of IPRs, namely, the promotion of the dissemination of knowledge, the preservation of public domain, and the protection of authors (Patterson and Lindberg 1991, pp. 49–55). In its report on the *Berne Convention Implementation Act* (1988), the US House of Representatives stated that copyright legislation must consider—in addition to the term of protection for inventions and exclusive rights—the costs and benefits to the public for the protection of individual rights and interests. This suggests that the protection of the interests of creators and the promotion of the dissemination of knowledge should be the twin objectives of IP legislation. Based on these objectives, it is important for the international regime of IPRs protection to establish the principle of public interest and ensure its implementation. It is worth noting that the three basic principles mentioned in this chapter have different implementation effects and outcomes. The principle of non-discriminatory national treatment and the principle of a high-level minimum protection have been effectively incorporated in the implementation of contemporary international conventions, while the principle of public interest has been neglected. One of the crucial topics in the reform of the current international regime of IPRs protection is the coordination of the relationship between IPRs and human rights, as well as the balancing of the interests of developed and developing countries. In a word, is the issue of the effective implementation of the principle of public interest.

16.3 Historical Evolution of the International IPRs Protection System

The international regime for IPRs protection has been in place for more than a century. Countries and organisations around the world have concluded and enacted over thirty comprehensive or specialised, global or regional treaties and model laws on IP. Based on these international conventions and relevant international organisations, the development of the international regime for IPRs protection may be divided into three distinct phases:

16.3.1 The Paris and Berne Unions Period: Formation of the System

The establishment of the international regime for IPRs protection began with the 1883 *Paris Convention* and the 1886 *Berne Convention.* After the two conventions entered into force, the Members of the *Paris Convention* formed the Paris Union, while the Members of the *Berne Convention* formed the Berne Union. Each union had its own executive body, named its "International Bureau." The two International Bureaus governed the two international conventions, under the supervision of the Swiss Federal Government.

In 1893, the Swiss Federal Government decided to merge the two International Bureaus into the "United International Bureau for the Protection of Industrial Property and Literary and Artistic Property", later renamed the "United International Bureau for the Protection of Intellectual Property" (BIRPI). The BIRPI governed not only the *Paris* and *Berne* conventions, but also the "special agreements" concluded under the *Paris Convention.* As an international organisation that aimed to protect IPRs, the main tasks of the BIRPI were to promote countries' IPRs protection, to prepare revisions of the conventions in order to further improve them, and so on. The United Nations was established in 1945 after the Second World War. As a specialised agency of the UN, UNESCO has presided over the conclusion and administration of many important international conventions and has also become an agency for the promotion of international IPRs protection.

It was during the period of the Paris Union and Berne Union that international regimes of IPRs protection first emerged and were formed. The main features of this period are: first, the BIRPI focused on global or regional multilateral consultations among governments to promote the international coordination of IPRs protection towards a holistic and comprehensive development (Zhang 1999, p. 54). A relatively unified protection regime for IPRs was achieved within the members through the effective operation of the *Paris* and *Berne* conventions. Second, a series of industrial property conventions concluded by the international community were dominated by the *Paris Convention.* These led to either substantive protection treaties which were only open to member states of the Paris Union, such as the *Madrid Agreement for the Repression of False or Deceptive Indications of Source on Goods* (1891); or procedural treaties under the *Paris Convention*, such as the *Madrid Agreement Concerning the International Registration of Marks* (1891) and the *Hague Agreement Concerning the International Registration of Industrial Designs* (1925); or specific agreements on international classifications based on the implementation needs of the *Paris Convention*, such as the *Nice Agreement Concerning the International Classification of Goods and Services for the Purposes of the Registration of Marks* (1957) and the *Lisbon Agreement for the Protection of Appellations of Origin and Their International Registration* (1958). Third, UNESCO also played an active role in promoting international protection of IPRs during this period, especially in the field of copyright, having hosted the conclusions of both the *Universal Copyright Convention* in 1952 and the *Rome Convention* in 1961. Based on the former, another copyright protection regime parallel with the *Berne Convention* was created; and based on the latter, the international protection regime of neighbouring rights began to be established.

16.3.2 The WIPO Period: Development of the System

The establishment of WIPO meant that the international regime for the protection of IPRs had embarked on a new stage of development. In 1967, Members of the *Paris* and *Berne* conventions signed the *WIPO Convention* in Stockholm, Sweden. After coming into force in 1970, the WIPO Convention set up the "International Bureau of Intellectual Property" to replace the BIRPI of the Paris and Berne unions. In 1974 WIPO, headquartered in Geneva, Switzerland, became one of the special agencies of the organisational system of the UN.

The establishment of WIPO made it possible for the BIRPI to become independent of the Swiss Federal Government. It was renamed the International Bureau of Intellectual Property and became a specialised agency of the UN. The founders thought this change could have two benefits: first, the fact that WIPO's prerogative and mandate was to deal with IPRs could be recognised worldwide; and second, WIPO might have roughly the same number of members as the UN. In particular, they thought, more developing countries might participate in the organisation, whereas the number of developing countries initially participating in the BIRPI were very few (Tang 1999, p. 27).

The establishment of WIPO facilitated the process of consistency of IP legislation. Since 1967, more than 20 international treaties have been concluded under the auspices of WIPO and its predecessor, the BIRPI, including treaties providing substantive protection, treaties facilitating multinational access to IPRs protection, and treaties establishing international classifications. These treaties have been implemented through the domestic legislation of Members, thus creating a relatively unified regime for the protection of IPRs at an international level. At the same time, more countries accepted the *Paris* and *Berne* conventions under the effective operation and influence of WIPO: the number of countries participating in the two conventions was 78 and 60 respectively in 1967, while by 2013, these numbers had reached 175 and 166 respectively, greatly expanding the scope of the international regime of IPRs protection.

Since its establishment, WIPO has paid attention to providing assistance to developing countries, providing advice, training, and access to documentation and equipment. Specifically, the assistance includes assisting developing countries in enacting or modernising IP laws; offering collective or individual training to equip government, industry and law enforcement departments with more experts; providing patents information services and so on. It is worth noting that WIPO, through the committees of experts or the governments concerned, has established the *Tunis Model Law on Copyright for Developing Countries* (1976) and revised the *Model Law for Developing Countries on Inventions* (1974), together with the Model Law for Developing Countries on Marks, Trade Names and Acts of Unfair Competition, the *Model Law on Designs in Developing Countries*, drafted by the BIRPI. This has improved the developing countries' relevant legislative ability and played an important role in the implementation of the international regime of IPRs protection.

The establishment of WIPO has provided an international platform on which developing countries can fight for their IPRs interests. Since the 1960s, developing countries have used this forum to call for revision of the relevant provisions of international conventions on IPRs and the establishment of a new international regime of IPRs protection, so as to safeguard their economic interests and promote their cultural, scientific and technological development. In terms of industrial property, developing countries have advocated amending the provisions of the *Paris Convention* regarding national treatment. For example, they have demanded that patent owners in developed countries pay higher patent fees, be granted a shorter term of protection, and be subject to stricter obligations for patents enforcement than their own nationals, and also that the priority period for patent applications be extended in developing countries. With regard to copyright, they have demanded that obstacles to accessing foreign works be removed and preferential provisions be increased for developing countries. For example, they have advocated lower levels of protection for works originating in developed countries, and that the use of patented works for the purpose of educational and scientific research be made possible in developing countries via compulsory licensing.

16.3.3 The WTO Period: Transformation of the System

The establishment of the WTO and the *TRIPS Agreement* marked the advent of a new historical period for the international IPRs protection regime, a period that features high-level and consistent protection. On April 15, 1994, the final document of the Uruguay Round negotiation initiated by the *General Agreement on Tariffs and Trade* (GATT) was signed in Marrakesh, Morocco. The package of agreements negotiated in the "Uruguay Round" had two main outcomes: first, the declaration of the establishment of the WTO ended the provisional application of the GATT.

Second, a "package" of agreements, including the *TRIPS Agreement*, was concluded, and placed under the jurisdiction of the WTO.

The WTO has played a leading role in the new regime of international protection for IPRs. Before the Uruguay Round negotiation, protection regimes for IPRs had been established both domestically and internationally, but there were obvious shortcomings: first, many countries—especially developing countries—have unsound IPRs regimes with a low level of protection; and second, the membership bases of many international conventions on IPRs were too small, the relevant treaties lacked effective institutions to ensure their implementation, and there was no coordination mechanism among the conventions. As a result, the GATT was largely ineffective in the area of international protection for IPRs. As the *TRIPS Agreement* was established by, and remains under the jurisdiction of, the WTO, the above problems have been significantly improved. Firstly, the *TRIPS Agreement*, which sets high standards of protection, is an important part of the legal framework of the WTO. Secondly, the WTO has a broad membership base, and as compliance with the *TRIPS Agreement* is a prerequisite for joining the WTO, this has greatly expanded the scope of application for the international protection of IPRs. And thirdly, the WTO has set up a rather robust monitoring and enforcement mechanism to guarantee that its members comply with the *TRIPS Agreement*. This will promote the development of a new international trade system and international protection regime for IPRs in the twenty-first century.

WIPO attaches importance to cooperation with the WTO in the international coordination of IPRs protection. For example, the *Agreement Between the World Intellectual Property Organisation and the World Trade Organisation* was signed in Geneva in December 1995 by the Directors General of the two international organisations. The provisions in this Agreement include: cooperation between the two international organisations in the exchange and use of laws and regulations; responses to the implementation provisions of the *Paris Convention* regarding the emblems and official seals that cannot be registered as trademarks; responses to requests for legal technical assistance and cooperation for developing countries; and cooperation and information exchanges between the WIPO's International Bureau and the WTO Secretariat. While seeking cooperation, the two international organisations have also each done a great deal of work individually on international IPRs protection. WIPO has been committed to comprehensive promotion of the international level of IPRs protection, and has presided over the enactment of new treaties, including the *Trademark Law Treaty*, the *Copyright Treaty*, and the *Performances and Phonograms Treaty*, which have solved some issues that were not covered by the *Paris* and *Berne* conventions; while the WTO has made efforts to implement the *TRIPS Agreement*, coordinate the sharing of IPRs benefits between underdeveloped and developed countries, and arrange multilateral negotiations for the protection of geographical indications, traditional knowledge and biodiversity.

References

Cao, Xinming. 1995. Analysis of the principle of national treatment in international copyright convention. *Studies in Law and Business* 1

Liu, Wenhua. 2001. *Circumvention and Conflict of WTO and Intellectual Property System of China.* Beijing: China City Press

Luo, Wenzheng, and Gu, Zuxue. 2002. Analysis of the basic principles of international IP law. *Hunan Social Sciences in Hunan* 4

Patterson, L. Ray and Stanley W. Lindberg. 1991. *The Nature of Copyright: A Law of users right.* Athens: The University of Georgia Press

Stewart, S. M. 1983. *International Copyrights and Neighboring Rights.* London: Butterworth and Copublishers Ltd

Tang, Qingyang. 1998. *Theory and Practice of International Protection of IPRs.* Chongqing: Southwest University of Political Science and Law

Tang, Zongshun. 1999. *International Protection of Intellectual Property Rights.* Beijing: People's Court Press

United Nations. 1966. *International Covenant on Civil and Political Rights*

Wan, E-xiang. 2001. *International intellectual property laws.* Wuhan: Hubei People's Publishing House

Wu, Handong. 2005. Changes and developments in the international protection of intellectual property rights. *Chinese Journal of Law* 3

Xia, Xudong. 1993. *World human rights.* Beijing: Current Affairs Press

Yang, Zewei. 1998. *Studies on the New International Economic Order.* Wuhan: Wuhan University Press

Yuan, Yong. 1997. IP law and technological and cultural innovation. *Journal of Peking University (Humanities and Social Sciences* 5

Zhang, Mingyu. 2001. *Tutorial on IP Law.* Chongqing: Southwest University of Political Science and Law

Zhang, Naigen. 1999. *IP Law in International Trade.* Shanghai: Fudan University Press

Zheng, Chengshi. 1997. *Intellectual Property Law.* Beijing: Law Press

Chapter 17
International IPR Conventions Administered by WIPO

The World Intellectual Property Organisation (WIPO) is a specialised agency and international organisation affiliated with the United Nations, established by its member states to pursue common interests, promote understanding and cooperation, and strengthen international IPRs protection, on the basis of mutual respect for sovereignty and equality. In short, WIPO is an intergovernmental organisation responsible for the global protection of IPRs. The international IPRs protection regime under the WIPO framework is characterised by systematic, comprehensive and authoritative nature. Firstly, it has established the principles for the international IPRs protection system. This includes three basic principles of national treatment, minimum protection standards, and public interest, which are foundational tenets adhered to by all international IPR conventions. Even regional and international agreements and treaties concluded outside WIPO cannot deny or contradict these three principles. Secondly, it has built a systematic regime for international IPRs protection. The *Paris Convention* protects industrial property rights, the *Berne Convention* safeguards copyright, and the *WIPO Convention* covers the scope of IPRs as commonly understood to date. It can be said that WIPO has established a comprehensive and well-structured international coordination mechanism. Thirdly, it has set up an international union for the international IPRs protection. Although WIPO's membership is limited to countries only, it is highly inclusive and representative, with member states now accounting for over 90% of the countries in the world.

As one of the 16 specialised agencies of the United Nations, WIPO is specifically responsible for managing global IP issues. The international conventions that it administers constitute the core of the international regime of IPRs protection.

H. Wu, *Theorising Intellectual Property Rights from Chinese Perspectives*,
https://doi.org/10.1007/978-981-96-5867-1_17

17.1 WIPO Unions and Their Governing Conventions

The international unions administered by WIPO in the field of industrial rights include the Paris Union, the Madrid Union, the Union of Patent Cooperation, and the Berne Copyright Union. The international conventions administered by the organisation through its International Bureau are listed below (Table 17.1).

The above international conventions can be divided into three types to reflect their nature: first, treaties providing substantive IPRs protection, such as the *Paris Convention*, the *Berne Convention* and the *Geneva Convention*; second, treaties designed to facilitate access to IPRs protection in multiple countries, such as the *Patent Cooperation Treaty*, the *Madrid Agreement* and the *Budapest Treaty*; third, treaties establishing relevant international classifications, such as the *Nice Agreement* and the *Vienna Agreement.*

In addition to the above WIPO-administered conventions, UNESCO administers the *Universal Copyright Convention* (signed in Geneva on September 6, 1952 and revised in 1971).

17.2 The *Paris Convention*

The *Paris Convention for the Protection of Industrial Property* (the *Paris Convention*) is the first multilateral global convention in the field of IP Law. China formally acceded to the Convention in March 1985, and as of June 2013 the Paris Convention boasted 175 member states.

The *Paris Convention* states that the countries to which it applies constitute a Union for the protection of industrial property. The "Paris Union", as it is known, comprises a General Assembly, an Executive Committee, and an International Bureau. Each Member State of the Union must establish a specialised industrial property agency and a central service agency for communication to the public. The *Paris Convention* delineates the scope of industrial property protection, encompassing patents, utility models, industrial designs, trademarks, service marks, trade names, indications of source or appellations of origin, and protection against unfair competition.

The *Paris Convention* established three basic principles, namely, national treatment, right of priority, and common rules:

1. National treatment

Nationals of any country of the Paris Union shall, as regards the protection of industrial property, enjoy in all the other countries of the Union the advantages that their respective laws now grant, or may hereafter grant, to nationals. Nationals of countries outside the Union who are domiciled or who have real and effective industrial or commercial establishments in the territory of one of the countries of the Union shall be treated in the same manner as nationals of the countries of the Union.

Table 17.1 International conventions administered by WIPO

No.	Treaty name	Time and place	Status
1	*Paris Convention for the Protection of Industrial Property*	Adopted in Paris in 1883, last revised in 1967 and amended in 1979	valid
2	*Madrid Agreement for the Repression of False or Deceptive Indications of Source on Goods*	Adopted in Madrid in 1891, last revised in 1958 and revised again in 1967	valid
3	*Madrid Agreement Concerning the International Registration of Marks*	Adopted in Madrid in 1891, last revised in 1967, partly amended in 1979, additional protocol in 1989	valid
4	*Hague Agreement Concerning the International Registration of Industrial Designs*	Adopted at The Hague in 1925, last revised in 1967, additional protocol in 1975, partly amended in 1979	valid
5	*Nice Agreement Concerning the International Classification of Goods and Services for the Purposes of the Registration of Marks*	Adopted in Nice in 1957, last revised in 1977, partly amended in 1974	valid
6	*Lisbon Agreement for the Protection of Appellations of Origin and their International Registration*	Adopted in Lisbon in 1958, last revised in 1967, amended in 1979	valid
7	*Locarno Agreement Establishing an International Classification for Industrial Designs*	Adopted in Locarno in 1968, individually amended in 1979	valid
8	*Patent Cooperation Treaty*	Adopted in Washington, D.C. in 1970, and amended and modified in 1979 and 1984	valid
9	*Strasbourg Agreement Concerning the International Patent Classification*	Adopted in Strasbourg in 1971, amended in 1979	valid
10	*Vienna Agreement Establishing an International Classification of the Figurative Elements of Marks*	Adopted in Vienna in 1973	valid
11	*Budapest Treaty on the International Recognition of the Deposit of Microorganisms for the Purposes of Patent Procedure*	Adopted in Budapest in 1977, individually amended in 1980	valid
12	*Trademark Registration Treaty*	Adopted in Vienna in 1980	valid
13	*Trademark Law Treaty*	Adopted in Geneva in 1994	valid
14	*International Convention for the Protection of New Varieties of Plants*	Adopted in Geneva in 1961 and last revised in 1991. The current text in force is the 1978 version	valid

(continued)

Table 17.1 (continued)

No.	Treaty name	Time and place	Status
15	*Eurasian Patent Convention*	Adopted in Geneva in 1994	valid
16	*Berne Convention for the Protection of Literary and Artistic Works*	Adopted in Berne in 1886, last revised in 1971, partly amended in 1979	valid
17	*Convention for the Protection of Performers, Producers of Phonograms and Broadcasting Organisations*	Adopted in Rome in 1961	valid
18	*Convention for the Protection of Producers of Phonograms Against Unauthorised Duplication of Their Phonograms*	Adopted in Geneva in 1971	valid
19	*Agreement on the Protection of Printed Type and its International Preservation*	Adopted in Vienna in 1973	valid
20	*Brussels Convention Relating to the Distribution of Programme-Carrying Signals Transmitted by Satellite*	Adopted in Brussels in 1974	valid
21	*Multilateral Convention for the Avoidance of Double Taxation of Copyright Royalties*	Adopted in Madrid in 1979	valid
22	*Treaty on the International Registration of Audiovisual Works*	Adopted in Geneva in 1989	valid
23	*International Treaty on the Registration of Scientific Discoveries*	Adopted in Geneva in 1978	invalid
24	*Nairobi Treaty on the Protection of the Olympic Symbol*	Adopted in Nairobi in 1981	valid
25	*Washington Treaty on Intellectual Property in Respect of Integrated Circuits*	Adopted in Washington, D.C. in 1989	invalid
26	*WIPO Copyright Treaty*	Adopted in Geneva on December 20, 1996	valid

2. Right of priority

Any person who has duly filed an application for a patent, or for the registration of a utility model, industrial design, or trademark, in one of the countries of the Union, or his successor in title, shall enjoy, for the purpose of filing applications in the other countries, a right of priority during the periods hereinafter fixed (12 months for patents and utility models; 6 months for industrial designs and trademarks). Consequently, any subsequent filing in any of the other countries of the Union before the expiration of these periods shall not be invalidated by reason of any acts accomplished in the interval, and the date of the first application shall constitute the effective filing date in those other countries.

3. Common rules

The Convention lays down a few common rules that all Contracting States must follow. The most important are:

a. The main provisions with respect to patents include: independence of patents; the inventor's right to be mentioned in the patent certificate; conditions under which patens may be denied; the granting of compulsory licenses under certain conditions; and the stipulation that the use of patented inventions on board vessels, aircrafts, or land vehicles temporarily or accidentally entering the territory of another country shall not be considered as an infringement of patent rights.
b. The main provisions with respect to trademarks include: the independence of trademark rights and exceptions; the stipulation that the nature of goods to which a trademark is applied shall not affect registration; the protection of well-known trademarks; and the prohibition of certain signs or marks from being used as trademarks.

In addition to observing the above principles or rules, member states of the Union are free to legislate in the field of industrial property protection, including the power to:

a. determine that inventions in certain fields of technology shall be unpatentable;
b. decide whether an examination for novelty or other conditions of patentability shall be conducted prior to the grant of a patent;
c. fix the term of patent protection;
d. determine whether rights in a trade mark may be acquired through use or through registration;
e. decide whether applications for the registration of trademarks and industrial designs shall be examined to ascertain any conflict with prior applications or rights;
f. determine the duration of protection for industrial designs; and
g. establish all matters of procedure and administrative detail.

17.3 Major International Patent Treaties

In addition to the *Paris Convention*, the main international patent treaties include the *Patent Cooperation Treaty*, the *Hague Agreement Concerning the International Deposit of Industrial Designs* (the Hague Agreement), the *Budapest Treaty on the International Recognition of the Deposit of Microorganisms for the Purposes of Patent Procedure* (the Budapest Treaty), and the *Strasbourg Agreement Concerning the International Patent Classification* (the Strasbourg Agreement).

The *Patent Cooperation Treaty* is only open to members of the *Paris Convention.* China signed this Treaty in January 1994, and soon the Chinese Patent Office became the receiving office, the international search unit and the international preliminary examination unit of the Treaty. The Treaty had 148 members by July 2013. Its purpose is to speed up the transmission and utilisation of technical information, strengthen the legal protection of inventions, and promote the scientific and technological progress and economic development of the contracting states by simplifying the formalities and procedures involved in international patent applications. The formalities and procedures stipulated in the Treaty include the following aspects:

1. Unified application. An international patent application is one that is filed in one place (the receiving office), one language, one format, and with fees paid in one currency, and can obtain the same effect in other contracting states as the national patent application of the receiving office.
2. Two phases. The international patent application process is bifurcated into the international phase and the national phase. The international phase encompasses the handling of the application's receipt, publication, search, and preliminary examination. Specifically, an International Searching Authority conducts a search and produces an International Search Report. The International Bureau of WIPO shall publish the application together with the said report within a prescribed period. Subsequently, the application and the report are transmitted to the patent offices of the designated States. The national phase entails substantive examination and the granting procedure. At this stage, the patent office of each designated State examines and processes the application in accordance with its national law. It is at this juncture that the applicant may appoint a representative in the designated State, discharge the requisite fees applicable therein, and furnish a translation of the application where required.

The aforementioned operational framework serves to obviate duplication of effort in the retrieval of technical documentation and fosters cooperation amongst member States concerning the examination work undertaken prior to the grant of a patent. Concomitantly, it affords the applicant the facility of seeking patent protection in several, or indeed all, member States through the filing of a single application.

The *Hague Agreement* was concluded with the aim of facilitating access to design protection in multiple countries. The purpose of the Agreement is to set up the necessary formalities for the protection of an industrial design in several countries, so as to avoid duplication of procedures for the deposit and registration of designs, and to reduce the burden of costs on the applicant. Under the *Hague Agreement*, an applicant who wishes to obtain protection for an industrial design in a contracting state need only deposit the design (in the form of an application and relevant annexes and, if necessary, a sample) once at the International Bureau of WIPO. At the same time, the application must specify both the country/countries for which protection is sought, and the industrial product classification in which protection is sought. In such cases, the international deposit made by the applicant has the same effect as a separate deposit in each of the designated countries.

The main purpose of the *Budapest Treaty* is to reduce the issues around deposit of microbiological samples, avoiding the repetition of the complex procedures involved in microbiological deposits for the patent offices of various countries, and also reducing the cost burden on applicants. Prior to the Treaty, patent applications involving microbial inventions required the submission of microbial samples in addition to a written description. However, the deposit of microorganisms requires special institutions and facilities. If a patent application for a microorganism had to be filed in several countries at the same time, this would impose a heavy burden on both the receiving countries and the applicant. For this reason, the *Budapest Treaty* recognised an international institution for the deposit of microorganisms, replacing multiple depositories for microorganisms with one depository, thus realising international cooperation in the field of microorganisms.

The *Strasbourg Agreement* is designed to facilitate the international classification of patents. It establishes the International Patent Classification, which is divided into 8 divisions, 20 subdivisions, 118 major classes, 617 subclasses and more than 55,000 groups. The classification numbers, which are determined by the patent office and marked on the application documents and patents, are composed of a combination of symbols representing divisions, major classes, subclasses and groups. The International Patent Classification is necessary for retrieval of patent documents with current retrieval technology. At present, more than 70 countries and regions around the world have used this classification. China also uses this classification in its patent literature, although it has not joined the Agreement.

17.4 Major International Trademark Treaties

International trademark treaties, in addition to the *Paris Convention*, mainly include the *Madrid Agreement Concerning the International Registration of Marks* (the Madrid Agreement), the *Trademark Law Treaty*, the *Nice Agreement Concerning the International Classification of Goods and Services for the Purposes of the Registration of Marks* (the Nice Agreement), and the *Vienna Agreement Establishing an International Classification of the Figurative Elements of Marks* (the Vienna Agreement).

The Madrid Agreement is only open to Members of the *Paris Convention*. China officially became a member of the Agreement in October 1989, and by May 2013 it had 91 members. The Madrid Agreement is a supplement to the *Paris Convention* on the international protection of trademarks, and its purpose is to facilitate international registration of trademarks. This Agreement provides that once nationals of contracting states have registered their trademarks in their own countries, they may apply to the International Bureau of WIPO in Geneva for international registration of the trademarks. After the registration is approved, the International Bureau will publish it and notify those contracting states where the applicant requests protection; however, these contracting states may declare within one year that they do not protect the trademark, provided that they give a reason. The applicant may then appeal against the refusal to the competent authorities or the court of that country. If the country in question does not make such a declaration within one year, the international registration will have the effect of a domestic registration in that country for a period of 20 years. Domestic revocation of registration within five years of the international registration can lead to revocation of the international registration. The Agreement also provides that the applicant, after registering a trademark in his or her own country, need only file a single application in one language to the International Bureau and pay a single fee to request protection in each contracting state.

The main objective of the *Trademark Law Treaty* is to simplify and harmonize the trademark registration regime of its contracting states. The Treaty contains 25 articles, which mainly stipulate three phases of the trademark registration procedure:

1. The phase of registration application. The Treaty provides that application for the registration of a trademark shall include all or part of the following: a request for registration, the names and addresses of the applicant and the agent, the various elements of the trademark, and the classification of goods or services in which the registration is sought. Each Contracting State shall allow trademark applications for goods or services belonging to the Nice International Classification. The requirements for trademark applications stipulated by each Member shall not exceed the scope expressly provided for in this Treaty.
2. Changes after registration of a trademark. Changes to the name or address of the trademark holder and changes of ownership of the registration are clearly regulated in the Treaty, and the relevant regime of Contracting States cannot go beyond the existing provisions of the Treaty.
3. The validity term of the registration. The Treaty stipulates that each renewal period is 10 years. China has so far not acceded to this Treaty.

The main purpose of the Nice Agreement is to facilitate uniform classification of goods and services for the purpose of trademark registration. The Agreement is divided into 34 categories of goods and 8 categories of services for trademark registration according to the use of goods or services, raw materials and so on. This classification method provides countries with an international standard of classification which is not only convenient for retrieval of trademarks, but also conducive to the management of trademark use, and international exchange and cooperation regarding trademarks. The Agreement allows the contracting states of the Madrid Agreement and also countries outside the Nice Agreement to adopt the above international classification. China began to apply the Nice Agreement in 1989.

The Vienna Agreement has established an international classification method for the figurative elements of trademarks, with 29 major categories, more than 300 subcategories and more than 3,000 items. All figurative trademarks are handled in accordance with this classification method. The Madrid Agreement requires that the classification of figurative trademarks should be dealt with in accordance with the provisions of the Vienna Agreement. At present, China also adopts this classification method for figurative trademarks.

17.5 Major International Copyright Treaties

The main international copyright treaties are the *Berne Convention*, the *Universal Copyright Convention*, the *Convention for the Protection of Performers, Producers of Phonograms and Broadcasting Organisations* (the *Rome Convention*), the *Convention for the Protection of Producers of Phonograms Against Unauthorised Duplication of Their Phonograms* (the *Geneva Convention* or the *Phonogram Convention*), the *Brussels Convention Relating to the Distribution of Programme-Carrying Signals Transmitted by Satellite* (the *Satellite Convention*).

The *Berne Convention* is the world's first international convention on copyright. China acceded to it in October 1992, and by December 2012 it had 166 members. The main contents of the *Berne Convention* are:

1. The basic principles. First, the principle of national treatment, that is, all works by nationals of contracting states, or works first published in a contracting state, enjoy the same protection within any other contracting state as the law of that state gives to the works of its own nationals. Second, the principle of automatic protection, that is, authors who enjoy national treatment do not need to perform any formalities to obtain protection in contracting states. Third, the principle of independent protection, that is, contracting states protect the works of other contracting states in accordance with their own copyright laws, regardless of whether the works are protected in their originating countries.
2. Provisions of minimum protection. The level of protection granted to copyright owners by the legislation of contracting states shall not be lower than the standards stipulated in the *Berne Convention.*

The specific provisions are:

1. Protected works. The Convention provides for the protection of all works in the fields of literature, science and art, regardless of their forms or methods of expression.
2. The content of the protected rights. In the Convention the term 'property rights' covers the rights to translate, reproduce, perform, adapt, broadcast, publicly recite, film and so on, and personal rights including the right to authorship and the right to the integrity of the work.
3. Term of protection. The protection of personal rights remains in effect after the death of the author, at least until the expiration of the protection duration of their property rights. The term of protection of property rights shall be the life of the author plus 50 years after their death. In the case of cinematographic works, the countries of the Berne Copyright Union may provide that the term of protection shall expire 50 years after the work has been made available to the public. In the case of photographic works and that of works of applied art, the term shall last at least until the end of a period of 25 years from the making of such a work.
4. Special provisions for developing countries. The Convention provides for preferential provisions for developing countries, such as compulsory licensing of translation and reproduction, in order to enable developing countries to obtain legal use of foreign works without unduly increasing their economic burden.

The *Universal Copyright Convention* (UCC) is parallel to the *Berne Convention.* China acceded to the UCC in October 1992, and by April 2007 it had 100 members. The main content of the UCC is covered by the *Berne Convention*, and the level of protection within the former is slightly lower than that within the latter. The differences between them are manifested as:

1. The principle of national treatment. The UCC provides that a Contracting State may treat any person who has habitual residence in that State as its national in accordance with its own law. Unlike the *Berne Convention*, the Contracting States of the UCC have the right to choose whether to grant national treatment to foreigners who are domiciled in their countries.
2. Subjects and subject matter of rights. The UCC defines the subject of copyright as "authors and other copyright owners", unlike the *Berne Convention*, which limits the subject to authors. Additionally, the UCC does not list the types of protected works in as much detail as the *Berne Convention* does, and the scope of its subject matter is more general.
3. Content and protection term of rights. The UCC does not specify the personal rights of authors, it is up to the national legislation of Contracting States to decide whether to protect personal rights. It also does not specify property rights, only emphasising the rights to copy, perform, broadcast, translate and so on. In addition, the term of protection stipulated in the UCC is relatively short, i.e., the life of the author plus 25 years after their death for general works, and not less than 10 years for photographic works and works of applied art.
4. Copyright Marks. The UCC requires each copy of a work to bear the "copyright mark", the name of the copyright holder, and the date of first publication when the work is already published. In addition, the UCC stipulates that it is not retroactive, and that contracting states may not declare reservations to the provisions of the Convention.

The *Rome Convention*, the world's first international convention on the protection of neighbouring rights, is open only to members of the *Berne Convention* and the *Universal Copyright Convention.* The Rome Convention had 91 members by April 2013, and China has not yet acceded to it. The main content of the international convention on the protection of neighbouring rights are:

1. The relationship between neighbouring rights protection and copyright protection. The protection of neighbouring rights granted by the Convention will not change or affect the copyright protection of literary and artistic works: where permission from the author is required for the use of a work under copyright law, such permission shall not be affected by the Convention.
2. Protection of performers' rights. Performers are actors, singers, musicians, dancers, and other persons who perform literary or artistic works. The protection provided for performers by this Convention shall include the possibility of preventing: the broadcasting and the communication to the public, without the consent of the performer, of their "live" performance; the recording, without the consent of the performer, of their live performances; and the reproducing of original works recorded without the consent of the performer, or reproducing them beyond the scope of their permission.
3. Protection of the rights of producers of phonograms. Phonogram means any exclusively aural fixation of sounds of a performance or of other sounds. Producer of phonograms means the person who, or the legal entity which, first fixes the sounds of a performance or other sounds. Producers of phonograms shall

enjoy the right to authorise or prohibit the direct or indirect reproduction of their phonograms.
4. Protection of the rights of broadcasting organisations. Broadcasting means the transmission by wireless means for public reception of sounds or of images and sounds, including broadcasts by radio and television, but not broadcasts by cable. Broadcasting organisations have the right to authorise or prohibit the rebroadcasting of their broadcasts; the fixation of their broadcasts; the reproduction of fixations, made without their consent, of their broadcasts, or the reproduction of legally produced fixations of their broadcasts for unlawful purposes; and the communication to the public of their television broadcasts if such communication is made in places accessible to the public after payment of an entrance fee.
5. Term of protection of neighbouring rights. The above three rights shall be protected for a period of not less than 20 years.

The *Geneva Convention* is a convention on neighbouring rights for the protection of phonograms (and "phonogram" here refers to exclusively aural fixation, and doesn't include films or videos. China formally acceded to the Convention in April 1993, and by February 2013 it had 78 members. The Convention provides that no phonograms may be reproduced or imported for the purpose of distribution to the public without the producer's permission. The implementation method of the Convention is determined by the domestic legislation of contracting states. The Convention protects phonograms by granting copyright or neighbouring rights to phonograms or by applying anti-unfair competition laws and criminal laws. The minimum term of protection for phonograms under the Convention is the same as in the relevant provisions of the *Rome Convention.*

The *Satellite Convention* is a convention on neighbouring rights for the protection of broadcasts, to which China has not yet acceded. The Convention provides that each Contracting State undertakes to take adequate measures to prevent the distribution on or from its territory of any program-carrying signal by any distributor for whom the signal emitted to or passing through the satellite is not intended. The Convention does not apply to signals transmitted directly from satellites to users, but rather to indirect signals that are received and then distributed by terrestrial broadcasting organisations. The Convention stipulates that it is up to each member state to decide what laws it will take to stop the abovementioned violations.

17.6 The *WIPO Copyright Treaty* and the *WIPO Performances and Phonograms Treaty*

In December 1996, WIPO adopted the *WIPO Copyright Treaty* and the *WIPO Performances and Phonograms Treaty* (collectively referred to as the Internet Treaties) in Geneva, and they entered into force in March 2002 and May 2002 respectively. The *Copyright Treaty* contains 25 articles, of which 14 are substantive and 11 are procedural, while the *Performances and Phonograms Treaty* contains 33 articles, of which 23 are substantive and 10 are procedural. The procedural provisions of the two treaties are basically the same. These two treaties were formulated mainly to solve the issues related to copyright and neighbouring rights caused by the use of works in new communication technologies, especially in the digital technology and Internet environment. The adoption of these two treaties is one of the most important events in the field of international copyright and neighbouring rights in the past two decades: first of all, they meet the needs of the development of information and communication technologies and raised the level of protection of copyright and neighbouring rights. Moreover, developing countries are paying more and more attention to the protection of copyright, and are playing an increasingly important role in the field of international protection of copyright.

The substantive provisions of the *Copyright Treaty* mainly include the following aspects:

1. Preamble. The Preamble states that the purpose of the Treaty is to: develop and maintain the protection of the rights of authors in their literary and artistic works in a manner as effective and uniform as possible; recognise the need to introduce new international rules and clarify the interpretation of certain existing rules in order to provide adequate solutions to the questions raised by new economic, social, cultural and technological developments; recognise the profound impact of the development and convergence of information and communication technologies on the creation and use of literary and artistic works; emphasise the outstanding significance of copyright protection as an incentive for literary and artistic creation; and recognise the need to maintain a balance between the rights of authors and the larger public interest, particularly in the areas of education, research and access to information.
2. Relationship with the *Berne Convention*. The Treaty is a special agreement under the *Berne Convention*, and as such shall have no connection with treaties other than the *Berne Convention*, and shall not prejudice any rights and obligations arising under any other treaties.
3. Scope of copyright protection. Copyright protection extends to expressions but not to ideas, procedures, methods of operation or mathematical concepts. Contracting parties shall apply *mutatis mutandis* the provisions of Articles 2 to 6 of the *Berne Convention* in respect of the protection provided for in this Treaty. Computer programs shall be protected as literary works. Compilations of data or other material, in any form, which by reason of the selection or arrangement of their contents constitute intellectual creations, are protected as such.
4. Economic rights. Article 6 of the Treaty provides for the right of distribution: authors of literary and artistic works shall enjoy the exclusive right of authorising the making available to the public of the original and copies of their works through sale or other transfer of ownership. The separation of the right of distribution from the right of reproduction is a refinement of the rights which increases the level of protection. Article 7 provides for rental right: authors of computer programs, cinematographic works, and works embodied in phonograms shall enjoy the exclusive right of authorising commercial rental arrangement to the public of the

originals or copies of their works. However, this shall not apply in the case of computer programs, where the program itself is not the essential object of the rental; nor in the case of cinematographic works, unless such commercial rental has led to widespread copying of such works, materially impairing the exclusive right of reproduction. Article 9 provides for the right of communication to the public: authors of literary and artistic works shall enjoy the exclusive right of authorising any communication to the public of their works, by wire or wireless means, including the making available to the public of their works. This article extends the right of dissemination of musical works under the *Berne Convention* to all works, and it confirms the right of dissemination in the Internet environment.

5. Term of protection for photographic works. The term of protection for photographic works is the same as that for general works.
6. Limitations and exceptions. Contracting Parties may, in their legislation, provide for limitations and exceptions to the rights granted to authors of literary and artistic works under this Treaty in certain special cases that do not conflict with a normal exploitation of the work and do not unreasonably prejudice the legitimate interests of the author.
7. Obligations concerning technological measures. The treaty provides that "circumvention" of protection measures of right owners is illegal, and Contracting Parties shall provide effective legal remedies.
8. Obligations concerning rights management information. This Treaty provides that the electronic information about the work must not be removed or altered without authority and confirms that such actions are illegal. The purpose of this provision is to ensure the authenticity and accuracy of information about works on the Internet.
9. Other provisions. The provisions of Article 18 of the *Berne Convention* shall be applied to the Treaty's application in time. The Treaty requires Contracting Parties to take the necessary measures to ensure the application of the Treaty.

The substantive provisions of the *WIPO Performances and Phonograms Treaty* (WPPT) mainly include the following content:

1. Preamble. The preamble is basically the same as the Copyright Treaty.
2. Relation to other conventions. Nothing in the treaty shall derogate from the existing obligations of the Contracting Parties under the *Rome Convention*, shall affect the protection of copyright, or have any connection with any other treaties.
3. Definitions. Through the interpretation of the concepts of "fixation", "phonogram" and "communication", the Treaty limits fixation to the fixation of sounds rather than the fixation of images, and communication to the communication of sounds rather than the communication of images. This effectively limits the rights of performers to the performance of sounds and excludes the rights of performers to images. It was decided to develop a separate document to address the rights of performers to images.

4. Beneficiaries of this Treaty. The beneficiaries of this Treaty are performers and producers of phonograms. This Treaty applies the principle of national treatment.
5. Rights of performers. The moral rights enjoyed by performers include the right to claim to be identified as the performers of their performances, and to object to any distortion, mutilation or other modification of their performances that would be prejudicial to their reputations. The economic rights enjoyed by performers include the right to authorise the broadcasting and fixation of their unfixed performances, the right to authorise the reproduction of their performances fixed in phonograms, the right to authorise the distribution, the right to authorise the making available to the public of, and the right to authorise the commercial rental to the public and the communication to the public, of their performances fixed in phonograms, and the right to a single equitable remuneration for the use of such phonograms for broadcasting or for any communication to the public. The provisions of the right of communication to the public are conducive to solving the issues of neighbouring rights in network data transmission.
6. Rights of producers of phonograms. A producer of phonograms has the right to authorise the reproduction, the distribution, the commercial rental and the making available to the public of phonograms, and the right to a single equitable remuneration for the use of phonograms for broadcasting or for any communication to the public.
7. Term of protection. The term of protection to be granted to the rights of performers and the rights of producers of phonograms shall be at least 50 years.
8. Limitations and exceptions. Contracting Parties may provide for limitations and exceptions to the rights in certain special cases which do not conflict with a normal exploitation of the performance or phonogram and do not unreasonably prejudice the legitimate interests of the performer or of the producer of the phonogram.
9. Obligations concerning technological measures. The Treaty provides that "circumvention" of protection measures of right owners is illegal, and Contracting Parties shall provide effective legal remedial measures.
10. Obligations concerning rights management information. This Treaty provides that the electronic information about performances and phonograms must not be removed or altered without authority and confirms that such actions are illegal. The purpose of this provision is to ensure the authenticity and accuracy of information about works on the Internet.
11. Other provisions. The enjoyment and exercise of the rights provided for in this Treaty shall not be subject to any formality. The provisions of Article 18 of the *Berne Convention* shall be applied to the Treaty's application in time. The Treaty requires Contracting Parties to take the necessary measures to ensure the application of the treaty. Subject to the provisions of Article 15(3), no reservations to this Treaty shall be permitted.

17.7 The *Beijing Treaty on Audiovisual Performances*

In June 2012, the IPO held a diplomatic conference in Beijing and adopted the *Beijing Treaty on Audiovisual Performances* (known as the *Beijing Treaty*). International legislation on the protection of performers' rights began in the second half of the twentieth century, and the *Rome Convention* (signed in 1961) was the first international convention to protect performers' rights, but the rights provided in it were relatively limited, only including that: no broadcasting and communicating to the public of their performances (the right to live broadcasting of performances); no fixation of performances they had not fixed (the right to fixation of performances); and no reproduction of a recording of their performance (performer's right to reproducing a recording) are permitted without the performers' consent. The WPPT, adopted in 1996, mainly protects live performances by performers and performances fixed in phonograms (except those fixed in audiovisual fixation.) The adoption of the *Beijing Treaty* in 2012 has made up for the prior conventions' lack of protection of performer's rights by establishing an international protection regime for performers' rights, together with the *Rome Convention* and the WPPT.

The *Beijing Treaty* provisions include a preamble and a total of 30 substantive articles, which can be divided into four parts as follows:

1. Preamble. The main elements of the preamble emphasise the purposes and objectives of the treaty as follows: "desiring to develop and maintain the protection of the rights of performers in their audiovisual performances in a manner as effective and uniform as possible", "recognising the need to introduce new international rules in order to provide adequate solutions to the questions raised by economic, social, cultural and technological developments", "recognising the profound impact of the development and convergence of information and communication technologies on the production and use of audiovisual performances", "recognising the need to maintain a balance between the rights of performers in their audiovisual performances and the larger public interests, particularly education, research and accesses to information", and "recognising that the [WPPT] signed in Geneva on December 20, 1996, does not extend protection to performers in respect of their performances fixed in audiovisual fixations." These purposes stated in the preamble describe the context of the Treaty, namely the protection of performers' rights in response to the impact of new communication technologies; the principles of this Treaty are the maintenance of a balance between performers' rights and the public interest; and the purpose of the Treaty is the establishment of a system of performers' rights in audiovisual fixation and phonogram, together with the WPPT.
2. General Provisions. Articles 1 to 4 of the Treaty are general provisions. They refer to: "Relation to Other Conventions and Treaties." With the exception of the WPPT, the Treaty is not substantially related to other treaties (such as the *Rome Convention*), and is an independent international treaty, so its implementation shall not prejudice the rights and obligations provided for by any other treaties. (2) "Definition." The definition of performers, audiovisual fixations, broadcasting

and communication to the public follows the interpretation of Article 2 of the WPPT, with the exception that the object of protection provided for is audiovisual performances rather than pure performance of sounds. (3) "Beneficiaries of Protection." The dual principle of nationality and residence of the performer is adopted, and anyone who meets one of the criteria is a beneficiary of protection under the Treaty. (4) "National Treatment." This treaty, like the WPPT, limits national treatment to the exclusive rights it grants and the right to reasonable remuneration. The difference, however, is that the Treaty provides for reservation of reciprocity, that is, "a Contracting Party shall be entitled to limit the extent and term of the protection accorded to nationals of another Contracting Party to those rights that its own nationals enjoy in that other Contracting Party."

3. Performers' rights. Articles 5 to 11 of the Treaty provide for various rights of performers in relation to audiovisual performances, including: (a) "Moral rights." The Treaty provides for two rights: the right "to claim to be identified as the performer of his performances, except where omission is dictated by the manner of the use of the performance" (i.e., the right to be identified as performer), and the right "to object to any distortion, mutilation or other modification of his performances that would be prejudicial to his reputation" (i.e., the right to the integrity of the image of the performance). (b) "Economic Rights." The Treaty covers two kinds of rights: performers shall enjoy the exclusive right to authorise—as regards their performances—the broadcasting, communication to the public and fixation of their unfixed performances; and performers shall enjoy the rights to their performances fixed in audiovisual fixations, including the right to reproduction, distribution, rental, and making available of audiovisual fixations, as well as the right to broadcasting and communication to the public. These rights are similar to the WPPT's provisions regarding performers' rights to their performances of sounds. It is important to note that under this Treaty, the "right of broadcasting and communication to the public" includes the right to authorise the broadcasting and communication as well as the right to equitable remuneration for the authorised broadcasting and communication to the public; whereas the WPPT only provides that performers have the "right to equitable remuneration for broadcasting or communication to the public." However, Contracting Parties to the *Beijing Treaty* may reserve the rights under this article and opt for a provision similar to the WPPT.
4. Transfer of performer's rights. The provisions on transfer of rights were the most hotly debated and difficult issues, and the result was the compromise reached in the end. According to the provisions of Article 12 of the Treaty, once a performer has consented to fixation of his or her performance in an audiovisual fixation, there are three ways the performer's rights can be dealt with: the exclusive rights of authorisation shall be owned or exercised by, or transferred to, the producer of such audiovisual fixation. Contracting Parties may choose one of the provisions in their domestic laws. In the above cases, the performers and the producers of audiovisual fixations shall be in accordance with the provisions of domestic law, except if any contrary contracts are in place. In addition, the Treaty provides for a remuneration clause, which is independent from the above transfer provisions,

and domestic law or agreements of an individual, collective or other nature may stipulate that the performer is entitled to reasonable remuneration for any use of the performance.

5. Other provisions. Articles 13 to 30 of the Treaty provide for "limitations and exceptions", "term of protection", "obligations concerning technological measures", "obligations concerning rights management information", "formalities", "reservations and notifications", "application in time", and "provisions on enforcement of rights", as well as provisions concerning accession to, and the management and denunciation of the Treaty. The article on "limitations and exceptions" is similar to the relevant provisions of the WPPT, that is, Contracting Parties may, in their national legislation, provide for the same kinds of limitations or exceptions with regard to the protection of performers as they provide for, in their national legislation, in connection with the protection of copyright for literary and artistic works, provided these limitations and exceptions do not conflict with a normal exploitation of the performance and do not unreasonably prejudice the legitimate interests of the performer. The term of protection to be granted to performers under this Treaty shall last for at least 50 years (computed from the end of the year in which the performance was fixed), which is consistent with the term of protection in the WPPT but higher than the level of protection provided by the *Rome Convention.* In view of the characteristics of communicating audiovisual performances in the Internet environment, the Treaty follows the provisions of the WPPT requires Contracting Parties to provide appropriate legal protection and effective legal remedies regarding to the technical measures and rights management information of audiovisual performances.

Chapter 18
The *TRIPS Agreement* Within the WTO Framework

The emergence of economic globalisation and the formation of a new international trade system constituted a pivotal trend in the development of the world economy in the second half of the twentieth century, and this trend has profoundly influenced the landscape of the twenty-first century (Xu 1997, p. 11). The *General Agreement on Tariffs and Trade* (GATT) and its successor, the WTO, have played an important role in promoting economic globalisation. Unlike preceding international organisations and conventions, the WTO and its *TRIPS Agreement* have incorporated intellectual property protection into the international trade system, leading to a new developmental trajectory towards the integration and internationalisation of IPRs regimes.

The *TRIPS Agreement* is the most extensive and binding multilateral treaty on IPRs since the establishment of an international coordination mechanism in the *Paris Convention*. Firstly, the *TRIPS Agreement* covers almost all substantive areas of IP. The scope of IPRs protection extends not only to traditional patents, trademarks, and copyrights, but also to industrial designs, geographical indications, layout designs, and trade secrets. Secondly, the *TRIPS Agreement* regulates and expands the international obligations of contracting parties. By adopting the stipulations of "compliance" and "non-derogation", it has incorporated many substantive obligations from numerous conventions—including the *Paris Convention*, *Berne Convention*, *Rome Convention*, and *Washington Treaty*—into the contractual frameworks of member states. Thirdly, the *TRIPS Agreement* strengthens the enforcement and dispute settlement mechanism for IPRs. As an integral component of the WTO's "single undertaking" framework, it intertwines the international trading regime with the IPRs protection regime, coupling substantive norms with procedural disciplines, thereby enhancing the Agreement's binding force under international law.

As the *TRIPS Agreement* came into force, the IPRs regime has entered a new phase in which high-level protection and efficient implementation were provided. The Agreement has led to a dramatic paradigm shift in today's international IPRs regime, and at the same time has also given rise to controversial institutional deficiencies.

H. Wu, *Theorising Intellectual Property Rights from Chinese Perspectives*,
https://doi.org/10.1007/978-981-96-5867-1_18

18.1 Relationship Between the *TRIPS Agreement* and Other WTO Agreements

The *TRIPS Agreement*, with the *Multilateral Agreements on Trade in Goods* and the *General Agreement on Trade in Services*, constitute the three main regimes in the institutional framework of the WTO. The WTO legal system consists of organic laws, trade-in-goods laws, trade-in-services laws, and multilateral trade agreements. As a sub-agreement of a series of agreements related to the WTO, the *TRIPS Agreement* is an integral part of this legal system and is closely linked to other related agreements.

18.1.1 Consistency Between the TRIPS Agreement *and Relevant WTO Agreements*

The *TRIPS Agreement* stipulates matters related to IPRs protection. It has to be consistent with the fundamental law—the WTO Agreement and other multilateral trade agreements that are also laws for various sectors. Firstly, a member of the WTO is also a party to the multilateral agreements, and vice versa. According to the WTO Agreement, all original contracting members of the WTO must accept both the Agreement and the multilateral trade agreements of its Appendices I, II and III, as well as the General Agreement on Tariffs and Trade documents. Moreover, anyone who wants to become a member of the WTO must accept the WTO Agreement and the multilateral trade agreements of its Appendices I, II, and III.[1] That is to say, a contracting party of the WTO agreements must accept both the WTO Constitution and also the multilateral trade agreements in Appendix I of *the Final Act of the Uruguay Round of GATT Negotiations*, and vice versa. At the same time, a country can be either both a member of the WTO and a contracting party of multilateral agreements, or neither. Failure to join, or withdrawal from, multilateral agreements also mean losing membership of the WTO, and vice versa. Secondly, the IPRs Council and the General Council of the WTO are coordinated. The Council for Trade-Related Aspects of Intellectual Property Rights, established under the *TRIPS Agreement*, is a body of the General Council of the World Trade Organisation that oversees the operation and implementation of the *TRIPS Agreement*. It indicates that the regulatory mechanism for IPRs protection is relatively independent but remains consistent with that of the WTO. Lastly, the *TRIPS Agreement* apply to the basic principles of the WTO and its dispute settlement mechanism. Regarding fundamental principles, the *TRIPS Agreement* follows the common basic principles established by the WTO, such as the principle of non-discrimination, the principle of preferential treatment, and the principle of transparency. As the basic principle of the WTO and the primary principle of the *TRIPS Agreement*, the principle of non-discrimination belongs to the principle of national treatment. The principle of preferential treatment is the

[1] See Article 11, Article 12 of *the Agreement Establishing the World Trade Organization.*

basic guideline of the WTO in dealing with the relationship between developed and developing countries, and the *TRIPS Agreement* also makes principal provisions in this regard. The principle of transparency is the basic principle of the WTO's dispute settlement mechanism, and the *TRIPS Agreement* also contains specific provisions.[2] In addition, according to the *TRIPS Agreement*, the specific practices of the WTO dispute settlement mechanism can apply without exception to its consultation and settlement mechanism for disputes.

18.1.2 Conflicts Between the TRIPS Agreement *and Relevant WTO Agreements*

The regulation of IPRs within the framework of the WTO necessarily involves the rules formulated by the GATT and the multilateral trading system. Article 16 of the *Agreement Establishing the World Trade Organisation* stipulates that "in the event of a conflict between its provisions and a provision of any multilateral trade agreement, its provisions shall prevail to the extent of the conflict." It can be seen that relevant conflicts and their rules are as follows:

1. The *TRIPS Agreement* vs. The agreement establishing the World Trade Organisation

In the legal system of the WTO, its constitution is regarded as the basic law, and it ranks higher than other sector laws. Thus, as the other multilateral trade agreements—including the *TRIPS Agreement*—are sector laws, they shouldn't conflict with the WTO's constitution, and if they do, the corresponding provisions of the constitution prevail.

2. The TRIPS vs. the GATT in 1994

The essential contents of the GATT in 1994 are similar to the GATT in 1947, and neither involve IPRs issues. The *TRIPS Agreement* established a new legal system related to trade, so its norms are irrelevant to the GATT, except that its dispute settlement shall adopt certain rules and procedures that are laid out in the GATT.

3. The TRIPS vs. other trade agreements

The multilateral trade agreements under the WTO's constitution, including the *TRIPS Agreement*, have equal legal status, none has priority.

[2] For the principles of national treatment, preferential treatment, and transparency, see articles 65,66,67, and 63 of *the TRIPS Agreement*.

18.2 Relationship Between the *TRIPS Agreement* and Other Pre-Existing International IPR Conventions

The *TRIPS Agreement* is an integral part of the multilateral trade rules under the WTO system, and an essential legal document in today's international IPRs protection system. There are many differences between the *TRIPS Agreement* and traditional international conventions on IPRs, so the framers of the Agreement have formulated corresponding rules and principles on its applicability to the original international conventions, to prevent and resolve the conflicts between the Agreement and the relevant conventions.[3] Here "original international conventions" refer to the four conventions administered by WIPO: the Paris, Berne, Rome and Washington conventions.

The relationship between the *TRIPS Agreement* and other international conventions on IPRs is manifested in the following aspects:

18.2.1 Incorporation and Preservation of Pre-Existing Conventions by TRIPS

The *TRIPS Agreement* emphasises that it has to be consistent with the existing obligations recognised in the four conventions administered by WIPO.[4] The above provisions reflect the succession and reservations to the original conventions. So, all parties to the Agreement, whether or not they are members of these conventions, shall be subject to the substantive provisions of the conventions. In other words, when it comes to the validity, scope, acquisition, and protection of IPRs, the provisions of the Agreement take the existing obligations arising from the substantive provisions of the conventions mentioned above as the starting point, which is an affirmation of the relevant contents of the original conventions. In addition, the provisions of the *TRIPS Agreement* do not explicitly state the validity of other conventions administered by WIPO, such as the "sub-conventions" of the *Paris Convention.* However, Paragraph 1 of Article 2 of the Agreement emphasises that within the scope of Parts II, III, and IV, all members shall comply with the provisions of Article 19 of the *Paris Convention.* Academics have different views concerning the validity of the Agreement and the *Paris Convention*'s "sub-conventions." One view is that the Agreement recognises the validity of the sub-convention, and members shall comply with the obligations arising from the sub-conventions (Zheng 1994). The other view is that the Agreement does not recognise the validity of the sub-conventions but the validity of Article 19 of the *Paris Convention,* and therefore members are not obliged to comply with the sub-conventions (Zhang 1997). The author believes Paragraph 1 of Article

[3] As for the unification and conflicts between *the TRIPS Agreement* and other relevant agreements, see (Zeng 1996; Gu 2002).

[4] See the provisions of Articles 2, 9, and 35 of *the TRIPS Agreement.*

2 of the Agreement requires members to comply with the provisions of Article 19 of the *Paris Convention.* This provision means that, to the extent that it is not in conflict with the *Paris Convention*, the Contracting Parties may conclude several special protection treaties for the protection of industrial property. In fact, among the industrial property conventions administered by WIPO, except for the *International Convention for the Protection of New Varieties of Plants*, they are almost specialised treaties arising from Article 19 of the *Paris Convention*, including *the Patent Cooperation Treaty*, the *Madrid Agreement Concerning the International Registration of Marks*, and the *Agreement for the Protection of Appellations of Origin and their International Registration.* The *TRIPS Agreement* does not emphasise that members must comply with these sub-conventions of the Paris Convention. Instead, it allows members to enter into specific treaties on IPRs, as long as they do not violate the minimum obligations and standards of IPRs.

18.2.2 Modification and Supplementation of Pre-Existing Conventions by TRIPS

Based on inheriting and retaining the "reasonable core" of the original conventions, the *TRIPS Agreement* has made a breakthrough and development in the design and regulation of the international protection of IPRs, and this is the most crucial point that distinguishes it from those original conventions. Specifically, this breakthrough is manifest in two aspects. First, there is an amendment to the relevant provisions of the original conventions on the matter of international protection of IPRs: the parties to the Agreement must apply the new provisions of the Agreement, rather than the original provisions of the conventions. The second aspect is that the Agreement provides additional provisions in areas of this matter that the original conventions failed to cover. In this case, the parties must apply these additional provisions. The *TRIPS Agreement* shows the breakthrough and development of the original conventions in various aspects, including basic principles, substantive obligations, protection measures, enforcement procedures, and preferences for developing countries and least developed countries. The features of the *TRIPS Agreement* as a new IPRs protection regime are described below (Kong 2002).

18.2.3 Exclusion and Negation of Pre-Existing Conventions by TRIPS

The *TRIPS Agreement* mainly succeeds and develops the existing obligations under the original conventions, and only rejects a few of their provisions, specifically in two aspects. First, it denies the moral rights of authors as stipulated in Paragraph 2 of Article 6 of the *Berne Convention.* The authors of the Agreement do not explain the motivation for this, but scholars believe there are two reasons: (1) all IPRs protection under the WTO framework is trade-related. The *TRIPS Agreement* reinforces the idea of a global market in which intangible goods protected by IPRs are considered together with goods and services. The result of this is that the Agreement emphasises the commercial and economic aspects of copyright, and gives the moral rights of authors secondary importance. (2) The protection system of authorial rights in common law countries differs from the relevant laws in civil law countries. Due to these historical differences in copyright legislation, the United Kingdom and the United States did not protect the moral rights of authors for a long time. However, they both later added such systems to their domestic laws due to the need to participate in the *Berne Convention*. However, the level of protection is low.[5] Such provisions of the *TRIPS Agreement* are more appropriate to the traditional US. The second aspect where the Agreement contravenes the provisions of the original conventions is its rejection of the "non-retroactive" provision of Article 20 of the Rome Convention. According to Article 20, on the one hand, this Convention does not affect a member state's rights that have been protected before it acceded to the convention. On the other hand, the Convention doesn't require a member state to protect performance, broadcasting, or phonograms that took place before it acceded to the convention. The *TRIPS Agreement* confirms the effects of the *Rome Convention*, but provides that the "retroactivity" provision of Article 18 of the 1971 *Berne Convention* applies to performers' and producers' rights in sound recordings. The "retroactivity" in the *Berne Convention* means that each member state must protect not only works that originate in other member states and have been protected after its accession to the Convention, but also works that existed in other member states before its accession to the Convention and have not yet entered the public domain in their country of origin. This means that members of the *TRIPS Agreement* can no longer invoke the "non-retroactivity" clause of the *Rome Convention*, Article 20. As long as performance, broadcasts, or sound recordings are still in the exclusive domain of the country of origin, new members of the agreement must grant retroactive protection.[6]

[5] *The British Copyright Law* of 1956 already had anti-counterfeiting signatures. Although *the Copyright Law* of 1988 stipulates moral rights, there are many restrictions. For example, the exercise of the right of authorship must be based on a prior declaration of the reputation of the author; moral rights may be waived. *The Visual Artists Rights Act* enacted by the United States in 1990 strictly restricted the protection of moral rights, such as literature, drama, musical works, audio-visual works, and electronic publications are excluded; moral rights are protected only for the work in a single copy that is signed by the author, or for a limited edition of 200 copies or fewer that are signed and consecutively numbered by the author.

[6] See Article 70 of Paragraph 2 of *the TRIPS Agreement*.

18.3 Core Characteristics of the *TRIPS Agreement*

The *TRIPS Agreement* is one of the final documents resulting from the Uruguay Round negotiations, and one of the primary documents of the WTO. Historically, the Agreement is also the first intellectual property convention explicitly linked to international trade, and the first international convention to integrate various intellectual property regimes—such as copyright, patent, and trademark rights—into one. The basic features of the *TRIPS Agreement* can be summarised as follows:

18.3.1 Integration with the International Trade System

The full name of the Agreement is the *Agreement on Trade-Related Aspects of Intellectual Property Rights*—so it is apparently related to international trade. However, the introductory provisions of the Agreement do not relate directly to trading issues, but are concerned with intellectual property protection. From this perspective, the content of *TRIPS Agreement* is not in accord with its name (Kong 2002). Nonetheless, scholars generally agree that the *TRIPS Agreement*, unlike traditional IPR conventions, is an essential organisational component of the new international trading system, and has as its primary objective the promotion of economic globalisation and legislative integration. Firstly, the Agreement establishes its purpose as being to reduce distortions and resistance in international trade, promoting adequate and effective protection of IPRs, and to ensure that intellectual property enforcement measures and procedures do not become obstacles to legitimate trade.[7] That is to say, the main intention of the Agreement is to raise the level of IPRs protection and unify the system by promoting the integrated protection of IPRs under the WTO system so that the level of protection for all members will reach the standard previously available only in developed countries. In this way, through the effective operation of the WTO system, IPRs protection has become part of the international trade regime. Secondly, the Agreement extends the principles and institutions of the GATT and the WTO on trade in goods to protection of IPRs. For example, as the primary principle in international trade, the principle of most-favoured-nation treatment was introduced into the intellectual property convention for the first time, and became the basic obligation that each member of the Agreement must fulfil. Prior to this, the basic rule that parties were required to implement, in order to achieve the fairness of trade practices in the GATT, was the principle of transparency. The Agreement invoked the principle of transparency in order to disclose each member's judicial system, to avoid legal explanations and conflicts. The dispute settlement mechanism under the WTO system is directly applicable to general trade disputes and this applicability has been extended to intellectual property disputes. This institutionalised multilateral dispute resolution mechanism helps to prevent acts of unilateral retaliation, such as the US "Sect. 301" in the trade act of 1974 (Kong 2002).

[7] See the preamble to *the TRIPS Agreement*.

18.3.2 Establishment of a New IPRs Protection System

The *TRIPS Agreement* is not an international convention on protecting a specific intellectual property right. However, it covers various fields of intellectual property, including copyright, trademark, geographical indication, industrial design, patent, layout design of integrated circuits, and trade secrets rights. Before this agreement, all international conventions on intellectual property protected only one or certain types of intellectual property. For example, the *Paris Convention* only has provisions on industrial property rights, not copyright and neighbouring rights, while the *Berne Convention* only deals with the protection of copyright in literary and artistic works, and the *Rome Convention* is a special convention dedicated to protecting neighbouring rights. In contrast, the IPRs system in the *TRIPS Agreement* includes not only traditional copyright, patent rights and trademark rights, but also emerging IPRs systems, such as the right to new plant varieties[8] and the right to layout designs of integrated circuits, and also places trade secrets, which have never been recognised by specific international conventions, in the IPRs system. It is noteworthy that the Agreement does not provide for the right of the invention and the right of discovery, which are recognised by the *Convention Establishing the World Intellectual Property Organisation* (the *WIPO Convention*), nor does it provide for the right of trade name protected by the *Paris Convention.* It may be argued that the former does not cover private property rights, and the latter has little connection with trade and therefore is not considered in the *TRIPS Agreement*. Nevertheless, the Agreement is still the most comprehensive and robust international agreement for building intellectual property systems.

18.3.3 Elevation of IPRs Protection Standards

Both the protection standard and the protection period of the *TRIPS Agreement* take into account and refer to the requirements and practices of developed countries. Its specific manifestations are:

1. The expansion of the scope of rights. In the fields of copyright and neighbouring rights, computer software and databases are protected as written works, and the rental rights of computer software, cinematographic works, and sound recordings are newly added. In the field of trademark rights, it is stipulated that it should be possible to obtain trademark registration under prevailing circumstances for any sign or combination thereof with "distinctive character", and well-known trademarks are specially protected with their scope of protection extended to service marks as well. In the field of geographical indications, members are obliged to prohibit the confusion of geographical indications (especially in the

[8] According to Article 27 of *the TRIPS Agreement*, members may adopt patent protection, exclusive rights protection, or a combination of both modes of protection for new plant varieties.

case of alcohol and wine; in the field of design rights and patents, the right to import is granted to the rights holder; in the field of layout design rights of integrated circuits, the protection is extended beyond the layout design and the circuit which is itself composed of the layout design, and also extends to items using the layout design. Similarly, in the field of trade secrets rights, it is stipulated that such intellectual property protection shall also cover pharmaceuticals and agrochemical products.
2. Extension of the protection period. The term of copyright protection, including computer software, is at least 50 years and the term of patent protection is at least 20 years, while industrial design protection and integrated circuit layout design protection are 10 years.
3. The effective non-existence of reservation clause. Article 72 of the Agreement stipulates that no reservation may be made to any provision of the Agreement without the consent of other parties. Unlike the reservation clauses in previous international conventions, the potential implication of this provision is that a member wishing to make a reservation to a provision of the Agreement in its domestic law must obtain the consent of the other members. In a sense, the reservation clauses provided for in the Agreement are, in fact, prohibited reservation clauses.
4. Restrictions on the limitation of rights. The Agreement allows members to restrict IPRs where they would affect social welfare, prevention of abuse of rights, and other considerations. However, it also gives counter-restrictions which explicitly require that the restriction of rights shall not conflict with the regular use of rights, shall not reasonably prejudice the interests of the right holder, or shall not harm the legitimate interests of third parties.

18.3.4 Strengthening of IP Enforcement Procedures and Protective Measures

In order to encourage members to strengthen the implementation of the intellectual property protection system, the *TRIPS Agreement* stipulates specific obligations concerning administrative and judicial procedures, provisional measures, and border measures. It is a significant feature and an essential innovation of the Agreement, and it didn't exist in the international conventions governed by WIPO. Specifically, the main elements are as follows:

1. Judicial review system. Litigants have the right to seek judicial reviews of final decisions of an administrative nature, and also of legal issues that are at least judicially decided in the first instance of the case.
2. The civil procedures. It means the implementation of fair and impartial civil procedures. Members must protect the defendant's right to litigate, allow the parties to hire a lawyer to participate in the proceedings, guarantee the parties' right to proof, and identify and protect confidential information.

3. Damages. The judicial authority has the right to order the infringer to pay sufficient damages to the IPRs owner, to compensate for their loss.
4. Temporary measures. The judicial or administrative authorities, for "immediate infringement" and other foreseeable and not unfounded inferred infringement preparatory activities, must take "temporary measures", including pre-litigation injunction, property preservation, and preservation of evidence.
5. Border measures. This means Members' judicial or administrative authorities must take measures and their customs must enforce those measures to suspend the importing and exporting infringing products.

References

Gu, Zuxue. 2002. *International Intellectual Property Law*. Beijing: Law Press
Kong, Xiangjun. 2002. *The TRIPS Agreement of the WTO and its Domestic Application*. Beijing: Law Press
Xu, Ming. 1997. *Twenty-seven Problems to be Solved in Contemporary China*. Beijing: China Today Press
Zeng, Lingliang. 1996. *The WTO Law*. Wuhan: Wuhan University Press
Zhang, Hanlin and Huang, Wei. 1997. *The Guardian of Intellectual Property—A Comparative Study on the International Protection of Intellectual Property Rights*. Beijing: China Economic Press
Zheng, Chengsi. 1994. *Intellectual Property Rights in GATT and WTO: Detailed Explanation of the TRIPS*. Beijing: Beijing Press

Chapter 19
International Protection of IPRs and Human Rights

As a fundamental legal instrument of the WTO, the *TRIPS Agreement* establishes a new institutional framework for the international protection of IPRs. It is the most comprehensive international convention to date in terms of the scope and standard of IPRs protection, and may rightly be regarded as the "code of IPRs protection" (Cao 1999, p. 312). However, despite its core position in the international IPRs protection regime, the *TRIPS Agreement* has revealed certain deficiencies in its implementation. From the *Doha Declaration on the TRIPS Agreement and Public Health* (also known as the *Doha Declaration*) to the decision on the implementation of Paragraph 6 of the Declaration reached prior to the Cancún Ministerial Conference, it is evident that the legal framework of the *TRIPS Agreement* is continuously evolving and improving. This development is driven primarily by the conflict between IPRs and human rights, and by the need to achieve a balance between the two (Zhang 2004).

19.1 Conflicts Between International IPRs and International Human Rights

Since the advent of the post-*TRIPS Agreement* era, the international community has paid significant attention to the relationship between IPRs and human rights. In fact, IP issues in international trade and human rights issues in international politics have been described as two preeminent challenges in contemporary international relations. In 2000, the *UN Sub-Commission on the Promotion and Protection of Human Rights* issued the report *Intellectual Property and Human Rights*, which examined the implications of the *TRIPS Agreement* for international human rights. It declared:

> Since the implementation of the *TRIPS Agreement* does not adequately reflect the fundamental nature and totality of all human rights, including the right of everyone to acquire scientific progress and the benefits derived from there, the right to enjoy health care, the

H. Wu, *Theorising Intellectual Property Rights from Chinese Perspectives*,
https://doi.org/10.1007/978-981-96-5367-1_19

right to enjoy food, and the right to make decisions. There is an apparent conflict between the intellectual property regime in the *TRIPS Agreement* on the one hand and international human rights law on the other.[1]

The implementation of international IPR conventions should take complete account of the obligations stipulated in international human rights conventions. Furthermore, the social role of national legislation in protecting IPRs should be consistent with international human rights obligations. In accordance with international human rights standards, the international IPRs protection regime has the following actual or potential problems.

19.1.1 Moral Rights and Deficiencies in Author Protection

The recognition of creators' rights to receive moral and material interests from their intellectual work is an essential criterion for considering IPRs as human rights. The *Berne Convention* provides equal protection for the economic and moral rights of authors, i.e., "one right, two attributes", and stipulates that the protection period for the right to authorship and integrity of a work shall be no less than the protection period for economic rights. WIPO, in its 1994 Seminar on the Future of Copyright and Neighbouring Rights, noted that the *Berne Convention* protects both the moral rights of authors and their economic rights as "human rights." Therefore, it is consistent with the *Universal Declaration of Human Rights* (as cited in Zheng 1996, p. 96). While the *TRIPS Agreement* incorporates the substantive provisions of major international IPR conventions, such as the *Berne Convention,* which serves as the basis for the Agreement, it states: Members shall not have rights or obligations under this Agreement in respect of the rights conferred under Article 6bis of that Convention or of the rights derived therefrom.[2] This is an explicit exclusion of the moral rights protected by the *Berne Convention.* Arguably, the *TRIPS Agreement* accommodates the inherent traditions of the US copyright system, while departing from the long-standing propositions of international human rights law. This provision has two consequences. The first consequence is the imbalance of the right system. The *TRIPS Agreement* emphasises the protection of "trade-related" IPRs while ignoring the existence of "non-trade" IPRs, particularly those that cannot be measured economically. The second consequence is an imbalance between rights and obligations. Parties to the *TRIPS Agreement* and the *Berne Convention* are obligated to protect moral rights, while parties to the *TRIPS Agreement* alone can be exempt from that obligation because they are not parties to the *Berne Convention.* In this case, when the Agreement undermines moral rights, the dispute settlement mechanism of the WTO cannot be applied to it.

---

[1] See UN Commission in Human Rights: Intellectual Property and Human Rights, 2000, E/CN1.4/Sub.2/2000/7.

[2] See Article 9 of paragraph 1 of *the TRIPS Agreement.*

19.1.2 Freedom of Expression and Limitations to Exclusive Rights

Freedom of expression (i.e., the freedom to express ideas and opinions) is recognised by international human rights conventions as a political right to which citizens are entitled. Freedom of expression is closely related to copyright, as the information that the former involves—including news, knowledge, information, data, ideas, and opinions—can be regarded as works with exclusive rights. When the two legal interests' conflict with each other, how can the priority of their protections be determined? It is generally believed that freedom of expression occupies a prominent place in the system of fundamental human rights. Compared to economic freedom, freedom of expression is superior and regarded as a legal value of higher priority (Du 1995). It is recognised that freedom of expression precedes economic freedom in constitutional theories and practices. In this case, it means that the exclusive property of copyright should not constitute an obstacle to expression of ideas and exchange of information. In this regard, scholars argued that the protection afforded by copyright may act against unlawful competitors, but it must not obstruct the public's fair use of works and that the public dissemination of information is of such paramount importance that the public interest of a free and democratic society must not be subordinated to private exclusivity under traditional notions of copyright" (Rosenfield 1980, p. 302). Although fair use (or fair dealing) is a common feature of national copyright laws, a prevailing trend is the imposition of stringent counter-restrictions on the limitations of such exclusive rights at the international level. The *TRIPS Agreement* does not replicate the relevant provisions of the *Berne Convention* on fair use. Instead, it reiterates and underscores the strict conditions governing limitations and exceptions to exclusive rights, namely that such limitations or exceptions shall:

1. be confined to certain exceptional circumstances;
2. not conflict with the normal exploitation of the work; and
3. not unreasonably prejudice the legitimate interests of the right holder.

The 1996 *WIPO Internet Treaties* (WCT and WPPT) further extends these principles restricting fair use into cyberspace. While the provisions of these conventions mentioned above are stringent, they remain relatively general, leading to divergent interpretations among contracting parties as to what constitute permissible restrictions or exceptions. In general, developed countries have sought to impose stringent restrictions on the fair use of printed, electronic, and even digital works, whereas developing countries have focused on making more information available to the public through online technologies.

19.1.3 Privacy Rights and the Expansion of Database Rights

The privacy right is the right of citizens to be free from unlawful interference, disclosure, collection, utilisation, and dissemination of their private life tranquillity and personal information. It is recognized both as a personal right under civil law and a fundamental human right under international human rights law. Article 12 of the Universal Declaration of Human Rights states: "No one shall be subjected to arbitrary interference with others' privacy, family, home or correspondence", while Article 17 of the *International Covenant on Civil and Political Rights* (United Nations 1966) provides: "No one shall be subjected to arbitrary or unlawful interference with others' privacy, family, home or correspondence." The legislative rationale for privacy protection was stated in the 1973 report of the UN's Secretary-Respect entitled *Respect for Individual Privacy*: "Massive invasions of privacy are engaged in by both governmental and private organisations… Such practices inhibit free expression and make free discussion impossible." These actions create "a general sense of insecurity which inhibits spontaneity and the assumption of responsibility, and which produces conformity induced by fear" (as cited in Wang 1995, pp. 405–406).

Echoing the above-mentioned documents, scholars have summarised the meaning of privacy into three aspects:

1. Privacy interests protected by law, derived from constitutional freedom such as secrecy of correspondence;
2. Privacy interests based on the need for a life of dignity, seeking freedom from intrusion; and
3. Privacy interests concerning the control over one's personal data, necessitated by the prevalence and sophistication of modern automated information processing. (Xu 2001, p. 54).

Since the conceptualisation of privacy in the nineteenth century by Warren and Brandeis based on the legal protection of private correspondence, the right to privacy has evolved from a traditional negative right of "freedom from interference in personal life" to a modern positive right encompassing "informational privacy" and "data privacy." However, "society is not evolving in a direction favourable to the protection of citizens' personal privacy. On the contrary, advancements in modern technology, particularly electronic information technology, coupled with the profound and pervasive influence of mass media on civil life, have rendered the protection of citizens' right to privacy more urgent than ever." (Zhang 1997, p. 26). The key to the ethical foundation of privacy lies in the right to control information about oneself, but this right is increasingly jeopardised by technological advances.

The primary reason is that information has become a commodity in the information society. Data such as personal preferences, communication records, medical records, personality traits, credit reports, criminal records, and employment details can be digitally processed and stored in databases. Without effective control of the above information, personal privacy will be rendered transparent by information commercialisation. Information commercialisation in the field of IP revolves around the issue of databases. The international copyright community considers the protection for databases under compilation copyright as "weak protection", as third parties are generally free to use material from a compiled database to create a competing one. Under such circumstances, several developed countries are actively pursuing the establishment of a *sui generis* database protection regime—a distinct right separate from copyright—aimed at protecting the interests of database investors.[3] While the copyright community focuses on the reconciliation of interests between database investors and users, the conflict of rights between the sources of the database (i.e., the data subjects whose information is collected) and its database owners should be considered from the perspective of human rights. In essence, it is the conflict between the right to privacy and copyright (or the *sui generis* database right). The key to resolving the problem lies in strengthening the legal protection of personal data, specifically by expanding the scope of the right to privacy and granting citizens with the right to control personal data or the right to information self-determination. This entails the rights concerning the limitation of personal data collection, data accuracy, the right to access and correct data, the right to receive notification of data collection, and the right to be informed of the existence of data concerning oneself. The objective is not merely freedom from interference, but crucially, control and dominate over one's own data (Liu 1989, p. 214). In summary, while establishing database rights regimes to foster the development of the information industry, legislators must accord greater attention to the interests of the data subjects, who are the bearers of the right to privacy. Currently, special rights protection for databases is advancing on three levels: domestic protection that the US is attempting to establish, regional protection established by the EU, and international protection proposed by WIPO.

19.1.4 Right to Health and Obstacles to Accessing Pharmaceutical Patents

The right to health denotes the entitlement of living subjects to enjoy health recognised by law. Numerous international human rights conventions recognise it as a universally accepted human right. Article 25 of the *1948 Universal Declaration of Human Rights* states that everyone has the right to enjoy a standard of living adequate for the health and well-being of themselves and their family, including food, clothing, housing, medical care, and necessary social services. Article 12 of the 1966 *International Covenant on Economic, Social, and Cultural Rights* recognises the right of everyone to enjoy the highest attainable standard of physical and mental health, and sets out targeted steps to be taken by the parties for the full realisation of this

---

[3] At present, the special rights protection of database is advancing at three levels, namely the domestic protection that the US tries to establish, the regional protection already established by the European Union, and the international protection proposed by the WIPO. See Xue (2000, p. 94).

right. According to international human rights standards, the current IPRs regime negatively impacts the realisation of the right to health (Chapman 2001).

Firstly, due to the monopolistic nature of patent rights, right holders can control the production and distribution of pharmaceuticals. As a result, the exorbitant prices of patented medicines are often beyond the financial capacity of impoverished patients, thus impeding access to treatment for residents of less developed countries. Secondly, due to restrictive conditions of patent enforcement, rights holders can obstruct others from accessing pharmaceutical patent technology, and even restrict developing countries and their people from obtaining compulsory licensing with the support of their governments. Thirdly, driven by the profit-driven nature of patent rights, R&D investors in the pharmaceutical industry primarily targets diseases promising the highest market returns, without taking into account the needs of developing countries. Fourthly, as patents are granted for novel products that have therapeutic effects similar to existing patented medicines, the production and distribution of certain types of patented medicines become increasingly concentrated among a few corporations. These circumstances demonstrate an apparent conflict between the patent rights of creators of new medicines and the right to health of the consumers of those medicines. UN human rights experts assert that both rights are valuable in their own contexts and are recognised by the international community. Nevertheless, following the principle of the precedence of human rights, certain human rights may take priority over others in specific situations (Vilamandri 1997, pp. 209–210). Specifically, those products which are essential for human life and well-being must, once created, become the property of the humankind as a whole, with the proviso that the creator is entitled to remuneration. In such exceptional cases, the right to health should precede IPRs, including patent rights.

Amidst disputes concerning patents and public health, and following concerted efforts by Third World nations, the WTO Ministerial Conference adopted the *Doha Declaration on the TRIPS Agreement and Public Health* (Doha Declaration) in January 2001. At the Conference, appeals from developing countries, represented by South Africa, to respect the right to life and the right to health, and safeguard the public interest, received a constructive response from developed countries in the field of IP. The Doha Declaration recognises the seriousness of the public health problems that afflict many developing and least-developed countries (LDCs), stresses the importance of IPRs protection for the development of new medicines while acknowledging concerns about the impact of such protection on prices, and agrees that the *TRIPS Agreement* should not be a barrier that prevents parties from taking measures to protect public health. The measures to protect public health are facilitated through an interpretative clarification of the *TRIPS Agreement*'s flexible provisions about public interests:

1. Members have the right to grant compulsory licences and the freedom to determine the grounds upon which such licences are granted.
2. Members have the right to determine what constitutes a national emergency or other circumstances of extreme urgency, including public health crises relating to HIV/AIDS, tuberculosis, malaria and other epidemics.

3. Members have the right to establish their own regime for the exhaustion of intellectual property rights, subject to the provisions on most-favoured-nation and national treatment.
4. Developed countries are obliged to provide incentives to their enterprises and institutions to promote technology transfer to least-developed countries. Least-developed countries were granted an extension until 2016 to provide patent protection for pharmaceuticals.

The adoption of the Doha Declaration marked a significant event in international intellectual property. By upholding the principle of public interest and employing the precedence of human rights to reconcile the conflict between pharmaceutical patents and the right to health, the Declaration represents a crucial adjustment to the intellectual property regime in the post-TRIPS era.

19.1.5 Right to Development and Impediments to Transfer of Proprietary Technology

The right to development is a vital element of third-generation human rights or collective human rights. According to *the International Covenants on Human Rights* (1966), it is the right of all peoples to "freely pursue their economic, social, and cultural development", reflecting the emergence of the Third World nationalism and its demand for a global distribution of power, wealth, and other essential resources (Xia 1993, p. 116). The 1974 *Charter of Economic Rights and Duties of States* interpreted the right to development as a universal right: "every state has the right to share the benefits of scientific and technological progress to enhance its economic and social development." The right to development is particularly urgent and essential for developing countries, and the Charter requires that "all states should promote international scientific and technological co-operation and the transfer of technology" and "assist developing countries in the establishment… of advanced technology". However, the right to development in developing countries has yet to be fully realised in the international IPRs protection system. The *International Conference on the Establishment of an International Code on the Transfer of Technology*, held in Geneva in 1978, failed to reach an agreement between developed and developing countries partly due to divergent interests concerning IPRs. Conversely, the entry into force of the *TRIPS Agreement* in 1994 achieved the strategic goal of developed countries to establish a higher standard, firmly enforced global IPRs regime, thereby further maintaining the technological advantage of developed countries in international trade—a technological advantage underpinned by IPRs. Statistics show that in the global economy, industrialised countries currently hold 97% of all patents worldwide, and multinational corporations in developed countries earn 70% of copyrights and licensing revenues (as cited in Chapman 2001). Although the *TRIPS Agreement* provides for the promotion of technology transfer and knowledge dissemination in principle, and emphasises that developed countries should encourage their enterprises and institutions to transfer technology to LDCs, the facts after the implementation of the Agreement have shown that these principles largely unrealised. International human rights experts argue that under conditions of high-levels IPRs protection, the primary beneficiaries are often foreign multinational corporations, with no guarantee of stimulating local research and innovation. Moreover, because developing countries often lack the infrastructure and capacity to utilise advanced technologies effectively, they cannot fully share the benefits of scientific and technological advances, thereby their disadvantaged position regarding social development (Chapman 2001).

19.2 Coordination Between International IPRs and International Human Rights

Human rights issues in international politics and IP issues in international trade and commerce are two focal points in contemporary international society. Noticeable conflicts exist between the extant international IPRs protection regime and the international human rights regime. Such conflicts necessitate resolution through international legal regulation to achieve equilibrium, that is, "the establishment of an intellectual property system consistent with human rights objectives" (Zheng 2006, p. 18). While dealing with the relationship between IPRs and human rights, the following two basic principles must be pursued:

19.2.1 Principle of Primacy of Legally Protected Interests

The principle of priority protection of legal interests dictates that when conflicts arise between different legal interests in the system of rights or interests, the legal interests with fundamental values should be protected in priority over others. Human rights—whether inalienable freedoms that are indispensable for the existence of human beings as subjects, or conditions necessary for human survival and development—constitute fundamental human rights. Relative to intellectual property rights, which are proprietary in nature, these fundamental human rights occupy the highest echelon within the hierarchy of rights. In 2000, the UN Sub-Commission on the Promotion and Protection of Human Rights reminded governments of the primacy of human rights obligations over economic policies and agreements in its adopted *Resolution on Intellectual Property Rights and Human Rights*.[4] This provision signifies that human rights obligations take precedence over IPRs obligations. Specifically, IP, being a private property right or an instrument of government economic policy, lacks binding legal force when it conflicts with human rights obligations and must yield to the latter, which are imperative. The aforementioned principles are

[4] See UN Commission in Human Rights: *Intellectual Property and Human Rights*, 2000, E/CN1.4/Sub.2/2000/7.

clearly defined in international law. Article 103 of the *UN Charter* stipulates that the obligations undertaken by Member States under the Charter shall take precedence over their obligations assumed under other international treaties. This means that international human rights law occupies a superior legal hierarchy to other bodies of international laws. Consequently, modern IP law must conform not only to the provisions of international IPR conventions, but also to international human rights conventions.

19.2.2 Principle of Interest Balancing

The principle of balance of interests dictates that in a system of rights or interests, equilibrium should be sought between conflicting legal interests in order to achieve a balanced and harmonious development of all such interests, thereby achieving a balance of rights. Article 15 of the *International Covenant on Economic, Social and Cultural Rights* enumerates three rights that party states must recognise, namely the right of everyone to take part in cultural life, the right to enjoy the benefits of scientific progress and its applications, and the right to benefit from the protection of the moral and material interests resulting from any scientific, literary or artistic production of which he or she is the author. It is thus clear that the international human rights conventions, while recognising the rights of creators, also emphasise the rights of the public to participate in cultural life and to benefits from knowledge creation. It is contended that in the traditional human rights system, IPR is a human right; moreover, private property right, including IPR, constitutes a fundamental right for the realisation of other human rights. This is an essential precondition in the quest for coordination between these rights. Following the principle of interest balancing, the IPRs regime should delineate a reasonable scope of private exclusivity that will stimulate creators' incentive for intellectual innovation whilst simultaneously ensuring that the fruits of intellectual progress are shared by society at large. Therefore, regarding knowledge products, the distribution of benefits among parties and between individuals and society should be in line with the value of fairness. IPRs should be conducive to the realisation of human rights and should develop in harmony with them (Torremans 2004). At the institutional level, this is linked to some rights restrictions and utilisation systems. This signifies that, for the sake of public interest and out of respect for fundamental human rights, IPRs should be restricted under certain circumstances to ensure reasonable public access to and utilisation of intellectual products.

The conflict between IPRs and human rights has garnered great concern among international organisations and triggered profound reflection among most countries on the deficiencies of the *TRIPS Agreement*, and a strong impetus to reform the international IPRs protection regime. It can be argued that following the principles of "priority protection of legal interests" and "balance of interests", coordinating the relationship between IPRs and human rights and balancing the interests of developed and developing countries will be pivotal themes in the reform of the contemporary international IPRs protection regime. The *Doha Declaration* adopted by the WTO Ministerial Conference addressed the resolution of issues concerning public health and the utilisation of IPRs. This represents a significant milestone, albeit merely an initial step; the task of institutional reform in the post-TRIPS era remains substantial.

Presently, politicians and scholars globally have proposed various recommendations and conceptual frameworks to resolve the conflicts between the international IPRs protection regime and international human rights protection regime. It is suggested that the international community should direct its attention to the following issues:

Taking Legal Measures to Enhance Human Rights Rules

International human rights conventions must transcend their current state of "soft law" characterised by the absence of implementation rules and safeguards. Indeed, the legally binding force of international IPR conventions also underwent a development process. During the pre-TRIPS period, relevant international conventions mainly provided for substantive aspects of international IPRs protection. However, they were less concerned with the provisions of implementation procedures, particularly lacking essential enforcement measures and dispute settlement mechanisms. Consequently, so some treaties remained "soft laws" with insufficient legally binding force (Sun 2002). For the first time, the WTO's *TRIPS Agreement* translates enforcement procedures of IPRs protection, which are traditionally matters of domestic legislation, into binding international rules under the convention. As a result, these procedural rules, alongside substantive norms, became international obligations that contracting parties are bound to implement rigorously. Thus, the traditional "soft law" acquired potent legal enforceability. In contrast, human rights conventions are mostly declarative, largely flexible, and contain many flexible mechanisms. Reform of the international human rights regime should progress in the following two directions.

Firstly, the justification of economic, social, and cultural rights should be accelerated. The impact of IPRs on human rights will undoubtedly prompt human rights bodies to develop a transparent and explicitly interpretable set of rights rules within the framework of international human rights instruments in order to counter the precise and refined set of rules in *the TRIPS Agreement* (Zheng 2006).

Secondly, the legal responsibility of states parties for breaches of international human rights obligations should be strengthened. Within the framework of international human rights conventions, the original non-coercive human rights responsibilities, based on "encouragement, promotion, and recommendations", should be replaced by enforceable and mandatory human rights measures. States parties should be required to adopt domestic legislation to guarantee the realisation of human rights, akin to their obligations concerning IPRs protection. At the same time, the Agreement provides legal consequences for violations of human rights obligations: international human rights bodies can provide "equitable remedies" for victims of IPRs abuses when these abuses undermine human rights. According to international human rights scholars, "equitable remedies" for human rights harm include investigation of violations, compensation or other reparations, termination of violations, deterrence of subsequent violations, and revision of the law of the violating state.[5]

Protecting the Public's Right to Utilise Intellectual Products

Public utilisation of intellectual products is both an exercise of their fundamental human rights and a restriction on the IPRs of others. In international conventions on IP, fundamental human rights such as public health, economic development, freedom of expression, and public education all involve the issue of public interests. The primary way to realise the public interest is to balance the interests of the right holder and the public interest. Concerning the relationship between the two, American scholars have pointed out that the existence of IPRs should benefit the public interest first and the rights holders themselves second (Chapman 2001). In the implementation of the *TRIPS Agreement*, the principle of non-discriminatory "national treatment" and the high level of "minimum standards of protection" has been strongly implemented in various countries, while the public interest principle has been unduly neglected. Given this, the international community must improve two aspects: First, improve the behavioural norms for the restriction and utilisation of IPRs and provide necessary restrictions and reasonable use of privatised IPRs; and second, refine the rules of the public's rights to use intellectual products, so that the "right to participate" and the "right to share" in the general sense become "user's rights" in the sense of private rights.[6]

Promoting Reform of the International Intellectual Property System

The future trajectory of the international IPRs protection regime must involve reform and innovation. In the post-TRIPS era, the international community must address the following issues: Firstly, deficiencies in the system of limitation and exceptions require rectification. The aforementioned public health issues, technology transfer and utilisation, and full public access to information need to be addressed through the revision of international conventions. Secondly, the expansion of the rights system must be curbed. Some developed countries have reached so-called *"TRIPS-plus Agreement"* through bilateral negotiation, seeking additional benefits or concessions exceeding the protection standards of the *TRIPS Agreement*. This elevation of IPRs protection standards risks exacerbating the imbalance of interests in the

[5] According to international human rights scholars, the "equitable remedy" measures related to human rights damage, comprising infringement investigation, compensation or other compensation, termination of the infringement, prevention of subsequent infringement, and revision of the laws of the infringing country. See Godshall (2003, p. 497).

[6] American scholars refer to the interests of knowledge products in which others enjoy exclusive rights as the rights of users, along with the rights of creators and the rights disseminators. Representative works including Goldstein (1989), Patterson and Lindberg (1991).

international IP field, and the international community and international human rights institutions must act to curb this trend. Thirdly, breakthroughs are required concerning novel property regimes. New forms of property rights, such as those for traditional knowledge and genetic resources, have attracted significant attention from some international organisations. WIPO has set up a special unit to conduct research on this issue, and the WTO has convened dedicated meetings to address it. Besides, the protection of traditional knowledge and genetic resources has been widely discussed in international forums on human rights, culture, trade, food and agriculture, indigenous rights, labour standards, sustainable development, land, environment, and biodiversity, involving international organisations such as UNESCO, the United Nations Environment Programme, the Food and Agriculture Organisation of the United Nations, the United Nations Conference on Money and Development, the United Nations Development Programme and the World Health Organisation. However, this issue has yet to receive a positive response from some developed countries; more concerted efforts from the international community are needed to transform relevant protection measures into universally observed international rules.

References

Cao, Jianming. 1999. *World Trade Organisation*. Beijing: Law Press

Chapman, Audrey R. 2001. Taking intellectual property rights as human rights: Obligations related to paragraph 1(3) of Article 15. Trans. Yuewei Liu. *Copyright Bulletin* 3

Du, Gangjian. 1995. On the principles of the guarantee of freedom of expression. *Chinese and Foreign Law* 2

Godshall, Lauren E. 2003. Making space for indigenous intellectual property rights under current international environment law. *Georgetown International Environmental Law Review* 15

Goldstein, Paul. 1989. *Copyright Principles: Law and Practice*. Kentucky: Little, Brown and Company Limited

Liu, Jiangbin. 1989. *On Information Law*. Taipei: San Min Book Co., Ltd.

Patterson, L. Ray and Lindberg, Stanley W. 1991. *The Nature of Copyright: A Law of Users' Right*. Georgia: The University of Georgia Press

Rosenfieid, Harry N. 1980. T*he American Constitution, Free Inquiry, and the Law, Fair Use and Free Inquiry*. New York: Ablex Publishing Co.

Sun, Haochen. 2002. WTO and WIPO: Discussion on conflict factors and cooperation opportunities in the framework of the *TRIPS Agreement*. *Comparative Law Research* 2

Torremans, Paul L.G. 2004. *Copyright and Human Right*. Kluwer Law International

United Nations. 1966. International covenant on civil and political rights

United Nations. 1999. The United Nations development programme: The human development report 1999

Villamandri, C. G. 1997. *Human Rights and the Development of Science and Technology*. Beijing: Knowledge Press

Wang, Liming. 1995. *Personality Right and Infringement of News*. Beijing: China Founder Publishing House

Xia, Xudong et al. 1993. World human rights. Beijing: Current Affairs Press

Xu, Wenyi. 2001. *On the Law on the Protection of Personal Data*. Taipei: San Min Book Co., Ltd.

Xue, Hong. 2000. *Intellectual Property Law in the Internet Age*. Beijing: Law Press

Yan, Yonghe. 2006. *On the Protection of Intellectual Property Rights of Traditional Knowledge.* Beijing: Law Press
Zhang, Naigen. 2004. On the relationship between intellectual property rights and human rights under the framework of *the TRIPS Agreement. Jurist* 4
Zhang, Xinbao. 1997. *The Legal Protection of Privacy*. Beijing: Mass Publishing House
Zheng, Chengsi. 1996. *WTO's IPRs Related to Trade.* Beijing: Renmin University of China Press
Zheng, Wanqing. 2006. *Intellectual Property Rights and Human Rights Under Globalisation.* Beijing: Intellectual Property Press

Chapter 20
International IP Lawmaking in the Post-TRIPS Era

Intellectual property (IP) has emerged as a focal issue of international attention today, and the main institutional basis of the knowledge-based economy. Globally, with the expansion of economic, scientific, and cultural exchanges among various countries, the IPRs protection system has evolved into a universally binding set of rules governing cross-border interactions. The entry into force of the WTO's *TRIPS Agreement* has directly integrated IPRs from the traditional field of intellectual creation into the international economic and trade order, and marked a new stage of high-level IPRs protection. Although the *TRIPS Agreement* has been effectively implemented and is recognised as "the most important IPRs treaty of the twentieth century", it remains "the most controversial international convention" in modern jurisprudence (Drahos and Braithwaite 2002, p. 452). In the post-TRIPS era, developed and developing countries have put forward their respective new demands for the equitable allocation of IPRs benefits. This has engendered extensive multilateral consultations concerning the *TRIPS Agreement*, as well as the proliferation of bilateral and multilateral protection mechanisms operating beyond the agreement. Such developments reflect a transformative shift in the international IPRs protection system. Against this backdrop, it is imperative to adopt a holistic, strategic, and forward-looking approach in analysing critical issues arising from the international IP legislation. Concurrently, there exists a pressing need to formulate coherent policy responses to optimize China's engagement with the evolving global IP regime. This undertaking carries substantial practical significance for contemporary legal and economic governance.

H. Wu, *Theorising Intellectual Property Rights from Chinese Perspectives*,
https://doi.org/10.1007/978-981-96-5867-1_20

20.1 Multipolarisation and Fragmentation of International IP Lawmaking

In the post-TRIPS era, particularly in the new century, developed and developing countries have held divergent positions and attitudes regarding the implementation of the *TRIPS Agreement*. Developing countries have raised concerns over the rationality and appropriateness of the Agreement in its enforcement. In 2003, the United Nations Development Programme (UNDP) issued a report on the global trading system, stating that "the appropriateness of *the TRIPS Agreement* for much of the developing world is highly questionable", and recommended that developing countries initiate dialogue on "adopting alternative IPRs paradigms to replace *the TRIPS Agreement,* and during a transitional period, revise the methods by which *the TRIPS Agreement* is interpreted and implemented" (Helfer 2004). In contrast, developed countries have criticised the effectiveness of the implementation of the Agreement, and expressed dissatisfaction with the prescribed standards of protection. They have sought to establish new international conventions with higher protection thresholds and stricter enforcement mechanisms, circumventing the *TRIPS Agreement* by advancing new global standards through regional and bilateral agreements. Specifically, the post-TRIPS era has witnessed the following trends in international IP legislation:

20.1.1 Negotiation on New International Treaties

Since the turn of the century, international organisations such as the World Trade Organisation (WTO), the World Intellectual Property Organisation (WIPO), the International Union of New Varieties of Plants (UPOV), the Asia–Pacific Economic Cooperation (APEC), and the Asia-Europe Meeting (ASEM) have conducted a series of multilateral consultations and negotiations on the reform of IPRs regime. However, the WTO Doha Round negotiations failed to reach consensus on critical issues such as public health, geographical indications, genetic resources, and traditional knowledge. Meanwhile, WIPO's initiative to enhance protections for audiovisual performers under the existing copyright framework led to the signing of the *Beijing Treaty on Audiovisual Performances* (the *Beijing Treaty*) in June 2012 with the support of over 50 countries. Nevertheless, the multilateral consultation mechanisms of existing international organisations have achieved limited breakthroughs in advancing international IP legislation.

Against this backdrop, developed countries have pursued "regime shifting", engaging in IP treaty negotiations among themselves to further raise the standard of IPRs protection. A notable example is *the Anti-Counterfeiting Trade Agreement* (ACTA), adopted by the European Parliament in 2011 under U.S. leadership, with active participation from the EU, Japan, Canada, Australia, Switzerland, and South Korea. This agreement aimed to "combat copyright and trademark infringement."

The United Nations Economic Development Organisation estimates that the global trade in counterfeit and pirated goods has surged from USD100 billion in 2000 to USD 250 billion in 2007. ACTA introduced stricter, more detailed and explicit provisions on IPRs protection across six key areas, including civil enforcement, criminal enforcement, border measures, information sharing, international cooperation, and enforcement supervision. In essence, ACTC is a new international treaty with a strong stance in IPRs protection. However, from its drafting to provisional adoption, the agreement lacked meaningful participation from developing countries. Rather than serving as a post-TRIPS instrument for global IP harmonisation, it functioned more as a trade weapon wielded by developed countries against developing countries. Proponents of ACTA sought to persuade major developing countries, particularly China and Russia, to accede to the agreement, thereby elevating its standards from a multilateral to a truly international level, akin to the *TRIPS Agreement*. Although ACTA did not enter into force, primarily due to opposition within the EU, it signalled a broader trend, that is, developed countries are increasingly bypassing multilateral frameworks such as the WTO and WIPO, opting instead for regional or bilateral negotiations with like-minded countries to establish new rules that exceed the *TRIPS Agreement*.

20.1.2 Resurgence of Regional and Bilateral Agreements

The international law-making process for IPRs, outside the WTO system, has primarily advanced through free trade agreements (FTAs), facilitated by regional and bilateral negotiations. FTAs—a predominant form of bilateral and regional trade arrangements—have long existed since the inception of General Agreement on Tariffs and Trade (GATT), the predecessor to the WTO. As exceptions to international trade rules, FTAs achieve partial market liberalization through intergovernmental negotiations. Their underlying principle of "internal liberalisation and external protection" often conflicts with the WTO's most-favoured-nation (MFN) principle (Yang 2013, p. 9). Nevertheless, FTAs serve the general purpose of promoting free trade within specific regions, complementing the multilateral system and the global liberalisation process. For this reason, the designers of the GATT framework conditionally recognised the legitimacy of free trade areas.[1]

Since the turn of the century, the WTO has made concerted efforts to advance multilateralism and global free trade, yet with little success. Meanwhile, the resurgence of regional and bilateral FTAs has emerged as a dominant force in the global economy. According to the *World Trade Report 2011*, WTO members have signed over 300 bilateral and regional FTAs outside the WTO framework. In the process of regional trade integration, the US and the EU have been playing pivotal or leading roles. Guided by the principle of "America First," the US has adopted a

[1] For the terms of the legality of free trade zones, see Article 24 of *the GATT* (1947) and Article 24 of *the GATT* (1994).

multi-pronged trade policy of multilateral, regional, and bilateral negotiations. By concluding bilateral and regional FTAs, it seeks to establish an "American model" of regional economic integration, thereby securing dominance in the formulation of international trade rules, including those governing international IPRs protection. The EU, as the largest and most integrated regional economic and trade organisation in the world today, has significantly recalibrated its trade policy in response to the stagnation of multilateral negotiations. Adopting an FTA strategy aimed at enhancing its global competitiveness, the EU has entered into agreements with over 50 external partners, setting a benchmark for regional economic integration. Most of these regional and bilateral FTAs—mostly "package deals" on trade rules, investment provisions, and IPRs protection—effectively setting new trends in international IP law-making, and are likely to influence the future evolution of the international IPRs protection system. The following are key regional agreements worth noting:

1. NAFTA and USMCA

The US, Mexico and Canada signed the *North American Free Trade Agreement* (NAFTA) in August 1992, establishing what was then the world's largest regional free trade organisation, and pioneering the linkage of investment, trade and IPRs within a single trade agreement (Zhan 2016). In November 2018, the US reached a new trade agreement with Mexico and Canada, the *United States-Mexico-Canada Agreement* (USMCA), the text of which includes over 30 chapters covering market access, agriculture, trade remedies, investment, digital trade, dispute settlement, and IPRs and other areas.

2. TPP and CPTPP

The Trans-Pacific Partnership (TPP), known as the "economic NATO," stands as a significant free trade bloc in the Asia–Pacific region. 12 pan-Pacific countries, including the US and Japan, finalised the TPP on 5 October 2015, and signed it on 4 February 2016. In March 2018, the US under the Trump administration withdrew from the TPP, leaving Japan to assume leadership. On 30 December 2018, the *Comprehensive and Progressive Trans-Pacific Partnership* (CPTPP) came into force, incorporating amendments to the original text. The US-led TPP introduced TRIPS-plus provisions that exceeded conventional IPRs protection standards. Examples include:

- Trademarks: Registrability not contingent on visual perceptibility; protection of well-known marks irrespective of registration; validity of trademark licences not subject to record;
- Patents: Extension of patentability to new uses of known products, novel methods or processes for using products; enhanced protection for experimental data; supplementary protection periods for pharmaceutical patents.
- Copyright: Extended protection terms; recognition of temporary reproduction rights for authors; performers and producers of phonograms; and the right of communication to the public for performers and phonogram producers.

- Enforcement: Stricter border measures, disclosure of infringement information, disposal of infringing goods, and criminal penalties.

These provisions reflect the evolving demands of developed countries in international IP legislation. Although the CPTPP later modified certain IP clauses, the parties indicated that once the US rejoin, the original TPP standards would be reinstated.

3. Rcep

The *Regional Comprehensive Economic Partnership* (RCEP), initiated by ASEAN in 2012, comprises 16 parties: 10 ASEAN member states, China, Japan, South Korea, India, Australia and New Zealand. The agreement aims to establish a unified free trade area by reducing tariff and non-tariff barriers. Beyond addressing market access for goods, services, and investment, RCEP also covers IPRs, e-commerce and legal mechanisms. China has actively participated in and promoted RCEP negotiations, contributing to economic globalisation and regional economic integration, including the evolution of international IPRs protection rules.

20.1.3 Rise of "South-South Cooperation" in IP Among Developing Countries

Developing countries have actively engaged in "South-South cooperation," seeking international IPRs protection strategies that align with their interests in areas where they hold comparative advantages, such as genetic resources, traditional knowledge, and knowledge-sharing.

Developing countries have pursued a human rights-based approach to interpreting IPRs, aiming to establish a development path that is in harmony with their economies, societies and cultures. In recent years, thanks to the efforts of developing countries to secure their development space, the concept and initiatives of coordinated and harmonious development have gradually gained recognition and attention within the international community. The United Nations Economic and Social Council (ECOSOC), as the promoter and interpreter of the *International Covenant on Economic, Social and Cultural Rights* (ICESCR), proposed for the first time in 2001 to interpret IPRs from the perspective of human rights, and issued the *Report on Human Rights and IPRs*, which initially analysed the significance of the Covenant for IPRs and advocated that IPRs should be viewed within the broader framework of economic and social rights. In 2006, the Council further commented on the relationship between IPRs and human rights. It emphasised that human rights are fundamental and inherent to people, noting the distinction between the rights outlined in the International Covenant on Economic, Social and Cultural Rights (ICESCR) and other human rights on one hand, and most rights recognised under the IPRs protection system on the other. In contrast, IPRs are a tool for states to incentivise innovation and encourage the dissemination of knowledge.[2] These documents and reports contain fair critiques of the *TRIPS Agreement* and the expansion of IPRs, while also acknowledging common goals and other similarities between human rights and IPRs regimes.

Through UNESCO, developing countries have advocated for greater attention to the importance of "cultural diversity." In October 2005, UNESCO adopted the *Convention on the Protection and Promotion of the Diversity of Cultural Expressions* (the *Cultural Diversity Convention*). The Convention, which was initiated mainly by Francophone developed and developing countries, initially aimed to unite Francophone countries in preserving their own distinctive cultural traditions. The Convention asserts that the protection of cultural diversity respects human rights, such as freedom of expression, information and communication, and the principle of openness and balance, manifested in the protection of national cultures and the acceptance of foreign cultures. Enhancing the flow of cultural goods and services between countries can promote cultural diversity and the development of a country's domestic cultural industries. The key controversy during the development of the Convention, and the reason why the US strongly opposed the Convention, was the establishment of a definition of "cultural diversity." The US believes that the *Cultural Diversity Convention* could lead to the misuse of the concept in certain countries, thereby contravening the objectives of UNESCO. The Convention allows signatory parties to implement differential treatment in the production, distribution, dissemination, and consumption of domestic cultural products, which contradicts the *TRIPS Agreement*'s advocacy for free trade. The Convention can be regarded as an attempt by developing countries to protect their cultural industries and to construct their own IP systems that are in line with their developmental stages.

Leveraging the influence of non-governmental organisations (NGOs), developing countries have sought to address their "public health" challenges. In 2005, international NGOs, public health experts, economists, and jurists proposed the *Medical Research and Development Treaty (Draft)* at the World Health Assembly. The draft treaty aimed to establish a new legal framework to move beyond established pharmaceutical patents and monopolies, promoting medical research and development, equitable cost-sharing for pharmaceutical research and development among governments, and the sharing of medical innovations with developing countries. On IPRs protection, the *Draft Treaty* required contracting states to set minimum exceptions for patents involving pharmaceutical research, and stipulated that inventions derived from public-domain materials should not be patented for a specified period. At the same time, to ensure smooth adoption and implementation, the *Draft Treaty* also alignment with other international conventions and expressed deference to the *TRIPS Agreement* in resolving intellectual property disputes. While the treaty's remains uncertain, it reflects the efforts of developing countries to address the need for IPRs protection in the field of pharmaceuticals and public health.

Using WIPO as a platform, developing countries have actively sought to transform the focus of international IP legislation from "promoting IPRs protection" to

[2] See Committee on Economic, Social and Cultural Rights Thirty-fifth Session Geneva,7–25 November 2005 *General Comment* No.17(2005) E/C.12/GC/17, January, 2006.

"fostering creativity through non-proprietary means." In light of the *TRIPS Agreement*'s adverse effects, developing countries have increasingly turned to WIPO to advance their positions on international IP legislation. In October 2004, the WIPO General Assembly adopted a proposal from Argentina and Brazil to establish a new "Development Agenda" reflecting the perspectives of the "Friends of Development" group (an organisation of developing countries) and other non-governmental organisations., The outcome of these efforts was the *Geneva Declaration*, which asserted that humanity is facing a global crisis in the management of knowledge, technology, and culture. Accordingly, WIPO should work to prevent the expansion of monopolistic privileges in the field of IP and focus on the following key issues: (1) the economic and social costs of IPRs protection; (2) the reform of existing IPRs rules; (3) non-proprietary innovation mechanisms, such as Wikipedia, Creative Commons, free software, and distance-learning tools. Additionally, within this "Development Agenda," another initiative concerning IPRs in developing countries emerged, namely the *Access to Knowledge Treaty* advocated by some NGO representatives. The *Access to Knowledge Treaty* (The *A2K Treaty*) is an important outcome of the "Access to Knowledge Movement."

In contrast to the "minimum standard of protection" upheld by existing international IP conventions, the *Draft Treaty* advocates for "maximum standards of protection," seeking to impose limits on the expansion of IPRs. The ultimate aim of such restrictions is to ensure that public goods such as culture and education can benefit from the progress brought about by IP.

20.2 Global Trends in IP Legislation and China's Position

The establishment of the international IPRs protection regime possesses a certain historical inevitability. Although the *TRIPS Agreement* was propelled by developed countries and their industrial interest groups, it is also the outcome of cooperation between developed and developing countries. Objectively, it reflects, to a certain extent, the inherent demands of the development of the global knowledge-based economy. The current landscape of international IP legislation features two central frameworks, WIPO and the WTO, alongside a pluralistic legislative mechanism of regional/bilateral FTAs. For developing countries, seeking discursive power and seizing the initiative is their fundamental position in participating in international legislative activities.

The conduct of international IP rule-making through regional/bilateral FTAs has emerged as a defining feature of the international transformation of IPRs in the post-TRIPS era. This phenomenon, characterised by regime-shifting, novel issue areas, and dynamic mechanisms, serves as a significant complement to the WTO's legislative framework and the *TRIPS Agreement*'s international rules. Simultaneously, it poses challenges to the established centralised systems and their standardised norms.

First, the diversification of participants in the legislative process marks a key trend in IPRs regime shifting. Under traditional IPRs regimes, IP legislation was predominantly the domain of sovereign states, with the WTO and WIPO serving as central legislative bodies.

In the post-TRIPS era, while these two major international organisations retain their dominant roles, and have established mechanisms for division of labour and cooperation,[3] many other international organisations and legislative institutions have also taken a keen interest in IP issues. Consequently, the legislative framework has shifted from a "centralised" regime to a "pluralistic" one. This transition is largely attributable to the rise of non-state actors—including alliances, private groups, transnational networks, and non-governmental organisations (Yu 2009)—which have become pivotal players in international IP legislation. Second, another trend in IP regime shifting is the expansion of the scope of subject matters of protection. Although the *TRIPS Agreement* remains the international treaty with the highest standards, broadest scope, and strongest effect of protection, its provisions suffer from a legislative lag, failing to accommodate subsequent technological advancements, new knowledge forms, and emerging industries. Many regional/bilateral FTAs have addressed this gap by legislating on novel subject matter such as genetic resources, business methods, experimental data, domain names, character images, and data programming, thereby providing a constructive supplement to the *TRIPS Agreement.*

Thirdly, interactive institutional arrangements are increasingly adopted in international IP legislation. Negotiations under FTAs frequently employ issue linkage and trade-offs to reconcile competing interests the interests of all parties, ultimately yielding IP-related institutional arrangements (Yang 2013, p. 17). This pragmatic and utilitarian orientation underlying institutional choices has given rise to various "TRIPS-Plus provisions." These include not only the high-standard IP protections advocated by developed countries—such as expanded subject matter eligibility, enhanced content of rights, extended period of protection, stricter enforcement, and narrower limitations and exceptions—but also provisions promoted by developing countries concerning the supplementary IPRs protection regarding traditional knowledge, genetic resources, folklore, access to essential medicines, and alternative innovation models.

China, the world's largest developing country and an important member of the WTO, possesses the world's most rapidly expanding domestic market of considerable scale, a large pool of IP professionals, and formidable capabilities in international negotiations. It is thus incumbent upon China to actively engage in the formulation of international IP rules. This constitutes both an international obligation befitting China's role as a responsible major power and a matter of strategic significance in projecting its soft power on the global stage. The author proposes that China ought to adopt the following strategies in international IP legislation:

Firstly, China must adhere to its fundamental stance as a developing-country. During the negotiations for its accession to the WTO, there was considerable debate within the international community regarding whether China should be classified as a developing or a developed country. China's accession to the WTO as a developing

[3] In 1995, the WTO and WIPO reached a consensus on a series of cooperation issues on intellectual property issues.

country was not only a political decision, but also a reflection of its economic conditions at that time (Liang 2012). Although remarkable economic progress has been made over the past decades since its WTO accession, China's GDP per capita and composite socio-economic development indicators remain comparatively modest, situating it within the ranks of developing countries. This underscores that upholding the position of a developing country and representing the interests and collective will of the broader developing world is an imperative in China's participation in the formulation of international IP rules.

Secondly, China should forge a strong IP national image. Today, China has taken a position of considerable influence in global politics, economics, science and technology, culture, and education. The second decade of the twenty-first century marks a critical period in China's transition form a big country to a leading global force. In the international IP arena, China must establish its image as a major power, leverage its negotiating prowess to safeguard its legitimate interests, and strive to establish a more equitable and rational international IP legal order for the benefit of developing countries.

Thirdly, China ought to assume a leading role among developing countries. Brazil, India and other countries have been very active in international IP affairs, emerging as the "frontrunners" amongst developing countries in the fight against the "imposition" of IPRs regimes by developed countries. Whether during the negotiations of the *TRIPS Agreement* or in the subsequent meetings of the *TRIPS Agreement* Council, these major developing countries have been striving to maintain their own position on IPRs, and have vigorously articulated various proposals for the reform of IPRs regimes. Among these major developing countries, China wields greater international stature and influence, and thus should take the lead in uniting and mobilizing developing countries to play a greater role in international IP governance.

Fourthly, China should advocate for the appropriate transformation of the international IPRs regime. The concept of "international regimes" was developed by international relations scholars in 1982 to refer to the principles, standards, rules, and decision-making procedures that participants are expected to develop in order to tackle a given issue (Krasner 1982, p. 186). In international relations theory, regime shifting denotes a strategy employed by both states and non-state actors, within existing power constraints, to evolve international regimes in a manner that more accurately reflect their interests. This entails efforts to alter the status quo by shifting from one international arena to another through activities such as treaty negotiations, legislative initiatives, or standard setting. It can be argued that regime shifting affords an opportunity for both state and non-state actors to generate "counter-regime norms" (Helfer 2003). Instances of regime shifting are commonplace in international IP legislation:

- In the 1950s, the US, through regime shifting, formulated the *Universal Copyright Convention* under the auspices of UNESCO while persistently refusing to accede to the *Berne Convention* administered by WIPO.

- Since the 1980s, developed countries led by the US have shifted the focus of international IP rulemaking from WIPO to the *General Agreement on Tariffs and Trade* (GATT), establishing a new order centred on the *TRIPS Agreement*.
- At present, relative to traditional regimes such as the WTO and WIPO, developing countries—including China—may exploit multilateral forums addressing biodiversity, cultural diversity, public health, international human rights, and development to establish new regimes with moral authority, thereby driving the transformation of the international IP protection system.

20.3 China's Strategic Responses to International IP Lawmaking

China is both a traditional developing country and an emerging industrialised country. In the process of internationalisation of its IPRs protection system, tailored strategic measures should be formulated in accordance with China's different developmental stages. At the present stage, it is necessary for China to balance immediate interests with forward-looking vision. While adhering to international conventions to protect foreign high technologies, China must also safeguard IP resources with local advantages from a national standpoint. Specifically, China should focus on the following aspects in the internationalisation of its IPRs protection system.

20.3.1 Alignment of Domestic and International Standards

Establishing and regulating the basic principles, minimum standards, and general requirements of IPRs protection across countries through the conclusion and amendment of relevant international conventions is a prerequisite for the internationalisation of IPRs regime. Since its formal accession to the Convention Establishing the World Intellectual Property Organisation in 1980, China has successively acceded to multiple IPRs protection conventions (see Table 20.1).

In order to adapt to the advancements of information and communication technologies and to protect the interests of copyright holders in the digital field, the Chinese government formally submitted its accession to WIPO regarding the *WIPO Copyright Treaty* (WCT) and the *WIPO Performances and Phonograms Treaty* (WPPT) on 6 March 2007. These treaties came into force in China on 9 June 2007. On 26 June 2012, the Chinese government signed the *Beijing Treaty on Audiovisual Performances*. These developments demonstrate that China has elevated its IPRs protection regime to a higher standard.

In light of its national circumstances and global trends, and in accordance with relevant international conventions, China has established and refined its IP laws and regulations, culminating in a legal framework that aligns with both domestic developmental needs and international standards. The scope and level of IPRs protection

Table 20.1 Major international IPRs protection conventions that China has joined

(Year of accession)	Convention name
1980	*Convention Establishing the World Intellectual Property Organisation*
1985	*Paris Convention for the Protection of Industrial Property*
1989	*Madrid Agreement Concerning the International Registration of Marks* *Treaty on IPRs of Integrated Circuits*
1992	*Berne Convention for the Protection of Literary and Artistic Works* *World Copyright Convention*
1993	*Convention for the Protection of Producers of Phonograms Against Unauthorised Duplication of Their Works* *Convention for the Protection of Performers, Producers of Phonograms and Broadcasting Organisations* *Patent Cooperation Treaty*
1994	*Nice Agreement Concerning the International Classification of Goods and Services for the Purposes of the Registration of Marks*
1995	*Budapest Treaty on the International Recognition of the Deposit of Microorganisms for the Purposes of Patent Procedure*
1996	*Agreement on the International Classification of Industrial Designs*
1997	*Strasbourg Agreement on the International Patent Classification*
1999	*International Treaty for the Protection of New Varieties of Plants*
2001	*Agreement on Trade-Related Aspects of IPRs (TRIPS)*
2007	*World Intellectual Property Organisation Copyright Treaty* *World Intellectual Property Organisation Performances and Phonograms Treaty*
2012	*Audiovisual Performance Treaty*

in China are largely in line with the provisions of international conventions, and in certain aspects, exceed their requirements.

The author contends that, in order to achieve a convergence between domestic and international norms, greater emphasis should be placed on the study of flexible and open clauses in international IPR conventions. For instance, Article 8 of the *TRIPS Agreement* (concerning public health issues and restriction of IP abuse), Article 27 (permitting members to exclude inventions from patentability on grounds of "public order and morality"), Article 31 (compulsory licensing of patents) and Article 71 (review of TRIPS implementation by the Council for Trade-Related Aspects of IPRs) can be used to explore the viable methods for coordinating domestic and international standards. China should take into account its current levels of economic, technological, and cultural development, and. At this stage, legislative standards should not be unduly elevated, provided that the minimum protection thresholds under international conventions are met, so as to strike an optimal balance between legal localisation and internationalisation.

20.3.2 Engagement with Pluralistic Lawmaking Mechanisms and Responses to Bilateral Agreements

Currently, the WTO and WIPO, both dominated by developed countries, continue to play leading roles in international IP legislation. Through a division of labour between the two international organisations, they collaborate in shaping the present and future landscape of global IP governance. As a complement to this dominant system, many other international organisations and legislatures have also engaged with IP issues, giving rise to a pluralistic legislative mechanism characterized as "two central bodies, multiple channels, North–South contention, and a trend towards equilibrium" in international IP legislation. This dynamic reflects the different positions and interests of sovereign states, non-state entities, IP rights holders, and society at large. China should make full use of the pluralistic legislative mechanism and secure a stronger voice in international IP legislation.

At the same time, China should prudently navigate bilateral agreement mechanism to forestall excessive IPRs protection standards. In the post-TRIPS era, owing to the collective assertiveness of developing countries in multilateral fora such as the WTO—evidenced by the failed negotiations at the 2001 Seattle Ministerial Conference and the 2003 Cancún Summit—developed nations, led by the United States and the European Union, have increasingly resorted to bilateral treaties to impose IP protections that surpass TRIPS standards in scope, stringency, and enforceability.

These bilateral agreements primarily target developing countries, but also extend to other developed countries. For example, the US has signed FTAs with Chile (2003), Singapore (2003), Australia (2004), the five Central American countries (2004), Morocco (2004), Bahrain (2004), and South Korea (2007). Similarly, the EU and its member states have concluded bilateral treaties with Sri Lanka (1995), the PLO (1997), Tunisia (1998), South Africa (1999), Mexico (2000), Jordan (2002), and Syria (2004). These IP-related bilateral agreements extend the minimum period of protection in the *TRIPS Agreement*, expand new domains of IPRs protection, introduce stringent IPRs enforcement measures, or disregard the legal protection of public health, biodiversity, and traditional knowledge, while marginalising public interest principles and limitations and exceptions to IPRs. Faced with the bilateral free trade negotiation mechanism led by developed countries, China should remain vigilant against the risks of inflated IPRs protection standards and resist unreasonable demands in bilateral negotiations.

20.3.3 Exchange Between Domestic Institutions and International Organisations

The primary objectives of international exchange and cooperation in IPRs are, firstly, to reform the global IP protection regime and rectify the current imbalance of

IPRs interests between developed and developing countries; and secondly, to facilitate knowledge-sharing, capacity-building, and coordinated action, thereby enabling China to refine its IP legal framework and foster sustainable IP development.

China has actively engaged with international organisations in the field of IP. It has participated in the initiatives of international organisations such as the WTO, WIPO and APEC, while strengthening bilateral and multilateral exchanges. Notably, China has established the *EU-China IP Dialogue Mechanism*, the *US-China IP Working Group*, and the *China-Japan-Korea Trilateral IP Dialogue and Cooperation Framework*. Additionally, China has pursued IP cooperation with Hong Kong, Macao, Brazil, Mexico, ASEAN, and other jurisdictions. In 2002, the China National Intellectual Property Administration (CNIPA) and WIPO signed a *Cooperation Framework Agreement* in Beijing. In 2008, China co-hosted the *2008 International Copyright Forum* with WIPO, the *Sino-German Symposium on Intellectual Property Law* with Germany, and the *EU-China High-Level Forum on Geographical Indications* with the European Commission.

Through such international engagement, China demonstrates its commitment to IPRs protection, addresses the escalating demands of certain developed nations, fosters mutual trust and recognition within the global IP community, and integrates itself into the international IPRs protection system. Moreover, China benefits from the experiences of other nations in IP governance, leveraging international norms to refine and enhance its domestic legal regime.

20.3.4 Participation of Domestic Experts in International Lawmaking Processes

The contemporary framework for international IPRs protection has been predominantly shaped by developed nations. It is imperative that China engages actively in relevant international legislative processes, based on thorough understanding and participation. When the Chinese IP legislation was first initiated, the principal international IPRs regimes had already been established and finalised. Throughout the over-century-long evolution of IP legislation, China's involvement in international IP legislation has been more reactive than proactive.

Following the 1990s, international economic relations and environments changed significantly. In November 1990, the draft of the *TRIPS Agreement* was concluded during the multilateral trade negotiations of the General Agreement on Tariffs and Trade (GATT Uruguay Round), and this marked the emergence of new international standards for IPRs protection. The Chinese government actively participated in this negotiation process and made substantial efforts to facilitate the adoption of the Agreement.

At the turn of the new century, China has taken a more active part in the formulation of the international rule of law. During the drafting of the UNESCO's *Convention on the Protection and Promotion of the Diversity of Cultural Expressions*, China's

Ministry of Culture, multiple Chinese ministries, including the Ministry of Culture, the General Administration of Press and Publication, and the National Intellectual Property Administration, formed a "Leading Group for Participation in the Formulation of the Convention on the Protection and Promotion of the Diversity of Cultural Expressions." China's active engagement in the negotiations yielded favourable outcomes. The negotiations not only successfully reinforced the "sovereign principle" in cultural diversity but also secured the independent status of the Convention, ensuring it would not be subordinated to other international conventions. Through China's efforts in the negotiations, the provisions that are inconsistent with China's relevant policies and legal provisions were either diluted or removed (Fan & Yang 2006).[4] It is particularly noteworthy that the *Beijing Treaty*, formulated under the auspices of WIPO, was adopted at a diplomatic conference held in Beijing in June 2012. The General Director of WIPO, Francis Gurry, hailed the Treaty as another milestone in international copyright legislation, filling the gap in the protection of audiovisual performers in the international copyright regime, and also exemplifying the cooperative nature of multilateral processes. This Treaty thus completed the comprehensive protection of performers under the international copyright regime (WIPO 2012). The *Beijing Treaty* is the first international IPR convention named after a Chinese city, representing the collective achievement of international organisations, China, and other member states.

At present, negotiations on the amendment of the *TRIPS Agreement* and the international protection of geographical indications are still underway within the WTO framework. Simultaneously, the WTO has initiated a new round of consultations on IPRs, addressing the inclusion of "biological diversity" and "traditional knowledge" Within the scope of IP. China should actively participate in the relevant negotiations and legislative processes to incorporate provisions favourable to developing countries.

20.3.5 Synergy Between Domestic Institutional Innovation and International Institutional Reform

The ongoing transformation in international protection of IPRs not only highlight reforms to the existing regimes (e.g., gene patents, digital copyrights, and online trademarks), but also heralds breakthroughs in entirely new systems (e.g., traditional knowledge, genetic resources). Among them, the emergence of novel property rights systems, such as those for traditional knowledge and genetic resources, has given a significant impetus to the development of international IPRs regimes, making it possible for developing countries to gain a competitive edge in the global allocation of IP resources.

[4] It is mainly the "media diversification" and other provisions that may involve the diversification of capital structure.

The institutional approach to protecting traditional resources involves both considerations of national interests and the functioning of international coordination mechanisms. At the international level, it not only reflects the formation of a new landscape of interest but also signifies the evolving trajectory of the development of the IPRs regime in the post-TRIPS era. In the face of external pressures, China should adeptly leverage international coordination mechanisms to counter demands from developed countries for heightened IPRs protection that exceed TRIPS standards and domestic conditions. By capitalising on its strengths as a cultural and resource-rich nation, China must secure a voice in international rule-making and strive for favourable conditions to preserve and develop traditional resources favourable (Wu 2005). In various international forums, China and other developing countries should commit to institutional innovation, adopting protection mechanisms for traditional resources that are different from existing IPRs regimes, thereby avoiding legal changes that could undermine the foundation of IPRs regimes. At the same time, China should seek the understanding and support of the majority of countries in the world, and gradually establish a legal system for the utilisation and protection of traditional resources on the basis of consensus, thereby ensuring robust international legal protection for IP resources where developing countries hold comparative advantages.

China's current IP laws are broadly in line with national conditions and meet the requirements of international standards, though certain inconsistencies remain. It is imperative to monitor international legislative developments and address domestic needs by expediting revisions to the Trademark Law, Copyright Law, and Anti-Unfair Competition Law, and enact standalone legislation such as the Trade Secrets Protection Law. Additionally, progress should be made in other areas of legislative protection. For instance, WIPO's 2000 Draft Objectives and Principles for the *Protection of Traditional Cultural Expressions/Expressions of Folklore* addressed national policy objectives for the protection of traditional culture, the choice of specific IPRs models, and the feasibility of non-IPRs protection methods. UNESCO's 2005 *Convention on the Protection and Promotion of the Diversity of Cultural Expressions* emphasised that cultural diversity is a fundamental characteristic of humankind and should be cherished and preserved for the benefit of all humankind, bringing traditional culture which were not covered by modern IP under its regulatory scope as cultural activities, content, products, and services. As a cradle of ancient civilisation with a wealth of traditional cultural resources, China should accelerate the formulation of administrative regulations, such as those for the protection of folk literature and art, to achieve comprehensive domestic legal protection in areas of comparative advantage, including traditional knowledge and intangible cultural heritage.

References

China National Intellectual Property Administration. 2002. *Intellectual Property Protection in China*

Drahos, Peter and Braithwaite, John. 2002. Economic politics law and health: Intellectual property, corporate strategy, globalisation: TRIPS in context. Wisconsin International *Law Journal* 20

Fan, Fan and Yang, Ying. 2006. The whole process of the negotiation of the convention on the protection and promotion of the diversity of cultural expressions. *China Publishing* 2

Helfer, Laurence R. 2004. Mediating interactions in an expanding international intellectual property regime. *Case Wisconsin Reserve Journal of International Law* 36

Helfer, Laurence R. 2003. Regime shifting: The *TRIPS Agreement* and new dynamics of international intellectual property lawmaking. *Yale Journal of International Law* 29

Krasner, Stephen D. 1982. Structural cause and regime consequences: Regime as intervening variable. *International Organisation* 36

Liang, Yeqian and Lu, Dasheng. 2012. Long Yongtu: It is China's political choice to join the WTO as a developing country. http://news.sina.com.cn/c/293551.html. Accessed 3 November

The IPRs Protection Working Group. 2008. *China's Action Plan on IPRs Protection.* 2008

WIPO. 2012. WIPO Beijing treaty on audiovisual performance is concluded, http://www.wipo.int/pressroom/en/articles/2012/ Accessed 28 June

Wu, Handong. 2005. The institutional reform of intellectual property in the post-TRIPS era and China's coping strategy. *Studies in Law and Business* 5

Yang, Jing. 2013. *Research on the Intellectual Property Provisions of the Free Trade Agreement.* Beijing: Law Press

Yu, Peter K. 2009. The global intellectual property order and its undetermined future. *The WIPO Journal* 1

Zhan, Ying. 2016. New trends of international legislation of intellectual property rights under the background of regionalisation of international trade system. *International Economic and Trade Exploration* 4

Chapter 21
International Reform and Global Governance of IPRs Regimes

Since the second decade of the twenty-first century, amid the rise of anti-globalisation sentiments, the multilateral system centred on the WTO and the international IPRs protection system anchored by the *TRIPS Agreement* have faced significant challenges. International trade disputes and IPRs conflicts have drawn high attention and deep reflection from the global community. Confronted with the complexities of the evolving international landscape and the intrinsic demands of China's development, we must uphold a global governance perspective, a developmental approach, and a rule-of-law mindset in IP. Grounded in the construction of a new type of international relations with mutually beneficial cooperation as the core, we should steer the international order for IPRs protection and the global governance system towards a more just and equitable direction.

21.1 Basic Requirements for the International Rule of Law in IP

IPRs protection is a focal issue of the international community. International economic and trade rules, encompassing trade regulations, investment norms, and IPRs protection standards, collectively form the legal framework governing scientific, cultural, and economic exchanges among countries. Through institutional platforms such as WIPO and the WTO, a body of international legal rules and orders has emerged in the field of IP.

Within the international IPRs protection system, the WTO and its *TRIPS Agreement* play a leading role. The modern integration of IP laws exhibits three key characteristics. The first is the integration of the international legal systems with the global trade framework. IPRs protection constitute a critical component of the international economic and trade regime, functioning under the WTO as binding

H. Wu, *Theorising Intellectual Property Rights from Chinese Perspectives*,
https://doi.org/10.1007/978-981-96-5867-1_21

"trade rules" for contracting parties. This means that while each party enjoys non-discriminatory most-favoured-nation (MFN) treatment within the international trade system, it must also commit to providing adequate and effective IPRs protection, ensuring that IPRs enforcement measures do not create barriers to legitimate trade.[1] Building on this foundation, the second characteristic is the integration of legal protection standards among contracting parties. Under the "minimum standard of protection" principle enshrined in international conventions, no contracting party may provide IPRs protection below the baseline prescribed by the agreement. These "minimum standard"—or "uniformity standards"—cover fundamental aspects such as subject matter, acquisition, scope and enforcement of IPRs, serving as reference norms for domestic legislation of contracting parties. The universal application of this principle has led to the convergence of IP laws, wherein, international law prevails over domestic law, national laws align with one another, and domestic statutes comply with to international obligations. The third characteristic of legal integration is the unification of substantive and procedural rules in international IPRs protection mechanisms. Historically, earlier international conventions primarily addressed substantive aspects of international IPRs protection, while lacking binding enforcement measures or effective dispute resolution mechanisms, earning them the label of "soft law" (Gu 2002). The *TRIPS Agreement* has strengthened enforcement procedures and protection measures, providing for judicial review, civil procedures, damages, provisional measures, and border measures. Moreover, it established a comprehensive dispute settlement process involving consultation, meditation, adjudication, appeals and enforcement, and ensues the normal implementation of IPRs protection through the WTO dispute resolution settlement mechanism (Samahon 2000). Under the constraints of the WTO trade system and its enforcement and dispute settlement mechanisms, IPRs protection has attained both high standards and high efficiency, epitomising the essence of the legal integration in this field.

From the above characteristics, it is evident that the WTO-centred multilateral system imposes basic requirements on each contracting party: while enjoying MFN treatment in international trade, each contracting party must condition such privileges on IPRs protection; their commitments to protect IPRs must adhere to the "minimum standard"; and any inter-member IP disputes must be submitted to the dispute resolution mechanism, precluding unilateral actions.

21.2 Significant Changes in the International Rule of Law in IP

The world is undergoing a period of major development, transformation and adjustment. A series of significant changes have taken place in the field of international rule of law, among which IP stands out as the most impactful and disruptive, showing a complex and multi-polar developmental trend.

[1] See the preamble to *the TRIPS Agreement*.

21.2.1 Shifts in the International IPRs Protection Order

In the era of knowledge economy and globalisation, the international political order, international economic and trade order, and international IPRs order constitute the three major components of the international order, each influencing the others.

As a critical mechanism for global distribution of benefits, IPRs determine a country's wealth creation and accumulation. A few developed countries advocate for IPRs protection standards that are higher and more stringent than the *TRIPS Agreement*, seeking to establish an international order of IPRs that favours their political and economic dominance. In contrast, most countries, including China, argue for modifications and adjustments to certain provisions of the *TRIPS Agreement*, aiming for a more reasonable and equitable framework that establishes balanced international IP rules. Here, differing demands for IPRs protection—whether through confrontation or compromise—will inevitably lead to a reconstruction of the international order.

21.2.2 Evolution of the International IP Lawmaking Mechanisms

The WTO and WIPO continue to play leading roles in IP legislation. Beyond these dominant mechanisms, many international human rights organisations and legislative bodies have assumed or are assuming significant roles, resulting a pluralistic legislative framework. This includes the rulemaking activities of international human rights organisations, the United Nations Economic and Social Council (ECOSOC), UNESCO, the FAO, and the WHO, many of which are related to IPRs protection. This pluralistic legislative mechanism reflects a structure of "two central bodies, multiple channels, North–South contention, and a trend towards equilibrium" in international IP legislation (Liu 2006). It must be acknowledged that this structure is healthy and beneficial, as it allows for the representation of different perspectives and interests of sovereign states, non-state entities, IP owners and the general public in the IP domain. It prevents the international IPRs regime from being disproportionately favouring the interests of certain developed countries and their IP owners while neglecting the negative impacts of IPRs protection on public interests, social welfare, and international human rights. For developing countries, it is essential not only to seek a stronger voice within dominant mechanisms like the WTO and WIPO, but also to take proactive roles in these pluralistic legislative forums.

21.2.3 Developments in the International IP Dispute Resolution Mechanisms

The WTO has established an effective multilateral dispute settlement mechanism characterised by a "high degree of uniformity" and a "certain level of enforceability" (Zeng 1996, p. 166). However, since its inception, WTO members have signed over 300 bilateral and multilateral free trade agreements (FTAs). While these agreements supplement WTO rules, they also undermine the authority of its rules. The majority of IP disputes are now resolved through these FTAs. More notably, there has been a resurgence of "unilateralism," where bilateral IP disputes are addressed through unilateral sanctions. For instance, the United State, based on its domestic laws, has initiated "Sect. 301 Investigations" and "Special 301 Reviews" (targeting trade partners), "Sect. 377 Investigations" (targeting companies entering the U.S. market), and "Review of Notorious Markets" (targeting foreign e-commerce platforms and physical markets). This revival of unilateral measures in recent years, as a part of a "de-globalisation" trend towards trade protectionism, has drawn significant concern from affected countries and the broader international community.

21.2.4 Changes in the Global IP Power Structure

The balance of global power has undergone rapid shifts, with the rise of emerging market economies and the growing collective strength of developing countries, reshaping the global IP landscape. These countries are striving to integrate their values and national strategies into existing international systems while pushing for new institutional arrangements that better serve their interests (Wu 2016). Emerging economies, such as China, India and Brazil, have rapidly advanced in technology and economic development, each adopting IP as a core strategy for innovation-driven growth. This has altered the dynamics of the international IP order.

The profound changes in the international rule of law concerning IP reveal a critical truth: the globalisation of the IPRs regime is an inherent product of broader globalisation. While it has universalised IPRs protection standards, it has also globalised systemic risks. Within the international IP domain, different types of countries exhibit divergent claims to rights. This divergence manifests as confrontations between national stances, opposition among principal organisations, and clashes in individual values and interests. Protectionist and unilateralist practices pose significant threats to the multilateral framework and its legal systems. It is therefore imperative that the international rule of law for IP adheres to the following fundamental tenets: (1) Establishing international norms as the benchmark for IPRs protection; (2) Applying the principle of cooperation as the central theme in handling IP affairs; and (3) Utilising consultation as the primary mechanism for resolving IP disputes.

21.3 China's Role and Strategy in the Global IP Governance

In the face of a profoundly complex world situation, we must study, comprehend, and implement Chinese President Xi Jinping's ideas on global governance and the rule of law. Key concepts such as "building a community of with a shared future for mankind," "pursuing peaceful development," "fostering a new type of international relations featuring win–win cooperation," and "promoting a more just and equitable international order and global governance system" serve not only as advanced guiding principles for China's foreign engagements and participation in global governance, but also as the correct guiding framework for China's involvement in the construction of the global IP governance system and its response to international IPRs regime reforms. In the post-TRIPS era, we need to not merely comply with the standards of the *TRIPS Agreement* but also, reassess the evolving pattern of the legal integration of IPRs and make corresponding strategic choices from the perspective of global governance of IPRs.

21.3.1 Upholding the "TRIPS Standards" and Promoting "Regime Shifting"

The international trade system led by the WTO and the international protection regime for IPRs centred on *the TRIPS Agreement* have played a significant role in advancing economic globalisation and maintaining the international IP order. The "*TRIPS standards*" provide the most critical foundation for the integration of IP laws. To this day, emerging economies have widely accepted these standards, using them not only as the basis for domestic legislation but also as the benchmarks for regional and bilateral IP cooperation. Simultaneously, emerging economies advocate for "appropriate regime shifting" in global governance. As noted in international relations theory, "regime shifting" refers to a strategy employed by state and non-state actors to evolve international regimes in ways that more accurately reflect their interests within established constrains. This involves efforts to alter the status quo by shifting treaty negotiations, legislative initiatives, and rulemaking activities from one international forum to another. Such practices are commonplace in the construction of international IP order. At this stage, developing countries, including China, can leverage various international forums, such as those addressing biodiversity, cultural diversity, public health, international human rights, and development, to establish new regimes with moral legitimacy, thereby driving reforms in the international IPRs protection system. Additionally, through the design of IPRs provisions in regional and bilateral free trade agreements, China can overcome the institutional limitations of the *TRIPS Agreement* standards and address issues such as the protection of emerging high-tech subject matter and the protection of traditional knowledge and genetic resources. Whether within the WTO framework or in regional or bilateral contexts involving "regime shifting", China should adhere to the basic principle of "building a community with a shared future for mankind." It must commit to "forging partnerships based on equality, consultation and mutual understanding; creating a security architecture that is fair, just, and shared by all; pursuing open, innovative, and inclusive development that benefits all; and increasing inter-civilisational exchanges that promote harmony in diversity and are mutually enriching" (Xi 2017). This means opposing hegemonic practices of institutional imposition and rule dominance, and instead advocating for a co-constructed, shared international IPRs protection system through collective deliberation.

21.3.2 Dual Role as a Major Developing Country and an Emerging IP Power

As a major developing country, China's status during its WTO accession negotiations was a subject of international debate—whether it should be classified as a developed or a developing country. China's decision to join the WTO as a developing country was not only a political choice but also a reflection of its economic status at the time. Although China has made remarkable progress over the past two decades since its accession, securing a significant position in the global innovation system, its per capita income and comprehensive socio-economic development indicators remain relatively low, keeping it within the ranks of developing countries. This underscores that adhering to a developing-country stance and advocating for the interests and aspirations of the broader developing world constitutes China's fundamental role in global IP governance.

At the same time, China is also an emerging major developing country, holding a prominent position in global politics, economy, science and technology, culture and education, and has become a veritable IP power. Its foreign policy as a "responsible major power" is evolving from "keeping a low profile and biding its time while getting things accomplished" to "striving for achievement" and "proactive engagement." In IP diplomacy, China should adhere to the principle of cooperation over confrontation, seeking "common ground while reserving differences" with developed countries such as the United States and Europe, pursuing "win–win cooperation" with emerging economies, and extending "inclusive and equitable benefits" to less-developed countries. In the field of IP protection, China should transition from being a follower and adherent of international rules to an active participant, contributor, and defender. Key measures include: (1) Promoting reforms in the global governance system of IP to enhance the representation and voice of developing countries in international affairs; (2) Contributing more Chinese proposals and wisdom in the formulation of international IP rules; (3) Facilitating North–South dialogue and South-South cooperation to properly resolve international IP disputes.

21.3.3 Interplay Between China's FTZs, International FTAs, WTO, and WIPO

In the "post-TRIPS era," WTO and WIPO provide a platform for multilateral cooperation, with the *TRIPS Agreement* and other international conventions on IP setting minimum standards for IPRs protection for each party. Regional and bilateral free trade agreements (FTAs) also prioritise IP clauses, creating a cyclical process of legal integration of IPRs involving bilateral, regional, and multilateral approaches. Against this backdrop, China's participation in global governance of IP has formed an interactive and interrelated operational mechanism, namely, a three-dimensional network linking domestic Free Trade Zones (FTZs), international Free Trade Agreements (FTAs), WTO and WIPO. Among these, FTZs serve as experimental zones and critical bridges connecting domestic and international IPRs regimes. These pilot free trade zones aim to test innovative policies, align with international trade rules, implement pre-establishment national treatment and negative lists, and foster an internationalised, market-driven, and rule-of-law-based business environment. FTAs, meanwhile, function as key platforms for China to advance its IP policy positions and legal initiatives. Bilateral and regional mechanisms, centred on win–win cooperation, drive institutional innovation in international IPRs protection through dialogue. The multilateral frameworks of WTO and WIPO represent the ultimate stage and authoritative forums for China's engagement in global IP governance of international IP affairs. Economists widely agree that the multilateral trading system is superior to bilateral or regional FTAs (The World Bank 2005, p. 125). This also applies to IPRs regimes, where the IPRs protection standards recognised by WTO and WIPO hold universal applicability. The above mechanisms China employs and participates in are not isolated but highly interconnected, forming an interactive framework that collectively supports the country's overarching strategy in global governance of IP.

References

Gu, Zuxue. 2002. *International Intellectual Property Law*. Beijing: Law Press
Liu, Sung. 2006. New trend in international creation of intellectual property. *Legal Studies* 3
Moratorium. 2000. Non-violation and situation complaints against developing countries. *Law and Policy in International Business* 31
Samahon, Tuan N. 2000. TRIPS copyright dispute settlement after the transition and moratorium: Non-violation and situation complaints against developing countries. *Law & Poly Intl Bus* 3
The World Bank. 2005. *Global Economic Outlook*. China Finance and Economic Press
Wu, Zhicheng, and Dong, Zuozhuang. 2016. International institutional transformation and China's response. *The Contemporary World* 5
Xi, Jinping. 2017. Jointly building a community with a shared future for mankind—speech at UN headquarters in Geneva. *People's Daily*, January 20
Zeng, Lingliang. 1996. *World Trade Law*. Wuhan: Wuhan University Press

Conclusions

Conclusion for Part I

IPRs and ownership rights are distinct terms used to differentiate the legal forms of rights over intangible property and tangible property. IPRs, together with "intangible property rights" and "information property rights", serve as specialised designations for property rights in the realm of intellectual creations. International conventions elucidate the nature of IPRs from the dual attributes of private rights and human rights, affirming that IPRs should essentially be a unity of private rights and human rights. IPRs are characterized by their "exclusiveness", "territoriality" and "temporality." However, these features are merely generalisations and descriptions of relative significance. The common legal feature unifying all categories of IPRs is the intangibility of their subject matter.

The subject system of IPRs possesses unique characteristics: the legal facts of original acquisition involve the creative activities of inventors and the authorisation of state organs; the legal consequence of derivative acquisition is that there are several subjects of rights on the same intellectual product; and the subject qualification of foreigners is governed by the principle of conditional national treatment.

Regarding the subject matter of IPRs, scholars in China and abroad have adopted terms such as "intellectual property," "intangible property," "intellectual achievements," and "intellectual information", but "intellectual products" would be more appropriate. Intellectual products encompass three categories: creative achievements, commercial identifiers, and business goodwill, all of which are creative, immaterial and public.

The utilisation of IPRs includes both statutorily prescribed uses and contractually agreed uses, with the object of such utilisation being certain rights rather than the intellectual products themselves. The protection of IPRs primarily involves delineating the scope of validity of various types of rights.

In addition to restrictions on the effectiveness of territorial space and duration, the main limitations of IPRs are those on the scope of the rights, such as fair use,

H. Wu, *Theorising Intellectual Property Rights from Chinese Perspectives*,
https://doi.org/10.1007/978-981-96-5867-1

statutory licensing, compulsory licensing, exhaustion of rights, prior use, parallel imports, all of which constitute institutional frameworks for restricting IPRs.

Intellectual property infringement is an unlawful factual act, the object of which is the exclusive rights of another party. The principle of attribution of liability for intellectual property infringement should adopt a dual system of fault liability and presumption of fault. Victims may resort multiple remedies, including civil, criminal and administrative measures, though their application differs from that in cases involving ownership rights.

The construction of an IPRs system involves its position within the civil law framework, wherein it is categorized alongside traditional property ownership under a unified property rights system. IPRs are an open, dynamic and continuously evolving legal system. It encompasses typical IPRs recognized by international conventions, such as copyright, patents and trademarks, as well as broader categories of IPRs, including goodwill rights, credit right, and publicity rights.

Conclusion for Part II

The IPRs regime is a product of the development of science and technology, and commodity economy in modern times, as well as the result of institutional innovation in private law. IP law has evolved from its inception to maturity, undergoing continuous refinement and improvement since the twentieth century. The modernisation driven by the new technological revolution and the integration brought about by the new international trade system represents the dominant trends in the contemporary transformation of IP law. The IPRs regime has its own theoretical foundations. The concept of *res incorporales* (incorporeal things) and its related doctrines developed by the Romans have provided pivotal conceptual tools and useful ideological resources for the IPRs regime. Economists have used the theory of knowledge value to clarify the economic rationality of the IPRs regime, while philosophers have employed metaphysics to address the general issues of the IPRs regime with theories such as "social justice", "free will," and "property personality." The IP culture is nourished as a private law culture featuring individualism, a spirit of free will and rational pursuits, serving as the ideological foundations of the IPRs regime. In the present context, it is necessary to draw on the advanced principles of Western legal culture and identifying the rational core of traditional Chinese culture to achieve the transformation and reconstruction of China's IPRs regime. The values of IP law consist of both universal values for general laws and special values (mainly justice, efficiency, and innovation) for division laws. Thus, the "inviolability of private rights" and "the balancing of interests" constitute the basic legal concepts of the IPRs regime. The IPRs regime, centring on the above legal values, protects IPRs, balances interests, and promotes both scientific progress and economic growth. In the context of a risk society, cultural risks, ecological risks, genetic technology risks, and cyber risks, among others, represent "endogenous" risks inherent to the IPRs regime. Thus, we should take supplement and alternative risk response measures in regard to the current IPRs regime to reduce the risks in accordance with "the unity of value rationality and instrumental rationality," "the unity of rights and obligations," and "the unity of legal control and the regulation of technology." From the perspective of policy science, the IPRs regime plays a significant role in a government's public policy, protecting legitimate IPRs and promoting the advancement of human knowledge. Although IP law and anti-unfair competition law are of different institutional designs, they share the same legislative objectives. The latter serves a supplementary role in IPRs protection, regulating acts such as trade counterfeiting, false advertising, commercial defamation, and infringement of trade secrets. IP law and anti-trust law share common policy objectives and complementary functions of regulation. IPRs abuse is subject to anti-trust law regulation, even though the "existence" of IPRs is an exception to the rule. IP law falls under civil law, and its legislative models include separate statutes, a special code, or incorporation into the civil code. China's IP law should be included in the civil code as general provisions, while retaining *lex specialis* within the civil scope.

Conclusion for Part III

The international regime for the protection of IPRs has evolved over more than a century, progressing through the "era of the Paris and Berne Unions," the "period of the World Intellectual Property Organisation (WIPO)," and the "phase of the World Trade Organisation (WTO)." It is both a product of the continuous development of international economic and trade relations and a result of the intrinsic transformation of the IP system itself. The principles underpinning the international protection of IPRs—primarily national treatment, minimum standards of protection, and public interest—are characterised by their direct applicability and universal relevance.

As the principal intergovernmental organisation responsible for the international protection of IPRs, WIPO administers various international unions, including the Paris Union, the Berne Union, the Madrid Union, and the Patent Cooperation Union, and oversees nearly thirty international conventions, such as the *Paris Convention* and the *Berne Convention*, through its International Bureau.

Within the WTO framework, the *Agreement on Trade-Related Aspects of Intellectual Property Rights* (TRIPS), alongside the *Agreement on Trade in Goods and the Agreement on Trade in Services*, constitutes the organisation's three foundational systems, and also the most significant international IPR convention of our time. These agreements closely integrate IPRs protection with the global trade system, establishing a new IPRs regime, elevating IPRs protection standards, and exerting a profound influence on the IP legislation of various countries.

Today, the international IPRs regime faces conflicts with international human rights law and divergences with other IPR conventions, necessitating further reform and continuous refinement. Moreover, debates in international IP forums—such as those concerning the protection of traditional knowledge, genetic resources, and geographical indications—have led to the emergence of new interest dynamics within the field, driving innovation and development in the international IPRs protection system. The *Convention on Biological Diversity* (1992) and the *Convention on the Protection and Promotion of the Diversity of Cultural Expressions* (2005) represent significant efforts by the international community to improve and reform the contemporary international IPRs protection system.

In light of the complex and shifting global landscape, we must proceed from the vision of building a "community with a shared future for mankind" to collectively deliberate, construct, and share a global governance system for IP. In the process of internationalisation of the IPRs regime, China should maintain its stance as a developing country and respond at both international and domestic levels. This entails collaborating with other developing countries to promote appropriate transformation of the international regime and reform of the international IPRs system, while also addressing local realities by refining domestic legislation and enhancing IPRs protection standards.

MIX
Papier aus verantwortungsvollen Quellen
Paper from responsible sources
FSC® C105338

If you have any concerns about our products,
you can contact us on
ProductSafety@springernature.com

In case Publisher is established outside the EU,
the EU authorized representative is:
Springer Nature Customer Service Center GmbH
Europaplatz 3, 69115 Heidelberg, Germany

Printed by Libri Plureos GmbH
in Hamburg, Germany